Corel PHOTO-PAINT™ 8
The Official Guide

About the Author...

I hate biographies where you write about yourself in the third person, so I am writing this in the first person –does this make my wife the first lady? I have been around the computer industry a long time, a real long time. Hey, I turn 50 later on this year. The first computer I ever worked on was larger than a tank, water-cooled and it had over 80 KB of iron core memory. Don't laugh at the 80 KB, in those days a megabyte of RAM cost nearly half a million dollars! Where was I - oh yes…

I started using CorelDRAW when it had just been updated to Version 2.0. Dr. Cowpland used to answer the phones in those days if you had a tough technical question. I began writing PHOTO-PAINT books with PHOTO-PAINT 5 –seems so long ago. I have written every single PHOTO-PAINT book since. I write monthly articles on (you guessed it) Corel PHOTO-PAINT for *Corel Magazine*, *CorelDRAW Journal*, *Corel User* (UK), *Corel Magazine* (Germany), and *The Intergalactic Journal of Non-Terrestrial Corel Users* (not really, I just wanted to see if you were paying attention). My big event this year has been winning the World Design Contest for June, making me a finalist. The good news about that is I could win a giant mountain of cash, the bad news is I have to wear a tux (sigh). I have a lovely wife to whom I have been married for the past 24 plus years. Many are amazed that (1) my wife could put up with my lame jokes for almost a quarter of a century (She's a saint) (2) how we could stay married that long. What's the secret? Two little words are the secret to a lengthy marriage. They are: "Yes dear." We also have two great kids. Our son Jonathan is 21 and a pre-med major at the local institute of higher learning, and our daughter Grace is 16 and still looking for Mr. Right. In my spare time I… what spare time?

I can be reached at dhuss@texas.net. Feel free to drop me a note and tell me what you like about the book and what you would like to see in PHOTO-PAINT 9.

Corel PHOTO-PAINT™ 8
The Official Guide

David Huss

Osborne **McGraw-Hill**

Berkeley   New York   St. Louis   San Francisco   Auckland
Bogotá   Hamburg   London   Madrid   Mexico City   Milan
Montreal   New Delhi   Panama City   Paris   São Paulo
Singapore   Sydney   Tokyo   Toronto

Osborne **McGraw-Hill**
2600 Tenth Street
Berkeley, California 94710
U.S.A.

For information on translations or book distributors outside the U.S.A., or to arrange bulk purchase discounts for sales promotions, premiums, or fund-raisers, please contact Osborne/**McGraw-Hill** at the above address.

Corel PHOTO-PAINT™ 8: The Official Guide

234567890 AGM 901987654321098

ISBN 0-07-882445-1

Publisher: Brandon A. Nordin
Editor-in-Chief: Scott Rogers
Acquisitions Editor: Megg Bonar
Editorial Assistant: Gordon Hurd
Project Editor: Jennifer Wenzel
Technical Editor: Jennifer Campbell
Copy Editors: Gary Morris and Dennis Weaver
Proofreaders: Karen Mead and Sally Engelfried
Indexer: Valerie Robbins
Computer Designers: Jani Beckwith and Michelle Galicia
Illustrator: Lance Ravella
Color Insert: Peter F. Hancik
Cover Design: Regan Honda

**This book is dedicated to Elizabeth,
my "Beautiful Lady" for the past 25 years.**

CONTENTS AT A GLANCE

PART V

Extending the Power of PHOTO-PAINT

PART I

Introduction and Digital Fundamentals

CONTENTS

PART II

Basic Photo Editing Techniques

PART III

Exploring PHOTO-PAINT Tools

12   Working With Fills and the Shape Tools 335

PART IV

Filters—Using the WOW Stuff

PART V

Extending the Power of PHOTO-PAINT

WORKSHOPS AT A GLANCE

"A picture is worth a thousand words."

Unlike many outdated adages, this one remains relevant in the Age of Information, especially in the realm of communication strategies. Whether surfing the Web, leafing through a magazine, or strolling through a shopping mall, we find ourselves enticed and enriched by an ever-changing landscape of extraordinary images. Many of these images are created by individuals like you, using tools such as Corel PHOTO-PAINT® 8 to extend their artistic reach.

The ability to use Corel PHOTO-PAINT 8 to produce outstanding digital images requires product knowledge, design experience and a little inspiration. For those of you who would like to learn more about this innovative product, David Huss provides an excellent overview of the application interface and the general principals of digital imaging. This valuable guide provides helpful step-by-step exercises, creative projects, techniques, tips, and tricks. Those familiar with earlier versions of Corel PHOTO-PAINT will benefit from Dave's explanation of the many new features and capabilities of this release.

Dave's easy, conversational style and hands-on approach to basics reflect his extensive knowledge and long-standing relationship with Corel PHOTO-PAINT, making this book an inspiration to us all.

Doug Chomyn
Product Manager, Corel PHOTO-PAINT 8
Corel Corporation

PREFACE

Corel PHOTO-PAINT™ 8: The Official Guide represents the latest CorelPRESS™ title in the series of books dedicated to of Corel ® software. CorelPRESS™ titles provide both a solid grounding in product fundamentals and the knowledge necessary to master advanced features of the product. The author, along with the PHOTO-PAINT product team at Corel, has spent many hours working on the accuracy and scope of this book, and we hope you enjoy it.

This edition provides an in-depth overview of Corel PHOTO-PAINT 8 and a first look at exciting new features. New users, as well as those who have purchased upgrades, will find significant value in these pages, and the hands-on workshops will teach you to make excellent use of the exciting features of this new version of Corel PHOTO-PAINT. The book reveals tips and tricks that have been developed over several versions of the software by the most experienced users, and also includes a gallery of beautiful images created with Corel PHOTO-PAINT to illustrate the power of the product.

The CorelPRESS series represents an important step in the ability of Corel to disseminate information to users with the help of Osborne/McGraw-Hill, the fine author, technical reviewers, editors, and all others involved in the series. Congratulations to the CorelPRESS team at Osborne on the creation of this excellent book!

DR. MICHAEL C. J. COWPLAND
PRESIDENT AND CEO
COREL CORPORATION

The acknowledgement portion of a book is like a secret compartment since generally only those mentioned in it ever read it. It is late in September and the book is ready to be put to bed (with milk and cookies of course). I have only just returned from CorelWORLD Europe in London a few days after Princess Diana's funeral and am packing for the Corel Summit in San Diego. In the middle of all that, it's fun to look back and think about all that was involved to get this book into your hands.

Of course, my family once again must be given thanks for giving up father and husband in exchange for the grumpy old man that I become when writing a book under deadline. As always, my family got to see more of the back of my head than the front.

The creation of a technical book is always a challenge to everyone involved. To have a book ready to ship with the product meant it was necessary to write about things in PAINT during the beta cycle. Now that's entertainment. A typical telephone conversation begins with "When I move the cursor it changes shape. Is it supposed to do that or is it a bug?" I think we were successful because of the efforts of several people up Ottawa way. Ottawa, Canada is where Corel is—you knew that, right? First and foremost I must thank Doug Chomyn, head of the PHOTO-PAINT development team, who once again endured a ceaseless barrage of questions during the creation of this book. My other PHOTO-PAINT technical wizard is David Garrett, who never ceases to amaze me with what he knows about the product—must be why he does PHOTO-PAINT quality assurance. A great big thank you—for a giant of a man—Mike Bellefeuille (that's pronounced like Delphi with a B). Hey, if I can learn to spell it, you can learn to pronounce it right. Mike wears so many hats up at Corel that I am thinking that investing in a hat company might be a sound financial move. Of course, for the lady who I am convinced can do almost anything—Michelle Murphy—a CD-ROM containing over 10,000 thank-yous.

My thanks to Jennifer Campbell who worked during her family vacation to complete the copyedit so we could get this book to the printers in time to ship with the product. I felt bad it took away from her vacation, but then how exciting can Idaho be? Just kidding—please no e-mail from Idaho.

I must tip my non-existent hat to Russell Roberts, my boss at MaxServe (Yes, I do have a "day job.") who tolerated my lengthy absences so this book could get out on time. Russell is the best boss one could ask for. We share the same taste in beer (What else matters?).

xxxi

ACKNOWLEDGMENTS

Finally, (it keeps going and going and..) my editor Megg Bonar who makes the task of getting a book out on time almost fun. Wouldn't even trade her for a beer—now that's serious. Also a thank you and farewell to Gordon Hurd, who worked with me on this book and the last one as well. He finally got that night job he always wanted at the local corner convenience store. Ah, to be young and have a career path. Once again, I would be remiss if I didn't mention the head honcho at the Osborne ranch—Scott Rogers. You've been mentioned.

Last, but surely not least, my daughter Grace (still 16) wanted to remind all of you reading this book she is still looking for a boyfriend. I guess the Boyfriend-in-a-box I bought her last week didn't work out. So if you are either Prince William or another dashing member of the opposite gender, send her e-mail at my address (dhuss@texas.net). And if you are really interested remember—I own a gun and have a shovel.

So there you stand next to a multicolored wall of computer titles, most of which are nearly as thick as phonebooks for major metropolitan cities. You ask yourself, "Will this book help me learn PHOTO-PAINT 8, or will it become another dust collector?" Your puzzlement is understandable. After all, the word "idiot" or "dummy" doesn't appear anywhere in the title. By now you have already looked at the dazzling color inserts and noticed it wasn't the typical collection of award-winning art produced by people with years of experience and way too much time on their hands. Instead you've seen a large collection of images that YOU will create using the step-by-step exercises in this book. If you owned one of the previous editions of the book, you also have noticed that the exercises are different from the previous editions. Yet, you may still hear that small voice in the background (not to be confused with the store announcement of the half-off sale on all organic chemistry textbooks) saying you won't be able to do stuff like that. Let me assure you that you will.

 CAUTION: *This book contains exercises and information about digital photo-editing that could be harmful to your non-computer literate status.*

My "day job" (as in "don't give up your day job") involves talking to thousands (OK, dozens) of people every day who begin their conversations by telling me how stupid they are regarding their computer knowledge. That is generally just before they hand the phone over to their 8-year-old. These people are not stupid. However, they have come to believe that they are; convinced by a legion of techno-babble-talking computer types, many of whom simply need to date more often. In creating this book I have worked with the following assumptions:

1. You have not received the Nobel Prize recently.

2. Your IQ is higher than that of mayonnaise.

3. You would like to learn to use the computer for something other than solitaire or Duke-Nukem 3D.

4. You are not a graphic arts expert. In fact, you may even be wondering if graphic art is the stuff they hang in motel rooms and sell by the truckload at "Starving Artist" sales.

In short, if you want to learn PHOTO-PAINT—this book is for you. There is one tiny secret I must share with you if you really want to learn how to use PHOTO-PAINT. It is: READ THE BOOK and DO THE EXERCISES! Contrary to rumors in the computer industry you cannot learn anything in this book by any of the following methods:

1. **Osmosis**   Keeping the book near you at all times so the knowledge of the product migrates into your mind.

2. **Sleep teaching**   Sleeping with a copy of the book as a pillow hoping that it will somehow jumpstart one or more of your brain cells.

3. **Super Speeder Reader method**   Thumbing through the pages wondering what all of the pictures mean.

4. **Proximity method**   Placing the book close enough to the computer so the PHOTO-PAINT program can get smarter and do what you want it to do.

5. **The musical "Annie" method**   I'll figure it out—tomorrow. Bet your bottom dollar that tomorrow it'll make sense. (Sung to the tune of *Tomorrow*).

6. **The Impress Your Friends technique**   Keeping a copy of this book on your shelf so your friends (or your boss) will think you are really getting into the program. Actually, this technique does work except you never really learn anything, you just impress your friends.

Enough already. Here is the short version. Using PHOTO-PAINT isn't brain surgery; it's electronic finger-painting without the mess to clean up afterwards. As I always tell people at the PHOTO-PAINT seminars, if you're not having fun with PHOTO-PAINT, you're probably doing something wrong. Buy the book and then check out that sale on organic chemistry books.

PART

I

Introduction and Digital Fundamentals

1

An Introduction to PHOTO-PAINT 8

You are about to begin an incredible journey into the world of photo-editing and digital wizardry. (Is it me, or does that last sentence sound like the preview for a new movie?) This was once the exclusive domain of multimillion-dollar computer systems and dedicated graphic artists.

With Corel PHOTO-PAINT 8, you will quickly correct and produce images that can make your desktop projects dazzle. Photo-editing programs have traditionally been labor intensive. They required many hours of tedious effort in order to manipulate images (removing trees, adding people, changing sky color, etc.). PHOTO-PAINT 8 greatly simplifies this time-consuming process. Just as CorelDRAW enables you to achieve professional computer graphic effects with little effort, Corel PHOTO-PAINT 8 will allow you to reach that same professional level in the manipulation of photographs, paintings, and other bitmap images. The bottom line is that PHOTO-PAINT 8 is fun to work with, period. The fact that you can quickly produce professional results is a bonus. Next, Dave's genuine history of PHOTO-PAINT.

A Brief History of PHOTO-PAINT

Corel PHOTO-PAINT began its life as a software product called Photofinish, created by Z-Soft. It was introduced as Corel PHOTO-PAINT 3 in May 1992. It was then, at best, an interesting bitmap-editing package that was very similar to Microsoft PAINT, which Z-Soft also wrote.

When Corel PHOTO-PAINT 4 was released in May 1993, there were many improvements, and only a small amount of the original Z-Soft program remained in it. PHOTO-PAINT 4 had limitations in the size of the image files it could handle, and the absence of several other key features prevented it from being a first-class product. In fact, it resembled Microsoft PAINT on steroids.

PHOTO-PAINT 5, which Corel originally released in May 1994, showed marked improvement. There were many changes still in progress when the product had to ship. Those changes appeared when the maintenance release (E2) was shipped in September. PHOTO-PAINT 5 began to draw serious attention from the graphics community with its support of objects and layers and other features.

PHOTO-PAINT 6 entered the world of 32-bit applications, offering a very robust set of photo-editing tools coupled with the power of a 32-bit architecture. If all this talk about 32-bit power is confusing, then—to borrow some terms from *Star Trek*—think of 32-bit power as warp drive and 16-bit as impulse power.

PHOTO-PAINT 7, which was released in November 1996, remains a 32-bit-only application that ranks among the best in the area of photo-editing applications. While retaining the general form and structure of PHOTO-PAINT 6, it provides greatly improved speed and functionality over the previous release. During its brief reign as Corel's premier photo-editing application, it won the coveted Editor's Choice award from *PC Magazine*.

With PHOTO-PAINT 8, released in November 1997, the program continues to build on its previous successes. Nearly all of the improvements in PHOTO-PAINT 8 are "under the hood." Some of the basic roll-ups have changed into docking windows which makes them available at all time. Both performance and precision of many of the PHOTO-PAINT tools have been substantially improved. On the exciting side a few new paint brush controls like Orbits and Symmetry have been added.

For PHOTO-PAINT 5 Users

PHOTO-PAINT 8 has changed substantially from the PAINT 5 release. Keyboard assignments, drop-down lists, filter names, mask and object methodology, and dialog boxes have all been modified to improve the product. Throughout the book I have attempted to leave notes like this to alert PHOTO-PAINT 5 users of specific changes.

For PHOTO-PAINT 3 & 4 Users

UPGRADE!

Before We Get Started

One of the things that makes PHOTO-PAINT such a powerful package is that there are so many combinations of tools and functions available. Of course, these qualities also make PHOTO-PAINT confusing for the novice. If you are new to photo-editing programs, I have included a section in this book to help you understand the sometimes complex world of bitmap images. For the experienced Photoshop user, I have tried to associate Corel names with their equivalent Adobe Photoshop names wherever appropriate.

If you have worked with PHOTO-PAINT 5, you may be overwhelmed at first by the changes that have been made. Truth is, after writing both the PHOTO-PAINT 5 Plus user manual and the third-party book on the product, when I first attempted to use the beta version of PHOTO-PAINT 6 in early 1995, I wondered if I would ever get used to it. In short, don't get discouraged. Follow the basic exercises and you will be using the program like a professional in no time at all.

If your experience has been with PHOTO-PAINT 6 or 7, the good news is that the PHOTO-PAINT 8 interface has only minor differences. The exciting news is in the program itself—the changes that were made have continued to enhance and streamline an already superior product. But I'm getting ahead of myself. First, let me formally introduce you to PHOTO-PAINT 8.

PHOTO-PAINT 8:
A Premier Photo-Editing Program

Corel PHOTO-PAINT 8 is first and foremost a photo- or image-editing program. It is in the same league as Adobe Photoshop, but it costs hundreds of dollars less. As a photo-editing program, it offers all of the features you should expect from a professional photo-editing package, and in several areas you can do more with PHOTO-PAINT 8 than with its main competitor. In case you are wondering why I mention Adobe Photoshop, it's because before PHOTO-PAINT came along, Adobe Photoshop was the unchallenged leader in digital photo-editing. Corel is not so quietly changing that.

One of the more useful tasks you can perform with PHOTO-PAINT 8 is to take a poorly composed, overexposed, scratchy photograph and make it look as if the photographer did a great job. Only you and PHOTO-PAINT 8 will know the truth. People today tend to get excited about all of the breathtaking, surrealistic effects they can achieve with photo-editing packages such as PHOTO-PAINT 8. In truth, I get excited, too. But it is the everyday work of making the images in our documents look as professional as possible, with the least amount of effort, that makes PHOTO-PAINT 8 such an important addition to your desktop publishing library.

Changing Reality (Virtually)

With PHOTO-PAINT 8 and this book, you will learn how simple it is to add people or objects to existing images. You can easily create things that don't exist, as shown in Figure 1-1, or, more commonly, remove unwanted objects like scratches, stains, or old boyfriends, as shown in Figure 1-2. You will even be able to change the way people look. I recently did a brochure for our church. The photo of one of the pastors had been taken several months and over 20 pounds ago. No problem. With PHOTO-PAINT 8 I took off those excess pounds in less than an hour—which is more than the pastor or the diet industry can say.

Altering people's appearance (removing blemishes, changing hair color, and so on) has been done by professionals for a long time. I knew a guy who was one of the kings of the airbrush (back in the predigital days), and was greatly appreciated by more than one playmate-of-the-month. Now, like my friend, you will be able to change the way people look. The only difference is that PHOTO-PAINT 8 doesn't require an airbrush, long hours, or years of experience.

What else can you do with PHOTO-PAINT 8? We have been talking up until now about changing existing images, but you can also create original images. If you're not an artist, don't feel excluded from this discussion. Like CorelDRAW, PHOTO-PAINT 8 lets you take clip art and assemble it to make exciting images.

Genie style floating in the tile tunnel

FIGURE 1-1

Breaking up may be hard to do, as the song goes, but removing a boyfriend from a photograph is simple using PHOTO-PAINT 8

FIGURE 1-2

Corel has provided an assortment of objects that can be placed together to make a composite image. Using the PHOTO-PAINT filters and its powerful editing tools, you will quickly learn to create all kinds of original images, logos, and what-have-you's (and still maintain your I'm-not-an-artist standing). You can take the background from one photograph and place it seamlessly with another. Figure 1-3 shows how you can make an object stand out by replacing the background. Can you find the can of Coke? It's hidden under his paw—and I wouldn't want to fight him for it.

What's New in PHOTO-PAINT 8?

Here is a list of the important features in PHOTO-PAINT 8.

ORBITS   One of the new features that demand your attention is Orbits. It is not a new brush;the Orbits feature is more like drugs for your Paintbrush. Enable Orbits on a plain old ordinary paintbrush and you will see results as shown in Figure 1-4. In addition to the many presets, you have all of the controls to make your own complex brushstrokes and save them. Orbits can be applied to masks and paths, or just applied like a normal brush using one of the many presets provided such as those seen in Figure 1-4. Even the names of the presets are entertaining. But why limit

Background
replacement
enhances
the subject

FIGURE 1-3

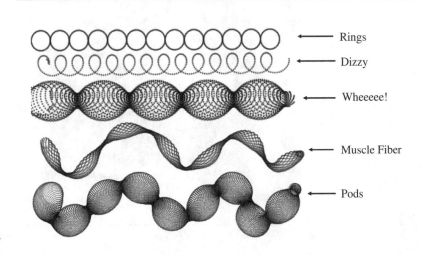

← Rings

← Dizzy

← Wheeeee!

← Muscle Fiber

← Pods

The new
Orbits
feature
turns
ordinary
brush tools
into
powerful
effect tools

FIGURE 1-4

Orbits to the normal brush tools? You can use it with the Image Sprayer and get results like that shown in Figure 1-5.

SYMMETRY Closely related to Orbits is Symmetry. When enabled, this feature turns your brush tool into a kaleidoscope. When you combine the power of both of these features, you can quickly create incredible and strange things like the one shown in Figure 1-6. Later in the book you will learn how to use Orbits and Symmetry together to produce the doily shown in Figure 1-7.

PERSPECTIVE DROP SHADOWS The Drop Shadow command was introduced with PHOTO-PAINT 7. In PHOTO-PAINT 8 the command has been expanded to automatically make perspective drop shadows like the ones shown in Figures 1-5 and 1-6.

CLIP MASKS So how did I get the rope through the ring in Figure 1-5? Using Clip Masks of course. Clip Mask is a new feature that attaches a mask to an object so the

Using
Orbits with
the Image
Sprayer tool
creates 3D
results

FIGURE 1-5

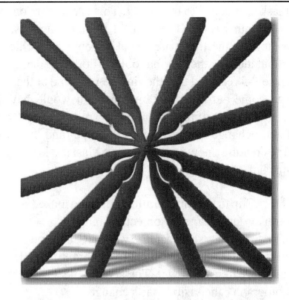

The power
of Orbits
and
Symmetry
together can
produce
fantastic
shapes

FIGURE 1-6

In Chapter
10 you will
learn how
to use
Orbits and
Symmetry
to create
this doily in
only a few
quick steps

FIGURE 1-7

effect of the mask is attached to the object. This is one of two new "nondestructive" editing effects (the other is Clip to Parent). I call them nondestructive because they allow the user to edit the transparency of an object by changing its Clip Mask properties without altering the original object. For example, to achieve the illusion you see in Figure 1-5 required that the ring be removed at the two points where the rope appears to come out. Before Clip Masks, it would have been necessary to permanently remove a part of the ring with the Transparency Brush. Then, if a client decided to slightly change the position of the rope (and they always do), it would have required re-creating a new ring. With Clip Masks, it is simply a matter of erasing and reapplying changes to a mask.

CLIP TO PARENT   Clip to Parent also allows users to make (nondestructive) changes to the transparency and shape of objects. Figure 1-8 was created by placing a photograph of a car over a text object (the word "RED") and selecting Clip to Parent. This feature makes the parts of the object (photograph) visible at every point where it is over the object (parent) below it. The actual object is unchanged. As you move the object (photograph), the visible parts change.

DOCKING DIALOGS   PHOTO-PAINT 7 introduced the Property Bar in a big way. Now in PHOTO-PAINT 8 we see the introduction of *docking windows,* shown below, that make it possible to have the equivalent of several roll-ups easily available without the sacrifice of precious screen real estate. If you are concerned that the

Using Clip to Parent allowed the quick and easy creation of this image

FIGURE 1-8

roll-ups are gone, don't worry; they are still available—but I wouldn't be surprised to find them on an endangered species list.

IMPROVED MMX SUPPORT Most people didn't know that PHOTO-PAINT 7 supported MMX. That support has been increased and improved in PHOTO-PAINT 8. This means if you own an MMX-based computer, PHOTO-PAINT works faster and you get done sooner.

LOW-RES Those who are tired of waiting for commands to be applied to large images now have the option of loading them as low-resolution images. When you load an image as Low-Res, you are working on a file that is many times smaller, which makes all actions much faster. On the screen the image appears the same as if it had been loaded at its normal resolution. When you have finished, PHOTO-PAINT renders the image at the resolution that the job requires. Another real time-saver.

ONSCREEN PREVIEW   Tired of squinting at a tiny preview window attempting to see how a particular effect will look on an image? Well, squint no longer. The built-in filters now feature an option that lets you view the effects on the actual image. Did I hear the faint sound of applause?

IMPROVED SCISSORS MASK TOOL   This hybrid of several mask tools follows edges in an image, automatically making the creation of complex masks much easier. The improved part is that it now works, and quite well I might add.

STITCH   This nifty new command puts images together, either vertically or horizontally. Don't make the same mistake some of the beta testers did and think this command is just for those still holding on to their hand scanners. It's great for making panoramas for VRML pages in Web sites or for just putting images together. I love to take two images like those shown in Figure 1-9 and use the Stitch command to make them into one, as shown in Figure 1-10.

IMPORT 3D IMAGES   PHOTO-PAINT users are no longer restricted to making objects in their images look like they're 3-D. Users can now import actual 3D models—rotating, positioning, and adjusting the lighting before rendering them and placing them as objects in the PHOTO-PAINT image.

This is only a partial list of the improvements that have been made to PHOTO-PAINT 8. I hope you're excited about some of the things you'll be able to do with this program. But before you run, you must learn to walk and that walk begins with a quick tour of PHOTO-PAINT 8.

A Quick Tour of PHOTO-PAINT 8

There is a lot of useful information in this chapter, so I urge you to look through it. If you are a first-time user of PHOTO-PAINT, I recommend that you familiarize yourself with (don't memorize) the terms and concepts described in this chapter before you begin to use the program. Time invested here will pay off in later chapters.

Two
completely
different
photographs
of Italy

FIGURE 1-9

Elements of the PHOTO-PAINT Screen

Figure 1-11 shows the Corel PHOTO-PAINT 8 main screen. Your screen may look quite different depending on how it is configured (you'll learn about this in Chapter 3). The following are the key elements that comprise the PHOTO-PAINT screen:

A panorama
created
using the
Stitch
command

FIGURE 1-10

The Onscreen Color Palette

The onscreen color palette is used to select the *Paint* (foreground color used by the brushes), *Paper* (background), and *Fill* colors. These three terms are used

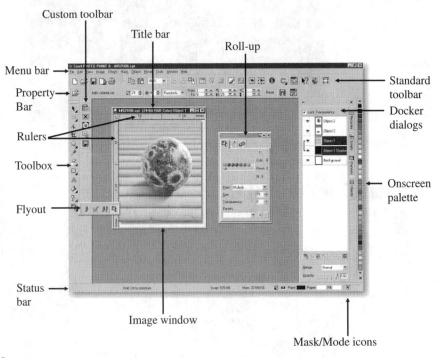

Custom toolbar

Title bar

Roll-up

Menu bar →

Property → Bar

Rulers →

Toolbox →

Flyout →

← Standard toolbar

← Docker dialogs

← Onscreen palette

The main
screen in
Corel
PHOTO-
PAINT 8

Status → bar

Image window

Mask/Mode icons

FIGURE 1-11

throughout PHOTO-PAINT, so you should try to remember them. To choose a Paint color—that is, to change the color of a brush—click a color on the palette with the left mouse button. To choose a Fill color, click with the right mouse button. To select a Paper color, hold down the CTRL key and click the left mouse button.

TIP: *If you don't enjoy memorizing mouse button/keyboard combinations, click and hold the right mouse button over the desired color. After two seconds, release the mouse button and a pop-up menu (Figure 1-12) appears allowing you to set the Paint, Paper, or Fill to that color.*

Onscreen Color Palette Pop-up Menu

In addition to selection of colors, the Pop-up menu allows you to view the Properties dialog box by choosing Properties. The title appearing on the dialog box is determined by the color palette currently selected. In Figure 1-12, the Custom palette is loaded. Other choices from the pop-up menu move the displayed portion of the Onscreen palette to either the beginning or the end, and most aspects of palette editing.

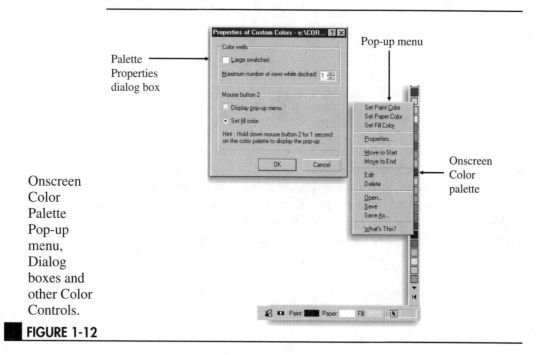

Palette
Properties
dialog box

Pop-up menu

Onscreen
Color
palette

Onscreen
Color
Palette
Pop-up
menu,
Dialog
boxes and
other Color
Controls.

FIGURE 1-12

The Menu Bar

Press any menu heading in this bar in order to access dialog boxes, submenus, and commands. Access is also available by depressing the ALT key followed by the highlighted or underlined letter in the command.

The Title Bar

This displays the application title or the image title (image filename). While it's nice to know the title, the important thing about the Title Bar is the background. The background color of the Title Bar indicates whether an image window is selected, which is important when you have several image files open and want to know which one you are about to apply an effect to.

Roll-ups

Roll-ups were designed to streamline operations using commands that are repetitively accessed. They are opened through the Roll-ups command in the View menu on the Menu Bar (shown below) through keyboard combinations, or through the Roll-up toolbar if it is open.

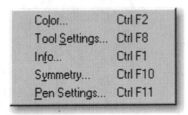

A roll-up provides access to controls for choosing and applying fills, outlines, text attributes, and other options. Roll-up windows contain many of the controls found in dialog boxes: command buttons, text boxes, drop-down list boxes, and so on. But unlike most dialog boxes, the roll-up window stays open after you apply the selected options. This lets you make adjustments and experiment with different options without having to continually reopen a dialog box.

Docker Windows

Most probably the successor to roll-ups, dockable windows are parked on the side and provide the same functionality as the equivalent roll-up. There are four docking dialogs in PHOTO-PAINT 8: Objects, Channels, Script Manager, and Command Recorder.

Rulers and Guidelines

Selecting Rulers from the View command in the Menu Bar or the keyboard combination CTRL-R toggles the display of the rulers on the image.

Rulers are important in PHOTO-PAINT because they provide the only visual indicator of how large an image actually is. We will explore why this happens in Chapter 2. For now, be aware that it is possible for a photograph to completely fill the screen and yet be smaller than a postage stamp when you print it. That's why rulers are important. Guidelines are new to PHOTO-PAINT 8 and provide a necessary alignment tool when setting up multiple objects in an image. Rulers, guidelines, and grids are explored in Chapter 4.

Toolbars

In PHOTO-PAINT 5 there is a single ribbon bar; in PHOTO-PAINT 6 several more toolbars were added and with PHOTO-PAINT 8, that single toolbar from PAINT 5 has returned and brought its entire family. There are now 17 toolbars in all (counting the Toolbox and the Property Bar). If they were all open and floating at the same time, there would be no room for the image you need to work on. The good news is that only a few of them have to be open at any given moment. Right-clicking on the Toolbox brings up a menu where you can select or deselect from the list of 15 or more (you can add custom toolbars).

The Image Window

This is the image-display window. The zoom factor of each image window is controlled independently by the Zoom command in View or by the Zoom control in the Ribbon Bar. The default setting of Zoom—100 percent—is set in the Options section of the Tools menu. If you have a medium- to high-performance graphics board in your system, you can choose Best Fit. But for an accurate representation of the image on the screen, you should always use 100%.

TIP: *When you choose a zoom factor that is less or greater than 100 percent, the image may have a poor appearance. This is a result of the way it's displayed by the graphics adapter under Windows 95 and does not reflect the actual image quality.*

Toolbox/Flyouts

This contains all of the tools used for image editing. Many of the buttons in the Toolbox have flyouts to allow access to additional related tools. Most flyouts are identical to their toolbar. For example, compare the Mask flyout shown below with the Mask Tools toolbar that was placed alongside it.

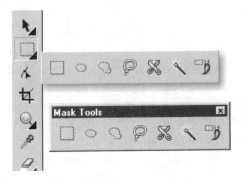

Availability of a flyout is indicated by a tiny black arrow in the lower right-hand corner of the button.

To open a flyout, you can click and hold the cursor on the button for more than a second or click directly on the black arrow. Clicking on any tool in the flyout places the selected tool button at the head of the flyout.

The Status Bar

The Status Bar contains a wealth of information. By default, it is located at the bottom of the screen. Refer to Chapter 3 for information on how to customize the Status Bar for your desktop needs.

Mask and Mode Icons

The mask icons are displayed in the Status Bar. The three icons are the Mask mode, Mask Present, and Object mode icons. These icons are more important than you might imagine. You will sometimes try to apply an effect or use a brush stroke and either nothing will happen or what happens is not what you expected. More often than not, this is because you have a mask somewhere in the image that is preventing whatever it is that you are trying to do, or you have the mask in something other than Normal mode. Make a habit of looking for the Mask icon when things don't work as planned.

The Property Bar

The Property Bar is a great productivity enhancement. Most of the common Tool settings items now appear on Property Bars, relieving the screen from overcrowding by too many roll-ups. Put simply, the Property Bar displays the most-often-used commands for whatever mode is selected by the user.

The Standard Toolbar

The Standard toolbar is enabled by default. The first seven buttons of the Standard toolbar, shown below, are common Windows functions. Several new buttons have been added with the release of PHOTO-PAINT 8. The remaining buttons of the Standard toolbar will be discussed in greater detail as we learn to use them.

Button	Function
	Activates the Create A New Image dialog box for creating new image files.
	Activates the Open An Image dialog box to open existing files.

	Saves the currently selected image. This button is grayed out (unavailable) until the selected image has been modified.
	Used to make a copy of the currently selected image in another graphics format
	Allows printing of selected image.
	Cuts (removes) the defined (masked) area and copies it to the Clipboard.
	Copies a defined (masked) area to the clipboard.
	Pastes (copies) the image in the clipboard into the selected image as an object. (Note: Unlike the Paste *command*, which gives you a choice of pasting as an object or as a new document, the Paste as Object *button* does not give you a choice.)

Where to Find Help

Most users don't take advantage of the extensive help features built into products. I can't say for sure why they don't use them, but I can say that Corel has built a lot of help features into PHOTO-PAINT 8 that will answer many questions for you without the need to reference either this book or the manual that shipped with the product. Here is a brief summary of what and where they are.

Corel Tutor

It's hard to miss this one—it's one of six possible choices on the opening screen. Selecting Corel Tutor opens the Corel Tutor main menu. This is a step-by-step tutorial that teaches you how to use PHOTO-PAINT 8 to accomplish many tasks in photo-editing. Another way to launch the Corel Tutor is to click the Apple button on the Standard toolbar shown below. (Sorry to disappoint those of you who thought it launched the Macintosh version.)

 TIP: *If you cannot find some of the buttons mentioned in this section, there is a good chance their current setting is too large to fit on your display. To change the size of the buttons, select Toolbars... in the View menu and change the Button size slider so that all of the buttons in the Standard toolbar fit the display.*

Context Help

The button with the question mark and the arrow shown next to the Corel Tutor button above is the Context Help button. Clicking this button changes the cursor to an arrow with a question mark. It remains in this mode until clicked on a tool on the main screen. Clicking on a tool brings up the context-sensitive help screen that explains the purpose of the item clicked.

What's This?

Placing the cursor on a feature anywhere on a tool or feature inside of a dialog box and clicking on it with the right mouse button produces a small rectangle with the message "What's This?" This provides a brief description of the function selected. The trick to making it work is to click the "What's This?" message box with the left mouse button *after* you right-click the feature. The message box and the resulting description are shown below.

 TIP: *Don't forget to click on the message box that contains the message "What's This?" to access the information.*

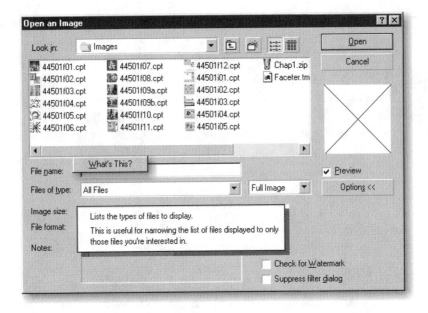

The Help Manual

Throughout the book I have included tips to direct you toward the more useful help files. These files provide all of the information that you would expect to find in the PHOTO-PAINT 8 reference manual. Speaking of which...

The manual that shipped with both the CorelDRAW 8 suite and the stand-alone version of PHOTO-PAINT 8 is an excellent reference. I am not just saying this because this is a CorelPRESS book. The crew that Corel assembled created a robust manual that is a vast improvement over the pathetic 48-page insert that was included with the original CorelDRAW 5 release.

Help on the Web

There are several Internet sites that provide answers to questions, including the Corel Web site (www.corel.com). Another useful site is the *Corel Magazine* home page (www.corelmag.com), which also has a wealth of back issues and other resources available. As Corel PHOTO-PAINT continues to increase in popularity, expect to see an even greater number of resources appearing.

Before finishing this chapter, we need to discuss some hardware requirements that are recommended for those about to venture into the land of PHOTO-PAINT 8.

Setting Up Your System—Do You Have What It Takes?

This is more than just a cute title. Corel PHOTO-PAINT 8 requires some substantial systems resources in order to work properly. To make sure that you have sufficient system resources, it is necessary to spend a little time understanding what's "under the hood" with the system you already have. (Good news for you techno-wizards: If you already know everything about hardware, go directly to the next chapter.)

Hardware Considerations

The minimum requirement to run PHOTO-PAINT 8 is that you must have Windows 95 already installed and running. While the minimum hardware necessary to run Windows 95 is not insignificant, it is not sufficient for photo-editing. Let's consider some realistic system requirements for using PHOTO-PAINT 8.

RAM

According to Microsoft, it is possible to run Windows 95 on 4MB of RAM (lots of luck). The minimum amount of RAM that you should be using is 8MB, but even that's tight. According to all of the computer magazines, Windows 95 runs well with 16MB of RAM. They call it the "sweet spot." It is even said that increasing the amount of RAM above 16MB doesn't provide any significant boost in performance. While this is true for many Windows 95 applications, it is not true for programs that manipulate large bitmap images—like PHOTO-PAINT 8. If you can afford it, I recommend you running with a minimum of 32MB RAM installed. I am running with 64MB RAM while working on this book. The reason for this large amount of RAM is because the price of RAM memory collapsed in the last half of 1996 and it was too good a deal to pass up. The performance increase you will realize with additional RAM installed greatly outweighs the dollar/benefit increase you will see with almost any other hardware purchase.

CPU

I would recommend a Pentium (P5) system. The difference between a 486 CPU and a Pentium will be noticed mostly when applying the Effect filters. While working on this book, I am using the new AMD K6 (233 MHz) processor and it is really fast.

How fast, you ask? I can actually finish a photo-editing project before I start. Now that's fast!

The Hard Disk

Your hard disk drive should have at least a 500MB capacity. If that figure gave you a start, take a look at your local computer superstore. In the latter part of 1997, 2GB drives were selling for $189 or less! So how big a drive do you need? After CorelDRAW 8 is loaded, you should have at least 50 to 100MB of free disk space remaining. Bitmap images take up a lot of space. So does Windows 95, for that matter. If you are going to be working on a lot of images and not constantly archiving them on tape or floppies, get yourself a drive large enough to handle the load. I am currently using a Seagate 4GB and I have already filled up most of it. Scary, isn't it?

That's all for this chapter and the first part. Next we will learn about digital images, resolution, and color. If you think that pixels are mythical winged creatures that fly in the forest, you really need to read Chapter 2.

2

Understanding Digital
Images

As the field of digital imagery expands, many people are getting deeply involved with computer graphics, with little or no background on the subject. While there are many books about graphics on the shelves today, most of them assume that you know the terminology and the technical material that serves as the foundation of computer graphics. The end result is frustration for the user. This chapter will try to help you fill in some of the gaps you might have in your graphics background.

Basic Terms in Digital Imaging

Before we dive into computer terms and acronyms, there is something you must first understand: There are many terms in the computer industry that are nonstandard, colloquial, or just plain dumb. This has led to one of my theorems regarding computer terminology: *The only thing that is universally accepted in the computer industry is that nothing is universally accepted in the computer industry.*

I don't expect the Pulitzer Prize for that one, but it goes a long way toward explaining why there are so many different terms to describe the same thing in the computer industry. I am also a strong believer in using the terminology in common use rather than the "technically correct" term. When it comes to communicating ideas, the popular or commonly used term is more important. In this book, I will always try to use the commonly used term (even if it isn't accurate) as well as the technically correct term. Here are a few terms we need to know something about.

Bitmap and Vector Images

When it comes to computer images, there are two types: *bitmap* (also called *paint*) and *vector* (also called *freehand*). The following photograph of a jet is a typical example of a bitmap image. The image file is composed of millions of individual *pixels* (picture elements—see Figure 2-1). Bitmap files tend to be much larger than their vector counterparts and resolution dependent (we will explore resolution dependency later in this chapter).

The jet from the CorelDRAW clip-art collection that appears to be taking off from on top of the photograph is a vector image. The original clip-art image contained no pixels and was composed of lines and fills. Vector images tend to be complex—meaning they may be composed of thousands of individual objects—and have a much smaller image file size than their bitmap equivalent. The complexity of the vector-based image is shown below as it appears (wireframe view) in CorelDRAW. Corel PHOTO-PAINT only works with bitmap images, so when a vector-based image file (like the jet) is loaded into Corel PHOTO-PAINT, it must first be converted, or *rasterized,* to a bitmap as it is loaded.

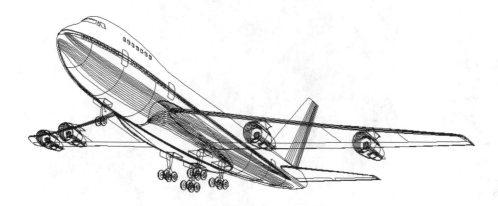

To work effectively with bitmap images, it is necessary to understand why they act differently than the object-based images in CorelDRAW. Let us begin by defining our terms.

Pixels

These are not little elf-like creatures that fly through the forest at twilight. Bitmap images are composed of pixels. The term "pixel" is short for PIcture ELement. Bitmap images are composed of pixels. They are the individual squares that make up an image on a computer screen or on hard copy. One way to understand pixels is to think of a wall mural created with mosaic tiles. When you get close to a mural made of mosaic tiles, it looks like someone had a bad Lego day. This is because you are so close you are looking at individual tiles. But step away a few feet from the mosaic and the individual tiles begin to lose their definition and visually merge. The tiles have not changed their size or number, yet the further back you move, the better the image looks. Pixels in bitmaps work much the same way. I have created a sample image, shown in Figure 2-1, to illustrate how pixels make up an image. The area surrounded by the white rectangle on the left has been zoomed in to 1,600 percent and displayed on the right. It shows that as you zoom in on an image, the individual

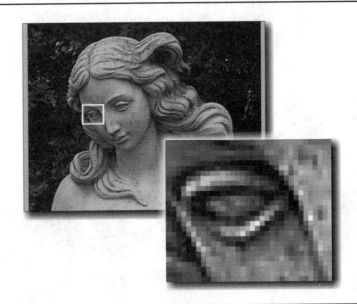

The pixels that compose the image become evident at a Zoom factor of 1,600 percent

FIGURE 2-1

pixels begin to stand out more and the image they produce becomes less and less evident. Returning to our mosaic tile analogy, there are, of course, major differences between pixels and mosaic tiles. Pixels come in a greater selection of decorator colors (more than 16.7 million, to be exact), and pixels don't weigh as much as tiles. However, mosaic tiles and pixels operate in the same way to produce an image.

Color Depth

What is *color depth*? It is the number of bits necessary to describe an individual pixel color. If a color image has a depth of 4 bits, that means there are 16 possible combinations of bits (4^2) to describe the color in each pixel. Another way to say it is there are 16 possible colors available, or the image has a 16-color palette. There are several different color depths available with PHOTO-PAINT. They are 1-bit (2 colors), 4-bit (16 colors), 8-bit (256 colors), 16-bit (65K colors), and 24-bit (16.7 million colors). There is also 32-bit color, but it is used for prepress and essentially only represents 16.7 million colors using a different type of color model. The greater an image's color depth, the more shades of color it contains, as shown in Table 2-1. The drawback is that as the color depth of an image changes, the file size changes, as shown in Table 2-2.

Color Depth	Type of Image	Color(s) Available
1-bit	Black-and-White	2 colors
8-bit	Grayscale	256 shades of gray
4-bit	Color	16 colors
8-bit	Color	256 colors
16-bit	Color, also called high color	65,000 colors
16-bit	Grayscale	65,000 shades of gray
24-bit	Color, also called true color or RGB color	16.7 million colors
32-bit	Color, also called CMYK	16.7 million colors
48-bit	Color	281 Billion

Color Depth for the Various Image Types

TABLE 2-1

File Size as a Function of Color Depth	Color Depth	32-bit (16.7 million)	24-bit (16.7 million)	8-bit (256 colors)	1-bit (2 colors)
	Size	793KB	632KB	395KB	28KB

TABLE 2-2

 NOTE: *Corel PHOTO-PAINT does not support conversion of an image to 16-bit color depth although it does convert to 16-bit grayscale.*

All image file formats have some restrictions regarding the color depth that they can accommodate, so it becomes necessary to know what color depth you are working with in order to recognize what kinds of colors and other tools you can use with it.

If color depth is new to you, you may be wondering, "Why do we have all of these different color depths? Why not make all of the images 24-bit and be done with it?" There are many reasons for the different image types. One of the major factors of color depth is the physical size of the image file that each type produces. The greater the number of bits associated with each pixel (color depth), the larger the file size. If an image has a size of 20KB as a black-and-white (1-bit) image, it will take more than 480KB as a true-color (24-bit) image. If an 8 x 10-inch color photograph is scanned in at 600 dpi (don't ever do it!) at a color depth of 24-bit, the resulting 64MB+ file will probably not even fit in your system. Not to mention that every operation with this image will be measured in hours instead of seconds. There are other factors associated with the different color depths. Let's take a closer look at the various types of color depth used in the industry today.

Black-and-White Images

The term "black and white" has caused some confusion in the past because old movies and television shows are referred to as being in black and white. They are actually grayscale, not black and white. Don't try to educate anyone on this subject. Just remember that the old *Andy Griffith* and *Dick Van Dyke* shows are really in grayscale, not black and white.

In real black-and-white images, one bit of information is used per pixel to define its color. Because it has only one bit, it can only show one of two states, either black or white. The little pixel is turned either on or off. It doesn't get any simpler than this.

Black-and-white images are more common than you would imagine. The following illustration shows a black-and-white image that was scanned from a clip-art book. It is common to associate this kind of image with old Victorian woodcuts, but as you can see, there are contemporary examples of black and white as well.

There is a lot that can be done with a black-and-white image, also called *line art.* Users of Adobe programs may refer to them as bitmap images. This can be confusing since most photographic images are referred to as bitmaps. It is possible to use black and white (1-bit) to produce photographs that appear to be grayscale. It approximates the grayscale look by a process called *dithering.* Dithering can be thought of as pseudo-grayscale when it comes to black-and-white images. While dithering can simulate grayscale, quality suffers greatly when a dithered image is resized.

Besides line art, there are three different types of black-and-white images that can be produced with PHOTO-PAINT 8 by selecting Convert to… in the Image menu and choosing Black and White (1-bit). To illustrate the differences between them, I have created a composite image in Figure 2-2 to show the results of these conversions. I have displayed only one of the two possible diffusion methods since they appear nearly identical. The original grayscale image that we converted is shown in Figure 2-3. The left panel of the image was converted to black and white using *error diffusion,* a dithering process that arranges the black-and-white pixels to appear to the viewer's eye as grayscale. Error diffusion is more complex than the other method, ordered diffusion. The difference in speed is almost unnoticeable on most Pentium computers.

TIP: *While Error Diffusion dithering produces the best-looking results, it distorts the most when the image is resized.*

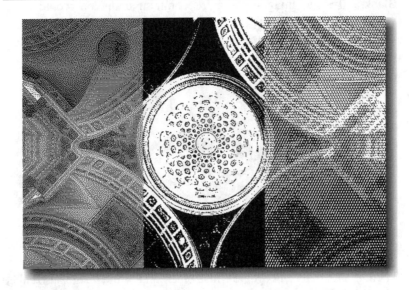

The result of converting an image to black and white using error diffusion (left), line art (middle), and halftone (right)

FIGURE 2-2

A grayscale image uses 256 shades to represent the continuous tone photograph

FIGURE 2-3

The middle panel was converted using the Line Art setting. This method measures the shade value of each pixel in the original image and converts it to either a black or a white dot. The *threshold value* determines whether it becomes black or white. Any value greater than the threshold becomes white; any below becomes black. While the default value is set to the middle of the range (128 out of a possible 256), I changed the value of the Threshold to 150 to get more of the detail in the dome.

The last panel in Figure 2-2 was created using the halftone screen. Halftones are discussed in greater detail in the section of this chapter dealing with resolution.

 *NOTE: For more information about halftones, in PHOTO-PAINT, press the F1 function key and select the index tab. type in **Halftone Types** and click the display button. select overview: working with bitmaps and halftone screens.*

Grayscale Images

What we call black-and-white photos are in fact grayscale images. Photographs (color and grayscale) are *continuous tone* images, so called because the photo, unlike a digital image, isn't composed of square pixels but rather continuous areas of different colors or shades. To represent this information in a digital format requires dividing the image into pixels using eight bits of information for each pixel, producing 256 possible shades of gray. The shade of each pixel ranges from a value of white (0) to black (255). Grayscale is used for many other things besides "black-and-white" photos. When you learn about masks (beginning in Chapter 7), you will find out that most of the masks used in photo-editing are actually grayscale images.

4-Bit and 8-Bit Color

With the explosive growth of the Internet, 256-color (8-bit) images have become very popular. If you are using PHOTO-PAINT 8 to create images for the Web, you will be using them a lot. With the exception of some Windows and Web Page icons, 4-bit color is rarely used, so we will devote most of this discussion to 8-bit or 256-color images. Referred to as *paletted* or *256-color,* an 8-bit color image can only have one of a possible 256 combinations of color assigned to each pixel. This isn't as limited as you might imagine.

When an image is converted to 8-bit, PHOTO-PAINT creates a reference palette to which all of the colors used in the image are assigned—hence the term "paletted."

Many people are under the impression that 8-bit color is markedly inferior to 24-bit color. That used to be true, but the process of converting the image from 16- or 24-bit to 8-bit color has been so dramatically improved that in many cases it is difficult, if not impossible, to tell the original image from the paletted one. We will explore some techniques that allow us to create vivid 256-color images from 24-bit color photographs in Chapter 5.

16-Bit Color (65K Color)

The 16-bit color depth reminds me of the EGA monitor standard. There was a brief time when CGA wasn't enough. There is nothing worse than seeing a graphic computer game in CGA, and so EGA came next. It offered more colors and slightly better resolution than CGA. EGA was quickly replaced by VGA. In a way, 16-bit color (65K color) is like that. It came at a time when 24-bit color was just too expensive and 8-bit (256 color) wasn't enough. Most of the higher-performance cards now offer 24-bit color support and 16-bit is losing popularity.

Using 16 bits to define the color depth provides approximately 65,000 colors. This is enough for almost any color image. I have seen 16- and 24-bit images side by side, and it is almost impossible to tell them apart. All things being equal, most of the photo-editing public could work with 65K color from now until the Second Coming and never tell any difference. What are the advantages of 16-bit color? Lower-cost graphics card and faster performance because you are moving one-third fewer bits. When will you use 16-bit color? Even though PHOTO-PAINT doesn't support 16K color, you may see it if you have a limited amount of video RAM on your display adapter card and you increased your resolution setting. Many times, the display adapter will change the display color depth from 24-bit to 16-bit.

 TIP: *If your display adapter is set to display 16-bit color, it does not affect the image quality, only the display of the image.*

24-Bit (True Color)

True-color images may use up to 16.7 million colors. They are so closely associated with the RGB color model that they are sometimes referred to as RGB 24-bit. (We will talk about color models later in this chapter.) RGB stands for Red-Green-Blue. Your monitor makes all of its colors by using combinations of these three colors. Your eye perceives color the same way: red, green, blue. The three colors that make up the RGB models each have eight bits assigned to them, allowing for 256 possible shades of each color. Your monitor creates colors by painting the images on the inside of your display with three electronic beams (called guns). Each color gun in the color monitor can display 256 possible shades of its color. The mixing together of three sets of 256 combinations produces a possible 16.7 million color combinations. While true color doesn't display every possible color, it gets pretty close. It is the model of choice for the desktop computer artist.

32-Bit Color

Look back at Table 2-1. Do you notice anything unusual about 32-bit color? Although the color depth is increased by 25 percent over a 24-bit image, the number of colors remained the same. Why is that?

There are two answers, because there are two types of color depth that involve 32 bits. The first is more commonly seen on the Mac side of the world. When they say something is 32-bit, they are referring to a 24-bit RGB model with an additional 8-bit *alpha channel.* Apple reserved the alpha channel, but it has never specified a purpose for this data. Alpha channel has come to be used by most applications to pass grayscale mask information.

The other 32-bit type of color image expresses a CMYK (Cyan-Magenta-Yellow-Black) model.

NOTE: *Most of the graphic processors are advertising that they offer 32-bit, 64-bit, and now 128-bit graphic processor boards. This has nothing to do with color depth. It is a reference to the width of the data path. The wider the data path, the greater the amount of color data that can be moved, and therefore the faster the screens are redrawn.*

File Compression

Because bitmap image files tend to be very large, there is a need to use compression to conserve space on the hard drive. This compression is not related to any compression that you may already be using on your disk drive. There are several compression schemes that are either built into the file formats or are offered as an option when saving the file. Before we look at the individual file formats, we need to know a few things about compression and its benefits and drawbacks. Compression is generally divided into two categories: lossy and nonlossy.

Lossy Compression

Lossy compression offers the greatest amount of compression, but at a price. As the name implies, some of the image quality is lost in the process. Lossy compression schemes can reduce very large files from several megabytes in size to only a few kilobytes. Most of the time, the loss in quality is not apparent. The most popular example of lossy compression is the JPEG format. Another compression method that is becoming popular is Wavelet compression, which also supports 24-bit color. This file format stores bitmap information at very high compression levels.

 TIP: *Whenever you save an image using lossy compression, it is no longer necessary to close and reopen the file to see the effect of the compression.*

Table 2-3 compares JPEG and Wavelet compression. The Best quality value was the one chosen by Corel PHOTO-PAINT 8 when the Suppress filter dialog option on the Save an Image to Disk dialog box was enabled. The Maximum compression category was based on the maximum compression that produced a small amount of image degradation.

Nonlossy Compression

Nonlossy compression has been around longer than lossy compression. It generally offers a significant amount of compression without any loss of image information (quality). Most of these compression schemes offer compression ratios between 2:1 and 4:1. The more popular versions of nonlossy compression found in Corel PHOTO-PAINT 8 are LZW and Packbits.

Comparison of File Compression Results	Original File Size	Wavelet Best quality	Wavelet Maximum Compression	JPEG Best quality	JPEG Maximum Compression
	5.02MB	202KB	78KB	634KB	104KB

TABLE 2-3

Image File Formats

Now that we have discussed the type of images that exist in a digital world, we need to understand some of the different ways these images can be saved. There are many different file formats for saving images. Each has its strong and weak points when it comes to storing different types of image files. Some formats cannot store more than 256 colors, some cannot be compressed, and others produce enormous files. Corel PHOTO-PAINT gives you a large assortment of file formats to choose from when you save a file. If you are not familiar with the choices, this blessing of a wide assortment can become confusing. In this section, we will try to take some of the mystery out of these formats with strange-sounding names.

Understanding File Formats

For some, the question will be, "What is an image file format?" The answer is an image file format defines a way of storing an image and any related information in a way that other programs can recognize and use. Each format has its own unique form, called a *file structure,* for saving the image pixels and other related file information such as resolution and color depth.

Each format is unique and is generally identified by its three-letter file extension. For example, the three-letter extension "CPT" on a filename identifies the file format as a Corel PHOTO-PAINT file. This extension is important because many programs use the three-character extension to identify the type of File Import filter to select. If the wrong extension or a unique extension is used, it may be difficult, perhaps impossible, to import the image.

Corel PHOTO-PAINT is aware of the color depth of the image you are attempting to save and changes the selection of available file-format choices automatically. For example, if you have a 32-bit color image, the drop-down list will be reduced from the normal selection to the few file format choices that support 32-bit color.

The Wavelet compression format represents another entry in the field of image file compression that was introduced in with PHOTO-PAINT 7.

Because there are dozens of file formats, it would be confusing to try to cover them all. Instead, we will look at the major ones supported by Corel PHOTO-PAINT and discuss a few of their strengths and limitations.

NOTE: *For more information about file formats, in PHOTO-PAINT, select Technical Support for tahe Help menu, and click the Contents tab. Choose Import, Export, and OLE and click on List of Export File Formats. Locate the file format that you want more information on and either double-click on it or click on it and then click the Display button.*

CPT (Going Native)

This is a native format of Corel PHOTO-PAINT. The term *native* means it is unique to the application. CPT (Corel PHOTO-PAINT) is the best format for your originals. Saving in a CPT format retains all of the unique PHOTO-PAINT information about the image being saved. Saving in other image formats results in the loss of this information.

The principle limitation of the CPT format is portability. To my knowledge, there are no non-Corel applications that can load an image saved as a CPT file. The image file can be saved as compressed (non-lossy). With the PHOTO-PAINT 8 release, there are two possible CPT file formats available: Corel PHOTO-PAINT image (CPT) and Corel PHOTO-PAINT 6 image (CPT). Although they have the same file extensions, the native format of PHOTO-PAINT 8 (CPT) can only be read by PHOTO-PAINT 7 and 8. The new version of CPT loads significantly faster than images saved in the PHOTO-PAINT 6 image (CPT) format.

Windows Bitmap (BMP, DIB)

BMP (Windows Bitmap) is the native image format for Microsoft Paint, which is included with every copy of Microsoft Windows and supported by nearly every Windows program. Corel PHOTO-PAINT supports BMP images up to 24-bit color (16.7 million colors). This is a popular format that decorates everyone's computer screen these days, but it does not offer compression and is generally used only for small image files (less than a few hundred kilobytes in size).

GIF (GIF)

CompuServe created GIF (Graphics Interchange Format) a long time ago as a means of compressing images for use over their extensive online network. Many people think CompuServe owns it. In fact, they bought the rights to use a patented compression scheme (LZW) from Sperry-Univac. Now if that's not trivia, I don't know what is. GIF has become a very popular format, especially now that everyone is jumping on the Internet. As a way to send pictures over phone lines, it can't be beat. It has a major limitation of supporting only 8-bit (256-color) images. Corel PHOTO-PAINT does not offer an option to compress images saved as GIF files because it is already a compression format.

Corel PHOTO-PAINT offers the ability to save GIF files in 89a and 87a format. These formats provide the capability to save a file with transparency and interlacing options, which is becoming increasingly important for creating Web graphics for use on the Internet.

Paintbrush (PCX)

PCX is one of the original file formats, created by Z-Soft for PC Paintbrush back when Noah was working on the Ark. It is unquestionably one of the most popular image file formats around, mainly because PC Paintbrush is the oldest painting program for the IBM PC. Corel PHOTO-PAINT supports PCX images up to 24-bit color. The only concern with using PCX images involves importing them into older applications. Because the PCX format has been around so long, there are many versions of PCX import filters around. It is possible, even likely, to find an older application that imports PCX files but cannot read the file exported by Corel PHOTO-PAINT.

EPS (Supports 32-bit)

EPS stands for Encapsulated PostScript. PostScript is a page description language used by imagesetters and laser printers. This format is a favorite of your friendly neighborhood service bureau. Many people do not think about using the EPS format when working with PAINT's bitmap images because of its association with vector-based drawings like CorelDRAW. Actually, EPS does work with bitmap images... for a price. By that I mean a bitmap image saved in the EPS format will be roughly three times as large as the same file saved in the TIF format. So, why use EPS? It was once the only way to place an image into CorelDRAW without the white background. This is no longer true; CorelDRAW can import CPT files with the object/layers intact. For more information, see Chapter 5. If you must send work to a service bureau, it may be the only format they will accept, especially for separations.

PICT

This is a problematic format, but I am including it because Corel PHOTO-PAINT can import it. Apple developed PICT as the primary format for Macintosh graphics.

Like PostScript, it is a page description language. This format has not been reliable for importing images into Corel, PageMaker, and other programs. The rule with PICT is simple. If the image you are using is in PICT format, you have no choice but to import it as a PICT file and hope for the best. If you are saving an image so that it can be used on a Macintosh, use JPEG or TIF. They are both excellent formats for the Mac, and are much more dependable than PICT.

TARGA (TGA, TVA)

This format was originally created for TARGA display boards. If you haven't seen this image format before, it is probably because it is used by a small segment of the professional market that works with high-end color and video. In Corel PHOTO-PAINT, this file format supports up to 24-bit color. TARGA does not support 32-bit color (CMYK). TARGA does support 32-bit images—24-bit color with an 8-bit alpha channel, which can be used to retrieve mask information by Corel PHOTO-PAINT 6–8. Corel PHOTO-PAINT 5 cannot read the alpha channel information in TARGA file format. Many people believe that TARGA is technically superior to any other format on the marketplace. Others feel it is only good for multimedia because it is a niche format that is not widely used. It is becoming popular with the growing 3-D market because it can process all the information that a 3-D image requires.

TIFF (Tagged Image File Format, TIF)

TIFF is probably the most popular full-color bitmap format around, supported by every PC and Mac paint program I have ever seen. TIFF is clearly the image format of choice. It is used as a default setting for every scanning program on the marketplace today.

You may have heard that there are many different versions of TIFF, which can conceivably cause some compatibility problems when moving images between programs. To date, the only problems we have experienced with TIFF files involved saving images as 24-bit color TIFF files and trying to read them on an application that doesn't offer 24-bit color support.

Corel PHOTO-PAINT supports all color-depth settings in TIFF format, including 32-bit color (CMYK). However, don't save your images in 32-bit color unless it is specifically requested. Because 32-bit color (CMYK) is new, you may end up with a TIFF file that some older applications cannot read. Remember that 32-bit (CMYK) TIFF contains the same color information as 24-bit color TIFF.

Scitex CT Bitmap (SCT, CT)

Unless your service bureau specifically requests this file format, don't save in it. High-end commercial printers use Scitex computers to generate color separations of images and other documents. Corel PHOTO-PAINT can open images digitized with Scitex scanners and save the edited images to the Scitex CT (Continuous Tone) format. Because there are several restrictions regarding the transfer of images from the PC to a Scitex drive, you will probably want to consult with the person using the Scitex printer before saving to the CT format. It is possible that a TIFF or JPEG (compression) format is preferred. Scitex is only available when the image is in 32-bit color (CMYK).

Now that you understand a few terms, let's move on and learn about resolution.

Resolution—A Term with Too Many Definitions

Without an understanding of resolution and its effects, you may find yourself creating beautiful images that fill the entire display screen in PHOTO-PAINT, yet appear to be smaller than postage stamps when you print them. Resolution is a very misunderstood concept in desktop publishing, the confusion compounded by the fact that this term may have entirely different meanings depending on the device you are talking about. In this chapter, we will learn what resolution is and what it does for us in PHOTO-PAINT 8. The information about resolution that is discussed in this chapter applies to all image editing applications, not just PHOTO-PAINT.

Resolution and the Size of the Image

As I said in the introduction to this section, the term *resolution* represents one of the more elusive concepts of digital imaging. In a vector-based program, we describe an image's size in the popular unit of measure for the country or culture we live in. In the United States, we refer to the standard letter-size page as being 8.5 x 11 inches. Image size in photo-editing programs is traditionally measured in pixels. The reason for using pixels is that the size of an image in pixels is fixed. So when I speak of an image being 1,200 x 600 pixels, I know from experience approximately how big the image is. If we use a unit of measure other than pixels—say, inches—the dimensions of the printed image are dependent on the resolution of the image.

So What Is Resolution?

Resolution is the density of pixels per inch (ppi) that make up an image, and it is measured in dots per inch (dpi). In other words, it is a measure of how closely each pixel in an image is positioned to the one next to it.

Let's assume we have an image that is 300 pixels wide by 300 pixels high. So how big will the image be when I import it into CorelDRAW? This is a trick question. There is not enough information. Without knowing the resolution of the image, it is impossible to determine the size when it is imported into DRAW. If the resolution of this image is set to 300 pixels per inch, then the image dimensions are 1 x 1 inches when imported into CorelDRAW. If the resolution is *doubled* (set to 600 dpi), the image would be *half* the size, or .5 x .5 inches. If the resolution is *reduced by half* (150 dpi), the *image size doubles* to 2 x 2 inches. We can see that resolution exhibits an inverse relationship, which means that if one value increases, the other decreases. The physical size of an image in PHOTO-PAINT is most accurately expressed as the length (in pixels) of each side. Resolution tells you how many pixels are contained in each unit of measure.

To show the effect of changing resolution, I duplicated a photograph with PHOTO-PAINT, making four identical copies. Next, I changed the resolution (resampled) of each of the copies so that I had four photographs at four different resolutions. Even though each of the images in Figure 2-4 is a different resolution,

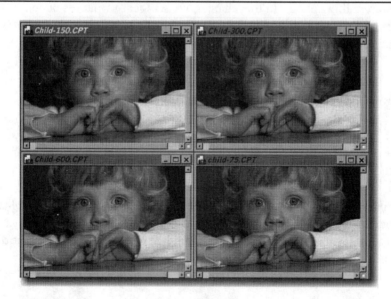

An identical photograph saved at four different resolutions displayed in PHOTO-PAINT

FIGURE 2-4

they appear the same size in PHOTO-PAINT. When all four files were imported into CorelDRAW, the results are as shown in Figure 2-5. Why do the photos appear to be the same size in Figure 2-4, you ask? Because the physical size of the images (in pixels) remained unchanged—only the resolution changed.

Screen Resolution

No matter what resolution you are using, Corel PHOTO-PAINT displays each pixel onscreen according to the zoom ratio. That'is why all of the photos in Figure 2-4 appeared to be the same size even though they were at different resolutions. At a zoom ratio of 100 percent, each image pixel is mapped to a single screen pixel. The display's zoom setting has no effect on the actual image file. If you are a little fuzzy on monitors and pixels, read on. If you know them cold, skip ahead to "Resolution and Printers."

When you bought your monitor and/or display card, you may have been bewildered by such terms as 640 x 480, 800 x 600, and so on. These figures refer to the number of screen pixels that the monitor can display horizontally and vertically. For example, let's say you have a plain vanilla VGA monitor. The standard resolution for this monitor is 640 pixels wide by 480 pixels high (640 x 480). If you open a file that is 800 pixels wide by 533 pixels high, the image at 100% zoom is too large to

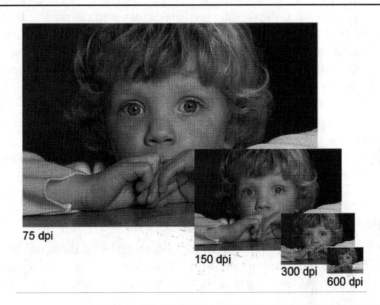

The same four photos imported into CorelDRAW

75 dpi

150 dpi

300 dpi

600 dpi

FIGURE 2-5

fit into the screen. With the screen resolution changed to 800 x 600 (also called Super VGA), the display area now contains a width of 800 pixels by a height of 600 pixels. The image appears smaller than in the previous figure, but it is still too large to fit into the screen area because of the menus and toolbars around the edge of the work area. The size of the photograph hasn't changed, but the screen (or display resolution) resolution has. To make more pixels fit into the same physical screen dimensions, the actual pixels must be smaller. With the resolution changed to 1024 x 768, all of the original photo can be seen on the screen. Again, the photograph remains unchanged, only the screen resolution has increased. Screen or display resolution operates under the same principle we discussed in the previous paragraph. As the screen resolution increases, the image size decreases proportionally.

Many people have been surprised to discover that after spending a lot of money to get a high-resolution monitor and display card, their screen images only appeared smaller rather than sharper. Now that you know the secret of the screen resolution game, have your friends buy you lunch and you can explain it to them, too.

Screen Setting Recommendations

With all of the exciting ads for high-resolution displays and graphics adapters, it is difficult not to get caught up in the fever to upgrade. If you have a 14- or 15-inch monitor, you should be using the VGA or Super VGA screen resolution setting on your graphics card. If you go for a higher resolution on a 14- or 15-inch display, even if your monitor supports it, your friends may start calling you Blinky, because you will be squinting all of the time to read the screen. Also, be cautious about recommendations from the retail clerk/computer expert at your computer superstore. Remember that last week your "expert" might have been bagging groceries and may know less about computers than you do.

With the price of 17-inch displays dropping, more people are investing in a few extra inches on their display. Just because you have a 17-monitor does not mean you have a moral obligation to run it at the highest resolution that it and your display adapter will support. I use 800 x 600 or 1,024 x 780 most of the time with my 17-inch monitor and it works very well.

Resolution and Printers

If this were a perfect world, image resolution would be the same as printer resolution (which is also measured in dpi). Then, if we were printing to a 600-dpi printer in our perfect world, we would be using a 600-dpi-resolution image because each image pixel would occupy one printer dot. However, it is not a perfect world. First of all, pixels are square and printer dots are round. When we talk about printer resolution, we are talking about the size of the smallest dot the printer can make. If you are using a 600-dpi laser printer, the size of the dot it produces is one-600th of an inch in diameter. The dot it creates is either on or off. There is either a black dot on the paper or there isn't. If we are displaying a grayscale photograph, we know that each pixel can be 1 of 256 possible shades. So how does the laser printer create shades of gray from black-and-white dots? Using halftones cells. What? Read on.

Creating Halftones

If I take an area on the paper and create a box that has a width of 10 dots and a height of 10 dots, it would have a capacity to fit 100 dots in it. If I were to place printer dots at every other possible point, it would only hold 50 printer dots. The result when printed on paper would appear to the eye as 50% gray. This is the principle behind the *halftone cell.* The halftone cell created by the laser printer is equivalent to the pixel—not exactly, but close enough for the purposes of discussion. The number of halftone cells a laser printer can produce is a function of its *line frequency,* which some of us old-timers still refer to as *screen frequency.* Companies that produce advertisements to sell their printers to the consumer marketplace never discuss line frequency, expressed as lpi (lines per inch). And why not? Because, in this hyper-advertised computer marketplace, bigger is better (except for price). And which sounds better—a 600-dpi printer or a 153-lpi printer? The 153-lpi printer would have a resolution of around 1,200 dpi. Names and numbers are everything in selling a product. This resolution specification hype also adds general confusion to the scanner market as well. (We will learn more about scanners and scanning in Chapter 5.)

So what resolution should you use? I have included the values in Table 2-4 for use as general guidelines when setting up the resolution of an image in PHOTO-PAINT.

In the next chapter, we will take a look at color to understand some basics of how it works and, more importantly, how to get what comes back from the printer to look like what we see on the display.

Basic Color Theory

Color is everywhere. Even black and white are colors (really). Color has the greatest and most immediate effect on the viewer of any factor in graphic design.

Image Type	Final Output	Recommended Resolution
Black-and-white	Laser printer (600 dpi)	600 dpi
Black and white	Display screen	Convert black-and-white image to grayscale and use 72–96 dpi
Grayscale	Laser printer	150–200 dpi
Grayscale	Imagesetter	200–300 dpi
Grayscale	Display screen	72–96 dpi
Color	Color inkjet printer	100–150 dpi
Color	Imagesetter	150–200 dpi
Color	Display screen	72–96 dpi

Recommended resolution settings

TABLE 2-4

Psychologists confirm that color has an enormous capacity for getting our attention. To use color effectively, we must have a basic understanding of it, both technically and aesthetically. Let's begin with the basics.

I knew I wasn't going to like high school physics the first day of class. We were asked to calculate the direction we would have to steer a rowboat up a fast-moving river in order to get to a pine tree on the other side. My answer was to row toward the pine tree. I got half credit. I mention this because if you were looking for a detailed discussion on complex mathematics of color models, you won't find it here. If you are looking for information on setting up PHOTO-PAINT to work with different color models, check the index again. What you will find here is a nontechnical discussion of the basic concepts and terminology of color.

Knowing how color works in the natural world and how this "real-world" color operates in a computer will help you when dealing with the complexities of the aforementioned color models. It is going to be simple, and I think you will find it interesting.

Why Is an Apple Red?

One of the first things they taught me in that physics class I didn't like was that without light there is no color. Pretty deep stuff. Light is radiant energy that moves in waves. Each color of light has a different wavelength (frequency). Here is the tricky part. As light radiates from its source and strikes an object, there are three things that can happen to the light waves. First, they can bounce off of the object; that is, they are *reflected*. They can also be *absorbed* by the object. If you doubt that objects absorb light energy, place a piece of metal painted a dull black in a Dallas parking lot for a few hours on a sunny August day and try to pick it up. Hot stuff! Lastly, the light waves can go right through the object—technically speaking, they are *transmitted*. An example would be a sheet of glass. The light strikes the glass and goes through it.

Depending on the composition of the object, all of the light striking it may be reflected, absorbed, or transmitted. Realistically, it will be some combination of the three. Pure, or white, light contains all of the colors of the visible spectrum. When white light strikes a banana, the blue component of the light is absorbed and the red and green components are reflected. The banana appears yellow because red and green reflected light combine to create yellow. An apple absorbs the green and blue light and we see the red component reflected—making the apple appear red. If an object absorbs all of the red, green, and blue components, it appears black. Conversely, if all of the colors are reflected, an object appears white. Reflection, absorption, and transmission are the guiding principles behind the two basic color models we are going to look at next.

Color Models

Color is made up of light components that, when combined in varying percentages, create separate and distinct colors. You also learned this in elementary school when the teacher had you take the blue poster paint and mix it with the yellow paint to make green. Mixing pigments on a palette is simple. Mixing colors on a computer is not. The rules that govern the mixing of computer colors change, depending on the color model being used.

There are many color models in available in PHOTO-PAINT 8. They provide different ways to view and manipulate an image. Regardless of the one selected, they fall into one of two basic categories: *additive color* and *subtractive color*. Additive color (also known as RGB) is the system used by color monitors, scanners, photography, and the human eye. Subtractive color (also known as CMYK) is used in four-color publishing and printing. Let's take a closer look at both.

Additive Color (RGB)

This model is said to use the additive process because colors are produced by adding one or more colors to produce additional ones. RGB (Red-Green-Blue) involves transmitted light as the source of color. In the additive model, color is created by adding different amounts of red, green, and blue light.

Pure white light is composed of equal amounts of red, green, and blue. For the record, red, green, and blue are referred to as the *additive primary colors,* so called because when they are added (combined), they can produce all of the other colors in the visible spectrum.

Subtractive Color

The subtractive model is so named because colors are subtracted from white light to produce other colors. This model uses the secondary colors: Cyan, Magenta, and Yellow. We have already learned this is called the CMYK model, because combining equal amounts of cyan, magenta, and yellow only produce black, in theory. When printed, they produce something closer to swamp mud than black; so, in order to create a vivid picture, black is added to compensate for the inability of the colors CMY to make a good black. In case you were wondering, K is used as the designator for the color black, since the letter "B" already designates the color blue.

CMYK is a printer's model, based on inks and dyes. It is the basis for almost all conventional color photography and commercial color printing. Cyan, magenta, and yellow dyes and inks simply transmit light better and are more chemically stable than red, green, and blue inks.

Describing Colors

If someone were to ask me to describe the color of my son's Jeep, it would be easy. It is black. The color of my wife's car is more difficult. Is it dark metallic green or deep forest green? The terms generally used to describe color are subjective. Even for simple classifications involving primary colors like red and blue, it becomes difficult to describe the exact color. Is it deep sea blue or navy blue? In the world of color, we need a way to accurately describe the *value* of color.

When creating or picking out a color in PHOTO-PAINT, you can specify the color either by defining values for its component parts or using a color-matching system. When using the RGB model in PHOTO-PAINT (it is the default color model), color values are expressed in shades of RGB. The maximum number of shades that a color can contain is 256. For example, the value of red in an RGB model is defined as 255,0,0. In other words, the color contains the maximum amount (255) of the red component and a value of zero for the green and blue components.

Let me interject here that in PHOTO-PAINT, you still pick colors from color palettes that contain recognizable colors like red, green, and blue. I didn't want you to think that you were going to have to sit with a calculator and figure out the value of puce.

In CMYK, the component values are expressed as a percentage, so the maximum value of any color is 100. The color red in the CMYK model is 0,100,100,0. In other words, the color red is created by placing the maximum values of magenta and yellow with no cyan and no black.

Color Matching

While defining colors as either number of shades in the RGB or percentage of tint in CMYK is accurate, it is not practical. Given that we cannot assign names to the millions of shades of color that are possible, there needs to be a workable solution. The use of color-matching systems like the Pantone™ Spot colors provided a solution. The designer and the printer have a book of print samples. The designer wants to use red in a two-color publication. He specifies that the second color is to be PANTONE Red 032 CV. The printer who gets the job looks up the formula in the Pantone book for the percentages of magenta and yellow to mix together and prints the first sample. She then compares the output with her book of print samples, called a *swatch book*. Most corporate accounts will use one of the popular color-matching systems to specify the colors they want in their logos and ads. Color matching in the digital age is less than nine years old. It has come a long way in its short life and is now finding its way into the design of Internet Web sites. No longer restricted to four- and six-color printing, the color-matching systems are dealing with the important issues of colors looking correct on the Internet, too.

RGB Versus CMYK

Each color model represents a different viewpoint on the same subject. Each offers advantages and disadvantages. If you are a Corel PHOTO-PAINT user creating multimedia and Web pages or just printing to inkjet or color laser printers, knowing how to get what you need out of RGB will more than satisfy your requirements. If you must accurately translate color from the screen to the printed page, you must get more deeply involved in CMYK. That is all we are going to learn about these two color models in this chapter. There are some other terms to learn to help you work in PHOTO-PAINT, described in the following sections.

Hue, Saturation and Brightness

The terms hue, saturation, and brightness (also called *luminosity*) are used throughout PHOTO-PAINT. *Hue* describes the individual colors—for example, a blue object can be said to have a blue hue. *Saturation* is technically the purity of the color. In practical terms, it is the balance between neutral gray and the color. If an image has no saturation, it looks like a grayscale image. If the saturation is 100 percent, it may look unnatural, since the image's midtones, which the gray component emphasizes, are lost. *Brightness* is the amount of light reflecting from an object or how dark or light the image is.

Color Gamut

It may come as a surprise to you, but there are a lot more colors in the real world than photographic films or printing presses can recreate. The technical term for this range of colors is *gamut*. There are many gamuts—for monitors, scanners, photographic film, and printing processes. Each gamut represents the range of colors that can actually be displayed, captured, or reproduced by the appropriate device or process. The widest gamut is the human eye, which can see billions of colors. Further down on this visual food chain is the color computer monitor, which can display 16 million colors. Photographic film can only capture 10,000 to 15,000 colors and a high-quality four-color printing process can reproduce from 5,000 to 6,000. We won't even discuss the limitations of color ink on newsprint.

Congratulations

If you have read through this chapter, you should have enough basic information to understand how the tools and commands in PHOTO-PAINT work. The good news is there won't be a test. Now, let's begin to work with PHOTO-PAINT 8. Were you thinking we weren't ever going to get to the actual program?

Setting Up Corel PHOTO-PAINT 8

As a larger-than-average person, I have come to discover that one size doesn't fit all. I also know that the same is true when it comes to the default arrangement and settings of tools of any software application—this includes PHOTO-PAINT. That's why Corel allows many of the features to be moved, removed, and otherwise customized.

One of the Great Lies . . . One Size Fits All

In this chapter, you will learn how to customize your PHOTO-PAINT workspace so that it is both comfortable and productive. Corel has put a lot of features into PAINT that allow you, to quote a famous fast-food chain, to "have it your way." There are literally several million combinations of tool settings possible, so we are not going to look at all of the configurable or customizable tools, just the commonly used ones.

You can configure existing toolbars, menus, and keyboard commands as well as create new ones. PHOTO-PAINT comes with 17 toolbars (plus the Property Bar) installed. You can add, remove, and rearrange buttons on both existing and new custom toolbars. The same can be done with the commands that are available in the Menu Bar. Many of the default keyboard combinations can be altered, or new combinations can be made. While all three areas—toolbars, menus, and keyboard commands—offer unique benefits, one, the configurable toolbars, offers some of the greatest productivity advantages.

Toolbars

The toolbar buttons are configurable in both size and content. Our first step when we set up PHOTO-PAINT is to get them to the right size for the display. Then we can fiddle with them.

Selecting the Right Button Size

Because monitors come in all sizes from 9 inches to 23 inches, Corel has made the size of the buttons, and therefore the size of the toolbars, configurable. One of the first steps in setting up PHOTO-PAINT 8 is to find the best fit for your monitor. Every size of button except the smallest may cause a portion of the toolbar to drop

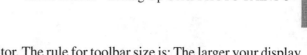

off the end of a standard monitor. The rule for toolbar size is: The larger your display (physically), the larger the toolbar button settings can be—as long as the toolbar fits the screen. The quality of the icons on the buttons varies with size; the middle-sized buttons look the best.

Changing the Toolbar Size and Shape

From the View menu, choose Toolbars. When the Toolbars dialog box opens, click the Options button to display the Size section as shown in the following illustration. (The actual dialog box doesn't have the wavy top; I created this effect with PHOTO-PAINT 8.) Move the Button slider to the desired size. Clicking the OK button in the dialog box applies the change to the toolbars. The Border slider increases or decreases the size of the border or bar that the buttons appear to sit on. Moving the slider all the way to the left means all button and no border; all the way to the right, and the border surrounding the buttons increases to its maximum.

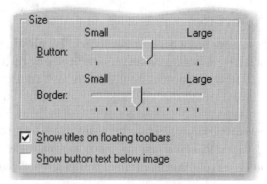

Selecting Toolbars That Are Displayed

If you choose to display all 18 of PHOTO-PAINT's standard toolbars, you won't be able to find the image. To make a toolbar visible, select Toolbars from the View menu and place a check by the desired toolbar as shown below. The first time you launch PHOTO-PAINT, there are three toolbars checked (visible): Standard, Property Bar, and Toolbox. Because toolbars take up screen space and the Property Bar provides much of the functionality of the other toolbars, I recommend that you initially keep only the default toolbars selected.

 TIP: *If you feel more comfortable with the Standard toolbar as it existed in PHOTO-PAINT 6, you can choose it in the Toolbar selection box.*

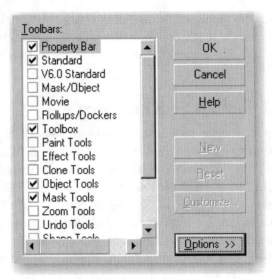

Placing the Toolbars

You can move the toolbar anywhere on the screen. By clicking on any part of the toolbar that doesn't have a button, you can drag it to any of the four sides of the window. When it gets close to a side, it will attach itself (dock) there. To make it a floating toolbar, move it away from the side.

 TIP: *Be careful when docking the toolbars. PHOTO-PAINT doesn't seem to mind if the toolbar you just docked is too long and some of the buttons go beyond the edge of the monitor, making them no longer visible.*

Customizing Toolbars

There are several ways to customize a toolbar. Here are some basic concepts about the buttons and the toolbars. Every command in PHOTO-PAINT has a button that can be placed on a toolbar. All of these buttons can be rearranged, moved to a different toolbar, or removed from a toolbar completely. To place a copy of a button, hold down the ALT key and drag the button to its new location. If you drag it off of the toolbar, the button will be removed. (See your user's manual for more details on creating new toolbars.)

I recommend that you spend some time working with PHOTO-PAINT 8 to get a feel for what arrangement will work best for you before you begin customizing.

If you are going to be doing the projects throughout this book, here is a simple project that creates a custom toolbar to make the other projects in this book easier and get you used to creating and modifying toolbars.

Building Your Own Custom Toolbar

The following procedure creates a custom toolbar. Before any customization can be done, an image must be open. I don't know why, but it must. The first step is to create an image that allows us access to the Customize... command.

1. Open a new file (CTRL-N), click the OK button when the dialog box opens, and minimize the image by clicking the Minus button in the upper-right corner.

2. Select Roll-Up Groups and then choose Roll-UP Customization from the Tools menu and click the Toolbars tab. The Customize dialog box shown here is divided into two areas: the Command categories (left) and Buttons (right).

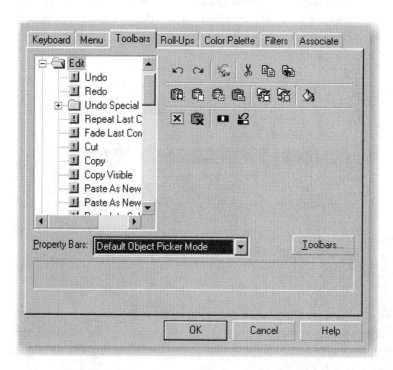

3. In the Command categories, locate Edit and click on the plus sign to the left of the folder icon. This action opens a list of all of the Edit commands that are available in PHOTO-PAINT and displays all of the icons in the Buttons area. Scroll down the list until you find the Clear command, and click on it once. This action surrounds the Clear button, which looks like an "X."

4. Click and drag the Clear button to the desktop. When you release it, it becomes a toolbar.

5. Repeat this procedure with the Fill button (also an Edit command). It isn't necessary to return to the Command categories side to select the button. Click on the button that looks like a bucket, and drag it over to the new toolbar. When you release it, the Fill button will attach itself to the new toolbar. If the button ends up below the Clear button instead of on the side of it, grab the left or right of the toolbar with the cursor and make the toolbar wider.

6. Give the new toolbar a name by clicking the Toolbars button in the lower-right corner of the dialog box. This opens the Toolbars dialog box. Scroll down until you find the new toolbar, which is named Toolbar x (x is a number). Name the toolbar by clicking on the name with the right mouse button. From the secondary menu that opens up, select Rename. The name of the toolbar is highlighted. Change the name to Custom. Click the OK button.

You have created your first custom toolbar. I always make a custom toolbar when I work on a project –like this book. My custom toolbar is shown below.

To remove a toolbar that you made, or if you accidentally made an extra one or two doing the above exercise, select Toolbars from the View menu, select the toolbar, and click the Delete button.

Menus and Keyboard Commands

The arrangement of the menus works in a similar fashion to the toolbars. An example of rearranging the menu structure would be moving a command that is nested several levels deep to the top of the menu for easy access. Another time-saver is the ability to assign a command to a keyboard shortcut. PHOTO-PAINT comes with a large set of default keyboard combinations. The operation of customizing a keyboard combination is pretty much self-explanatory. Assigning a keyboard combination to a command allows you to execute commands quickly without the need to click a button or access the menu. The only disadvantage of using keyboard combinations is the need to memorize the keyboard shortcut. Also, remember that you cannot use existing reserved combinations like CTRL-S (Save). Refer to the user's manual or online help for detailed information on using either the menu or keyboard command configurations.

Each of these methods—toolbars, menus, and keyboard commands—offers the PHOTO-PAINT user a wealth of productivity enhancements that can be applied to a specific project or to the program in general.

Making Your Preferences Known

The preference settings for PHOTO-PAINT 8, called Options, are located in the Tools menu or by pressing CTRL-J. The user interface for this area has changed considerably since PHOTO-PAINT 7 as shown in Figure 3-1. If it looks familiar, you probably have or use Netscape's Communicator for your browser. This has been designed to allow multiple configurations to be saved as individual workspaces.

The three major groups of preference settings are Workspace, Document and Global.

The first selection in the Workspace group on the Options dialog box is called General.

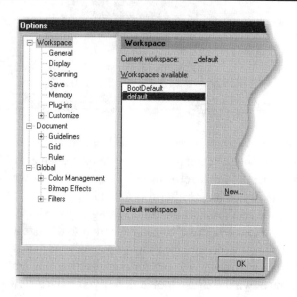

The Options
Dialog Box

FIGURE 3-1

The Workplace Settings

This grouping includes all of the settings that used to be in Options in PHOTO-PAINT 7. They are General, Display, Scanning, Save, Memory, Plug-ins and Customize.

The General Page

The General page, shown in the next illustration, contains many of the settings that determine how PHOTO-PAINT functions. The setting that determines what PHOTO-PAINT does when you launch it is found in the On startup setting. By default, it is set to the Welcome screen.

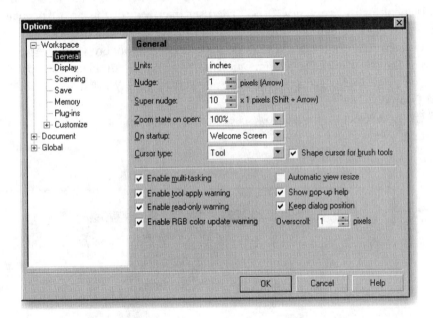

There are a few default settings in the General page that you should consider changing. I recommend keeping the Zoom state on open at 100%. If you have Best Fit or some other Zoom level selected, it may slow down the amount of time necessary to display an image after it is loaded.

In the Cursor section, an important setting is the Shape cursor for brush tool checkbox. When enabled, this changes the cursor to the size and shape of a selected Brush tool. This is important since this feature allows you to see the size of your Brush tool. The only reason I know for not selecting this feature is that the cursor shape can slow down the Brush tool action if you have a slow system.

Near the bottom of the page is the Automatic view resize option. This changes the size of the image window automatically so that it always fits the current size of the image anytime you change the Zoom level. As neat as this feature is, you may want to leave it unchecked when editing an image. This option keeps the edge of the image window tight to the edge of the image, which creates a problem as the cursor approaches the edge of the image window. The program thinks you want to take action on the image window size or placement on the workspace rather than on the image, making work near the edge of the image difficult. If you will be doing the projects in this book, I recommend leaving this feature off.

The Display Page

This page, shown below, contains the settings to change the colors, actions, and appearance of the marquees in PHOTO-PAINT. These settings are not intended to make the marquees more esthetically appealing, but to allow the adjustment of their colors and shapes for the types of images you are working on. For example, the Object marquee is blue, but against a blue background you cannot see it. Generally, these settings should be left in their default state unless the color of the image makes it difficult to see the marquees.

NOTE: *The Scanning page has only one option. By default, after you scan an image the TWAIN scanner interface closes. The option in this page allows you to keep it open after scanning. This can be handy if you are scanning multiple pages.*

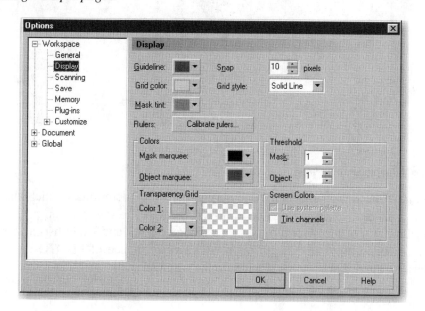

The Save Page

This page, shown in the following illustration, is where you can instruct PHOTO-PAINT to automatically back up the file you are working on at specific time intervals and enable backup copies of images to be produced when an image is saved. The automatic backup of an open image, called Auto-Save, sounds good, but keep in mind that the changes you make to the image you are working on will be saved at these intervals whether or not you actually want them to. If you choose to enable this feature (it is off by default), I suggest setting it to Save to checkpoint. The Checkpoint command creates a temporary copy of an image. This avoids changes being made to the original file before you are ready to save them. You should leave the other settings in their default state until you become more familiar with PHOTO-PAINT.

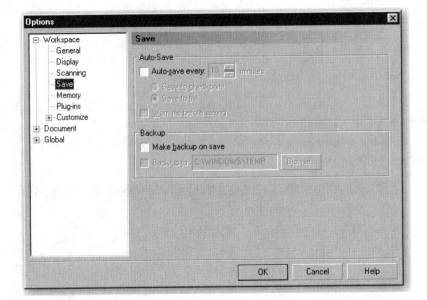

The Memory Page

The next illustration shows the Memory page, which determines which and how much hard disk space is available for PHOTO-PAINT to save temporary files, and the allocation of the system memory for image editing and Undo lists and levels. The correct settings in this tab improve the performance of PHOTO-PAINT by adjusting the use of system resources to the way you work.

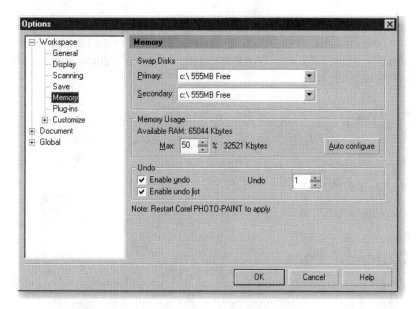

Because bitmap images require larger areas of memory than traditional Windows applications, PHOTO-PAINT uses space on your hard disk drive for temporary storage. This area is called a *swap disk.* If you have more than one hard disk drive, the program, by default, will select the first drive (alphabetically) as the primary swap disk and the second drive as the secondary swap disk regardless of the amount of available space on the drive. Check your settings to make sure that the drive with the greatest amount of available space is set as the primary swap drive. If one of the drives is slower than the other, select the fastest drive for the primary swap drive.

The Memory page has settings to enable and disable the Undo and Undo list commands. This is an important feature. The traditional problem with a photo-editing package is the lack of multiple undo levels. With PHOTO-PAINT 8, you can determine how many undo levels you have. Before you decide to set the undo level to 99, be aware that each level of undo keeps a copy of the image at that level, which uses up system resources. Setting to a high level can consume a lot of swap disk space and ultimately slow down your system. I recommend keeping the undo level to less than 3. Another feature that has been improved in PHOTO-PAINT 8 is the Undo List. Enabling this feature will allow you to undo as far back as you choose. It does this by recording each command that is applied to an image and then reapplying the commands (minus the ones you wanted to undo) in a sequential manner. While it is slower than the normal Undo, it does not consume the amount of system resources required by undo levels.

You can also determine the amount of RAM assigned to temporarily store images when you open and edit them. Allotting too much RAM for the images can result in slower performance of other Windows applications. I recommend leaving this setting at its default state.

NOTE: *Any change you make to the settings in the Memory tab requires the restart of PHOTO-PAINT for the changes to take effect.*

The Plug-ins Page

How to use the settings in this page is discussed in Chapter 14.

The Customize Page

This page offers many of the same selections for customization found in the Roll-up Groups | Roll-Ups Customization discussed previously in this chapter.

The Document Group

This grouping contains the settings for the Guidelines, Grids and Rulers. It can be accessed through this dialog box or directly through the Tools menu. Like many other things in WIN95, it has multiple paths to the same destination.

The Global Group

The Global Group contains some settings that used to be accessed through the View menu. The three pages in it are Color Management, Bitmap effects and Filters.

The Color Management Page

The Color Management page contains three separate pages: Color Management, General, and Profiles. Color Management, shown next, provides the controls for viewing colors accurately on the display. This page contains many of the items that used to be in the Color Correction category of the View menu. While it is great to have accurate color, I recommend keeping this disabled until you get down to the critical color adjustment phase of your project. I say this because this feature, when enabled, tends to slow down the refresh of the display. The General page of the Color

Management page includes selection of options that are primarily the concern of those working in prepress. The Profiles page displays the currently selected devices in the Color Profile Wizard and includes access to the Color Profile Wizard to add profiles for devices that are not currently installed.

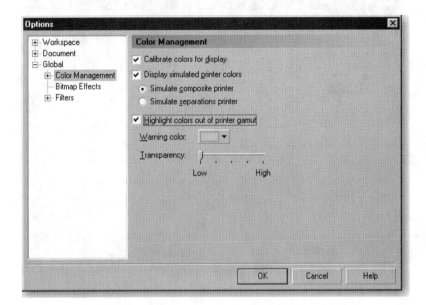

Bitmap Effects Page

This page controls how the filters in the Effects menu initially appear when selected. They also include an option that allows the filters to either keep the last value entered or reset to default every time they are closed.

The Filters Page

This page controls two major areas of the import and export filters. First it controls what import and export filters are installed and available in PHOTO-PAINT. This feature, if properly used, can be a real time saver. If you are always working in a limited number of formats, you can "turn off" the filters that you are not using so that your list of choices isn't miles long. This is especially handy if the file format you use always seems to be just out of sight when you open the file dialogs. The second area controlled by this page is the file associations. How many times have you double-clicked on a graphic file in My Computer or Explorer and the wrong application opened? In this page you can tell PAINT which file formats are associated with it by simply checking and unchecking boxes on the page shown below.

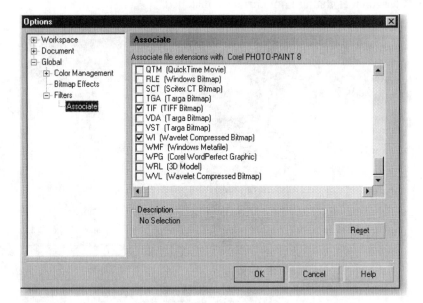

Roll-Ups

Unless this is your very first time working with Corel, you are already familiar with roll-ups. For those who have never heard of roll-ups, a *roll-up,* shown in Figure 3-2, is a dialog box that contains the same sorts of things most dialog boxes contain—command buttons, boxes, and so on. However, unlike most dialog boxes, roll-ups can stay open while you continue to work. Most roll-ups can be opened by double-clicking on the tool in the Toolbox. If you need to maximize your workspace but wish to keep the roll-up open, roll it up by clicking the arrow in the Title Bar. This leaves just the Title Bar visible. Click the arrow again to unroll it.

Onscreen Palette

The onscreen color palette first appears on the right side of the screen. Like the toolbars, it can be dragged and docked anywhere on the screen. You can change several of the color features by selecting Roll-Up groups and the Roll-Up

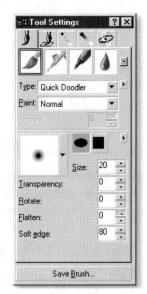

The Tool
Settings
roll-up
offers many
options for
controlling
the Brush
Tool.

FIGURE 3-2

Customization in the Tools menu and clicking on the Color Palette tab. From here you can configure the color wells and control how the right button on the mouse responds when clicking one of the color wells. I recommend keeping the default setting of Set fill color. It offers a quick and easy way to change fill colors.

TIP: *When configuring the color palette, you may want to disable the Use 3D wells setting if you are experiencing sluggish performance from your display.*

The Pen Is Mightier Than the Mouse (Pen Settings...)

If you are fortunate enough to own a digitizer tablet with a pressure-sensitive stylus, you can assign nine different parameters to the pressure output of the pen. The pressure-sensitive stylus responds to increases and decreases in pressure as the user presses it on the tablet. This pressure information is provided to PHOTO-PAINT, and the selected brush settings change with the pressure. If you do not have a pressure sensitive stylus and tablet, I want to assure you that you do not need one to use

PHOTO-PAINT. Even though I have an excellent Art Z II tablet courtesy of the Wacom Co., it is not necessary for completing any of the projects in this book.

 TIP: *A pressure-sensitive stylus is not a good substitute for a mouse. You will need to have both. All of the major manufacturers allow both the mouse and the stylus to be active at the same time.*

Setting Up the Pressure-Sensitive Pen

From the View menu, select Roll-Ups and choose Pen Settings roll-up as shown below. The keyboard shortcut to open the roll-up is CTRL-F11. The roll-up is available only when a tablet has been detected by the system.

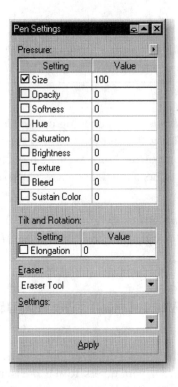

The settings of this box let you control the relationship between the pressure you apply with the pen to the tablet, and the effect produced by brush tools. As you press down on a drawing tablet with the pen, the effect produced by such tools changes. For example, if you set the Size option to 25% and apply pressure to the tablet, the nib widens to a maximum of 25 percent just as a real paintbrush does as you apply more pressure.

 TIP: *The Pen Settings Roll-Up can remain open while using the pen, allowing you to change and test the various settings.*

Just because there are multiple settings that can be applied doesn't mean you need to use all of them. For most photo-editing work, I don't even use the pressure information, since I just need the feel of a pen in my hand to finely control some touch-up work. I recommend that you start with the size setting and experiment with it in a blank image area. To add one of the settings to the pen, you must click the checkbox, change the value, and click the Apply button.

 NOTE: *For more information about setting up pressure sensitive pen settings, in PHOTO-PAINT, select Pen Settings from the Tools menu. When the dialog box opens, click the Help button in the lower-right corner of the dialog box. There is a wealth of information about each of the settings.*

Setting Up Color Management on PHOTO-PAINT 8

The primary purpose of color management is to get the colors you expect from your output device. To make the colors on your screen match the ones you get from your printer, you must first set up the Corel Color Manager 8. If you used this tool in PHOTO-PAINT 5 or 6, you'll notice it has been greatly improved. If you used it in PHOTO-PAINT 7, you'll see that it has been overhauled again and is now much faster. If the thought of calibrating PHOTO-PAINT to your monitor, scanner, and printers sounds difficult and complex, you will soon find out it isn't.

Who Needs Corel Color Management?

There is a misconception about who should be using the Corel Color Manager. This is not a feature that should be tagged "For Professional Use Only." The truth is, it is designed to operate with both high-end equipment and inexpensive color printers to produce the best colors possible. So if you are thinking the Color Manager isn't for you because you only have an low-cost color ink-jet printer, you are wrong.

However, if your printer is a color dot-matrix, you're right—Color Manager is not for you!

Why Colors May Not Look Right

If you work on a photograph of an apple and an orange, you want the scanned image on your monitor to look exactly as it did in the photograph. You expect to see accurate and clearly distinguished shades of red and green both on the screen and from the printer. Before inexpensive color printers became available, color wasn't important. After all, it is difficult to determine shades of red and orange on a grayscale image. Now that so many users are printing in color, they are noticing that their apples are not quite red and their oranges seem to be less orange and more green. Why? Color management is only part of the answer. There are a number of factors affecting color.

Color Gamut

Chapter 2 introduced the concept of the color gamut. Any device that detects or produces color is limited to colors in its color gamut. For example, since the human eye can detect the color purple, it is within our gamut, whereas ultraviolet is beyond us. Typically, desktop devices can produce a far narrower range of color than the eye can detect, and since each device uses a different technique, color model, or set of inks, each has its own unique gamut. All we need to understand about the gamut is that there are colors that are outside of the gamut for a device and therefore these colors are nonreproducible.

Corel PHOTO-PAINT provides a visual indicator for colors that are outside of gamut called, appropriately, a *Gamut alarm*. The Gamut alarm is enabled in the Color Management page in Tools Options under Global. Once the Gamut alarm is activated, any colors that cannot be reproduced by the printer will appear as a single shade of color. A word of caution about the information displayed by the Gamut alarm: An image may contain a large quantity of out-of-gamut colors and have the color still match the original. The Gamut alarm is only a visual indicator of colors that may not accurately reproduce.

 NOTE: *For more information about Gamut Alarms In PHOTO-PAINT, depress the F1 function key and select the index tab. Type in* **Gamut** *and select Gamut alarm, changing the color of. Click the Display button.*

Color Space

A *color space* is a geometric representation of gamut, containing all of the colors in a device's color gamut plotted as points on color models like RGB or L*A*B*. When different color spaces are "mapped" to the same model, it becomes easy to see where the capabilities of various devices differ.

To compensate for all of these device exceptions and limitations, we use the Corel Color Manager, which acts as a mediator between your hardware and all of the Corel graphics applications you use. It uses the CIE standard to map the color spaces of individual devices into device profiles and combines these devices to plot a common color space for your system. If you didn't understand that, the important part is the result: all of your devices will speak the same color language, and more importantly, they will produce the same colors. In other words, your apples will not only be red, but on the monitor they will look like the photograph you scanned. Most important, the output of the printer will look like what you see on the monitor—mostly.

Setting Up the Color Manager

The Corel Color Manager is a separate application that can be launched directly from the Windows Explorer or from within PHOTO-PAINT. To launch it from within PHOTO-PAINT, select Color Profile Wizard in the Profiles page under Color Management in the Global page. The dialog box opens, as shown in Figure 3-3.

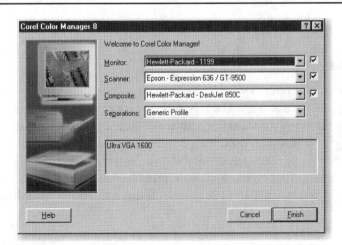

The Color
Manager
dialog box

FIGURE 3-3

Setting the Color Manager is simple. From the dialog box, select profiles for your monitor, printer, and scanner, if you have one. To select a monitor, click the checkbox at the far right. Click the down arrow button in the monitor space to open a list of monitors. Select your monitor from the list. Be aware that if you choose to load the profiles from the CD-ROM (#1), it will take several minutes for the profiles to load. If your monitor is not on the list, see the help file or the user's manual for information about manually creating a profile for your monitor. Select your composite printer and scanner the same way.

 TIP: *To get the most benefit out of Color Manager, you should be using a 16- or 24-bit display adapter. While 256 color (also called paletted color) produces good results, it is difficult to get accurate color.*

Monitor Calibration

Of all of the devices in the Color Manager, it is the monitor that benefits most from manual calibration. This is because as the monitor ages, its color characteristics change. For example, my monitor has a gamma value of 1.8 in its specification, yet when I manually calibrated it, the gamma value was closer to 2.5. The difference in the accuracy on the screen colors was noticeable.

 TIP: *When calibrating a monitor, make sure it has been on for at least an hour and that your room lighting is close to what it will be when working on images.*

Printers

The *composite printer* is either the printer that you use to proof your work or your final output device or both. The *separations printer* is your final output device. It is called "separations" because in commercial printing, the process of splitting colors in a composite image to produce a number of separate grayscale images, one for each primary in the original, is referred to as *making separations*. For example, for a CMYK image, four separations must be made: one each of cyan, magenta, yellow, and black. If your final output device is a composite device (your ink-jet qualifies), you don't need to set up a separations printer. You should disable it by clicking on the checkbox next to it.

Scanners

If the scanner selection is grayed out and you have a scanner, click the checkbox and select your scanner from the list. If you have an off-brand scanner without a TWAIN interface, don't waste your time looking for it in the selection list. The scanner needs to be set up in the Color Manager to use the Corel Scan Wizard. For more information on setting up scanners, check the online help and the user's manual.

 TIP: *If you are using a grayscale scanner, you do not need a profile and should leave the scanner selection checkbox unchecked.*

Other Selections

A few more features, located in the Color Management page, deserve mention. The Display simulated printer colors setting can be set to either composite printer or separations printer. Depending on which printer it is set to, the Color Manager will attempt to display an accurate representation of what the final output color will look like. The Gamut color swatch allows you to change the color used to indicate areas on the image that are out of gamut. The only time you would need to change this setting is when you have colors in the image that are too close to the gamut warning color, making determination of the out-of-gamut areas difficult.

Screen Calibration

After you have the color set up, the last step is to make sure that the image on the screen is physically calibrated. It is very important to ensure that one inch in your image really corresponds to one inch in your printed image. This makes the size of your image displayed on the screen accurate when you select the Zoom 1 to 1 level.

It is a simple operation that only requires a ruler (preferably a clear plastic ruler). From the Tools menu, select Options or use CTRL-J. When the Options menu opens, choose Workspace and then the Display page and click the Calibrate rulers button.

The screen is filled with a horizontal and a vertical ruler a portion of which is shown in the next illustration. Change the vertical and horizontal adjustments until the tick marks on the screen rulers match the ruler, you hold on the screen. When it matches, click the OK button and close the Options dialog box.

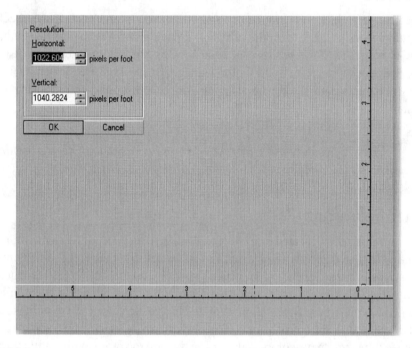

With our system set up, we can move on to the next chapter and learn about the basic PHOTO-PAINT tools and how to use them.

PART

II

Basic Photo Editing Techniques

4

Basic Tools and Procedures

Corel PHOTO-PAINT 8 provides an assortment of tools to make working on images easier. Rulers, grids, and guidelines are provided for aligning and positioning objects and masks in an image. While these alignment tools are generally associated with vector-based (CorelDRAW) or page layout (Corel Ventura) programs, they can be used for tasks other than accurate positioning of graphic elements. In addition, there are navigation tools to help us quickly get around large images and Zoom tools that magnify areas for accurate retouching and other image manipulation. As capable as these tools are, the ones we appreciate most are those that help us undo our mistakes. Fortunately, Corel PHOTO-PAINT 8 offers a lot of ways to help us, even beyond the traditional last-action-only Undo command. We also must be able to save our images in a format that can be either archived or transported to another location. We will explore some of the potential pitfalls of file compression and other image management issues.

Rulers, Guidelines, and Grids

Apart from providing one of the few visual indicators that show the physical dimensions of a PHOTO-PAINT image, rulers are the source of guidelines. The guidelines are useful when cropping an image or aligning elements in an image to a fixed point. With the Snap to guidelines feature, guidelines can be used like the grids, but with the added advantage of being placed where needed rather than at fixed intervals like grids. The grids, which are nonprintable, serve as both an alignment tool for placing graphic elements in an image and a way to proportionally arrange them.

Rulers

In Chapter 2 we learned it is possible for a photograph to completely fill the screen, yet print smaller than a postage stamp. By displaying rulers on an image, you can see the dimensions of the image in inches. Here is a quick exercise that demonstrates why rulers are so important.

A Ruler/Resample Demonstration

This demonstration is to familiarize you with the rulers and to visibly display the effects of changing the resolution of an image.

1. Select Open from the File menu (CTRL-O). From the Corel CD-ROM, select the file EXERCISE\OBJECTS\BALLOON4.CPT.

2. Select Duplicate from the Image menu, and when the dialog box opens, name the duplicate image COPY.CPT.

3. From the Window menu, select Tile Vertically. Two identical copies now fill the screen, as shown here:

4. With COPY.CPT selected, choose Resample from the Image menu. We will explain resampling further in Chapter 6. For now, you only need to know it can change the size of the image. When the Resample dialog box opens, check the Maintain original size checkbox. In the Resolution section, double-click on the value for Horizontal, change it from 300 to 75, and click the OK button.

5. With COPY.CPT still selected, display the rulers (CTRL-R) or select Rulers from the View menu. Click on the Title bar of BALLON4.CPT and display its rulers (CTRL-R).

6. If the rulers on this file are displayed in pixels, double-click the ruler to open the Grid & Ruler Setup dialog box, as shown in Figure 4-1, or select Grid and Ruler Setup in the Tools menu. Enable the Same units for Horizontal and Vertical rulers checkbox and select inches from the Horizontal drop-down list in the Units section. Click the OK button. Even though both images appear to be the same size, an examination of the rulers shows that they are not.

 TIP: *The quickest way to open the Grid & Ruler Setup dialog box is to double-click either on a ruler or a gridline on the image.*

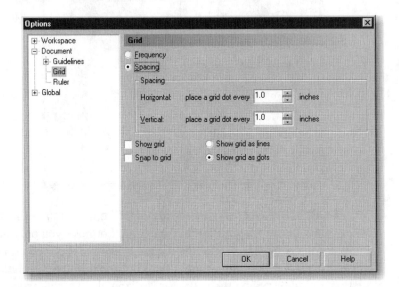

The Grid & Ruler Setup dialog box

FIGURE 4-1

7. To see the images in their actual size, make sure BALLOON.CPT is still
selected (Title bar is highlighted). In the Standard toolbar, change the
Zoom level from 100% to 1 to 1. Select COPY.CPT and change it to a
Zoom level of 1 to 1. The following illustration shows the result of
changing the resolution of both images when they are displayed using 1 to
1 Zoom level.

The ruler normally uses the upper-left corner of the image window as its point
of origin. To change this, click and drag the origin point to the new desired position.
The origin point is where the two rulers intersect.

When the cursor is in the image, dashed lines on the horizontal and vertical rulers
indicate the cursor position. To get a more accurate reading, increase the zoom level.
The information displayed in the ruler will increase as a function of the zoom level
as shown in Figure 4-2.

Repositioning the Rulers

You can place a ruler anywhere on an image. There are times when placing the ruler
at a different location allows you to see dimensions of a graphic element in the image
more clearly.

To reposition either ruler, hold down the SHIFT key, click the ruler you want to
move, and drag it to a new position. The ruler outline will appear as double-dashed
lines as you move it.

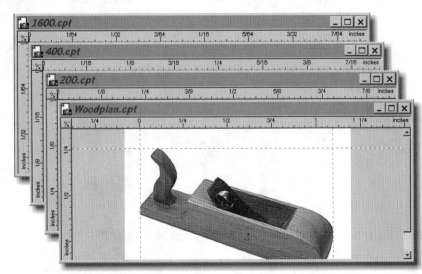

Ruler markings change with the zoom level's settings

FIGURE 4-2

To return either the horizontal or vertical ruler to the position of origin, hold down the SHIFT key and double-click on it. If you need to move both rulers at once, hold down the SHIFT key and drag the intersection point of the two rulers. To return both at once, hold down the SHIFT key and double-click at the intersection.

NOTE: *When you reposition and release a ruler, the image may jump a short distance (the width of the ruler—five pixels) the first time it is moved. Click and drag the ruler and reposition it a second time, and the image will not jump.*

Grids

Grids are very useful for performing a variety of design functions in PHOTO-PAINT. In Figure 4-3, I have shown a simple tile pattern that was created using a variety of Paint filters. The actual design of the pattern would have been impossible without the grids and the Snap to grid feature. In a similar manner, grids made the intricate pattern shown in Figure 4-4 that was duplicated with the Tile filter (2D Effects, Chapter 18). In fact, neither of the figures could have been made without grids. You can align objects and masks to grids as well when you work with objects

A simple
tile pattern
created with
grids

FIGURE 4-3

and layers. In Chapter 13, you will discover that the grid can be used with the New Object command to make tracing paper.

This more
complex
pattern also
required
grids to
create

FIGURE 4-4

Grid Properties

Grids are simple, so you don't need to spend a lot of time learning about them. Select Grid in the View menu to make the grid visible or invisible. From the Grid & Ruler Setup dialog box, you can change the frequency of the grid (number of grids per unit of measure) and other grid properties. An important property of the grid to remember is that it is nonprintable. Even though they appear on the display, the gridlines do not occupy space in the image. There may be occasions when you want to include the grid in the image. This can be done (as shown in the following illustration), but only by using a screen capture program such as Corel CAPTURE and bringing the image into PHOTO-PAINT 8.

Guidelines

Guidelines are created by clicking on the ruler with the left mouse button and dragging a guideline into the image. The guidelines can be either horizontal or vertical. For all practical purposes, you can make as many guidelines as you want. Double-clicking on a guideline with the Object Picker tool opens the Guidelines Setup dialog box. While there are several different guideline settings that can be controlled in this dialog box, the one to remember is the Clear All button. This removes all of the guidelines you created with a single action. For more details on the settings for the guidelines, refer to either the online help or the *PHOTO-PAINT 8 User's Manual.*

Guidelines are very handy for situations where you need to line up several objects in an image. Although you can use PHOTO-PAINT's built-in alignment commands to align both multiple objects and masks, there are times when you need a guideline to find the visual center of multiple objects in an image. In such cases, you will discover that they are very useful tools indeed.

Rules about Rulers, Grids, and Guidelines

Here are some little-known facts about rulers, grids, and guidelines:

- When a file is saved and later reopened, it uses its last ruler and grid settings.

- The grid is not always visible when a file is opened, even if the grid was visible when the image was saved.

- The Show Grid and Snap-to-grid modes are turned off when an image is first opened.

Zoom and Navigation Tools

The Zoom tools of PHOTO-PAINT 8 provide several ways of viewing and working on your image from as close up or as far away as necessary. Zoom tools magnify or decrease the size of your onscreen image without affecting the actual image size. You also have a wealth of navigation tools for moving to different locations in an image that is either too large or has a zoom level too high for the image to fit on the screen.

Working the Zoom Tools

You can change the zoom level several ways in PHOTO-PAINT. You can choose a preset zoom level from the drop-down list in the Standard toolbar or you can enter a value into the Zoom Level box and press ENTER.

 NOTE: *The preset zoom levels can no longer be selected from the View menu.*

There are several new zoom settings that are available in PHOTO-PAINT 8. A list of available settings, as shown below, appears when you click the DOWN ARROW in the Standard toolbar.

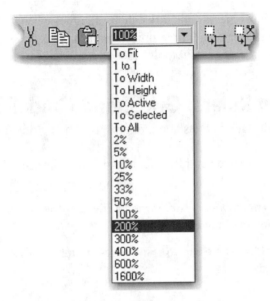

In addition to the percentile preset zoom level settings, there are seven other zoom settings: To Fit, 1 to 1, To Width, To Height, To Active, To Selected, and To All. What follows is a description of the least obvious settings.

Zoom 100% Vs. Zoom 1 to 1

The first time I saw these two commands back in PHOTO-PAINT 6, I thought they did the same thing. I was wrong. Zoom 100% matches pixels in the image with screen pixels in the display. Zoom 1 to 1 should be called "display in actual size," since it changes the zoom level to display the image at its physical size.

Zoom 100%, on the other hand, provides the most accurate possible representation of the image you are working on. I mention this because there are times when images in the display will appear to be degraded. This is often the result of the image being at some zoom level that is difficult for your video adapter to properly display. In the following image, a screen capture of the word "ZOOM" was made at zoom levels of 100 percent and 88 percent. The 100 percent zoom-level text looks smooth, with no sign of the "jaggies," those irregular edges that primarily appear on the diagonal portions of an image. The 88 percent text below appears to be very ragged. The insert to the left of the image is a magnification of the first letters.

TIP: *Always use Zoom 100% to see the most accurate representation of an image in PHOTO-PAINT.*

To Width/To Height

This one is pretty self-descriptive. Selecting either one changes the zoom level so that either the entire width or height fits in the image window.

To Active/To Selected/To All

These three Zoom options are only available when the image contains PHOTO-PAINT objects. If you haven't learned about objects yet, don't worry: that's covered in Chapter 13. To Active and To All are always in the list when an image has objects. To Selected appears in the list when an object is selected.

TO ACTIVE This zoom setting zooms in on the object that is currently active in the Objects Dialog. This setting really gets up close and personal. By that I mean if the active object is small, PHOTO-PAINT will zoom up until it fills the image screen (up to 1600%).

TO SELECTED With this setting, the zoom level is chosen by PHOTO-PAINT so that any and all selected objects fit in the image window.

TO ALL This is just like To Selected except it applies to every object in the image. In all three of these options, the zoom setting does not include areas outside of the image. For example, if part of an object is hanging over the side of an image, and To All is selected, you will not be able to see the portion of the object that is not in the image area.

Zoom to Fit

This option changes the zoom level so that the image fits into the current window. The keyboard shortcut is F4. This is very handy when you want to quickly see the entire image. Remember that when you use Zoom to Fit, your zoom setting may change from 100% and you may no longer be viewing an accurate representation of the image.

The Zoom Tool

The Zoom tool shown here, found in the Toolbox, allows you to magnify or decrease the size of your onscreen image without affecting the actual image size. To use it, click on the image to zoom in to the next preset level, right-click to zoom out to the next preset level, or click and drag a rectangle around the area you wish to zoom in on.

TIP: *The quick way to activate the Zoom tool is to hold down the Z key while any other tool is selected. After you have finished using the Zoom tool, click the SPACE bar to return to the previous tool.*

Right Mouse Button Zoom Feature

The Zoom Tool Settings roll-up, accessed by double-clicking on the Zoom button in the Toolbox, contains a single checkbox for enabling or disabling the right mouse button as a means of zooming out on an image. If the checkbox is disabled, a right-click causes a pop-up to appear, listing a variety of zoom options. Regardless of the checkbox, you can always zoom out by holding down the SHIFT key while clicking the image with the left mouse button.

The Hand Tool

If you zoom in enough so that the entire image is no longer visible, you can move around the image by clicking the scroll bars that appear at the side and bottom of the image window. An easier method is to use the Hand tool, shown here, and drag the image. As you click and drag the image, it moves inside the window. You can select the Hand tool from the Zoom tool flyout or from the Property Bar when the Zoom tool is selected.

TIP: *A quick way to select the Hand tool is to click the "H" key. The Hand tool is selected as indicated by the cursor becoming a hand. Click the SPACEBAR to return to the previously selected tool.*

Navigator Pop-up

Introduced with the PHOTO-PAINT 7 release, the Navigator pop-up is an easy-to-use image navigation tool available whenever the entire image no longer fits in its window. Placing the cursor on the icon in the lower-right corner of the image where the scroll bars meet and holding down the left mouse button displays the Navigator pop-up, as shown in the following illustration. The Navigator remains open as long as the mouse button is held. The cursor moves the rectangular box in the Navigator, and as the box moves, the image moves. Releasing the mouse button closes the Navigator.

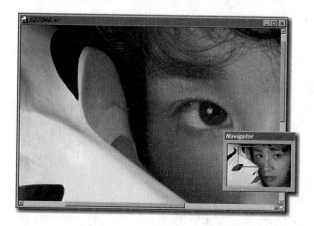

Tools for Correcting Mistakes

Corel PHOTO-PAINT 8 has more ways to undo mistakes than any previous version. Tools in this genre fall into two overlapping categories: those that remove previous actions and those like the Eraser that remove portions of the image as the tool is dragged over them. One of the frustrations considered normal for users of photo-editing programs was that the Undo feature only allowed the last action to be undone. That has all changed in PHOTO-PAINT 8. Besides having as many Undo levels as your system memory resources allow, the Undo list actually works very fast. There is another innovation that I consider the ultimate Undo tool: Clone From Saved which we will learn about later in this chapter.

The Eraser Tool

 Found on the Undo Tool flyout in the Toolbox and on the Undo toolbar, the Eraser tool, shown here, is as simple as it gets. The Eraser tool changes the color value of pixels in the image with the Paper (background) color as it is dragged over them. This makes it look like that portion of the image is erased, though nothing actually is. The Eraser tool has a soft edge that makes the erased area less jagged. Don't confuse this tool with a similar-looking one in the flyout. The Eraser icon with the gray shadow is the Color Replacer tool, which we discuss later in this chapter.

 TIP: *Double-clicking on the Eraser tool button completely clears the image. Think about this the next time you want to open its Tool Settings roll-up by double-clicking on the button. If I had a nickel for every time I had accidentally done this…well, be careful.*

The Local Undo Tool

 Also located on the Undo Tools flyout (Toolbox) and the Undo toolbar, the Local Undo tool allows the selective removal of the last action that was applied to the image.

Something for You to Try with the Local Undo Tool

While the Local Undo tool works fine at removing portions of the last applied actions, it can also be used to create some interesting effects. This demonstration will quickly show you how you can use the Local Undo tool to make a composite image from two different ones

 1. Load EXERCISE\PHOTOS\680035.WI on the Corel CD.

2. Select Image, Resample, and enter 6 in the Width value box (units of measure should be inches). Click OK and the image should look like the one shown in Figure 4-5.

3. Select Fill from the Edit menu, opening the Edit Fill & Transparency dialog box. Click the Bitmap fill button (looks like a checkerboard), and click the Edit button. From the Bitmap Fill dialog box, click the Load button. From the Corel CD-ROM, locate the file EXERCISE\PHOTOS\680054.WI. Click Open. Click OK and click the next OK button. The fill covers the entire image as shown in Figure 4-6. Because we used the Bitmap fill, which is a PHOTO-PAINT tiling engine, only the upper-left corner of the photograph filled the image area. Why is the second photograph so much larger than the first? Because we reduced the size of the original by almost 50% by resampling in step 2.

4. From the Eraser flyout on the Toolbox, select the Local Undo tool. In the Property Bar, change the nib size of the brush to 30 (pixels), the soft edge to 20, and the transparency to zero. It is very simple. Just click and drag in an area. Everywhere the brush is applied, the original image is restored. Position the brush so that it removes the portions of the image illustrated in Figure 4-7.

Original
photograph
from
Corel CD

FIGURE 4-5

Entire
image
covered
with
another
photograph

FIGURE 4-6

Part of the
fill
selectively
removed by
Local Undo
tool

FIGURE 4-7

Just a couple of hints. First, there is no Undo with the Local Undo tool. You can't undo and undo. Try saying that five times real fast! Next, this isn't brain surgery, so don't spend a lot of time trying to be exact. Finally, try changing nib sizes to get into those hard-to-reach spots.

TIP: *If you are not sure which controls do what in the Property Bar (even I get confused) you can either leave the cursor over the tool in question and wait for a context box to open up or look at the Status bar for a description; select the Context Help tool in the Standard toolbar and then click on the control in question. As a last resort, you can open the Tool Settings roll-up (CTRL-F8). Don't double-click on the Local Undo button, as it will remove the whole thing.*

The Checkpoint Command

The Checkpoint command, located in the Edit menu in the Undo Special category, is one of the most frequently used commands when photo-editing. It lets you save a temporary copy of the current image that you can return to anytime.

TIP: *When doing any kind of work on an image, you should get in the habit of automatically selecting the Checkpoint command each time you begin to experiment with different effects and techniques.*

The temporary file created by the Checkpoint command is closed when the image file is closed or when exiting PHOTO-PAINT (whether you planned to exit the program or it crashes). To return to the image saved by Checkpoint, select the Restore to Checkpoint command located below the Checkpoint command. This command is only available after the Checkpoint has been activated.

NOTE: *The Checkpoint command is linked to the image; you cannot save a Checkpoint file in one image and open it in another.*

The Undo and Redo List— Try It, You'll Like It!

The Undo list shown in Figure 4-8 is essentially a command recorder that frees you to experiment by providing a way to remove one or more actions. If you make a

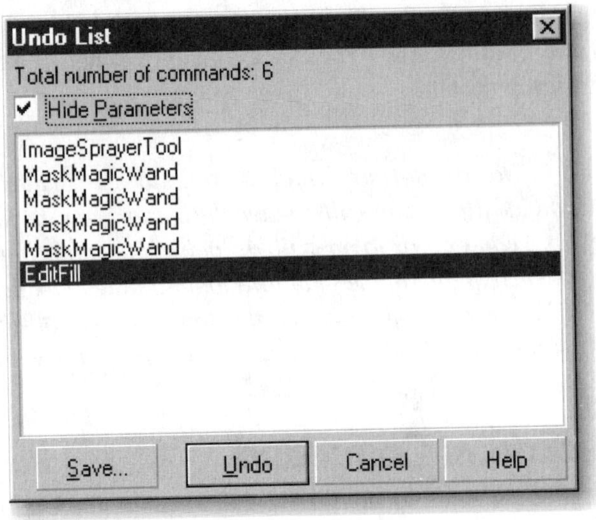

Undo List   ✕

Total number of commands: 6

✔ Hide Parameters

ImageSprayerTool
MaskMagicWand
MaskMagicWand
MaskMagicWand
MaskMagicWand
EditFill

[Save...] [Undo] [Cancel] [Help]

The Undo
list keeps
track of
every move
you make…
in PHOTO-
PAINT

FIGURE 4-8

change to an image that doesn't come out the way you thought it would, you can undo
the change or a series of changes, or even redo the changes you have just undone.

This list continues to grow until the file is saved or the Checkpoint command is
enabled. At that time, the list is cleared. The more actions that are on the list, the
longer it will take your system to replay the entire list without the commands you
removed, and the greater the possibility that it may not replay perfectly. Don't let
that last sentence scare you. If you haven't used the Undo list because you didn't
like earlier versions of it (PAINT 5 or PAINT 6), I strongly recommend you try it in
PHOTO-PAINT 8. You will be impressed—I guarantee it. So, what happens to the
commands that are removed? They go to the Redo list, of course.

TIP: *Select Hide Parameters in the Undo List dialog box feature to
remove all of the clutter that follows the command names.*

The Redo List dialog box, found by selecting the Redo List from the Edit menu,
lists the names of the operations performed on an image that were reversed using
the Undo List command. The command works in the same way as the Undo List
except it replays the commands that were removed.

With all that the Undo list does, it also functions as a true command recorder. Whenever the Undo list is active, you can save the list as a file for Corel Script. This means you can replay the list of commands.

Clone From Saved—the Ultimate Undo Tool

The Tool Settings roll-up for the Clone From Saved Brush tool, shown in Figure 4-9, allows you to selectively restore a portion of an image to its previously saved state. We will explore operation of Clone tools in greater detail in Chapter 11. The Clone From Saved tool is actually a brush tool that uses the contents of the last saved version of an image as the source and paints it onto the same portion of the current image. Any part of the image you brush with the Clone tool is restored to the last saved version of the image.

NOTE: *If you changed the size of an image since opening it, the Clone From Saved tool will not be available because the original and the current images are no longer the same size.*

The Tool
Settings
roll-up

FIGURE 4-9

Color Replacer Tool

 The last Undo tool in the flyout is the Color Replacer tool. On the surface it appears very simple. Like the other Undo tools, it is a brush that, when applied, replaces any pixels containing the Paint (foreground) color with the Paper (background) color. Not only does that seem simple, it also sounds pretty useless. If I can only replace one color with another, its use would be restricted to the areas of uniform color, of which there are darned few in a color photograph.

Well, the truth is, this little gem can replace a range of colors with a single color, which allows PHOTO-PAINT users to change day scenes to night and also remove the matting that sometimes appears on the edge of an object. In Figure 4-10a is a photograph of a TV remote controller (which someone at Corel categorized under computer equipment). Around the edge of the controller is the remainder of the original white background that got included when it was made into an object. Later in this book you will learn several different techniques to reduce or remove this fringe (correctly referred to as *matting*), but by selecting the color of the fringe for the Paint color and a color similar to the background for the Paper color, the Color Replacer can instantly replace the ring around the controller as shown in 4-10b.

(a)

(b)

(a) The white fringe around the controller is easily replaced using the Color Replacer tool (b)

FIGURE 4-10

To use the Color Replacer tool, use the Eyedropper (described next) to select the desired Paint and Paper colors and apply it either selectively with the Color Replacer brush or throughout the entire image by double-clicking it. Next we will find out how to use the Eyedropper tool.

Getting the Right Color with the Eyedropper Tool

As we discovered in the previous topic, the secret of using the Color Replacer tool is selecting the correct color. Since the chances of locating the exact color you need from the On-screen palette is close to impossible, the only way to do this is with the Eyedropper tool.

The Eyedropper tool is located in the Toolbox and is used to pick a specific color from an image by clicking on it. This tool has more uses than might first be apparent. For instance, while the Eyedropper tool is active, the color value of the pixel under the cursor is displayed in the status bar. I'll explain the usefulness of this in a moment. First, let's go through the basics of how to use the Eyedropper.

There are three color areas that can be selected using the Eyedropper tool: the Paint color, the Paper color, and the Fill color. The three color swatches on the Status bar display the currently selected colors.

- *PAINT color*   To select the Paint (foreground) color, click on the desired color with the left mouse button.

- *PAPER color*   To select the Paper (background) color, click on the desired color with the mouse button while holding down the CTRL key.

- *FILL color*   To select the fill color, click the right mouse button.

Eyedropper Tool Hot Key

To quickly select the Eyedropper tool, press the "E" key on your keyboard. This enables the Eyedropper tool. To return to the previous tool, click the SPACEBAR.

TIP: *The "E" key shortcut is a quick way to get a numerical color value for a spot or area. This information is very helpful when setting Color Tolerance values.*

Eyedropper Sample Size

The Tool Settings roll-up (CTRL-F8) shown in Figure 4-11 is used to set the sample size of the Eyedropper tool. By default, the Eyedropper tool samples an area one pixel wide to determine a color value. Sometimes when selecting colors for the Color Replacer tool or retouching photographs, you want an average color from an area. This is why PHOTO-PAINT gives you the ability to select different sample sizes.

To change the sample size, open the Tool Settings roll-up (CTRL-F8) and click an alternate sample size in the list box. The roll-up, shown in Figure 4-11, has a Custom setting as well as three preset sample sizes:

- *Point (1 pixel)*   Default setting

- *3 x 3 Area (9 pixels)*

- 5 x 5 Area (25 pixels)

- *Custom Area*   Enables you to use the Eyedropper tool to define any size sample area

With every sample size (except 1 x 1), the color selected when the mouse button is clicked represents the average of all the colors in the sample area. Obviously with

The Tool Settings roll-up for the Eyedropper offers a selection of different sample sizes for the Eyedropper

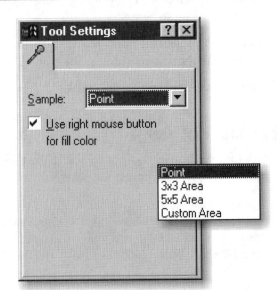

FIGURE 4-11

the 1 x 1 setting, it represents the color value of the single pixel underneath the cursor. Be aware when using samples larger than the default setting of 1 pixel on areas of high contrast that the averaged color may be different than any individual color in the sampled area. The settings made in the Tool Settings roll-up only affect the Eyedropper tool; they have no effect on other tools that may use an Eyedropper to define colors, such as Color Mask.

Notes on Using the Eyedropper Tool

If there are multiple objects on the image, the Eyedropper tool can only read the colors on the top object whether or not the object is active or selected. Good rule of thumb: If you can't see it, the Eyedropper can't see it either.

When a large area is sampled and averaged, the result may be a color that, while representing the average color in the image, may not actually exist in the image. An example of this would be an area that had the same number of white and red pixels. The resulting color would be pink, even though there was no pink in the image.

Use the Eyedropper hot key (E) when you want to see what the color value(s) are for a part of the image to help set the Tolerance Values. An example of using this is when determining where a Magic Wand mask in an image is to be created. I use the "E" hot key to see what the color value is of the starting area (where I click to start the mask).

 TIP: *Use the "E" hot key when retouching images. It provides a fast and easy way to pick up adjoining colors, which is critical when touching up an imperfection on a picture of someone's face.*

Making the Most of Image File Management

The opening and closing of image files in PHOTO-PAINT 8 is similar in operation to most Windows 95 applications, so I will not spend time explaining how to do it. If you need detailed information about this subject, you will find it in both the *PHOTO-PAINT 8 User's Manual* and the online help.

Lo Res

PHOTO-PAINT 8 added a new feature to the File menu called Lo Res. It loads a low-resolution copy of a large image for you to work on. When you're finished, PHOTO-PAINT will apply the actions you took to the original (larger) image. The benefit of working with smaller images is that many of the effects and other actions work noticeably faster when applied to a smaller file.

The operation of this new command is quite simple. Load an image selecting Lo Res in the File menu. Choose Open. From the Resample dialog box, select how much smaller you want the image to be. This action creates a smaller copy. Work on the smaller copy as you normally would and then from Lo Res, select Render. PHOTO-PAINT applies the effects to the larger original.

The default setting for the Lo Res is 25%, meaning the final image will be reduced by 75%. My recommendation for selecting a size is to choose a percentage that is small enough to display at 100% on your monitor. You may find keeping the units of measure in pixels helpful. For example, if you have an image that is 1400 pixels wide and your monitor is set for SVGA (800 x 600 pixels), you know that you are going to need to make it smaller than 800 x 600 pixels. Don't make the image so small that you have to squint to see it.

Here are a few suggestions about using Lo Res: Use it when you have an exceptionally large image for your system. What constitutes a large image? It is determined by the amount of RAM available on your system compared to the size of the image. There's no math formula, just common sense. For example, if you are running with 16MB of RAM on your system and want to load a 40MB image, you should consider loading it using Lo Res. Another thing to watch out for is when applying effects that use fixed-size brushes (like Paint Alchemy). Be aware that the appearance of the Lo Res version may differ slightly when the same size brush is applied to a larger image. Now on to resampling and cropping.

Resampling and Cropping

If you are opening very large images to be resampled or cropped, you should consider selecting this option on opening the file. Corel PHOTO-PAINT 8 offers the ability to crop or resample the image during the loading process, thus saving a lot of system resources that might otherwise be tied up opening a very large image and then having to either resample or crop it. Resample on Open is the same command that is executed when you open Lo Res. The difference is that this image doesn't have the Render command, which the Lo Res does.

 NOTE: *The Resample option available when opening files can only reduce file size—it cannot increase it.*

Going Native—It's the Best Way

Although some of this information was mentioned in Chapter 2, it bears repeating. You should always save your original files in the native CPT format. When an image is saved in PHOTO-PAINT format, all of the masks, objects, and layers are saved with it. The same cannot be said of other file formats. Pay special attention to which of the two available CPT formats you use. The native format of PHOTO-PAINT 8 cannot be read by any version of PHOTO-PAINT released prior to PHOTO-PAINT 7. If you think you may need to open the file with older versions of PHOTO-PAINT, Corel VENTURA 7, or CorelDRAW, you should consider saving in the CPT file format that is compatible with PHOTO-PAINT 6. This format is indicated in the Files of Type selection drop-down list.

Wonders and Dangers of Compressed Files

With your original safely saved as a CPT file, you can use the Save As command in the File menu to save the file in a different format suitable for archiving or distributing on the Internet. Compressed files have been around for some time. Corel PHOTO-PAINT offers several compression schemes for its files, including the CPT files. The types of compression fall into two general categories: *lossless* and *lossy*. These categories are also referred to as nondestructive and destructive compression, which should give you some hint about why we save an image in the CPT format before compressing it.

Lossless Compression

With lossless compression (Packbits, LZW), the process of compressing and decompressing is not destructive to the image. The compressed image is identical to the original image. While it is nondestructive, its compression ratio is usually only 2:1. This is why lossless compression is used for graphics files that are being archived or those going to the service bureau where the need for quality and accuracy is great. It is not a practical solution for the Internet.

Lossy Compression

During the process of compressing the graphic with lossy compression, some of the image information is forever lost. If you choose a high-quality compression, very little of the image information that can be detected by the human eye is lost; however, the greater the amount of compression, the poorer the resulting image quality will be. The most commonly used lossy compression is JPEG. Other lossy compression formats include the photo-CD (PCD) format and the new Wavelet format included in PHOTO-PAINT 8, which is increasingly popular on the Internet as more and more Web sites are supporting it.

Compression Comparison

A picture is still worth 1,000 words (50 if it is compressed). The Wavelet Compressed Bitmap (WI) option is located in the Save an Image to Disk dialog box. Wavelet compression has a quality range of 1 to 100, with a setting of 1 offering the best image and least compression, and a setting of 100 producing a very small but nearly unrecognizable image. With Wavelet compression, you can use settings up to 40 or 50 without any really noticeable image degradation. At a setting of 40, our 540KB file is reduced to a mere 16KB.

Using the highest quality JPEG setting of 2 compresses the image to 203KB. JPEG compression offers a quality factor range of 2 to 255. You can use a setting in the range of 140–160 without noticeable image loss. The same image compressed using this setting produces a 27KB file.

New with PHOTO-PAINT 8 is the ability to preview the effect of your compression setting. Prior to this, you had to decide on a compression setting and then close and reopen the image before you could accurately see the result of compression. This new preview mode, as shown below, is a real time-saver.

TIP: *If you have used any version of PHOTO-PAINT prior to PHOTO-PAINT 8, you could not see either the effect of the compression or the size of the compressed file. Now you can see both before you compress the file.*

Compression Considerations

The hazard of using compression formats results from either applying too much compression when initially saving the image or continually opening, changing, and saving using a lossy compression format. We have already discussed the problems of applying too much compression. Many users do not know that every time a lossless compressed image is opened, changed, and saved, more of the image quality is lost. The best way to make changes is to open the CPT original and then save the changed file as both a CPT and a JPEG.

Closing Thoughts

We have covered a broad range of PHOTO-PAINT tools. While I realize that some of them may seem about as interesting as 40 pounds of wet fertilizer, they make the day-to-day job of working with PHOTO-PAINT easier and more productive. Now that we know how to use the tools to handle an image, in the next chapter we are going to learn how to get images into PHOTO-PAINT from a wide variety of sources.

5

The Ins, Outs, and Abouts of PHOTO-PAINT

Unless you have a digital camera or a video frame grabber, or you are an artist doing all of your original work on the computer, you will have to find some way to get the source images that you need into the computer. Corel provides many ways to bring images into and out of PHOTO-PAINT. While the scanner is the primary way we get photographic images into PHOTO-PAINT, there are also CorelCAPTURE, Photo-CDs, and a wide variety of import and export functions that allow you to move images between PAINT and other Windows applications. In this chapter, we will look at these methods and how to use them.

Scanners, Scanning, and CorelSCAN

The most commonly used device to input photos, line art, or hand-drawn pictures into a computer is a scanner. Several programs within CorelDRAW support scanners. You need to use a scanner, either yours or one at a service bureau, to bring existing photos and artwork into PHOTO-PAINT. A *scanner* is a device that captures an image and converts it into a digital pixel map for computer processing. Think of it as a camera and a photocopier combined and connected to a computer. Like a camera, most scanners capture an image with depth (grayscale or color), whereas a copier records only black and white. As with a copier, the object being scanned is usually placed on a glass plate (the copyboard), where it is scanned. The image, however, is not captured on film or reproduced on paper; but rather is stored in a computer file where it can be opened with Corel PHOTO-PAINT and manipulated to the limits of one's imagination and work schedule.

Bringing Scans into PHOTO-PAINT 8

Corel provides two different paths for moving images from a scanner directly into PHOTO-PAINT:

- **The TWAIN driver provided with your scanner** Figure 5-1 shows an example of a TWAIN interface provided by the manufacturer, in this case it is Epson for their Expression scanner— I provided the picture. According to the tale, kissing the frog turns it into a prince. What do you get if you kiss an iguana? Back to business. TWAIN interfaces provided by scanner manufacturers range in functionality from the bare essentials to very sophisticated interfaces like the Epson software shown in Figure 5-1, which provides many presets and automatic scanning functions. Both of these methods of scanning into PHOTO-PAINT are available in PHOTO-PAINT 5, 6, and 7.

- **CorelSCAN** Available since the PHOTO-PAINT 7 release, CorelSCAN automates many of the operations, such as red-eye removal, tonal adjustments, and almost anything else that can be done on a scanner. The opening screen is shown in Figure 5-2. We will discuss the three methods as we learn how to scan.

Epson's UI —an example of an automated TWAIN scanner interface

FIGURE 5-1

The Story of TWAIN (Not Mark)

Not so long ago, it was the responsibility of every company that wrote paint (bitmap) programs to provide the software programs necessary to communicate with the scanner. However, every scanner spoke its own language, so to speak, and the result was that unless you owned one of the more popular scanners, you could not access the scanner from within your paint or drawing program. Most of the time, it was necessary to run a separate scanning program (provided with your scanner) to scan in an image. After the image was scanned, you could load it into your favorite paint or OCR program. That may seem like a lot of work, and let me assure you, it was.

Then one day all of the scanner people got together and said, "Let us all make our scanners speak one language" (sort of a Tower of Babel in reverse). So, they came up with an interface specification called TWAIN.

Why is the interface specification called TWAIN? This is one of those mysteries that might puzzle computer historians for decades to come. I have never received a straight answer to the question, only intriguing possibilities. My favorite explanation is credited to Aldus (now Adobe) Corporation. They say TWAIN means "SpecificaTion Without An Interesting Name." Logitech, one of the driving forces behind the specification, gives a different answer: "It was a unique interface that brings together two entities, application and input devices, in a meeting of the 'twain'."

Whatever the origin of the name, the TWAIN interface allows Corel PHOTO-PAINT (or any other program that supports TWAIN) to talk to the scanner directly through a common interface, and for that we should all be thankful.

Setting Up to Scan

The first step in initially setting up the system is to ensure that your scanner's TWAIN drivers are installed. The default installation for PHOTO-PAINT 8 does not install any scanner drivers. If you have already installed the software that came with your scanner, you probably have the necessary TWAIN driver installed. To determine what TWAIN drivers are installed, choose Acquire Image from the File menu. This

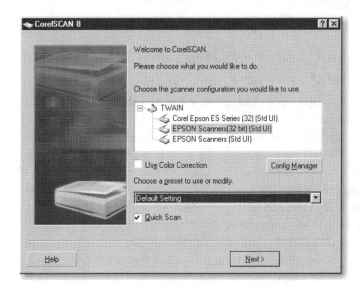

CorelSCAN—
the
automated
scanning
system in
PHOTO-
PAINT 8

FIGURE 5-2

action opens a drop-down list. Choosing Select Source opens the Select Source dialog box, as shown here, or a warning message, indicating no scanners are installed on your system.

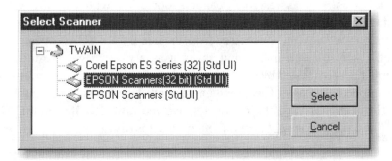

All of the installed TWAIN drivers in Windows 95 are on this list. If your scanner does not appear, its TWAIN driver is not installed. If there are no TWAIN drivers installed then a message will appear. You cannot use any scanner until one is installed. To install a TWAIN driver run the software that came with your scanner. If you are using an older scanner you must use a WIN95 TWAIN driver. If you do not have one, then contact the manufacturer of your scanner.

NOTE: *Some older or discontinued scanners do not have WIN95 TWAIN support and cannot be used to scan directly into PHOTO-PAINT.*

Scanning

To scan an image using the scanner's TWAIN drivers, choose Acquire Image from the File menu and select Acquire and your own scanner's dialog box will appear. You can also run CorelSCAN either as a stand-alone application or from within PHOTO-PAINT 8 by choosing Acquire Image from the File menu and selecting Acquire from CorelSCAN. This opens the beginning dialog box shown in Figure 5-2. CorelSCAN uses a wizard style of operation. The first time you use CorelSCAN after installing PHOTO-PAINT or a new scanner, it will run a series of tests to check the capabilities of your scanner and determine if it is safe to use without the driver's UI, check whether the scanner supports ADF, check what type of resolution it supports, etc. It stores the results in a configuration file, which is then used by CorelSCAN to optimize its scans.

Configuring and Testing the Scanner

To set up the configuration of your scanner click the Configure Scanner button on the opening screen of CorelSCAN that opens the Scanner Configuration dialog box shown in Figure 5-3. From this dialog box you can select your specific scanner configuration as well as test the scanners operation with CorelSCAN. After completing the configuration you can give it a unique name and save it. The configuration you save can be accessed from the initial CorelSCAN opening screen.

CorelSCAN scans an image and saves it as a raw image. From there, any processing that is requested by the user (red-eye removal, image enhancement, and so on) is applied to a copy of that raw image to produce the final output. When the scan is finished, you have the option to save the raw scan if CorelSCAN was launched as a stand-alone application, otherwise it is discarded.

Automated Scan Wizard

CorelSCAN does not require the user to understand the scanning process. It asks you a series of questions regarding the source material being scanned, such as, Is it a black-and-white photo? A picture from a magazine? and so on. Next, it asks what processing you want done—red-eye removal, image enhancement, for

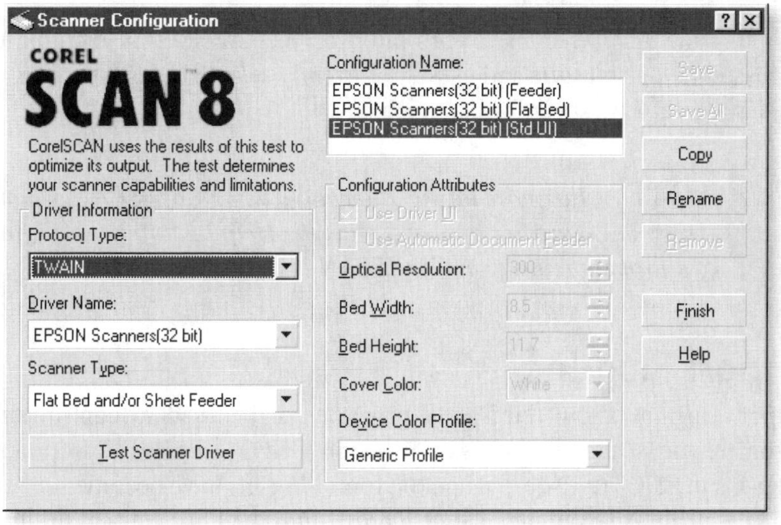

The
Scanner
Configuration
allows
you to
customize
CorelSCAN
for your
scanner

FIGURE 5-3

example—and where the final output of the scan is going to be used, for example, multimedia or laser printer. These answers help you determine how CorelSCAN will set up and process the scan. When using CorelSCAN, you should be aware that selecting "high quality art" will cause the image to be scanned at the highest optical resolution of the scanner using 24-bit color for the "raw" scan. This can take a long time and result in very large image files. I recommend that you change the value of CorelSCAN's recommended resolution from the maximum to one no larger than 200 dpi.

The automated features offered by CorelSCAN include dust and scratch removal, image enhancement, rotation, red-eye removal, and cropping. There are others, depending on the image type you choose to process. While all of these features can be accomplished in PHOTO-PAINT 8, CorelSCAN provides a wizard-like approach for scanning that you may find desirable. Regardless of which approach you take, you will end up with an image in PHOTO-PAINT 8—which was our original goal.

Once you have made your choices using the wizard approach, you can save these settings as a preset and access them the next time you scan an image. While Corel provides an excellent library of presets with CorelSCAN, you will find it quite helpful to add your own presets for the specific type of work you do.

Advanced Interface

Enabling the Advanced Interface option on the CorelSCAN opening dialog box bypasses the wizard style and uses the currently selected Preset to process the scan. This is a great time saver for batch jobs.

 NOTE: *For more information about using CorelSCAN, when the screen shown in Figure 5-2 appears, click the Help button. You will find a wealth of information there on CorelSCAN and its features.*

Import Plug-Ins

Import-Plug-Ins allow third-party programs to be used to control and at times automate the scanning process. Although PHOTO-PAINT 7 supported Import Plug-Ins in PHOTO-PAINT 8 it and Export Plug-ins have become separate items in the File menu. An example of such a program is the PhotoPerfect program shipped with UMAX scanners or the SilverFlash program shipped with Epson scanners. Both of these programs offer many automated features that provide the user with the best possible scans with the least amount of effort. Installing either the Import or the Export is simply a matter of installing the software per the manufacturer's instructions and then configuring PHOTO-PAINT to use them just as normal plug-ins as discussed in Chapter 14.

Some Basics About Scanning

Scanning is not difficult—we aren't talking brain surgery here. It is simply knowing a little and working a little to extract the most out of a printed image. Over the last few years, the price of desktop scanners has dropped while the performance has increased dramatically, resulting in more and more people owning and using them. Sadly, many users, including graphics professionals, do not understand some of the basics necessary to get the best-quality image from a scanner into Corel PHOTO-PAINT and out to a printer.

A Trick Question

During a recent 51-city Corel WordPerfect roadshow, I had the opportunity to ask literally hundreds of attendees the following question: *"If you are going to print a photograph on a 600 dots per inch (dpi) laser printer, at what resolution should you scan the image for the best output?"* More than half answered they would use a resolution of 600. Was that your answer? If so, read on. If you answered with any resolution from 100 to 150 dpi, you are correct. Take two compliments out of petty cash. For some of you, this may be review, but even if you knew the correct answer, I hope that in reading this part of the chapter, you either learn something new or remember something you once knew.

Scanning and Resolution… Making It Work for You

It seems logical that the resolution of a scan should be the same, or nearly the same, as that of the printer. The problem is that when we talk about the resolution of the scanner in dots per inch (dpi), we are not talking about the same dots per inch used when describing printer resolution. In Chapter 2, we learned about pixels. Scanners scan pixels, which are square, and printers makes dots, which are round. The resolution of the scanner is measured in dots per inch, which is incorrect because its resolution is more accurately described in samples per inch. Each sample represents a pixel.

The resolution of the printer dot is measured in dots per inch. The resolution of the printer determines the size of the dot it makes. For example, each dot made by a 600-dpi printer is 1/600 of an inch in diameter. These printer dots only come in two flavors: black and white. To produce the 256 shades of gray that exist between black and white on a printer, these tiny dots are grouped together to form halftone cells. For example, let's assume for the sake of illustration that each halftone cell made by our printer is 10 × 10 dots in size. Each halftone cell can hold a maximum of 100 dots. To print the shade 50 percent gray, the printer turns half of the dots on in each halftone cell and leaves half off. This gives the appearance to the eye of being 50 percent gray.

When we talk about scanner resolution, we are actually talking about samples per inch. Each sample of a scan at 600 dpi is 1/600 of an inch square (remember that pixels are square). Unlike the printer's dot, which can have only two possible values, each scanner pixel can have one of 256 possible values (for simplicity, we are assuming grayscale). The relationship between scanner pixels and printer dots is shown in the photograph taken during a conversation between the two of them, as shown here:

At this point, we can see that a scanned pixel is much more like a printer halftone cell than the original printer dot. So how do you determine how many halftone cells per inch your printer is capable of producing? If you look in the back of your printer manual, you won't find a setting for halftone cells per inch, but you may (I emphasize the *may* part) find a setting for either screen or line frequency. Line frequency is measured in lines per inch (lpi). An old rule of thumb for scanning used to be: Scan at twice the line frequency of the final output device. This rule has become pretty outdated. You should scan at roughly 1.5 times the line frequency of your final output device.

There is some serious math we could use to calculate the ideal resolution to match the scan to the output device, but there is a simpler way. The following sections give some basic recommended resolutions and tips for scanning different types of images. These recommendations are compiled from information provided by various scanner manufacturers and service bureau operators.

Scanning Text and Line Drawings in PHOTO-PAINT 8

Text and line drawings are truly black-and-white images. They are also called *line art* and *bilevel images*; Adobe refers to them as *bitmap images*. Regardless of what you call them, either a white dot or a black dot is scanned and then printed. We encounter these all the time. When you receive a logo or letterhead to scan, it is invariably line art. Unlike continuous-tone images (like photographs), which have smooth transitions, changes in line art are abrupt, which produces a sharp edge. It is because of this sharp edge that this type of image is most often scanned using the following rule:

> Scan line art and text with a resolution equal to the maximum resolution (in dpi) of the final output device, up to but not more than the scanner's maximum optical resolution, and apply sharpening with the scanner (if possible).

There is another way to scan line art into PHOTO-PAINT that deserves consideration. Sometimes the original has many fine lines that tend to plug up when scanned. Rather than scanning the image as line art, scan it as a grayscale image with sharpening. Then use the Threshold command located under Transform in the Image menu to remove any light gray background that appears as a result of the color of the paper the original was printed on.

Figure 5-4a shows an old woodcut printed on a poor grade of paper that was scanned as line art at 635 dpi without sharpening. There are a lot of fine lines in the feathers in the lower-left corner and around the eyes that have gone to solid black, thus losing detail. Figure 5-4b is the same image, but with sharpening applied during the scan. The sharpening brings out more detail in the feathers. In Figure 5-4c, the bird is scanned as a grayscale image with sharpening. In this scan, we have much more of the image detail, but the paper the original was printed on creates a background that is a light shade of gray. The way to remove the background is to apply the Threshold filter to convert everything below a specified threshold to white. After applying Threshold, we have an image that looks like a black-and-white image (Figure 5-4d), but with more image detail. The operation of the Threshold filter is discussed in Chapter 24.

a) 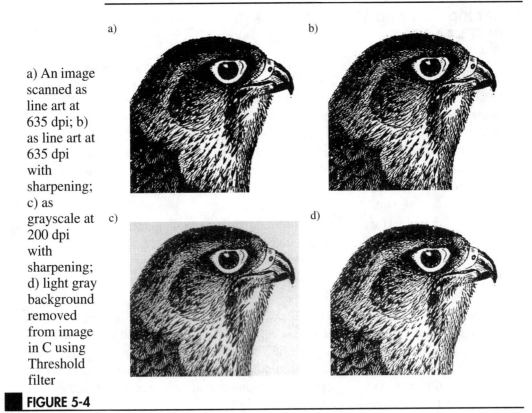 b)

a) An image scanned as line art at 635 dpi; b) as line art at 635 dpi with sharpening; c) as grayscale at 200 dpi with sharpening; d) light gray background removed from image in C using Threshold filter

c) d)

FIGURE 5-4

A word of caution if you scan at the maximum resolution of your scanner: You may find it causes problems with the RIP (raster image processors) when you are outputting to an imagesetter. RIPs seem much more sensitive to the high resolution of these images than they are to the image size. It is not uncommon for the RIP to output a 20MB grayscale image with a resolution of 200 dpi with no problems and have it throw a hairball when it gets a 1,000-dpi image, even if it is a small one.

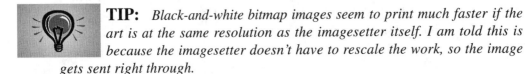

TIP: *Black-and-white bitmap images seem to print much faster if the art is at the same resolution as the imagesetter itself. I am told this is because the imagesetter doesn't have to rescale the work, so the image gets sent right through.*

Line art and text are the only things that should be scanned at the maximum resolution of the scanner. Because the color depth value of each pixel is binary (either on or off), the file sizes do not become extremely large. If you scan this type of image at a lower resolution, you will discover that it produces jaggies like the ones you saw in Chapter 4.

Color Text and Drawings

These images present a problem for scanning because they require high-resolution scanning with the addition of the overhead associated with color. In such a case, file sizes become as large as the federal deficit in a big hurry. There are several work-arounds to this. If your scanner supports it, scan the image in at 256 colors. If your scanner can only do 24-bit color, scan the image into PHOTO-PAINT and convert it to 256 colors using the Convert To command and the Paletted (8-bit) option in the Image menu. Converting the file to 256 colors reduces its file size by 66 percent.

 TIP: *When converting to 256 colors, choose the Optimized palette and not the Uniform palette. Keep dithering set to None.*

You could use CorelTRACE to convert color text and drawing to a vector image, or scan these images as black and white and replace the black in PHOTO-PAINT with colors similar to the original.

Photographs

Continuous-tone images (such as photographs) can be color or black and white. This type of image is less detailed and requires lower resolution than line art. The rule for this is simple: *Scan photographs at 100–200 dpi.*

Some variations to this rule are as follows:

- For 300-dpi laser printers, scanning at 100 dpi is usually sufficient.

- For 600-dpi lasers, scan at 150 dpi.

- For imagesetters (including high-resolution lasers that produce camera-ready art), scan at 200 dpi.

Why You Shouldn't Scan at Excessively High Resolutions

Even after going through all of the explanations about the best settings to get a good scan, some still believe that scanning at a higher than necessary resolution somehow gives their image extra detail or makes it look sharper. In fact, doing this rarely improves image quality and produces very large file sizes. Remember that each time resolution is doubled, the file size quadruples. Large image files take a long time to process, and time is money at your local neighborhood service bureau. Also, scanning at a resolution higher than the output device can reproduce tends to cause detail in the shadow area to be lost, and if the resolution is high enough and the image small enough, the final result may actually be a blurry picture. Let's move on to some other scanning-related commands and issues.

The Deskew Command

After scanning an image, if you notice it is crooked, lift the lid on the scanner, straighten the image, and scan it again. Sounds simple, right? You would be amazed at how many users will accept a crooked scan and not do that simple step. Don't be one of them. If you receive a scan with a crooked image, you can straighten it in PHOTO-PAINT using the Deskew command located in the Image menu. The Deskew command places imperfectly positioned images squarely in the image area, but the image being deskewed needs to appear against a light background that PHOTO-PAINT can recognize. The deskewing action works well and causes little to no distortion of the original image. This filter has no user-definable settings.

In the image shown below, I have deliberately misaligned a photograph of myself and my charming wife on the scanner. The image resulting from using the Deskew command is shown below the first.

Tips for using Deskew

Don't be concerned if the image is cropped closely, because the Deskew command will increase the size of the final image to fit the deskewed image. I want to qualify my next suggestion by saying that all of my testing done with this version of Deskew has been accomplished using a late beta so, check this theory out for yourself. I have found that scans that are very dark overall don't seem to deskew as well as lighter ones. I tested several scans and found that by lightening the scanned image (including the background) with some Gamma (Image>Adjust) many times improved the accuracy of the scan. By accuracy I am referring to how straight up and down the final image is.

 TIP: *The Deskew command in PHOTO-PAINT 7 requires a pure white background to operate. The Deskew command in PHOTO-PAINT 8 is much more tolerant of backgrounds that are something other than pure white.*

Removing Dust, Scratches, and Other Debris

When you apply sharpening to an image, all of the dust and other small artifacts in the image make themselves known. They have always been there—they just blend into the image until sharpening is applied. I want to warn you not to fall into the trap of spending hours removing specks of dust and debris from a scanned image with

PHOTO-PAINT that could have been prevented in the first place by either dusting the original photograph with a fine-hair brush or a can of compressed air, cleaning the glass on the scanner with some glass cleaner before scanning, or both. If you feel the glass on your flatbed scanner is clean and doesn't need this attention, try this test. Lift the lid and start a scan. Look at the glass from the side as the light moves. Surprised?

If the dust and debris are part of the image you have scanned, you may need to use the Dust and Scratch filter, which is discussed in Chapter 16.

So much for scanning. There are times when we need to get our image directly from the computer screen. This type of application is found mostly in technical documentation, including this book. For this purpose, Corel included CorelCAPTURE.

Using CorelCAPTURE

CorelCAPTURE, which has improved with each release of CorelDRAW, is one program I probably use as much as I use PHOTO-PAINT 8. Every image in this book, with the exception of the screen shots of this program, was captured in one way or another by CorelCAPTURE. Corel CAPTURE 8 has functionally remained the same as previous versions with the exception of the user interface. In earlier versions, CAPTURE would open, and when the Capture button was selected it would minimize to the task bar. In Corel CAPTURE 8, pressing the Capture button makes the program an icon in the WIN95 SYSTRAY (System Tray) located next to the clock in the Task Bar.

 TIP: *Can't find CorelCAPTURE? It is not installed using the Typical install. You must go back and select Custom install. It isn't necessary to reinstall all of the other programs, just CorelCAPTURE.*

CAPTURE works with any image that can be displayed on your monitor. The images don't even have to be in Corel. The operation of CAPTURE is very simple. After launching the program, the CorelCAPTURE bar opens as shown below.

Selecting the Source

You can specify which part of the image you want to capture on the Source drop-down list shown below. Most of the selections are self-explanatory. Here are some tips I learned while working with this page. If you need to capture a mask or other software marquee, use Full Screen. If you use anything less, only part of the marquee is captured. The best way to capture an image window, dialog box, and so on, is to use the Menu or control setting. If the Include border option is selected, the Title Bar on the image window will be included. The Elliptical Area and Rectangular Area features do not have a constrain key, so you must create your circle and square capture areas by using a steady hand on the mouse and your calibrated eyeball. If you use any setting that captures an area that is nonrectangular, the resulting capture will be in a rectangular image area.

Choosing the Hot Key

From the Activation drop-down list you can pick the hot key you want to use for activation of the program. By default, it should be set to the function key F7. If User defined is chosen, another dialog box opens as shown below.

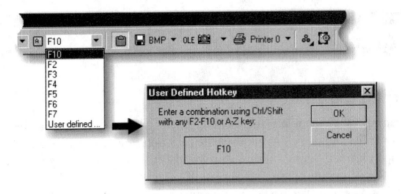

Selecting the Destination

The next two buttons allow you choose where to send the screen capture you create. There are two choices, Clipboard and File. Because I must make a lot of screen captures for books and articles, I often save the image to the clipboard and then use the New from clipboard command in the File menu in PHOTO-PAINT to make it into an image. The only caveat is that you have to remember that the clipboard can only hold one object at a time. More than once, I have saved a screen capture in the clipboard and then, before unloading it in PHOTO-PAINT, proceeded to copy some text to the clipboard while in another application, thus wiping out my screen shot. Other than this small consideration, the clipboard works best for me.

The other option worth discussing is the File setting, which creates a file containing the capture each time the hot key is selected. The type of file it creates is selected from the drop-down list shown below. Choosing Options... at the bottom of the list opens the Capture As dialog box. In this box, you specify the name of the file and—if you want to—use the automatic naming function, which is handy when saving a sequence of images. If you don't use automatic naming, the CAPTURE program will overwrite the same file each time you hit the hot key, just like the clipboard. While I personally have rarely used these options, you can also set the capture to a printer of your choice or even set it up to be made available to an OLE application (either to DRAW or PHOTO-PAINT) by enabling the button labeled OLE to the right of the file selection area. This action will actually launch the application selected when a screen capture occurs.

Just a few notes of interest. The default file format is BMP. I recommend not using any lossey compression format (JPEG, Wavelett, etc.) for images that you may later want to modify for reasons explained in detail in both Chapters 2 and 3. The Capture As Directory button is important because it determines where your files are going to be placed when they are created. The default location is an obscure area deep within the CorelDRAW program files. If you are recording a sequence of events, the Use Automatic Naming feature is handy and will, with each capture, create another file with a sequential numbered name beginning with the first number you place in the Start Naming At setting.

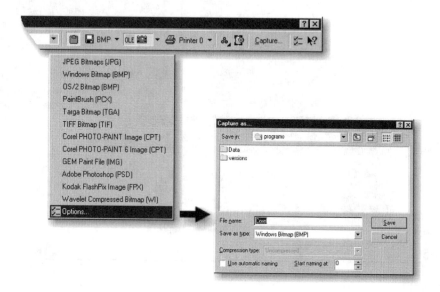

Printers, Colors, Resample et al

The remaining dialog boxes are shown in Figure 5-5. From the Printers button you can select the printer to send the Screen Capture to, if you have selected a printer as the destination. The drop-down list displays all of the available printers. The Options setting at the bottom of the list opens the Printer setup dialog box for the selected printer. The color depth of the image is selected by clicking the button to the immediate right of the Printer button. From its drop-down list you can choose which of the five color depths you want to use. The Resample button opens the Resample dialog box. You control the parameters of the image that CAPTURE produces. It has been designed so that you can pick the ultimate destination of the screen shot, and CAPTURE provides a recommended resolution. For multimedia and the Web, you should be using the Screen setting. A very helpful feature on this page is the Resizing section, which is activated with the Resample captured option.

Throughout this book I have included screen shots of the toolbars and buttons. These images are, by their nature, very tiny. You can capture them at screen

The
Resample,
Options,
Printers,
and Colors
toolbar
buttons
and their
corresponding
dialog boxes

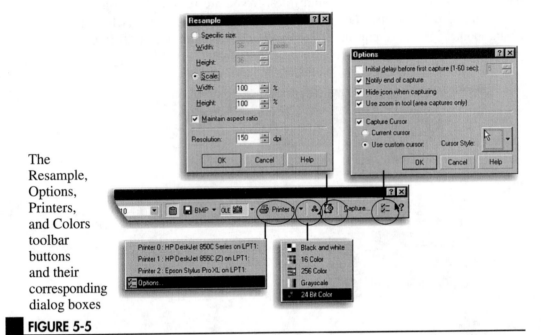

FIGURE 5-5

resolution and increase their size using the Resample command or set the Resizing
option for the size you want the final image to be.

The Options button offers control over a variety of features. The Capture cursor
feature, which is enabled by default, doesn't actually capture the cursor, but places
a cursor arrow on the captured image in the location of the cursor position. This
means that if you have some fancy cursor, or one of PHOTO-PAINT 8's many
cursors, that you wish to capture, it cannot be done. So where did I get the cursors
that appear in this book? Select Use custom cursor at the bottom of the dialog box
and from the Cursor style choose the file containing the desired cursor.

You can also set the delay for activation from this page. The delay feature is
necessary when you have a "shy" function. That is my term for a part of a program
you are attempting to capture that disappears the instant you hit the CAPTURE
activation key. An example of this would be the Pop-up Navigator. By using the
delay, you can activate the CAPTURE program with the hot key, open the "shy"
portion, and then wait for the capture to occur.

Photo-CDs

Developed by Kodak as a consumer file format, the photo-CD was a failure. Later, it become popular as a method of distributing photographic images, and has since become a common form of exchange for such images. Corel Corporation is the world's largest supplier of images on photo-CDs, although there are none in the CorelDRAW 8 release. Ironic, isn't it? Corel PHOTO-PAINT 8 provides several color correction methods for use with photo-CDs, which we will look at briefly in this section.

Picking the Right Size When Opening a Photo-CD

When a photo-CD is initially opened, the dialog box displays the Image tab, as shown in Figure 5-6. If color correction is not desired, the only choices that must be made are the size of the image and the color selection. The size choices and their size in pixels are Wallet (192 × 128), Snapshot (384 × 256), Standard (768 × 512), Large (1,536 × 1,024), and Poster (3,072 × 2,048). The available color selections are 16.7 million (24-bit), 256 colors (8-bit), and 256 grayscale. After you have the size and color, click the OK button to load the image.

 TIP: *Larger file sizes require large amounts of system memory, take longer to load and to apply effects, and require more disk space for storage. Therefore, always try to pick a size and color depths that are sufficient for your application.*

Applying Color Correction When Opening Photo-CDs

If you want to apply color correction, click on the Enhancement tab, which opens the color correction page of the dialog box as shown in Figure 5-7. Here, you can make some of the not-so-great Photo-CDs on the market look much better. Either of the two color correction systems, Gamut CD™ and Kodak Color Correction, will correct the color of the image before you load it into Corel PHOTO-PAINT. Any correction applied at this stage of the process is superior to any correction that might be applied after the image is in Corel PHOTO-PAINT.

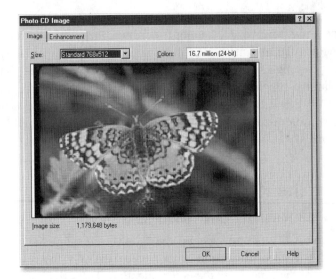

The
photo-CD
dialog box

FIGURE 5-6

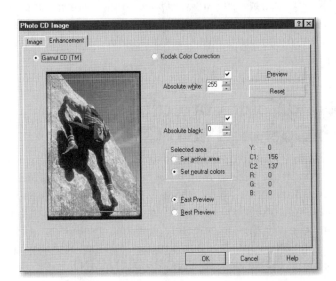

The Gamut
CD Color
correction
system
provides
automatic
color
correction
for
Photo-CDs

FIGURE 5-7

While most of the newer photo-CDs from the good digital stock agencies have already applied color correction, older or poor-quality Photo-CDs benefit from this enhancement. I have several old photo-CD images that had black backgrounds until I applied correction, and they turned out not to be black backgrounds after all. In one, a night shot of a wolf, the enhancement revealed that the "black background" was actually a forest.

Exploring the Gamut CD Color Controls

The following options are available using the GamutCD system.

Color Correction Methods

- **Gamut CD**   This color correction method uses gamut mapping to enhance the color fidelity and tonal ranges of the CD image. *Gamut mapping* is a system that ensures that colors in a computer image are reproducible by a printer. Of the two methods, I have had the greatest success with this one.

- **Kodak Color Correction**   The Kodak Color Correction method allows you to alter color tints and adjust brightness and saturation, as well as adjust the level of contrast. The Kodak system, while excellent, is not automatic, making it more complicated to use.

The Gamut CD option, available only with 24-bit color images, lets you select neutral colors (black, white, and grays) in the image. The software then maps these neutral colors to adjust the dynamic range of the image. Gamut, in short, is a system that knows what colors can or cannot be printed by Standard Web Offset Process (SWOP). Colors that cannot be printed are referred to as being "outside of gamut." The Gamut CD correction system ensures that all of the colors in the photo-CD are within gamut. The best part is that the Gamut CD color correction almost always improves the overall appearance of the image, even if you don't need the color correction for printing purposes.

NOTE: *Take notice of the difference in the arrangement of Figure 5-7 and 5-8. The dialog box automatically rearranges itself to fit either portrait or landscape orientation of the image*

Setting the Active Area Using Gamut CD

Generally, the default area should be used. If you need to change the Selected area, choose the Set active area option and click and drag the mouse to specify an active area within the image in the view field. This ensures Gamut CD will base its color correction on the area of the photo that you are going to use and helps cut out any black borders left over from the original scan that would interfere with accurate correction.

Set the Set neutral colors option by clicking on pure whites, blacks, and grays within the active area, which leaves a small "x" on the preview image in most displays. The more samples that are selected, the better the color correction.

- **Adjust white in image**   Choose this option if you have good white elements in the photo. If you do not have a white, disable this option since the gamut mapping will overbrighten your picture as it maps the lightest elements of your picture to white. This option will assist Gamut CD in enhancing the tonal range of your image and removing color cast. If your white is not pure white, you may wish to lower the 255 setting in the Absolute white number box.

- **Adjust black in image**   Choose this option if you have good black elements in the photo. If the image does not have blacks, disable this option as the gamut mapping will darken your picture as it maps the darkest elements of your picture to black. This option will assist Gamut CD in enhancing the tonal range of your image and removing color cast. If your black is not pure black, you may wish to raise the setting in the number box for Absolute black from 0.

- **Color Swatch and Values**   This option displays the YCC and RGB color value of the currently selected color from the image as the cursor is moved around the image in the preview window. The color swatch displays the color that is being assessed.

- **YCC**   The YCC color system is the color model of the Photo-CD. The Y represents the luminance or grayscale values of the image, and C represents the color chrominance values. The YCC color space is similar to the way television broadcast color is transmitted. The YCC values are of little help in setting up the Gamut CD system.

- **RGB** RGB represents the values of the Red, Green, and Blue color components in the image. It is the RGB information that is of the greatest help in establishing the neutral colors of the image.

- **Fast Preview** This option displays the effect the chosen Gamut CD settings will have on the image. The first time you preview, you may wonder why it is called "Fast Preview." Way back in the time when we thought that a 486 33Mhz was a real powerful machine, the Fast Preview setting saved you a lot of time. Now with the more powerful Pentium-based computers, the time savings is not measured in minutes but seconds.

- **Best Preview** This setting takes longer, but if color accuracy is critical, I recommend using it.

Using Gamut CD Color Correction

This is all great, but how do I use it? That was my question to the people at Corel way back when I was writing the Corel PHOTO-PAINT 5 Plus manual. Their answer surprised me: they hadn't used it that much themselves. I shouldn't have been surprised that these folks work their brains out writing code for PAINT and have little time for loading and correcting their favorite Photo-CDs. Since that time, they and I have learned a lot about using Gamut CD. So, here is Dave's handy-dandy method for using the Gamut CD color correction system, based on lots of practice and a little too much coffee.

The principle of this system is that you select the neutral colors (white, black, and gray) in an image. The Gamut CD system uses those colors for its gamut mapping to enhance the color fidelity and tonal ranges of the image, ensuring that the colors in a computer image can be reproduced by a printer.

1. **Open the photo-CD image.** When the photo-CD dialog box opens, pick the size and color desired.

2. **Click the Enhancement tab.** Ensure that the Gamut CD button is enabled. I highly recommend using the default Selected area, which is shown by the light-colored rectangle on the image in the preview window. If you needed to change the Active area, click the Set active area button and drag a rectangle in the preview window that includes the portion of the image you wish to be included in the color correction calculations.

3. **Click on the whitest white spot you can find.** Don't trust your eyes on this one. Watch the Color swatch on the right side of the dialog box as you move the cursor over the white area. Specifically, watch the numbers by R, G, and B. The whitest white will produce the highest numbers in RGB. This is basic color theory. Pure white reads 255 on each of the RGB channels. Make three or four white samples. The more you make, the more accurate the color correction will be.

4. **Click on the blackest black you can locate in the active area.** "Active area" is the key phrase here—do not click on the black border. The idea with these samples is to establish the dynamic color range of the image, so shooting some of the black off of the negative border will throw the correction off. You pick the black the same way you pick the white, by the numbers. In this case, you are looking for the lowest numbers in the RGB values.

5. **Find a good middle-of-the-road gray if there is one (optional).** This is used to set the midtones, and finding a gray can be very subjective. Use the numbers again. In this case you are looking for RGB numbers that are very nearly equal. In case you didn't know, anytime the values of RGB are equal, the result is gray. If you use gray, the result will be shifted slightly toward the warmer colors.

6. **Select the Preview option and click the Preview button.** On a good 24-bit color monitor, the difference can be very impressive. If you like the results, click the OK button. If not, reset the color correction by clicking the Reset button and start over again.

Notes on the Gamut CD™ Color Correction System

Here are some pointers about using GamutCD.

- There isn't a specific order to enter the neutral colors. The computer sorts it all out.

- If there isn't a good black (RGB less than 90) or a good white (RGB greater than 220), don't use them, and uncheck the respective Adjust White In Image or Adjust Black In Image checkbox.

■ If you don't like the results of the preview, click Reset and choose the color samples again. The image will appear the same, but the color values will be correct.

■ If the preview is too dark, try increasing the value in the Absolute Black In Image value box. If the preview is too light, try decreasing the value in the Absolute White In Image value box.

The Kodak Color Correction System

This color correction method, which is selected by enabling the Kodak Color Correction button in the Enhancement page, opens the dialog box shown in Figure 5-8. The Kodak system allows you to alter color tints and adjust brightness and color saturation, as well as adjust the level of contrast.

This is not an automatic system like the Gamut Image Enhancement System. You can control the tints of the three primary colors (red, blue, and green—RGB), the Brightness, and the Saturation (the amount of color in the image). There are several adjustments in the dialog box that are unique to photo-CD images. The effects of changing any of these settings do not appear in the preview window until

The Kodak color correction system's wide assortment of manual color correction tools

FIGURE 5-8

the Preview button is clicked. There is no automatic preview. The controls for this dialog box are as follows:

- **Contrast**   This allows you to adjust contrast by choosing preset amounts from a drop-down list.

- **Remove scene balance adjustment**   Enabling this button removes the scene balance adjustment, which is made by the photo-finisher at the time the original image was scanned and preserved on the photo-CD disc. You should remove this if the image looks lifeless or dull. It may result in some areas of the image blowing out (bright spots becoming large white areas).

- **Show colors out of screen gamut**   If the changes you've made are too extreme, the preview will display out-of-gamut pixels as pure red or pure blue. Colors that are out of gamut cannot be printed accurately, and it is important for critical prepress work for all colors to be within gamut boundaries.

Color correction takes time. If you have images that have not been color corrected, it is worth the time spent trying to apply correction at this stage rather than in Corel PHOTO-PAINT. Another source for images is CorelDRAW and other Windows applications. In the following section, we will look at some of the different ways we can move an image between these programs.

Moving Images Between Applications

Just because this is a book on PHOTO-PAINT doesn't mean that I think everything should be done in PHOTO-PAINT. In fact, the opposite is true. Get into the practice of deciding which program(s) to use to create a project *before* you begin.

Many of the rules you may have learned about moving images between applications using previous versions of PHOTO-PAINT have changed. This is good news, since PHOTO-PAINT 8 makes the movement of images between applications very simple. In this section, we will cover the basics of moving images between both Corel and non-Corel applications. This section of the chapter is like a cookbook—full of recipes for different ways to get from here to there and back again. If you are reading this book from front to back, you will encounter tools and terms that have not previously been introduced. I have included some brief explanations, exercises, and cross-references so that you won't get too confused.

PAINT to DRAW and Back Again

Since most people ask how to move images between PHOTO-PAINT and DRAW, we will cover it first. In previous releases, this was a little complicated, but now there are so many ways to move images between the programs that it is difficult to sort them out. Talk about an embarrassment of riches!

From PAINT to DRAW (Save Method)

This is the simple one. In PHOTO-PAINT, save the image in PAINT (*.CPT) format. In DRAW, select Import from the File menu. Locate the CPT file and click Import. The cursor changes to the filename, allowing you to click and drag to the size you want.

- The size of the image in DRAW is controlled by the resolution of the image in PAINT. The higher the resolution, the smaller the image. Use the Resample command in PAINT to change the size.

- If the PHOTO-PAINT image contains more than one object (bitmaps that float above the image), the objects will appear grouped as objects in DRAW.

- If the PHOTO-PAINT image contains a mask, only the area surrounded by the mask will appear on the image in DRAW.

- One of the objects will be a rectangle, which is the background. To remove the background, you must Ungroup the objects, select the background, and delete it.

The following session takes you through the procedure of bringing a PHOTO-PAINT image that contains an object into DRAW.

Importing PHOTO-PAINT images into CorelDRAW (Tutorial)

This is an easy exercise for importing a PHOTO-PAINT 8 image into DRAW.

1. In PHOTO-PAINT, create a new image. Make the image 5 x 5 inches, 24-bit color at 72 dpi.

2. Select Fill from the Edit menu. When the Edit Fill & Transparency box opens, click the Fountain Fill Tool button and then click the Edit button. When the Fountain Fill dialog box opens, click the down-pointing arrow at the right of the Presets value box and select Circular - Blue 02. Change the number of steps to 999. Click the OK button to select the setting and click the next OK button to apply the fill.

3. From the Effects menu, choose Fancy and then Alchemy. In the Paint Alchemy dialog box under Saved Styles, choose Bubbles Pastel from the Style drop-down list. Click OK. Now the blue image looks like it lost a fight with Lawrence Welk. Save the file as BLUE.CPT and close it.

4. In DRAW, select the Object Picker tool at the top of the Toolbox, and from the File menu, choose Import (CTRL-I). When the Import dialog box opens, locate the file BLUE.CPT and click Import. When the cursor changes, click and drag on the page.

5. Next, import FISH02.CPT in the EXERCISE\OBJECTS\ folder of the CD-ROM . Click and drag this image on top of the blue image. The result appears in Figure 5-9.

The fish
imported
with a white
background

FIGURE 5-9

6. To remove the white rectangle, you must first ungroup the fish from it. With the fish object still selected, click the Ungroup button in the Property Bar.

7. Click somewhere outside the images to deselect the two objects, and then click on the fish again. This time, only the top object is selected. Click the TAB key to change the object selected to the white background and click the DEL (Delete) key. Now we have the fish without the background. There is a better way. Leave DRAW and PAINT open while I explain.

From PAINT to DRAW (Copy to File Method)

Instead of saving the image using the Save, Save As, or Export command, we will use PHOTO-PAINT's Copy to File command located in the Edit menu. The Copy to File command saves the selected object, but unlike the Save command, it does not save the background. Here are some rules about the Copy to File command:

- If the image contains one object, only the object will be saved.

- If the image contains multiple objects, only the objects that are selected will be saved.

Back to our little exercise.

1. In PAINT, open the file EXERCISE\OBJECTS\FISH02.CPT. From the Edit menu, choose Copy to File. Save the file as GOLDFISH.CPT.

2. In DRAW, from the File menu, choose Import (CTRL-I). When the Import dialog box opens, locate the file GOLDFISH.CPT and click Import, then drag out the image. The fish is now swimming in the bubbles without the white rectangle background, as shown in Figure 5-10.

A Recap of What We Just Did

In the previous hands-on session, we imported a PHOTO-PAINT image that contained an object and a background. An *object* is a bitmap image that floats above the background. A background is…well, you know—a background. The image actually contained two objects: the background and the fish. CorelDRAW treats the objects in PHOTO-PAINT files just like regular objects in DRAW, even though it is

Using the
Copy to
File
command
saves the
image
without the
background

FIGURE 5-10

a bitmap and not a vector drawing. If the image has no objects, CorelDRAW imports the entire image as a bitmap image.

PAINT (with Masks) into DRAW

Some of the rules in this area have changed with the release of the DRAW 8 suite, so if you are an experienced PHOTO-PAINT 7 user, I recommend spending a few moments and reading through this section.

It isn't necessary to have objects in a PHOTO-PAINT image for the subject to be clipped to the boundary of the image. In PHOTO-PAINT, the subject of the image that you want to bring into DRAW can be defined by a mask. A *mask* is a layer over the entire image that is used to define areas in the image. For more information on masks, see Chapter 7. In previous releases, it was necessary to mask the desired portion of the image and save it as an Encapsulated PostScript file (EPS) for the mask to define the edges of the image with what is called a clipping boundary.

While this method is still necessary with other non-Corel applications, the DRAW 8 Import command now recognizes and defines the image clipping boundary based on the mask that is in the image. Say what? Let me show you this visually. A picture is still worth more than a thousand words, even accounting for inflation. Figure 5-11 is my favorite Corel Professional Photo of a child. The circle around his face is a mask. Saving this image as a CPT file with the mask and then importing it into CorelDRAW 8 produces the image shown in Figure 5-12 Notice in Figure 5-12 that the edge is not sharp and distinct. This is because I feathered the mask in PAINT. Don't be concerned if you don't know what feathering is at this moment; just remember that DRAW recognizes and applies mask attributes. Here are a few more rules about masks when importing into DRAW.

On importing, DRAW does not:

- Recognize or apply Lenses

- Apply masks to objects—only the background

- Recognize or apply Clip Masks

The mask
marquee
shown in
PHOTO-
PAINT 8

FIGURE 5-11

The mask
defines the
image
boundary
when
imported
into
DRAW 8

 FIGURE 5-12

Getting From PAINT to both Corel & Non-Corel Applications

To save an image so the subject will be clipped to the masked area, select Export in the File menu and save the image as an Encapsulated PostScript (EPS) file. When the EPS dialog box opens, as shown in Figure 5-13, check Save and then check the Image Enclosed by Mask option. (Don't be fooled by the preview window in the Import dialog box.) After the image is saved, you can, in DRAW, select Import from the File menu and only the masked area appears. If you are going to be sending the work out to a service bureau, I would strongly recommend exporting as an EPS file. This is because the service bureau or printer is used to working with, and understands, EPS files. When you import the EPS image, it may not display properly on the screen, meaning the white rectangle may remain but will not be printed as long as you print it on a PostScript output device.

TIP: *In previous releases of PHOTO-PAINT, you could use the Save As command to create an EPS file. Now, you must use the Export command.*

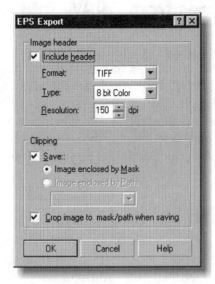

The EPS
Export
dialog box

FIGURE 5-13

EPS Export Dialog Box

The Image Header section allows you define what the bitmap file of
the file looks like. This header file is used for placement of the image
in another application. This is why an EPS image may sometimes look
very poor—because you are not actually looking at the image but at
the low-resolution header file.

The Clipping section is available if either a mask or path is present
in the image. When the Save feature is enabled, it saves the contents
of the mask marquee on the image in the EPS file. The program
converts the mask to a path before saving, so the process may take
some time, depending on how complicated the mask is. The sections
of the image that are outside the mask marquee are still in the image
but will not be visible, nor will they print, when you use the EPS file
in another application. You can still see those sections if you open the
image in Corel PHOTO-PAINT.

To delete the sections that are outside the mask marquee, enable the Crop
Image To Path/Mask When Saving option at the bottom of this dialog box.

Getting Images from DRAW into PAINT

Getting an image from DRAW into PAINT involves a process called *rasterization* (see the adjoining box). The Corel image, or the portion of the image, that you want to bring into PAINT is saved as a Corel CDR (vector) file. Unlike DRAW, the CDR file is not imported into PAINT—there is no Import command in PAINT—but is opened just like a PAINT file, with one exception. Opening any vector file opens the Import Into Bitmap dialog box, as shown in Figure 5-14. Select the settings and it will take a few moments to rasterize the image. After the image is loaded, it will be necessary to mask the area of the image you want and convert it to an object.

Rasterization and Dithering

When we go from CorelDRAW to PHOTO-PAINT (or any other bitmap application), it is necessary to convert the vector (or line) format into bitmap (or paint) format. This process is called *rasterization.* How the rasterization is accomplished determines how faithfully the image we import into Corel PHOTO-PAINT is reproduced.

When a color in the original image cannot be produced precisely (either because of display or color mode limitations), the computer does its best to make an approximation of the color through a process called *dithering.* With dithering, the computer changes the colors of adjacent pixels so that to the viewer, they approximate the desired color. Dithering is accomplished by mathematically averaging the color values of adjacent pixels. The use of dithering can also affect the process of getting an image from CorelDRAW to PHOTO-PAINT.

Import Into Bitmap Dialog Box

Use the Import Into Bitmap dialog box, shown in Figure 5-14, to specify how you want to rasterize the CDR or other vector-based image. Many users are intimidated by all the choices that are available to them in this dialog box. Never fear; after you read this section, they will begin to make sense.

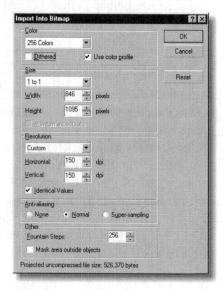

The Import
Into Bitmap
dialog box

FIGURE 5-14

Color

This directs PHOTO-PAINT to rasterize the CorelDRAW file either as a black-and-white image, as shades of gray, or color. The greater the number of colors, the larger the exported file, and the better the image will appear.

Use color profile

Uses the color profile assigned to the printer in the color manager.

Dithered

This dithers the colors of the DRAW file. Dithering is only available when you have selected a Color setting of 256 shades or less of color or the Black and White option (it is disabled in grayscale). If the image contains fountain fills or color blends, dithering can cause obvious banding in the exported bitmap. Here are some guidelines to help you decide whether to dither the bitmap:

■   If you are importing an image with 16 or 256 colors or black and white, use dithering.

- If you intend to scale this bitmap in PHOTO-PAINT, dithering is not recommended.

Size

This is the setting that ultimately determines the size of the image in PHOTO-PAINT. The Size setting specifies the dimensions of the resulting rasterized bitmap. If you choose 1 to 1, the image will be the same size as it was in CorelDRAW. You may also choose one of the preset sizes from the list box (not recommended) or choose Custom and type the dimensions in the Width and Height boxes.

By default, the size of the image in CorelDRAW is used, which is why I recommend the default setting of 1 to 1. Smaller bitmaps (with lower resolution) or larger bitmaps (with higher resolution) can be created by scaling the image up or down in CorelDRAW prior to exporting. When Custom is selected, make sure the Maintain aspect ratio checkbox is enabled.

 NOTE: *If you choose one of the preset sizes from the list box, the dimensions you choose may not be proportional to the bitmap's original aspect ratio. The exported bitmap will distort unless you place an empty border around your bitmap with the same ratio as the preset. For example, in DRAW, create a rectangle around your image 6.4 x 4.8 inches if you are exporting at 640 x 480. Then assign No Fill and No Outline to the rectangle. Now the aspect ratio of the image will be maintained when you export.*

Resolution

This specifies the resolution (in dots per inch) for bitmaps. The most popular choice is to use the 1 to 1 setting. The vector image is rasterized at a size of 1 to 1. If you choose one of the preset resolutions from the list box, you may be in for a surprise. For example, if you choose 640 × 480, it changes the aspect ratio (ratio of height to width) to match. In most cases, it will distort the image. Another choice is Custom, which is handy for making the image larger or smaller. Type the resolution in the DPI box.

 NOTE: *As resolution increases, so does the size of the export file and the time required to print the image.*

Anti-Aliasing

There are three choices for Anti-aliasing. Anti-aliasing produces smoother bitmap rasterization. By default, it is set to Normal. Super-sampling is a method that takes longer but produces superior results. You can also choose None.

Fountain Steps

This feature is new in PHOTO-PAINT 8. It allows you to determine the maximum number of fountain steps in the fills that replace blends.

Mask Area Outside Objects

Another new feature with PHOTO-PAINT 8, this option creates a mask that surrounds the background. Very handy.

The Express Route from DRAW to PAINT

This is so easy it's almost criminal. Use the Windows Clipboard as follows:

- In DRAW, select the object or objects you want to place in your PAINT image. Copy them to the Clipboard (CTRL-C).

- In PAINT, with the image open, click the Paste button on the toolbar and the DRAW objects will be rasterized to the resolution of the open image—no questions asked.

This next method, Drag and –Drop, used to produce badly dithered results, but not any longer.

The Drag-and-Drop Method

Another way to move an image from one application to another is *drag and drop*. This method is limited to screen resolution (72 dpi) only if there isn't an existing image open in PHOTO-PAINT 8.

Using Drag-and-Drop

If you decide to use drag and drop, you should follow these guidelines:

- Both applications must be open. This means that neither one can be reduced to a little icon in the Task bar.

- To drag an image from CorelDRAW, you must click on it and drag it into the PAINT application. When the cursor is over the paint application, the icon will turn into an arrow-rectangle icon.

- PHOTO-PAINT does not need to have an image area open. If an existing image is not open, a new image will be created with the resolution restricted to 72 dpi. If there is an existing image, it is rasterized at the resolution of the image.

- If you are dragging an DRAW object into an existing PAINT image you can use the right mouse button to drag it over and you will have the choice of copying (original remains in DRAW) or moving the object (original in DRAW is gone).

 TIP: *When dragging an image into PAINT, be patient. It sometimes takes longer than you might expect for the cursor to change into the arrow-rectangle icon. As Radar would say in* M.A.S.H: *"Wait for it."*

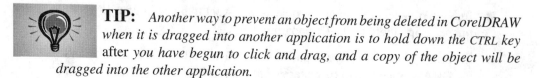 **TIP:** *Another way to prevent an object from being deleted in CorelDRAW when it is dragged into another application is to hold down the CTRL key after you have begun to click and drag, and a copy of the object will be dragged into the other application.*

- To restore the image that was dragged kicking and screaming out of CorelDRAW, just click anywhere in the CorelDRAW window (which makes it active again) and select Undo Delete from the Edit menu or press CTRL-Z.

When to use PAINT and When to use DRAW

You may want to use PHOTO-PAINT to enhance bitmap images and then bring them back into DRAW for adding text. An exception to this rule is if you need to apply special effects to the text. The reason for placing text in DRAW is that the resulting output text will be much sharper. When text is created in PAINT, the text is a bitmap image that is resolution dependent. In other words, the text is no longer text but a bitmap picture of the text. It is fixed to the same resolution of the image it is placed in. This means that text placed in PAINT will be the resolution of the image. If it is 300 dpi (dots per inch), then the text will be a bitmap image that is 300 dpi regardless of whether it is printed to a 300-dpi laser printer or a 2,450-dpi imagesetter. Text in a program like DRAW is resolution independent. Any text that is placed in DRAW remains as text. At printing time, DRAW sends the font information to the output device, allowing it to be printed at the maximum resolution of the device. If it is output to a 2,450-dpi imagesetter, then the resolution of the text will be 2,450 dpi. The result is sharper text.

How about CorelDREAM and other 3-D Stuff?

Will this chapter never end? The ability to import 3-D metafiles is new in the Corel 8 release. With this new capability, you can import any 3-D metafile (with the 3DMF extension). The settings are very similar to those in the Import into Bitmap dialog box. You can, using the dialog box controls, rotate the image along any axis, and control the different rendering engines with a selection of buttons on the dialog box. The image shown in the preview window of Figure 5-15 shows a 3-D model of an office chair.

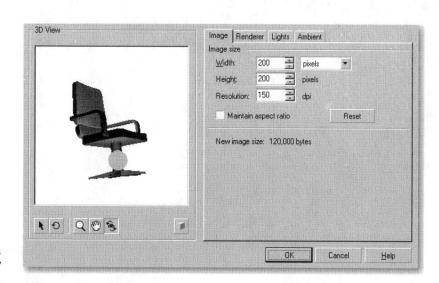

Now we can bring 3-D objects into PAINT

FIGURE 5-15

Using OLE

It is a widely advertised fact that the entire Corel line of products, beginning with DRAW 4, supports OLE 2.0 (Object Linking and Embedding). Corel PHOTO-PAINT 8 and CorelDRAW 8 now both support in-place editing. OLE is a powerful interapplication program that is routinely demonstrated by dragging an image from one application and dropping it into another. OLE is given a lot of hype by Microsoft and the press. On paper, OLE looks great; in practice, it carries a lot of overhead.

In-place editing means that when you place a PHOTO-PAINT image into a word processing application like Microsoft Word, you can actually open PHOTO-PAINT inside of Word by right-clicking on the image. By copying the image to the Clipboard and then using the Paste Special command in the Edit menu of Word or other OLE-compliant application, you can right-click the image and PHOTO-PAINT will open up within Word. For the average PHOTO-PAINT user, this isn't a big issue. Because of the resources needed for photo-editing in PHOTO-PAINT, I cannot recommend using OLE's in-place editing unless you have a really powerful system with lots of memory. Even then, I am not sure what the great advantage would be. I guess this means I will get a lump of coal in my stocking from Santa Bill Gates this Christmas. Enough said about OLE.

Closing Thoughts

We have covered a lot of material in this chapter, which I hope will help you use both Corel and non-Corel applications together to make some incredible projects.

6

Controlling Image
Size, Direction
or Format

J ust as images don't always come in the proper size, they also don't always come in the desired orientation. When you are laying out a newsletter, for instance, it seems that when you get the images you want, they are inevitably facing the wrong direction. You usually want them facing inward if they are on the outside edge, and facing outward if they are on the inside edge. (I knew you knew that; I just thought I would throw it in.) Corel PHOTO-PAINT offers a collection of commands to allow the image to be re-oriented quickly and easily.

The Duplicate Command

This command was introduced way back in Corel PHOTO-PAINT 6. In Corel PHOTO-PAINT 5 all of the commands in the Image menu produce changed copies of the image while leaving the original intact. Since many people complained that this created many unnecessary copies of the image cluttering up the main screen, Corel changed the commands so they did not produce duplicates.

The Duplicate command produces a new file that is a copy of the original image. When you select Duplicate in the Image menu, a dialog box opens. You have two decisions to make. First, you enter a name for the duplicate file or accept the name generated by Corel PHOTO-PAINT. Second, you must decide whether to use Merge Objects with Background. If you don't know what objects are, don't be concerned; they are explored later in the book. For now, objects are bitmap images that float on top of the picture. The Merge Objects with Background option gives you the choice of making the duplicate image with all of the objects as they are in the original or with all of the objects merged into the background. Once they are merged, they are no longer objects.

The Duplicate command becomes important when you must produce copies of a image to create things like Displacement maps—which are explored in Chapter 18.

For Corel PHOTO-PAINT 5 Users

There is a Duplicate command in Corel PHOTO-PAINT 5 as well. It is located in the Window menu. That Duplicate command does not make a new file; it produces only a temporary copy of a file. Any changes made to it are reflected on the original. Each file made with the Duplicate command in Corel PHOTO-PAINT 8 is a separate file and has no effect on the file it was duplicated from.

The Image Flip and Rotate Commands

Many users in their headlong rush to get to the fancy effects ignore the Image Flip and Rotate commands. These commands are more useful than you might think.

The Flip Command

This command is pretty much self-explanatory. Accessed through the Image menu, it makes either a vertical or horizontal mirrored copy of the original image. To use the Flip command, select Flip from the Image menu. A flyout appears, showing the two choices: Horizontally and Vertically. Clicking on either of these executes the command, producing a copy of the image with the selected effect.

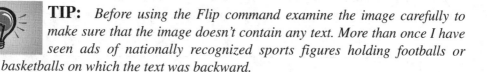 **TIP:**   *Before using the Flip command examine the image carefully to make sure that the image doesn't contain any text. More than once I have seen ads of nationally recognized sports figures holding footballs or basketballs on which the text was backward.*

Now, if these commands seem pointless to you, you are not using your imagination. Remember, the best tool in Corel PHOTO-PAINT is located between your ears.

The AIR SHOW image in Figure 6-1 began with a single jet, shown above. Using the Duplicate command, a second copy of the entire image was made. The Flip Horizontal command was used to make a horizontal mirror copy of the original. The Paper Size command was used to double the width of the original. The original was copied to the clipboard and pasted as an object into the duplicate. The text and shadows were created with the text tool.

The Rotate Command

Rotate offers the ability to rotate the entire image. Again, this may not seem like much, but there are many things you can do with this little command.

Let's say you are laying out a sports magazine. You have a story about the playoffs that needs a graphic to introduce it. Everybody uses the picture of the arena packed with screaming fans and sweaty players. You want something different. You find what you want in a stock photo, as shown on the next page. The problem is that

This began as a photograph of a single jet.

FIGURE 6-1

6

it is a vertical photo and you wanted something to cover several columns. No problem with the Rotate command.

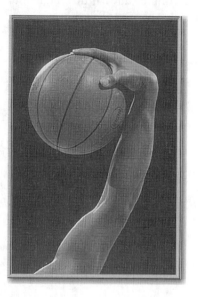

The original photo from the PhotoDisc library is great but it's not wide enough to cover several columns.

From the Rotate command from the Image menu, 90 degrees clockwise was selected.

That operation took less than two minutes, you met your deadline, your editor is happy with you. Of course, if you had more time (10 minutes) and had already learned how to create and rotate objects, you could have made the graphic shown in Figure 6-2. I only included this to show you some of the things that can be done with PHOTO-PAINT 8.

By using the Rotation command and a little imagination, you can create excellent banners for magazines, brochures, and so on.

Rotating an Image

To rotate an image, choose Rotate in the Image menu. A flyout appears with the available choices. Selecting Custom from the drop-down list opens the Custom Rotate dialog box.

NOTE: *If the original image has objects, they will all become visible in the rotated copy. They will not be merged. This includes the hidden objects. (If you are bewildered by those last few sentences, it will become clearer when you get to Chapter 13 on objects.)*

Rotating
objects
gives us
even more
creative
freedom

FIGURE 6-2

The Custom Rotate Dialog Box

The Custom Rotate dialog box enables you to rotate the current image by a specified amount. A new image is created from the results of the rotation. The variables are as follows:

- **Degrees**   Enter the amount of the rotation in whole numbers. It ignores decimal numbers. Warning: the dialog box accepts decimal numbers without giving any indication that it isn't using them.

- **Direction**   Determines the direction of rotation. Click the Clockwise or Counterclockwise radio buttons.

- **Maintain Original Image Size**   When this check box is selected, the image height and width dimensions are fixed. The rotated image is cropped at the image boundaries. If this is left unselected, the dimensions of the image are automatically calculated (adjusted) to fit the edges of the rotated image. The following images demonstrate the several uses of rotated images.

- **Anti-Aliasing**   When enabled, this check box reduces "jaggies" on rotated images but may soften the image being rotated.

- **Paper Color**   From the drop-down Color palette, you can define the color of the new background that is added when Maintain Original Size is not selected.

Here is a quick exercise to show how quickly you can make a placard for a café in no time at all. If you are reading this book from start to finish, you may not understand all of the commands but fear not, as you read on, they will begin to make sense.

1. From the File menu choose Open. Locate the file EXERCISE\ PHOTOS\569057.WI on the CD-ROM, highlight it and click Open.

2. Suddenly your screen is filled with food. From the Image menu choose Resample. Change the Width setting to 5.0 inches and click OK. Now it is down to a manageable size.

3. We are going to create a new Paper color from a color in the photograph. With the cursor over the image click the "E" key. The cursor becomes an eyedropper. Keep holding down the "E" key and hold down the CTRL key. Do you feel like you are playing twister? Place the cursor over the image so it is inside of the candle on the pottery. Click it once and the Paper color, as seen in the Status bar, changes to match it.

4. Select Rotate from the Image menu and choose Custom. From the Custom Rotate dialog box enter 15 in the Angle value box and check the Anti-aliasing box. Click OK. The result is shown below.

5. Change the Paint color to Yellow by clicking one time on the Yellow color swatch in the on-screen palette.

6. Click the Text button in the Toolbox (looks like the letter A). In the Property Bar change the Font to Playbill and the Size to 72. (The font isn't critical, if you don't have Playbill installed just pick one you like).

7. Click on the image and type NACHOS. Next, click on the Object Picker tool at the top of the Toolbox (the text becomes an Object) and move the type so it looks like Figure 6-3.

8. For the final step, select Drop Shadow from the Object menu. Select the settings you like and click the default setting (you may want to reduce the Opacity). Click the Apply button and you are done. The result is shown in Figure 6-3.

In a few simple steps we were able to create this colorful table placard.

FIGURE 6-3

TIP: *Anti-aliasing or not, the edge of this image has some minor "jaggies" after rotation. To correct this I chose the Blend brush from the Effect tools (Chapter 10) and smoothed over the rough edges—so to speak.*

Next we will learn how to take images and make them the correct size for use in other programs.

Manipulating the Image by Resizing

Resizing an image is a common practice in word processing and page layout programs. There is more to resizing than first you might imagine.

Why You Shouldn't Resize or Crop an Image in Other Applications

Many page layout programs like Corel VENTURA, Pagemaker, and Quark offer graphic cropping and resizing as part of the program. They are usually fine for very minor image adjustments, but for any significant changes, you should open the files in Corel PHOTO-PAINT and make the changes there. There are several reasons for doing so, as follows:

- If you crop a large image file in a word processing or page layout program, the file size remains unchanged. Even if you use only 5 percent of a 16MB image file, the entire file remains as part of the document file. Large document files create problems with lengthy print times and difficulty in transport to a service bureau. If you crop that same 16MB file in Corel PHOTO-PAINT, it becomes an 800KB file.

- Resizing bitmap files in these applications can cause image distortion, which often shows up as unwanted moiré patterns over the entire image.

There are many different ways to change the size of an image once it has been loaded into Corel PHOTO-PAINT. Most of the commands are found in the Image menu. Commands in the Image menu affect the entire image and cannot be applied to a portion of the image.

How to Display Information About an Image

Corel PHOTO-PAINT gives the current size and resolution of an image, along with other data, at the bottom of the Image menu, which displays information about a selected image file when you click the Info button.

Another way to see the Image Info window is to click on the Corel PHOTO-PAINT icon in the upper-left corner of the window of the image and select Info... from the drop-down menu.

Please note that the Image Info window is not a dialog box. Information is displayed but it cannot be edited. Once opened, the Image Info window must be closed by clicking the OK button before any other actions occur.

Image-File Information (Bigger is Not Better)

What follows is an explanation of the information that is displayed in the Info message box:

Name:	Filename of the selected image file
Width:	Displays width in the units of measure selected by choosing Options in the Tools menu in the General tab (pixels always shown in parentheses)
Height:	Displays height in the units of measure selected by choosing Options in the Tools menu in the General page
X dpi:	Resolution (horizontal) in dots-per-inch
Y dpi:	Resolution (vertical) in dots-per-inch
Size in Memory:	Size of the uncompressed file
Original File Size:	Size of file after it is saved
Format:	Type of image file format, i.e. Wavelet Compressed Bitmap (WI)
Subformat:	Displays compression information
Type:	Color Mode of Image, e.g., grayscale, 256 color, 24-bit color, etc.
Objects:	Displays number of objects in an image (Corel PHOTO-PAINT format only)
Status:	Indicates if any changes have been made to the image since it was opened

You will find yourself using the Info command more than you may expect. Generally I use it to check the size of my image file before I save it.

Resizing the Image Window

Although this is not directly related to image resizing, it is essential for working with images. To resize the Image window, move the cursor over the corner or sides of the Image window until the cursor becomes a double-headed arrow. Click and drag the Image window until it is the desired size. The image size remains unchanged and a gray border appears around the original image. It is very helpful to increase the image area size when working on an image close to the edge. When you are working with various Corel PHOTO-PAINT tools near the edge of the image, the program reacts when the cursor touches the Image window's border. Increasing the view area prevents the cursor from changing into a double-headed arrow any time the edge is approached.

TIP: *For a quick resize of the image to see it better, grab the corner of the window and drag it until it is the size you desire, then depress the Zoom to Fit (F4) key.*

Changing the Size of an Image

Images are rarely provided to you in the exact size that is required for your project. In the old days, when we needed to change the size of an image, we made a PMT (photo-mechanical transfer) of the image, which could then be reduced or enlarged. Fortunately, Corel PHOTO-PAINT provides several much simpler ways to change both the size and the surrounding working area of an image. There are several ways to change the size of an image. They include *resampling* and *cropping* and their variations.

Resizing Methods	Description
Resampling	This command makes the image larger or smaller by adding or subtracting pixels. It can also change the resolution of the image, which affects the printed size without adding or subtracting pixels.
Crop Tool	This tool acts like a traditional cropping tool. It allows you to define a specific area of an image and remove all of the area outside the defined area. In Corel PHOTO-PAINT 5, we did the same thing with a rectangle mask tool.
Changing paper size	This handy command uses a combination of resampling and cropping. The Paper Size command increases overall image size by increasing the size of the base image. It is as if you were to put a larger sheet of paper under the original. It can also be used to crop the image.

The Resample Command

The resolution and the dimensions of an image in Corel PHOTO-PAINT can be changed using the Resample command. One of the best aspects of the Resample command is that it can change the size of an image without the need for you to grab the old calculator to work out the math. Resampling should not be confused with the scaling features of CorelDRAW or other DTP programs like Pagemaker and Quark. These applications stretch or compress the bitmap images, often resulting in serious distortion. Resampling actually recreates the image, adding or subtracting pixels as required. Figure 6-4 shows the effects of resampling a photograph. The original sample (left) was resampled at 200 (middle) and 800 percent (right).

TIP: *Be aware that adding or subtracting pixels from an image decreases the quality of an image. Having said that, resampling remains the best way to change the size of an existing image. If you must resample, resample down (make the image size smaller) avoid resampling up (making the image larger.)*

Two Approaches to Resampling and Their Results

Resampling an image with Corel PHOTO-PAINT 8 falls into two general categories: fixed and variable resolution. Each method changes the image size, and each has its own advantages and disadvantages.

6

A graphic example of the effects of Resampling on a photograph

FIGURE 6-4

Fixed Resolution Resampling

With this method, the resolution of the image remains unchanged, while the dimensions are either increased or decreased. Wait! Didn't I explain in Chapter 2 that if the dimensions increased, the resolution had to decrease? I did. Because the resolution is fixed, Corel PHOTO-PAINT must either add or subtract pixels from the image to make it fit the new dimensions entered. When the space between the pixels increases, Corel PHOTO-PAINT creates more pixels to keep the resolution constant. When you resample, Corel PHOTO-PAINT goes through the entire image comparing pairs of adjacent pixels and creating pixels that represent the average tonal value. I told you that so you would know why your computer seems to take so long to resample an image.

Conversely, when the dimensions of the image decrease, as was the case with the original file of our Nacho exercise, Corel PHOTO-PAINT subtracts pixels from the image. This sounds ideal, doesn't it? Actually, you always lose some detail when you resample an image, regardless of whether you add or subtract pixels. There is no magic here. The greater the amount of resampling, the greater the amount of image degradation introduced.

If the Maintain Aspect box in the Resample dialog box is checked, any change made to one dimension will automatically change the other. By disabling Maintain Aspect, it is possible to change one value without causing the other to change. Whenever you change the aspect ratio of an image, you introduce distortion. The distortion will be noticeable if the values entered vary too greatly from the original aspect ratio.

Another consideration when using the fixed resolution method is the increase in file size. Table 6-1 shows how quickly file sizes increase when a photo-CD (300 dpi) file is increased in size using fixed resolution resampling.

How files increase in size geometrically when resampled at fixed resolutions			
100%	200%	300%	400%
1.01MB	4.03MB	9.82MB	17.23MB

TABLE 6-1

Variable Resolution Resampling

The other resampling method is the one I generally use (when I must use one). Variable resolution resampling is accomplished by clicking the button labeled Maintain Original Size. By forcing PAINT to keep the file size (number of pixels) unchanged, the resolution is changed to fit the newly requested image size. You can safely allow the resolution to be reduced to 150 dpi for grayscale and 100-120 dpi for color images.

The advantages of this method are that the file size remains the same and the operation is instantaneous. The reason it happens so quickly is that the image is not physically altered. Only information in the file header is changed. The resolution information is maintained in the header of bitmap image files. When PAINT changes the resolution of an image, it only needs to change two sets of numbers in the file. The disadvantage to this method is the loss of image detail that results from the lower resolution. In most cases, if you keep the resolution at the recommended levels for the type of image you are working with, you should be able to resize the image without any noticeable loss of image detail. I recommend disabling Maintain Aspect when using variable resolution resampling (Maintain Original Size enabled).

TIP: *When Resampling by changing resolution, you cannot see any physical change in the displayed image while in Corel PHOTO-PAINT. This is because the program maps each pixel of the image to a pixel on the display regardless of the resolution setting. To see the effect, you must save the image and print it.*

Resample Dialog Box Options

Here is a list of the Resample dialog box controls and what they do. Not very interesting reading, but handy information when you need it.

Option	Description
Units	Choose a unit of measurement from the drop-down list box.
Width/Height	Enter a number or use the scroll arrows to choose a size (entered in units of measure), or enter a percentage in the % box. The dimensions of the image remain proportional to the original. Any value entered in one box will cause the other box to change proportionally if the Maintain Aspect check box is checked.

Option	Description
Horizontal/Vertical	Enter a resolution value or let PAINT select a value for you. Resolution is measured in dots-per-inch (dpi).
Process	Selects the process to convert. Choices are Anti-alias and Stretch/Truncate.
Anti-Alias	This is the best selection. It creates a smoother image by removing jagged edges from the original. This is done by averaging or interpolating pixels. It takes longer to process, but it is worth it. Be aware that this option will soften some images with strong diagonal or edge components.
Stretch/Truncate	Only use this if you have a very slow system or you are resampling bitmap graphics like screen capture shots of menus in this book. It creates a rough image by stretching duplicated pixels and eliminating overlapped pixels. This process is very fast and the results less than great.
Maintain Aspect Ratio	When this is checked, the dimension/resolution values of the image remain proportional to the original. If you enable Maintain Aspect Ratio, values in the Width/ Height and Resolution boxes remain proportional to the original values. For example, if you increase the height by 50 percent, the width will be increased by 50 percent. The same is true of the Horizontal and Vertical resolutions. They remain equal.
Maintain Original Size	When selected, this keeps the file size the same as the original, regardless of the values of resolution or Width/Height selected. This option is used to resample the image by changing the resolution. Changes in resolution are not reflected on the display, only when printed.
Original Image Size	Displays the size of the original image.
New Image Size	Displays the calculated size of the resampled version based on the values entered in the dialog box.

Option	Description
Reset	Returns all the values in the dialog box to the values of the original image when the Resample dialog box was opened.

Resample on Open

The Resample option that is available on the Open an Image dialog box is identical to the Resample command with one exception. The Resample command can increase or decrease the image size, while the Resample option on Open an Image can only be used to decrease image size.

Additional Notes on Using Resample

When changing resolution, remember that resolution settings that are greater thanwhat the final output device can support will result in large image files that require extra printing time without improvement in output quality.

Cropping an Image

Cropping involves the removal of part of an image either to change its size or to enhance the composition of the subject matter. Cropping in Corel PHOTO-PAINT previous to release 6 can only be done with either a mask tool or the Paper Size command. The Crop tool is in the Toolbox located just under the Mask tool flyout.

Using the Crop Tool

There are several ways to crop an image. In Chapter 5 we discussed cropping an image when opening it. The Crop tool offers several different ways to select what is cropped and what is not. The choices are:

- Crop to Selection
- Crop to Mask
- Crop to Border Color

CROP TO SELECTION After you select the Crop tool, you draw a rectangular bounding box that surrounds the subject and excludes the area you wish to crop. You can move the rectangle or size it using the handles that surround the box. Double-clicking the rectangle crops the image to the shape of the rectangle.

Instead of double-clicking the left mouse, you may click the right mouse button and the available options for the Crop tool appear. The Crop to Mask option is grayed out (not available) if there are no masks in the image. Selecting Crop to Selection crops the image.

CROP TO MASK   This option operates like Crop to Selection except that it crops to a mask rather than to a rectangle created by the Crop tool. To crop an area, surround it with a mask. Select the Crop tool and right-click inside of the mask. Choose Crop to Mask.

Regardless of the type of mask you place on the image—circle, trapezoid, and so on—the Crop to Mask feature will calculate a rectangular area that will fit all of the points on the mask you have used. The final result will be a rectangular image. Figure 6-5 shows the original photograph with a circle mask on it.

After using Crop to Mask, notice that the photograph was only cropped to the edges of the mask as shown below.

CROP BORDER COLOR   The Crop Border Color command removes borders of a particular color from an image. An example would be the ugly black border that seems to surround so many of the early photo-CDs. The idea is to select the color of the border and click the button, and the black border disappears. In theory, that is the way it is supposed to work. The problem with the command has nothing to do with Corel PHOTO-PAINT. It is that nearly all borders are irregular, and since all crops must be rectangular, the result is that pieces of the original border do not get cropped.

a) Original
photograph
with a circle
mask

FIGURE 6-5

The operation of the Crop Border Color option is a two-step process. After you select the Crop tool, you right-click on the image to be cropped and select Crop Border Color from the pop-up menu. This opens the Crop Border Color dialog box, as shown below.

It is from the Crop Border Color dialog box that you select the color that will be used as the border color to be removed. The Crop Border Color dialog box lets you crop out the paper color, paint color, or a custom color you select from an image. The sensitivity of the cropping is controlled using the Tolerance sliders, which crop color based on similarities between adjacent pixels. These sliders control just how many shades of colors will be included in the cropping action.

A word of warning here. If the tolerance is set to zero, there is a chance that when you use the command nothing will happen. Let me explain. Let's say you have a black border surrounding a photo-CD image. You choose Paint (foreground) color, since the border is black (the default color for Paint is black). The Tolerance is set to zero, meaning that only the Paint color will be selected. Nothing changes after you execute the command. What happened? Because the Tolerance was set to zero, only an exact match of the Paint color would be cropped. While the black on the border looks black, it is only a close approximation. As you go through the book, you will learn about shading and numerical color values. To crop to the color, you can increase the Tolerance (a setting between 5-10 will suffice); don't go crazy and set the Tolerance to a large value of 200. When the Tolerance value gets large enough, it reaches a threshold that I call the avalanche point. When it is set this high, almost all colors in the image are included in the border color.

For border colors that are not black or white, I recommend you use the Eyedropper tool to select the color from the image to be cropped. Your chances of finding the right color in a standard palette are very slim. When using the Eyedropper tool to get a color match, remember that most border colors are not uniform and you will still need to increase the Tolerance if you are going to include the entire border. Corel PHOTO-PAINT offers you two Tolerance modes to choose from, Normal and HSB. Stay with Normal and don't worry about the HSB for the Crop Border Color command.

Using the Paper Size Command

Another command is in the Image menu to increase or decrease the size of the image area by creating a new image area in the specified size and placing the original image within it. It is called Paper Size because Corel refers to the background as paper. This command takes the original image and places it *unchanged* on larger or smaller paper (background). The new image (Paper) color is determined by Corel PHOTO-PAINT's Paper Color setting. If the paper size is decreased to a size smaller than the original image, the image is cropped. If the paper size is larger than the original image, it is placed on a paper based on the Placement selection made in the dialog box.

Paper Size Dialog Box

The operation of this dialog box is pretty much self-explanatory. The Width/Height determine the new width and height of the paper while Units selects the units of measurement for width and height. If Maintain Aspect Ratio is checked, the width and height values maintain their proportion to one another. Placement determines the placement of the image on the paper. The drop-down list box has the following options: Top Left, Top Center, Top Right, Center Left, Centered, Center Right, Bottom Left, Bottom Center, Bottom Right, and Custom. If you choose Custom, use the hand cursor in the Preview window to move the image to the correct location.

Making a Poster with the Paper Size & Duplicate Command

You will find that the Paper Size command in Corel PHOTO-PAINT is very useful for a variety of projects. In this hands-on exercise, we will create the background for a poster using the Paper Size, the Duplicate and the Flip command.

1. Open the file EXERCISE\PHOTOS\554026.WI. Select Resample from the Image menu and change the Width to 5 inches. Click the OK button.

2. Choose Duplicate from the Image menu and when the dialog box opens name the duplicate file RIGHTEYE.CPT.

3. Select Flip, Horizontally, from the Image menu.

4. Mask the entire image (CTRL-A) and copy it to the clipboard (CTRL-C). Minimize RIGHTEYE.CPT.

5. Select the original image and from the Image menu choose Paper Size. When the dialog box opens uncheck the Maintain aspect ratio box, change the Width value to 10 and select Center Left for Placement. Click the OK button. Press F4 to see the resulting image as shown in Figure 6-6.

6. Click the Paste as Object button on the Toolbar and the RIGHTEYE.CPT is pasted as an object.

7. Select Arrange from the Object menu and Align from the flyout and set it to Vertically: Center and Horizontally: Right. Click the OK button. The image now fills the image window. With the object still selected, move it to the left with the left arrow key. Until the graffiti in the middle is on top of one another as shown in Figure 6-7.

The Paper Size command is used to double the width of the image.

■ FIGURE 6-6

8. Select Combine from the Object menu and choose Combine Objects With Background.

9. Choose the Crop tool from the Toolbox. Place the cursor in the upper-left corner of the image, click and drag it to the lower-right corner of photograph. Do not include the white area on the right side. Click the right mouse button inside of the image and choose, Crop To Selection.

10. This completes the background for the poster. Your figure should look like Figure 6-8.

11. Save the file as WALLEYES.CPT; we will use it again in Chapter 19

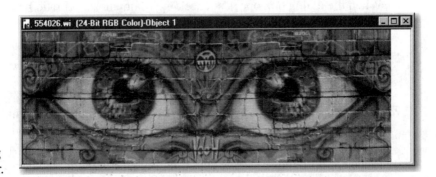

Both eyes are overlapping but together.

■ FIGURE 6-7

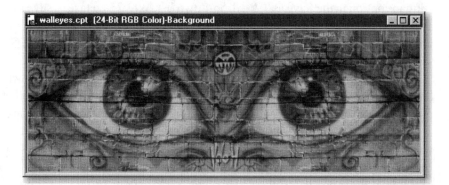

The
finished
eyes

FIGURE 6-8

 TIP: *As a reminder for users of Corel PHOTO-PAINT 5, the Paper Size command does not create a duplicate image. Rather, it creates the new images and deletes the original.*

Tips on Changing Paper Size

The Paper Size command can be used to precisely crop an image by changing the paper size to the desired value and selecting centered placement. By moving the image with the cursor, it is possible to place the image at the exact desired position on the new paper size. Paper size provides a method of placing an image on a larger background. You can make borders around an existing image. Try using Paper Size several times on the same image with complementary colors to make a quick border.

Image Conversion

One of the many features of PHOTO-PAINT is its ability to convert images from one graphics format to another. This section begins with a description of a new command in PHOTO-PAINT 8, the Export command.

The Export Command

Corel PHOTO-PAINT 8 has an Export command like the one found in CorelDRAW, which is used to save a copy of an image in a format that requires modifying an image. Does that make sense? Maybe not. Let me give you an example. If I have a PHOTO-PAINT image that contains masks and/or objects and want to save it as a

JPEG file, I no longer can choose Save As from the File menu and find the JPEG Bitmaps option in the Save as Type drop-down list. Why? Because to save the image as a JPEG requires removing the masks and flattening (combining the objects in the image with the background) the image. So to convert the image to a JPEG I must select the Export to option in the File menu.

We can also convert images in two other ways: by saving files in a wide variety of different formats (.EPS, .TIF, etc.), and by converting open images to different color modes (256-color, grayscale, etc.) using the Convert To command in the Image menu.

Converting color images to grayscale can save enormous amounts of disk space when producing graphics that will be printed in grayscale. Converting a 24-bit color image to grayscale reduces the image file to one-third of its original size. For example, if the original 24-bit color image is 1.1MB, converting it to grayscale will result in a file size of approximately 250-300KB.

Another use of this feature is viewing color images for pages that will be printed in grayscale. This book is an example of that type of work. All of the examples shown were originally in color. I have learned that it is very important to convert the images to grayscale so I can see what they will look like when they appear in the book. Often, in previous books, I would find an excellent example to show an effect or technique only to discover that the effect did not show up when printed in grayscale.

To Convert an Image

To convert an image, select Convert To in the Image menu. A drop-down list opens with the following choices:

Black and White (1-bit)	Converts the image to black and white (not to be confused with grayscale). This selection opens another dialog box with the following choices:
	Line Art: Produces an image containing only black and white pixels. A pixel is assigned either a black or a white value, depending on the grayscale value assigned to the pixel (1-256) and the threshold level setting in the Options box. There are no intermediate steps between the two extremes. No halftone is applied to the image.

Ordered: Controls the appearance of images with pixel depths greater than that of the display device. Dithering is performed at a faster rate than error diffusion by approximating pixel values using fixed dot patterns.

Error Diffusion: Controls the appearance of images with pixel depths greater than that of the display device. Provides the best results by calculating the value of each pixel using 256 shades of gray and spreading the calculation over several pixels.

Half Tone: Produces a continuous tone image such as a black-and-white photograph using dots of various sizes. On laser printers that cannot print different-sized dots, the halftone is produced by printing different numbers of dots in a given area.

Grayscale (8-bit)	Converts the image to grayscale.
Duotone (8-bit)	This is new in Corel PHOTO-PAINT 8. This converts a grayscale image image into a duotone image.
Paletted (8-bit)	Converts the image to 256 colors. (See additional discussion later in this chapter.)
RGB Color (24-bit)	Converts the image to 24-bit color (also called True-Color or 16.7 million color). It uses eight bits of data for each of the three channels of Red, Green, and Blue (RGB).
Lab Color (24-bit)	Converts to 24-bit color using eight bits of data for each of the LAB channels.

CMYK Color (32-bit)	Converts the image to 32-bit color. This is a 24-bit color image that is separated into four channels: Cyan, Magenta, Yellow, and Black (CMYK), which is the standard separation for four-color printing.
Multi-channel	Coverts the image into its three basic color channels. This is different than an RGB image whose 3 channels can be viewed separately.
Grayscale (16-bit)	Conversion to this format provides 65,000 shades of gray. Of course you can't print anywhere near that many, but this provides them and is generally used with high-resolution scanners.
RGB Color (48-bit)	Converts to three channels each containing 16 bits of information. Generally used with high-resolution scanners.

Duotones

The term duotone is used to describe bitmap images that have spot colors assigned to them. Up to four spot colors can be assigned to a bitmap creating monotones, duotones, tritones, and quadtones. The original purpose of duotones was to compensate for the fact that printing inks had a limited dynamic range when printing halftone images. When inks other than black or gray are used, duotones create striking effects. Technically, the term duotone refers to a two-color job, which is probably the most common type in the industry. Duotone has come to mean any combination of spot color/bitmap assignments. In other words, when someone is telling you they want a duotone, it is a good idea to verify actually what they want.

While the traditional approach has been to simply add a second color to the black image to give it a richer look, programs like PHOTO-PAINT are giving designers the tools to take a traditional technique and create some new looks.

Creating Duotones

With Corel PHOTO-PAINT the creation of duotones is simple. First, convert the image to grayscale and then select Convert To and choose Duotone (8-bit). This opens the Duotone dialog box shown below. If the image contains objects, you will receive a message asking you to combine all of the objects with the background before proceeding. If you wish to keep your original image with objects, you may want to use the duplicate command from the Image menu and make a Duotone from the duplicate. There are only two tabs, Curves and OverPrints in the dialog box, and the good news is you probably only need to use Curves.

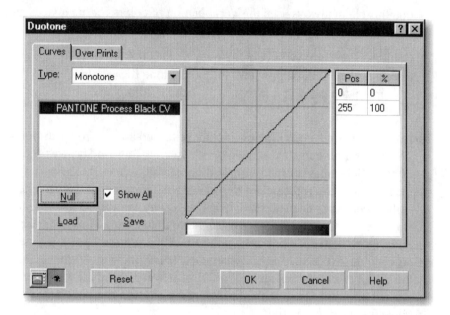

A Duotone Exercise

Possibly the best way to learn how to use this feature is to make a simple Duotone. Let's assume we are creating a duotone for a client that is creating a pamphlet on Asian children. In the interests of saving money the client has created a design that uses two inks - Black and Pantone 144CV. Let's make a duotone.

1. From the File menu locate and select the image EXERCISE\PHOTOS\ \538097.WI. The photograph needs to be 5 inches wide so choose Resample from the Image menu and change the width to 5 inches and click OK.

NOTE: *If we were actually printing this image we would change the resolution as well, but for the exercise we will leave it as it is.*

2. From the Image menu, choose Convert to and choose Grayscale (8-bit).

3. The Duotone dialog box opens and it is set to Monotone. We could change to Duotone in the Type section and then select the ink we want by double-clicking on the second ink and choosing the Pantone 144CV from a very large menu. We could do that but there is an easier way. As it turns out, this client always uses this combination of colors for his images and so we have wisely saved it as a duotone (*.cpd) file.

4. Click the Load button and double-click on DCOLOR1.CPD. Be aware there are no thumbnail previews for the duotone files so the more descriptive the name you assign it, the better your chance of finding it later.

5. If you are in on-screen preview the image turned a very brownish-orange. This looks a little intense and we decide to tone down the brown—hey, it rhymes. Select the Pantone 144CV if not already selected. The curve and the figures on the right side of the dialog box indicate that the Pantone 144CV curve has been accentuated. This is why the second ink appears so strong. Click the Null button and the curve flattens out. Now the image looks much better. If you click on the Black ink, you will see it is pushed down to make the black inks lighter. Don't click the Null button again or the picture will become very dark. OK so if you jumped the gun and clicked it, you can restore the file setting by clicking the Load button and reloading the duotone file.

6. Click OK and you have a duotone image. Close the file and do not save any of the changes.

So Now What Do You Do with the Duotone?

If you want a commercial printer to reproduce the duotone, you must print the image to color separations. Because PHOTO-PAINT has already specified the inks to use and how much of each ink to apply, all of the work has been done for you. If you are preparing the duotone to be imported into another program, save the image in the Encapsulated PostScript (EPS) format. The only other file format that supports duotone separations, other than native PHOTO-PAINT CPT, is Desktop Color Separations (DCS).

After all of that talk about two-color printing, what if you want to print a duotone in a CMYK document? No problem, convert the duotone to CMYK. Not only will all of the duotone shades be preserved, but you'll have the advantage of being able to adjust colors using PHOTO-PAINT's standard color correction commands and editing tools.

Over Prints

Fair is fair, I should tell you about this. The Over Print tab of the Duotone dialog box allows you to control the blending of colors. When you select this tab you are shown how each pair of colors will mix when printed. To change the color swatch, double-click on the color and the Select Color dialog box opens. The problem with this method is that it complicates the editing process. PHOTO-PAINT doesn't actually change the ink colors or transfer functions in keeping with your new specification; it just applies the new Over Print colors. You also will lose any changes you make in Over Print when you make any adjustment of the ink colors. Like I said at the beginning of this section, Why is it there? Because the Over Print method is necessary for certain types of printing. If you are new to duotones, stick with Curves.

One of the more common questions I get asked is, "How do I assign spot colors in an image and get spot color separations when I print?" The next section answers that question nicely.

Using the Convert To Command

Choose the desired format to which the image is to be converted. The formats that are unavailable are grayed out. With a Paletted (8-bit) image, for example, the Duotone option is grayed out because the image must be a grayscale to create a duotone. However, the Paletted option is still available because there are other valid choices.

The selection of a format begins the conversion process. Remember that this process does not create a copy of the image being converted as it does in Corel PHOTO-PAINT 5. If you convert an image from 24-bit color to grayscale, the original will be converted. If you do not want to change the original, then use the Export command to change the format or use the Save As command in the File menu to save the file under a new name before you convert it.

TIP: *Use the Convert To command when experimenting with different file formats. When I was making the screenshots for this book, I frequently converted images to grayscale to see what they would look like when printed. You can use the Undo command to revert to the original and try another color combination.*

Understanding Color Reduction

Before discussing the Convert to Paletted (8-bit) dialog box, we must understand some more basics of color images. When we reduce a color image from a palette of 16.7 million colors (24-bit) to a palette of 256 possible colors, something has to give. It is much like putting 16.7 millions pounds of flour in a 256-pound sack. Conversion is accomplished by using a color table. All 256 Color graphic images contain information about how color is supposed to be mapped in a feature called a *color table*. This produces a 256-color image that is indexed to the color table. This type of file is also referred to as indexed color file.

In a Super VGA World, Why Convert Images to 256 colors?

The answer is the Internet. The explosive growth of online services demands 256 colors. If you don't do a good job converting your image from 24-bit to 256 color, it can look terrible. Believe it or not, you can use some of the 256 color images in color publications and have them look as good as (or at least very close to) 24-bit quality.

 TIP: *Don't be too quick to dismiss the 256-color option because of previous bad experiences with a 256-color palette. Corel uses a proprietary 256-color palette that produces color that can be very close to 24-bit color but without the system overhead. (Image files in 256-color mode are two-thirds smaller than 24-bit files).*

The Convert to Paletted (8-bit) Dialog Box

This dialog box, as shown in Figure 6-9, has changed dramatically in PHOTO-PAINT 8. One of the most important new features is the ability to preview the results of conversion. In previous releases you had to convert the file and then open it to see if the results were satisfactory. The Convert to Paletted (8-bit) dialog box is opened by the selection of Paletted (8-bit) in the Convert To section of the Image menu allowing you to control almost every aspect of the conversion process.

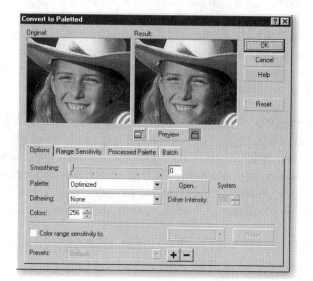

Convert To
Paletted
(8-bit)
Dialog Box

FIGURE 6-9

Dialog Box Options

The dialog box shown in Figure 6-9 is divided into 4 tabs. Options, Range Sensitivity, Processed Palette, and Batch. The selection that has the greatest influence on the output is the choice of the palette type that is used to convert the image. The options are Uniform, Standard VGA, Adaptive, Optimized, Black body, Grayscale, System, Microsoft Internet Explorer, Netscape Navigator and Custom.

UNIFORM PALETTE When we convert an image to a 256-color image using a Uniform palette with no dithering (we will discuss dithering in a moment), colors lose their smooth transitions between different colors, resulting in a posterized effect. Corel PHOTO-PAINT allows us to look at the palette that was created using the Color Table command in the image menu. The Uniform palette spreads out the colors across the entire spectrum, regardless of the color content of the image. With the Uniform Palette, there are usually colors in the palette that don't exist in the image. Because it includes the entire spectrum in the palette regardless of the image content, Uniform is rarely a good choice for palette selection.

STANDARD VGA   Based on the Standard VGA color table.

ADAPTIVE PALETTE   This palette is an improvement over the Uniform palette. It takes longer to process but the results are well worth the extra time. This method takes the overall range of hues (colors) and approximates the necessary palette to accommodate the greatest range of colors in the 256-color palette.

OPTIMIZED PALETTE   This is the best of all the palettes. It is a proprietary method that produces a palette that is as close to the original color as possible. It doesn't take much longer to process than does the Adaptive palette, but the results are noticeably superior on most images. There is still some image degradation, but it is very slight. There is a visual difference between the color palettes produced by the Adaptive and the Optimized, although the appearance of the palette is of little consequence.

BLACK BODY   Specialized palette for scientific work. In short, if you need this palette, you already know more about it than I do.

GRAYSCALE   Selecting this palette restricts the colors to the 256 shades available in the standard grayscale palette.

SYSTEM   Uses the current Windows system Palette.

NETSCAPE AND INTERNET EXPLORER   Selecting either of these palettes changes the palette to the respective palettes specified by Netscape or Microsoft (Explorer). Don't agonize over which one to pick. They are nearly identical palettes , just the order of the colors is different.

CUSTOM PALETTE   The Custom Palette allows you to pick all of the colors in the image. I cannot think of a single reason, other than for special effects, that you would ever want to use this option. The computer can do a far better job of creating a palette than any of us could ever hope to accomplish.

Dithering, or ... What Do You Do with the Leftover Colors?

When we convert an image that has many thousands of colors down to 256 colors, we are sometimes forced to practice a little visual sleight of hand to make the loss of color less apparent. We do it through dithering. *Dithering* is the placement of adjacent pixels in a bitmap image to create a value that the human eye sees as a color that does not really exist. Yes, it is eye trickery, plain and simple. If the color doesn't exist, then Paint creates a combination of adjacent colors to give an approximation of the missing color.

Three buttons determine the type of dithering performed when the image is converted. The choices are None, Ordered, and Error Diffusion.

None

The default is that no dithering is performed. This is the best choice if the image looks good without it. The colors in the image are limited to the 256 colors in the palette.

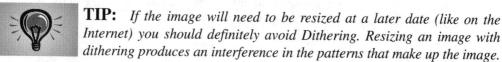 **TIP:** *If the image will need to be resized at a later date (like on the Internet) you should definitely avoid Dithering. Resizing an image with dithering produces an interference in the patterns that make up the image. This patterning is called Moiré patterns.*

Ordered

Ordered dithering is performed at a faster rate, but the result is less attractive. It is also known as *pattern* dithering. Each pixel that is not in the available 256-color spectrum is evaluated and two palette colors are applied to the two adjacent pixels to give the appearance of the missing color. For example, if the missing color is green, one pixel would be made yellow and the other blue. Together in close proximity, they would appear to be green. Of the two dithering options, this is the least desirable. The Ordered option is only available for Uniform palette.

Error Diffusion

This provides the best results, but is slower to process. It is the best of the two types of dithering. Error diffusion changes a color pixel whose value falls outside of the 256-color palette into an adjacent pixel's color. That pixel in turn replaces another pixel's color and this continues until the last pixel is determined to be close enough to one of the colors in the palette. This type of dithering produces the softest transitions between the areas of color that would normally have harsh lines of color separation.

Using Convert to Paletted (8-bit)

As complicated as the dialog box looks, it is quite simple to use. The most common way is to select a palette and dithering and see if the results in the preview window look acceptable. Regardless of the palette you choose the computer is going to decide which color (or range of colors) that PHOTO-PAINT will use to create the palette unless you select the Color range sensitivity checkbox. When this is enabled, you can either select the color from the image by clicking on and using the eyedropper tool (which is what you will do 99% of the time you decide to select this method) or select the color by clicking on the color swatch. Once the color is selected you can go the to Range Sensitivity tab and adjust the sliders to control how much or how little of the selected color you want in the palette. Regardless of the method you choose, the resulting palette is displayed by clicking on the Processed Palette tab.

We have covered a lot on information in this chapter and it is now time to move on to the next chapter and begin to learn about masks.

PART

III

Exploring PHOTO-PAINT Tools

7

The School of Masks

Now that we have covered some of the basics of applying enhancements to the entire image, we need to understand how *masks* operate. I call this chapter the School of Masks because it is in this chapter that we will learn many of the fundamentals and techniques necessary to create and control masks. It is the creation, manipulation, and transformation of masks and objects that form the foundation of any advanced work done in Corel PHOTO-PAINT. With that said, let us begin this chapter by introducing masks.

What Is a Mask?

One definition of a mask is "a defined area that covers part of an image or the entire image." Another way to say the same thing is that by using a mask, we can control exactly where on the image an effect will be applied. For example, in Figure 7-1 I have a photograph of London. To change the background but leave rest of the image

Original
photograph

FIGURE 7-1

unaffected, I need to make a mask that protects it from changes. With the help of a mask, we are able to change London, which is not known for it mountains, into a charming little town in a canyon, as shown in Figure 7-2.

Here's an analogy. If you have ever painted a room in a house, you know that one of the most tedious jobs is painting around the window sills and baseboards. The objective is to get the paint on the wall but not on the surrounding area, so either you paint very carefully (and slowly) or you get a roll of masking tape and put tape over the area where you don't want the paint to go. In using the tape, you have created a mask.

Another example of a mask is a stencil. When a stencil is placed over an object and then painted, only the portion of the stencil that is cut out allows paint to be applied to the surface. Both stencils and masking tape are examples of masks.

Corel PHOTO-PAINT masks are much more versatile than a stencil or masking tape (and not as difficult to remove when you are done). The masks used in Corel PHOTO-PAINT enable you to control both where and (in later chapters we will learn) how much of an effect is applied to a portion of an image.

 NOTE: *For Photoshop users. So you won't be confused, what is called a mask in PHOTO-PAINT is called Selection in Photoshop.*

7

With the help of a mask, we have mountains

FIGURE 7-2

How Masks Are Created

Corel PHOTO-PAINT provides a variety of mask-creation and selection tools. Figure 7-3 shows some of the mask-creation and mask-manipulation tools. The newest addition to the family is the Property Bar (not shown), which combines elements of all of the other toolbars. These tools, used in combination with their related commands, provide the Corel PHOTO-PAINT user with an almost limitless selection of masks.

Don't be concerned about the names of tools for the moment. We will be examining each one of these so that you can understand their functions and the best times to use them.

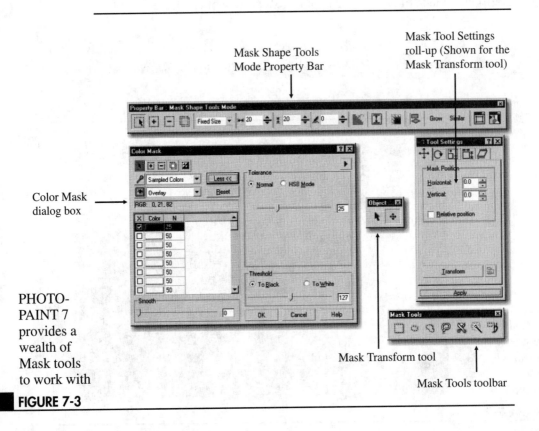

Mask Shape Tools
Mode Property Bar

Mask Tool Settings
roll-up (Shown for the
Mask Transform tool)

Color Mask
dialog box

Object...

Mask Transform tool

Mask Tools toolbar

PHOTO-
PAINT 7
provides a
wealth of
Mask tools
to work with

FIGURE 7-3

Two Groups of Masks

The mask tools shown in Figure 7-4 appear in PHOTO-PAINT 8 either as a flyout on the Toolbox or can be opened as a separate toolbar. The masks that can be created with these tools can be divided into two basic groups: *regular* Mask tools and *color-sensitive* Mask tools. Regular masks are created by the user, who defines their size and location within the image by using the mouse or other pointing device. The regular Mask tools are the Rectangle, Circle, and Freehand Mask tools. Unlike the regular mask, the boundaries of the color-sensitive masks are created by Corel PHOTO-PAINT based on information entered by the user in conjunction with the color values of the image. Color-sensitive Mask tools are the Lasso, Scissors Mask, and Magic Wand. The remaining button on the Mask Tools flyout are the Mask Brush tool and the Mask Transform tool, which are used to modify both the regular and color-sensitive masks.

Fundamentals of a Mask (Hands-on)

If you are unfamiliar with using masks, this hands-on exercise will lead you through the basic steps of creating and manipulating a mask. It will also introduce you to some of the properties of a regular mask.

1. Create a new file by clicking the New File button in the toolbar, selecting New... from the File menu or using the keyboard combination (CTRL-N).

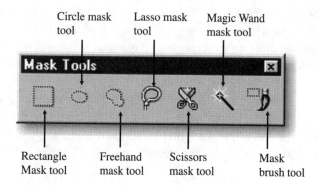

A reference to the Mask Tools buttons

Circle mask tool   Lasso mask tool   Magic Wand mask tool

Mask Tools

Rectangle Mask tool   Freehand mask tool   Scissors mask tool   Mask brush tool

FIGURE 7-4

This action opens the Create a New Image dialog box. Change the settings in your dialog box so that they match those shown in the image below and click the OK button. This produces a blank image window.

2. Select the Rectangle Mask tool, shown on the left, from the Toolbox. Place the cursor in the upper-left region of the image. Click and drag the mouse, creating a rectangle as the mouse is moved, then release the mouse button. You have created a regular mask. The size of the rectangle is not critical, but don't try to encompass the entire image. The boundary of the mask is indicated by a black-and-white marquee, which is always described as "marching ants" because of the motion. If a marquee is not visible, check the Mask menu and see if Marquee Visible has a checkmark beside it. If it doesn't, click on it or use Ctrl-H to toggle it on and off.

3. Select the Image Sprayer tool, shown on the left, from the Paint tool's flyout at the bottom of the Toolbox. The Image Sprayer allows you to load one or more images and then spray them across your image. The default image is the butterfly, but any image will work. Place the cursor on the image area, click the button, and drag it all over the image. Your result will look something like the image shown below.

4. Next, invert the mask, either by clicking the Invert Mask button in the Standard toolbar, shown on the left, using the keyboard combination (CTRL-I), or selecting Invert in the Mask menu. This action makes everything that was protected by the mask unprotected and the area outside of the mask is now protected. The marquee indicates the invert action.

5. We will demonstrate the effect of inverting the mask using the Fill command. Select Fill... from the Edit menu. When the Edit Fill & Transparency dialog box opens (Figure 7-5), click the Texture Fill button (indicated by the white arrow) and click the OK button. The image floods the image area outside of the original mask with the currently selected

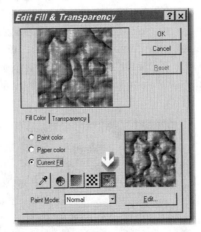

The Edit
Fill &
Transparency
dialog box

FIGURE 7-5

texture as shown in the illustration below. If you have a different texture
selected than the one shown, it will not affect the tutorial.

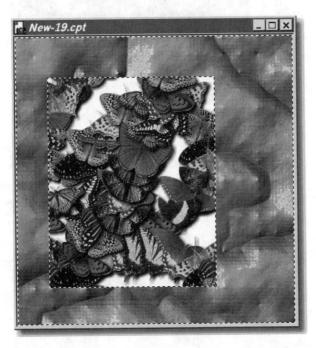

6. Close the file by choosing Close in the File menu. You do not need to
save the file as we will not be using it later in the book.

The Properties of Masks

From the previous tutorial, we learned a few things about masks. A mask restricts the application of effects to areas inside of the mask. For example, when we attempted to paint butterflies outside of the mask, nothing happened. The area outside of the mask, as indicated by the marquee, is protected. The area inside of the mask has no protection. Here is a summary of some basic mask properties:

- A mask "sits on top" or floats on top of the original image.

- A mask can be loaded as an image.

- Since a mask is an image, masks can be saved separately from the image and loaded later as masks.

- An image can have only one mask.

- A mask can be retained when the image is saved as a Corel PHOTO-PAINT (CPT) image.

- Several other graphic formats in addition to the CPT format support masks in the form of alpha channels.

If all we can do with masks is make rectangles, they would be pretty useless. As we move on through this chapter, we will learn more about mask properties as we explore the tools that create the masks and how the masks make tasks in PHOTO-PAINT easier.

The Basic Mask-Creation Tools

We will start our exploration with the Mask tools used to create regular masks. Unlike the color-sensitive Mask tools, these tools allow us to define where the boundaries of the mask will be. All of the following Mask tools are available either from the Mask flyout in the Toolbox or from the Mask Tools toolbar.

The Rectangle Mask Tool

This is the tool we already used in the previous tutorial. You will probably use this Mask tool more than any other in the toolbox. In case the name of the tool didn't give it away, it is used for making square and rectangular masks. A mask is made by clicking and holding down the left mouse button and dragging until the desired shape is achieved. Here is the part you didn't know. Holding down the SHIFT key produces a mask that increases or decreases proportionally from the center. If you hold down the CTRL key after clicking the mouse button, it constrains the shape of the mask to a square.

The Circle Mask Tool

The Circle Mask tool, shown on the left, enables you to define oval or circular masks. This mask works just like the Rectangle Mask tool except holding down the CTRL key after the mouse button is clicked constrains the mask to a circle.

The Mask Transform Tool

If you have used any of the previous releases of PHOTO-PAINT, your first question may be "Where is the Mask Transform tool?" The Mask Transform tool, shown on the left, has moved and shares a cozy little flyout with the Object Picker tool. The Mask Transform tool is not actually a Mask tool but a mask modifier. All of the masks that can be created with the Mask tools can be moved, scaled, rotated, skewed, have perspective applied— in other words, you can do just about anything you want to a mask with this tool.

When the Mask Transform tool is selected, eight handles appear on the mask. Clicking inside of the mask changes the shape of the handles, indicating a different transform mode. Figure 7-6 shows the control handles associated with the different modes and functions. There are many ways to manipulate a mask using this tool, but you will find its most commonly used function is to move a mask on an image or to change the size (scale) of a mask. The other transform functions are mostly used when working with objects, which is explored in more detail in chapter 13.

NOTE: *For more information on mask transformations: In PHOTO-PAINT 8, depress the F1 function key and select the Index tab. Type in **Mask Transformations** and click the Display button. For individual descriptions of the transform modes, click the How To button when the mask transformation description appears.*

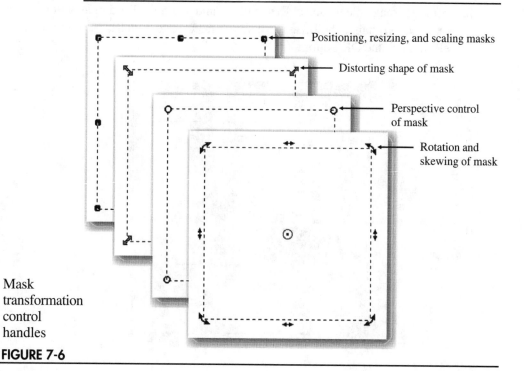

Positioning, resizing, and scaling masks

Distorting shape of mask

Perspective control of mask

Rotation and skewing of mask

Mask
transformation
control
handles

FIGURE 7-6

Circle Masks, Mask Transforms, and Selections (Hands-on)

The following hands-on exercise uses the Circle Mask tool and the Mask Transform tool, and introduces another aspect of working with masks—the *selection*. In this exercise, we are going to use several of the Mask tools to create and move the contents of a masked area from one part of an image to another.

1. Open the image EXERCISE\PHOTOS\554026.WI located on the Corel CD. After this image has finally opened (it takes a few moments for it to decompress), you will discover it is HUGE! We will change that in step 2.

2. From the Image menu, select Resample... and when the Resample dialog box appears, change the Image size Width from 16 to 5 inches as shown below. Click the OK button.

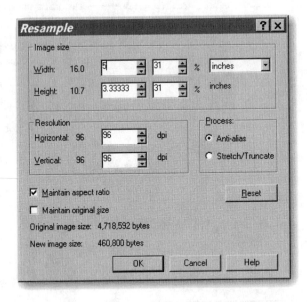

3. Select the Circle Mask tool from the Toolbox. Placing the cursor near the point shown by the arrow in Figure 7-7, hold down the CTRL key and drag a circle mask over the eye in the wall. It doesn't need to exactly fit. To try again, just click on the same spot. Each time you create a mask, it replaces the existing mask.

4. Select Checkpoint from the Undo Special category in the Edit menu. If at any point in this tutorial you take an action that cannot be corrected with the Undo command, select Restore to Checkpoint from the Undo Special category in the Edit menu.

5. With the Circle Mask tool still selected, place the cursor inside of the mask you just created. The cursor changes from the tool shape to an arrow. Now click inside of the mask and drag the entire mask up and a little to the right as

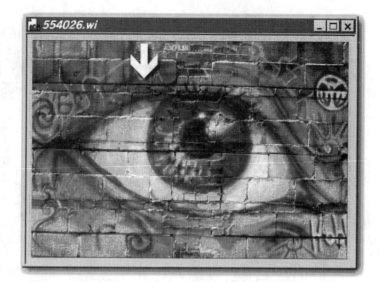

Arrow
indicates
starting
point for
Circle Mask
tool

FIGURE 7-7

shown in Figure 7-8. The contents of the mask moved with the mask and is now floating above the image. You have created a selection.

Selections

The bitmap image contained by the mask marquee it is called a *selection,* and it is said to be *floating*. While it may appear that the mask removed the image, leaving the original color, actually the area occupied by the mask been replaced with the current Paper color. This action is like the Cut command of the Clipboard. Dragging an existing mask with any of the Mask tools, except the Mask Brush tool and the Mask Transform tool, create floating selections. The selections remain floating until you click the Mask tool anywhere outside of the mask, select the Mask Transform tool, or choose Defloat from the Mask menu.

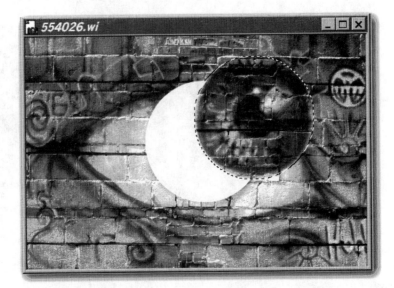

The contents of the mask has become a selection

FIGURE 7-8

6. Click inside of the mask (selection) with the Circle Mask tool again and drag it around the image. The contents of the selection (defined by the mask marquee) move with it; even if you move part of the selection off of the image, it may disappear but it remains unchanged. Any portion of the mask that is outside of the image will be cropped once the mask is defloated.

7. Now take the cursor and click it anywhere outside of the mask boundary and the contents of the selection are merged into the image. Before you take any other actions select Undo (CTRL-Z) and the selection is restored.

8. From the Object Picker's flyout in the Toolbox, select the Mask Transform tool. This action will display a message, shown below, that warns you that the contents of the selection will be merged into the image. Click the Yes button. The mask remains, but the contents of the selection are not part of the image.

9. Resize the mask by grabbing one of the handles and dragging it in or out. Click inside of the mask and move it anywhere within the image edge. Now drag it so part of the mask is beyond the edge of the image and bring it back again. The portion of the mask that went beyond the edge was removed and the shape of the mask permanently changed. In step 6, the mask did not change when we did this because it was a selection.

10. Select Restore to Checkpoint from Undo Special category in the Edit menu. Select the Circle Mask tool.

11. Hold down the ALT key and drag the mask down and to the left as shown below. This action creates a selection, but doesn't replace the original masked area with Paper color. Instead, a copy of the mask's contents is placed in the selection. This action cannot be done with the Mask Brush or Mask Transform tools.

12. Continue to hold down the ALT key and drag several more copies of the selection. Figure 7-9 shows the result of placing multiple copies throughout the image. It appears the "eyes" have it.

13. Now drag the selection off of the image on to the PHOTO-PAINT main screen. Figure 7-10 shows the selection is removed from the image, and it becomes a new image. The selection that was removed can restored by

The ALT key helps make many copies of our eye

FIGURE 7-9

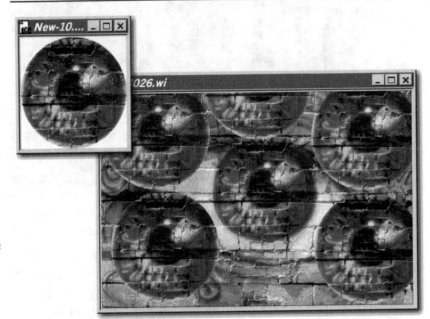

We can easily make the selection into an image

FIGURE 7-10

ensuring the original image is active (look at the title bar) and using Undo (CTRL-Z).

14. Close the both of the images and don't save the changes when asked.

Properties of Mask and Selection

Let's review some of the properties we observed when using the Mask tool in the previous tutorial. First, if you move an existing mask with a Mask tool (except the Mask Brush or Mask Transform tool), it becomes a selection. If the ALT key is held down when the selection is created, the original image in the masked area remains; if not, it is replaced with the current Paper color. A selection can be moved around an image, even beyond the edge of the image borders, and it will still maintain both its shape and contents. If a selection is dragged completely off of the image, it becomes a new image.

The Freehand Mask Tool

This Mask tool has changed considerably since Corel PHOTO-PAINT 5. For those of you familiar with Corel PHOTO-PAINT 5, the Freehand Mask tool is now a combination of the Polygon Mask and the Freehand Mask tools. Traditionally, a freehand-type tool is difficult to use with a mouse. By combining the two Mask tools, it becomes possible to use a mouse to mask irregularly shaped objects with some degree of accuracy. The concept behind the operation of this tool is as follows: As long as the left mouse button is clicked and held down, it acts as a traditional freehand tool. Wherever the cursor is moved, the mask is applied. What makes this Mask tool so good is that when the mouse button is released, the mask does not immediately join its end points. Instead, the mask can be continued until all of the subject is masked. Then, only by double-clicking the left mouse does the mask becomes complete. Here is a little exercise to familiarize you with the Freehand Mask tool, shown on the left.

Emphasizing a Subject with the Freehand Mask Tool (Hands-on)

Many times in photo-editing, we need to emphasize a subject. One way to do that is by masking the background and slightly blurring it. This produces a false depth-of-field effect. In other words, the object that is not blurred appears closer to the viewer than the blurred portion. It is one of the many techniques we use to fool the eye of the viewer. In this exercise, we will take a photograph of some native structures, produce a mask with the Freehand Mask tool, and blur the background.

1. Open the file EXERCISE\PHOTOS\ARCHITCT\539000.WI on the Corel CD. Again, this image is way too big, so we need to resample it. From the Image menu select Resample... and when the Resample dialog box appears, change the Image size Width from 15 to 6 inches. Click the OK button.

2. Select the Freehand Mask tool from either the Mask tool flyout or the Mask Tools toolbar, if it is visible.

3. Because we will be using the Freehand Mask tool on the very edge of the photograph, I recommend that you make the image area larger than the photograph. Place the cursor on one of the four corners of the image window. The cursor will change to a two-headed arrow. Click and drag the corner to enlarge it. Enlarging the window will prevent the Mask tool from interacting with the image windows border.

4. Let's mask. At the upper-left corner of the image, click the left mouse button on the arrow labeled A and release it. Now, move the mouse down to the point shown by the arrow labeled B in Figure 7-11 and you will notice that a line is attached to the cursor. Next, continue in a counterclockwise direction, clicking at the arrows shown in the figure. As with so many things, the selection of points to place the mask involves personal taste and technique. I choose to do the larger jumps between the points so the blurring will not require the mask to closely follow the edge of the buildings. Continue to do this until you reach the upper-right corner. If you place a point in the wrong place, clicking the DEL key removes the point. Continuing to click the DEL key removes each successive point in the mask.

5. Double-click the mouse and PHOTO-PAINT creates a straight line to the starting point to complete the mask. You have just completed a Freehand mask. Your mask should look like Figure 7-11. I have highlighted the mask in the figure with white paint to make it stand out more in the book. Don't worry if your mask is a little inside or outside of the building. It isn't critical in this exercise.

6. Now that we have the background and some of the buildings masked, select Blur in the Effects menu. From the drop-down list that appears, choose Gaussian Blur.... When the Gaussian Blur dialog box opens, set the Radius to 2 and click the OK button. The Blur filters and their use are

The points
on the path
for creating
a Freehand
mask

FIGURE 7-11

explained in Chapter 15 of the book. The Gaussian Blur makes the
background appear slightly out of focus. The results are shown in Figure
7-12.

7. Close the file and do not save any changes.

> **TIP:** *Consider using the Freehand Mask tool when creating a large and complicated mask, even if it doesn't have a single straight line in it.*

The Importance of Looking for the Mask Icon

Before we begin to explore mask modes, I want to impress something on you that
will save you frustration later on. Whenever a mask is created, one of four tiny icons
appear in the lower-right corner of the Status bar. These icons tell the user there is
a mask present on the image and what mode it is in. These tiny icons will save you
a great deal of frustration once you train yourself to look for them. *Make it a habit
to look for the icon.*

The
Freehand
Mask tool
allows
selective
application
of the
Gaussian
Blur filter

FIGURE 7-12

If you have created a small mask or have zoomed in on a corner of the image and can't see the masked area, Corel PHOTO-PAINT will not allow any effect to be applied to the image (other than in the masked area). Here's the best part: when you attempt to apply an effect, PHOTO-PAINT will tell you that it completed the action, yet nothing will have been done. Talk about frustration!

TIP: *If you are unable to apply an effect to an image, check first to see if the Mask icon is present. We will talk about the different mask modes later in the chapter. Even if you can't see the mask, the computer thinks the mask is there and will prevent you from applying any effect. Knowing this will save you time and money (for the cost of aspirin and tech-support calls).*

Mask Modes

In the previous tutorials, the creation of a mask caused any existing masks to be deleted. As we begin to work with more complex masks, this mode of operation (called Normal), prevents any modification of masks. As you may have guessed there are other mask modes available in PHOTO-PAINT 8 that allow us to add to, subtract from, and otherwise modify to our heart's content any existing mask. The four mask modes are pretty much self-explanatory. They are: Normal, Additive, Subtractive, and Exclusive OR (XOR). OK, so maybe only three of the four modes are self-explanatory. Mask modes can be selected either from the Mode setting in the Mask menu, through keyboard combination (real tricky keyboard combinations, that is), or through toolbar buttons. The mode of the currently selected Mask tool is indicated by an icon displayed in the Status bar and by the shape of the cursor. Figure 7-13 shows the Mask Mode buttons, their keyboard combinations, and the respective icon that appears in the Status Bar when the mode is active. We will be using these modes frequently throughout the book.

TIP: *Is something not working as you expect? Check the mask mode first.*

New Mask Mode Controls in PHOTO-PAINT 8

In order to make the selection of mask modes even easier, Corel has added some new keyboard mode selection keys. Holding the SHIFT key makes the mask mode Subtractive; holding the CTRL key makes it Additive. In previous releases, the CTRL

7

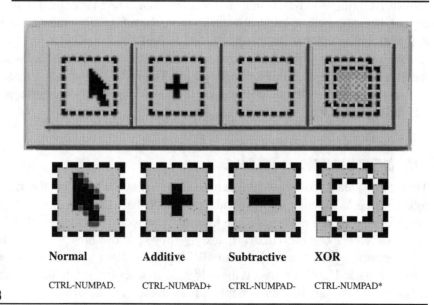

The Mask Mode buttons and their icons

Normal	Additive	Subtractive	XOR
CTRL-NUMPAD.	CTRL-NUMPAD+	CTRL-NUMPAD-	CTRL-NUMPAD*

FIGURE 7-13

key has been the constrain key for the Mask tools and the SHIFT key made changes from the center of the mask—and they still do. The difference is now they have become dual-purpose keys. Here are the simple rules for using them to create masks:

- Holding down the SHIFT key before clicking the mouse changes the mask to Subtractive mode while it is held down.

- Clicking the mouse key before holding down the SHIFT key creates a new mask that expands or contracts (depending on the direction you are dragging the mouse) from the center.

- Holding down the CTRL key before clicking the mouse changes the mask to Additive mode while it is held down.

Clicking the mouse key before holding down the CTRL key creates a new mask that is constrained to a square (Rectangle Mask tool) or a circle (Circle Mask tool).

 NOTE: *The above rules apply only to mask creation.*

The Mask Brush Tool

 This is the ultimate mask cleanup and touchup tool. The Mask Brush tool, shown on the left, enables you to brush or paint an area to be masked. Unlike a regular brush tool that applies color to an image, the Mask Brush tool can be used to apply or remove a portion of a mask. The size and shape of the Mask Brush tool is set from the Property Bar or the Tool Settings roll-up. The roll-up is accessed through the Roll-ups in the View menu or using CTRL-F8, which reflects the settings of the currently selected tool.

Color-Sensitive Masks

The previous Mask tools would create masks wherever we would drag the mouse. The following masks are color sensitive and create masks based on the color content of the image and the tolerance settings of the selected Mask tool. This category allows you to create incredibly complex masks quickly— if you know how to use them. The color-sensitive masks are: the Lasso mask, Magic Wand, the Scissors Mask tool, and the Color mask. The Color mask is the only mask tool not located on the mask flyout. It is accessed through the Mask menu. It is explored in Chapter 8.

The Lasso Mask Tool

If you are an experienced PhotoShop or PhotoStyler user, you might think you know what this tool does, but you'd be in for a surprise. The Lasso Mask tool, shown on the left, is a very handy tool that unfortunately bears the same name as a different tool in both of the aforementioned programs.

The lasso metaphor is perfect for this tool. On a ranch, a lasso surrounds an object, and when you pull on the rope, the lasso closes until it fits tightly around the object. The Lasso tool works very much in the same way, but without the rope.

How the Lasso Mask Tool Works

The Lasso Mask tool enables you to define a mask that is irregular in shape in much the same way as the Freehand tool. When the mouse button is released, the mask shrinks until it surrounds an area of colors that fall within the limits set by the Tolerance slider in the Tool Settings roll-up. The mask will contain the area surrounded by the Lasso Mask tool. It is used when it is necessary to restrict the region where the mask is to be placed.

Whereas the Magic Wand mask begins at the pixel starting point and *expands* until it reaches its limits, the Lasso mask *shrinks* until it reaches its limits.

How to Use the Lasso Mask Tool

The Lasso Mask tool operates much like the Freehand Mask tool.

- Click and hold either mouse button to anchor the starting point for the mask.

- Still holding the mouse button, drag the cursor around the area to be masked. This causes a line to be drawn around the object. The pixel underneath the cursor when the line is started determines the starting color value. You can also click and release the mouse button to create straight lines, just like the Freehand mask tool.

- Continue to drag the cursor around the area until you are near the starting point.

- When the button is double-clicked, the computer will complete the line and compute the masked area.

Replacing a Background Using the Lasso Mask Tool (Project)

Here is a common application. The client wants to use a specific type of picture to use in a brochure. Unfortunately, the photograph you have been given has several problems. The plane is too small (relative to the size of the entire image) and the sky is a dull blue. Your solution? You could hire a photographer (big bucks) or enhance the photograph yourself. Guess which one we are going to do in this exercise? You're right if you said "enhance the photograph." We'll be using the Lasso Mask tool and a few other commands to mask the subject of the photograph and replace the background.

1. In the Open an Image dialog box, select the Crop command (located to the left of the Options button) to open the file EXERCISE\PHOTOS\601039.WI located on the Corel CD-ROM. If we resample this large photograph, the plane remains small, so we are instead cropping the plane during loading of the file, as shown here.

2. When the Crop Image dialog box opens, enter in the settings shown in Figure 7-14 and click the OK button.

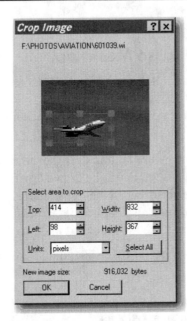

Cropping
the plane
instead of
resampling

FIGURE 7-14

3. Select the Lasso Mask tool from the Mask flyout or the Mask Tools toolbar, if it is open. Double-click the Lasso Mask Tool button. This action opens the Tool Settings roll-up , shown below, that is common for the color-sensitive masks (except for the color mask). The default value for this setting is 10 - change it to 12. The setting of 12 tells Corel PHOTO-PAINT to compare pixels as the mask is shrinking and to keep going until it reaches a pixel that is greater or less than 12 shades of the starting pixel value. It does this with all of the pixels in the enclosed area until it is finished. Anti-aliasing tells it to make the resulting mask smooth.

NOTE: *For more information about tolerance and how it works: In PHOTO-PAINT, depress the F1 function key and select the Index tab. Type in* **Tolerance** *and click the Display button. There is an excellent and detailed explanation of how tolerance settings work.*

4. Since we want to mask the background (and not the jet), select the Subtractive mask mode. This means the final mask will be inverted.

5. Click the cursor at the arrowhead tip in the upper-left corner indicated by the arrow in Figure 7-15 to establish the starting (anchor) point. Now click around the jet at the points indicated by the arrows until you have surrounded it completely with a rectangle. Double-click the last point and the mask is created. Switch the mode back to Normal when the mask is completed.

6. To replace the background with something more dynamic, we will use the Fill… command located in the Edit menu. Selecting it opens the Edit Fill

Setting Color Tolerance

Setting of the color tolerance correctly determines how accurately the color-sensitive Mask tools perform their job. The tolerance setting determines the range of effect for color-sensitive tools (and also fills). The higher the value, the more colors will be included in the operation. There are two methods of setting tolerance: Normal and HSB. The *Normal* method makes its selection based on the color similarity of *adjacent pixels* in the color mode of the current image. The tolerance value you choose controls how discriminating the color selection will be. The *HSB* method creates it selection based on the similarity of hue, saturation, and brightness levels between adjacent pixels.

The key to finding the optimum tolerance method and setting is experimentation. You should begin by using the default setting (10) in Normal mode. If that setting doesn't include enough of the colors (shades if working with grayscale), increase the setting to include more. If the mask or fill that was produced took in too many colors from the image, decrease the setting. You will get better results if you make several small changes rather than large ones.

As you approach a setting that seems to work, keep a few points in mind. Zoom in and look carefully at the where the boundary is being created. If the tolerance setting is too low, a portion of the background will remain in the form of a halo or edge glow. If it is set too high, the mask will actually go inside of the subject area, causing a portion of the area you are attempting to mask to be lost. There will be times when the best setting will cause the inclusion of similar edge colors in isolated areas. If this happens, use the Mask Brush tool to remove them. It is easier than taking a lower tolerance and adjusting the entire mask.

HSB mode should be used when the color values in the area you are attempting to mask are too similar to the background. By using the HSB mode, you may be able to differentiate between areas that seem impossible in Normal mode. I recommend starting with different Saturation or Hue settings first, since the Normal mode uses values very similar to the Brightness setting. In Chapter 8, we will explore how to use channels to increase the capability of color-sensitive Mask tools.

Arrows
display
points to
click mask
tool

FIGURE 7-15

7

& Transparency dialog box. Select the Fountain fill (third button) in the lower portion of the Fill Color tab and click the Edit button in the lower-right corner.

When the Fountain Fill dialog box opens, click on the down-pointing arrow in Presets: in the lower-left corner and select Circular - Blue 01. After selecting the preset, change the other values in the top portion of the dialog box to match those shown in Figure 7-16. Click the OK button and also click the OK button in the Edit Fill & Transparency dialog box. The result is shown in Figure 7-17.

7. Close the file and don't save the changes.

The Scissors Mask Tool

The Mask Scissors tool, shown on the left, was introduced with the release of PHOTO-PAINT 7. If you tried to use it in that release, you should try it again in PHOTO-PAINT 8. The performance of the tool has been drastically improved. Like a Lasso mask, it contracts around an image. Unlike the Lasso mask, it detects edges in your image, i.e., the outline of the areas that are in contrasting color to their surroundings, and places the mask marquee along that edge as you are outlining the mask. The key to the operation of this mask is the bounding box. When you select this Mask tool, a bounding box surrounds the Mask tool cursor. The bounding box

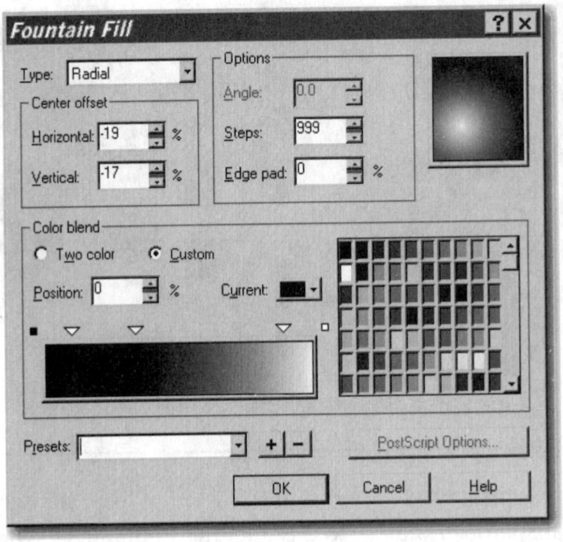

The
Fountain
Fill dialog
box

FIGURE 7-16

The
finished
photograph
is a
composite
of a
cropped
original and
a fountain
fill

FIGURE 7-17

defines the limit of the color tolerance for the tool. The Tolerance settings, which are set in the Tool Settings roll-up or the Property Bar, controls the sensitivity of the edge detection. A low Tolerance setting means that edges do not need as much contrast to be detected as they do with a high tolerance.

The Radius, which is also set in the Tool Settings roll-up or Property Bar, defines the perimeter of the bounding box (ranging from 10 to 999 pixels), which has dimensions equal to the value you type. This bounding box determines the area in which the automatic edge detection will work. When you move the cursor beyond the Radius you have defined, the Mask Scissors tool can no longer detect edges accurately.

The operation of the Scissors Mask tool is simple. Just click at a point on the edge of the selection. Click another point of the mask along the edge but within the bounding box. The only problem you may experience is when the color/shades that define the edge are too close. When this happens, either click many points close together or click and drag the mouse like a Freehand Mask tool.

The Magic Wand Mask Tool

The Magic Wand Mask tool, shown on the left, is used to create masks both quickly and automatically. Like the other color-sensitive Mask tools, the ability of the Magic Wand to make an accurate mask is dependent upon the Tolerance settings in the Tool Settings roll-up and the actual color-value composition of the image. In other words, it takes a little time to get the hang of using this tool correctly. However, once you do, it is a very handy tool to have. The Magic Wand Mask tool differs from the Lasso mask in that the Magic Wand mask expands from a starting point until all of the adjacent colors that meet the selection criteria are included where in the Lasso contracts inward until all of the pixels that meet the criteria are included.

How the Magic Wand Mask Tool Performs its Magic

Two simple facts about the Magic Wand tool are (1) there is nothing magic about it and (2,) it is very simple to use once you understand the concept behind its operation. In theory, you simply click on the area that needs to be masked or the area that surrounds the area to be masked and Corel PHOTO-PAINT does the rest. There are actually times when this will work as intended.

As with the Lasso Mask tool, Corel PHOTO-PAINT treats the pixel under the cursor when it is clicked as the starting point. The program reads the color value of the pixel, then, using the limits entered in the Tolerance setting of the Tool Settings roll-up, *expands* the mask pixel by pixel until it can no longer find pixels that are within the limits. For example, if the starting pixel has a hue value of 60 and the Tolerance value has been set to 50, the mask will continue to expand from its starting point until every adjacent pixel with a value between 10 (60 minus 50) and 110 (60 plus 50) has been included in the mask.

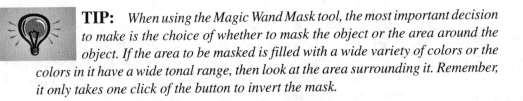 **TIP:** *When using the Magic Wand Mask tool, the most important decision to make is the choice of whether to mask the object or the area around the object. If the area to be masked is filled with a wide variety of colors or the colors in it have a wide tonal range, then look at the area surrounding it. Remember, it only takes one click of the button to invert the mask.*

Taking the Magic Wand Mask Tool for a Test Drive

Remember the photograph of London at the beginning of the chapter? In this hands-on exercise, we will use the Magic Wand tool to do a simple background replacement like we did with the Lasso Mask tool and the background.

1. Open the file EXERCISE\PHOTOS\509075.WI on the Corel CD. Make sure the Open an Image dialog box is changed back from Crop to Full Image.

2. Again, this image is way too big, so we need to resample it. From the Image menu, select Resample... and when the Resample dialog box appears, change the Image size Width from about 15 to 6 inches. Click the OK button and the photograph of London appears as shown in Figure 7-1.

3. Select the Magic Wand tool from the Mask flyout in the Toolbox. Set the mask mode to Additive. Double-click the Magic Wand button. When the Tool Settings roll-up appears, ensure the Tolerance value is set to 10 and

turn off Anti-aliasing to allow the mask to accurately follow the complex edges of the Parliament buildings.

4. Click anywhere on the sky in the upper part of the image and a partial mask appears to cover part of the sky. Now, at this point we could click the parts of the sky that were previously out of range for the Tolerance setting; but we have another mask command we can use. In the Mask menu or on the Property Bar, select Grow and the mask completes the action and fills the entire background.

5. To place another photograph in the background, select Paste from File in the Edit menu. This action opens the Paste an Image from Disk dialog box, which, except for the title, is identical to the dialog box for opening an image. Change the method for opening the file from Full Image to Resample. Click the Open button. From the Corel CD-ROM, select EXERCISE\PHOTOS\\392046.WI.

6. When the Resample dialog box opens, set Units to inches and change the Width value to 6 inches. Click the OK button. The resampling will take a little while. The mountain photograph is now floating (as an object) on top of the photograph of London and only the mask from the original photograph can still be seen, as shown next. Open the Align command (CTRL-A) and select Vertically Top, Horizontally Center. Click OK. Part of the object doesn't cover the bottom completely, but that won't make any difference.

7

The Grow Command

The Grow command found in the Mask menu and on the Property Bar uses the current color tolerance to expand the mask. The mask expands until it reaches pixels that are dissimilar in color (by a value greater than the Tolerance setting) to those located along the original mask marquee.

7. Our next step is to clip the object using the mask. From the Object menu, select Add Clip Mask and then From Mask. The portion of the object that was outside of the mask is removed, resulting in the image shown below. To see the image without the mask marquee, either turn off the marquee or click the Full Screen Preview (F9) key.

Well, we have covered a lot of material. If you have gone through each of the exercises, you have learned a lot about masks and how they work. In the next chapter, we will continue to learn more about these powerful tools.

Advanced Masks

T his chapter begins with the all important topic of mask management. We will then learn about using photographs as masks, the Color Mask and several PHOTO-PAINT mask commands buried in the Mask menu that are real gems. We will also take a brief look at the Path Node edit tool.

Mask Management

All masks created in Corel PHOTO-PAINT can be saved and reloaded. This ability to save masks is essential because:

- Only one regular mask can be on an image at a time.

- Masks are valuable. If you spent several hours creating a mask, it is essential to have a copy.

- It is a great way to copy the same size image area out of several different images.

How Masks Are Saved with Images

There are two ways that masks can be saved, either with the image or the mask can be saved as an image. An image containing a regular mask that is saved in Corel PHOTO-PAINT format (.CPT) will have its mask saved with the image automatically. In addition to Corel PHOTO-PAINT format, masks can be saved in Targa (.TGA) and TIFF (.TIF) formats. They are also saved as Alpha channel information when an image is saved as a Photoshop (.PSD) image.

The ability to save a mask apart from the image allows a mask created in one image to be loaded and applied to other images for special effects or accurate placement of objects. How another application uses the saved mask information depends on the application. For example, the mask information in a .TIF or .TGA file is interpreted by Photoshop as an alpha channel.

Saving a Mask

Saving a mask is just like saving an image file. The mask does not have a unique file extension. In fact you can save a mask in almost any graphics format you desire. After a mask has been created, it can be saved two ways. It can be saved to disk or saved in temporary storage in a channel. Use of the Mask channel is explained later in this chapter. The following procedure is for saving a mask to disk:

1. Choose Save from the Mask menu. At this point you have two choices: Save to Disk and Save As Channel. Select Save to Disk and the Save a Mask to Disk dialog box opens.

2. Choose from the Save as Type list, name the mask, and click the Save button. The mask has been saved and can be recalled at a later time.

When naming masks, try to include the fact that the file is a mask as part of the name (e.g., Mask for Project 22.CPT or Tree mask.TIF). One of the benefits of using WIN'95 is the ability to assign 256-character filenames.

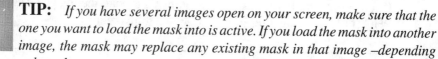

TIP: *Do not use a unique extension such as .MSK for the mask. This three-character extension is used by Corel PHOTO-PAINT and most other Windows applications to determine the correct import filter to use. Although the mask can be saved in any bitmap format (i.e. PCX, TIF, BMP, etc.), it is recommended to save masks in Corel PHOTO-PAINT's native CPT format.*

Loading a Mask

The Load Mask function allows a wide variety of image file formats to be loaded as masks. Loading a mask into an image involves the following procedure:

TIP: *If you have several images open on your screen, make sure that the one you want to load the mask into is active. If you load the mask into another image, the mask may replace any existing mask in that image –depending on the mask mode.*

1. Select the image to which the mask being loaded will be applied.

2. Choose Load in the Mask menu and then Load from Disk. The Load a Mask from Disk dialog box opens.

3. Select the file to be used for a mask. The mask will be a black-and-white or a grayscale image. Click the Open button, and the mask will load into the image and the mask outline will appear on the image.

Loading a Photograph as a Mask

Any image file can be used for a mask. Using photographs or other non-mask files may give unpredictable, although not necessarily undesirable, results. A non-mask file is any image file that was not created using the mask tools in Corel PHOTO-PAINT.

When loading a mask, it is important to be aware that Corel PHOTO-PAINT *will resize the mask to fit the image!* This used to be a problem prior to the release of PHOTO-PAINT 6. It required ensuring that the mask and the image were the same size. No more, now it works great and we will prove it in the next hands-on exercise.

Making the Lady in the Leaves

I stumbled upon this jewel when trying to come up with an easy exercise to show how to use a photograph for a mask. I call it Lady in the Leaves. In it we will load the photograph as a mask. The photograph we are using is 15" wide but PHOTO-PAINT will automatically resize it. Next we will invert the mask. This is because a mask acts like a negative when we apply effects we must first invert positive images before applying any effects. Lastly we will apply leaves from the Image Sprayer tool to the masked image.

1. From the File menu select New or use CTRL-N. Leave the Color mode at 24-bit color and the Paper color white. Change the image size to 6 x 4 inches at 96 dpi.

2. In the Mask menu, select Load and choose Load From Disk. Change the Look in: to the drive with the Corel CD-ROM that contains the photos. Locate and select the file EXERCISE\PHOTOS\527028.WI and click the Open command. It will take a few moments to load the image because PHOTO-PAINT must resample the image to make it fit.

Note for Corel
PHOTO-PAINT 5 users:

In Corel PHOTO-PAINT 5, the mask must be a one-bit (black-and-white) image file, while the Transparency mask is a grayscale image. Since the release of Corel PHOTO-PAINT 6, the two have been combined. The regular mask now is a grayscale image.

3. To see the mask, click the Mask Overlay button on the Toolbar. Click it again to turn off the Mask Overlay. Click the Invert Mask button on the Toolbar.

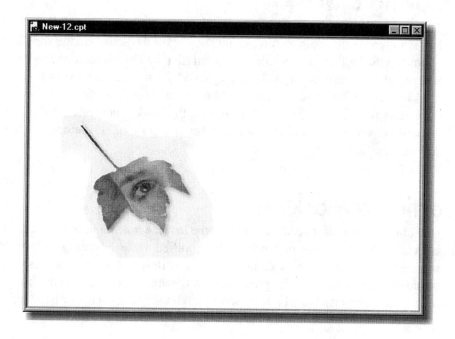

4. Click the Image Sprayer button from the flyout at the bottom of the Toolbox. Click the Load Image Sprayer List button located on the far left end of the Property Bar. When the Load Image List dialog box opens, change to the CD-ROM drive and locate and select the file \IMGLISTS\MAPLE.CPT. Open the Tool Settings Roll-Up and Change the Paint mode to Subtract.

5. In the Edit menu, select the Special undo and choose the Checkpoint command. Place the cursor in the image and click one time at a point as shown below. Because the Image Sprayer applies its image randomly yours will look different. If you don't like the leaf that was applied or where it was applied use the Undo (CTRL-Z) to remove it. That's all there is to it. Continue clicking until you have an image you like. To clear the image and start over again, select Restore to Checkpoint in the Edit menu. Figure 8-1 shows what my finished image looks like. Yours will be different -viva la difference!

The Lady in
the Leaves
is made
using a
photograph
for a mask

FIGURE 8-1

Removing a Mask

 There are several ways to remove a mask. One of the quickest is to click the Remove Mask button on the toolbar. A mask must exist on the active image for the mask buttons in the toolbar to be available. The mask may also be removed by selecting Remove in the Mask menu. A mask may also be removed with the DEL key if the mask is selected. The mask is selected whenever the Mask Transform tool is selected. (The mask will have control handles on it.) If the mask is not selected, *the contents of the mask will be cleared when the DEL key is depressed.* Therefore, use the DEL key with caution.

Inverting a Mask

One of the more useful mask functions is the Invert Mask command. When a mask is created, the area inside the mask can be modified while the area outside the mask is protected. The Invert mask command reverses the mask so that the area that was inside the mask now becomes protected and the area outside can be modified. The Invert mask command can be accessed through the Mask Menu, or by clicking on the Invert Mask button, or with the keyboard combination CTRL-I.

TIP: *Some masks are so complex it is difficult to determine what part of the image lies inside or outside of the mask. A quick way to check is to select the Mask Overlay button. The tinted area is protected the lighter area is not. The Mask Overlay is a display function and does not affect the operation of PHOTO-PAINT.*

Mask All

To mask the entire image, click the Select All button from the Toolbar or choose the Select All command in the Mask menu. You can also double-click any of the basic Mask selection tools in the toolbox: Rectangle, Circle, or Freehand. The mask will encompass the entire image inside of the image window. If the image is only partially visible because you have zoomed into an area, the entire image is still masked. In this situation, you will not be able to see the entire mask.

Mask Channel Operations

The mask channel is a temporary mask storage area, and if you do any amount of work with masks, you have got to love this feature. You can temporarily store masks in mask channels by using the Channels Roll-Up. When you create a mask, Corel PHOTO-PAINT makes a copy of the current mask and stores it in a channel where you can access and reuse it in the image as many times as you wish. You can also save a mask channel to a file or open a previously saved channel into the current image.

Once saved in a channel, a mask can be selected and reused within an image. When you change a mask in an image, you can reflect the changes in the channel by clicking the Update Channel button in the roll-up. There are also commands for saving a mask channel to a separate file or opening a previously saved mask channel. The contents of the Mask Channel are retained when an image is closed.

The Channels Docker Window

The Channels Docker window is one of four roll-ups that are referenced as docking dialogs. It can be opened several ways: pressing CTRL-F9, selecting the Channels tab on the docking or selecting the Channel button in the Property Bar. The Channels Docker window provides several different command functions buttons at the bottom. The Mask channels section displays the mask channels that are currently occupied. Figure 8-2 shows Docker windows with the Channels window enabled.

Exploring Channels

There have been improvements to the Channel Docker window that should be discussed. First of all, your Channel Docker probably looks much taller than mine does. I did a little photo editing and removed the blank middle. The top four entries are the RGB and then individual channels. The entry Current Mask is indicated in the title area. Whenever a mask is created, the current mask appears below the RGB channels. That's simple so far, right? As mentioned previously although an image can have only one mask at a time you can store many different masks with an image in the form of channels. Prior to PHOTO-PAINT 7, alpha channel information was not saved with the image.

Different Names and Colors

Referencing the example in Figure 8-2 we notice there is one channel below the Current Mask. If you have many mask channels, names are an easy way to keep track of them. You can assign names to channels either when you create them or by double-clicking the channel which opens the Channel Properties dialog box. This dialog box provide another way to differentiate between multiple mask channels by allowing assignment of different Mask overlay colors and transparency. Maybe in PHOTO-PAINT 9 they will add individual flavors –was that over the top?

Operating the Channels Docker or Many Ways to Do the Same Thing

You can covert a mask into a channel through the Mask menu (Mask, Save, Save as Channel) or Select the Current Mask in the Channels and click the Save Mask to New Channel button at the bottom of the roll-up. Conversely you can convert a channel into a mask though the Mask menu or through the Channels Docker window. Here are a few more tidbits before we move on. You can create a new channel without a mask by clicking the little option button in the upper right-corner of the Docker window and choosing New Channel. It looks like the Channel Properties box except it comes with 2 choices for colors—black or white.

That's enough for now. We will use Channels docker in a hands-on exercise later in this chapter.

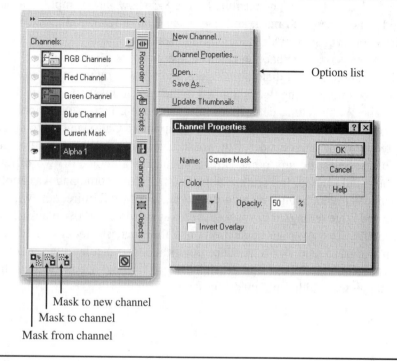

Options list

Channel Properties

The
Channels
Docker
window

Mask to new channel
Mask to channel
Mask from channel

FIGURE 8-2

Manipulating Masks

After a mask has been created we often need to modify it. Corel has provided several mask manipulation tools to help us do this. Probably the most-often-used mask manipulation tool is the Feather Mask command.

Feather Mask

Feathered masks are the means by which we can add or subtract images or effects without the viewer being aware of it. Technically speaking feathering a mask changes the transparency of the pixels located near the mask boundary. Any effect or command applied to the selection fades gradually as you get near the protected area. Feathering can be applied to a mask during or after its creation

It is particularly useful if you want to apply an effect to the masked area but not the surrounding area. Feathering a mask makes the transition between the two areas gradual, therefore less noticeable. Figure 8-3 shows an example of an object made with a non-feathered mask and one made from a feathered mask. See if you can figure out which one was made with the feathered mask.

When you select Shape and then Feather from the Mask menu or click the Feather Mask button, a small dialog box opens that allows you to set the direction, amount and type of feathering that is applied to the current mask.

The Width setting determines how wide the effect is to be applied to a mask edge. The Average Direction effectively applies a Gaussian blur to all of the pixels directly inside and outside of the mask. This provides the smoothest mask of the choices. Selecting any other Direction enables a choice of two different Edges: Linear and Curved. In Figure 8-4 the Feather Mask command was applied to three identical masks using Average direction, and Middle direction with Linear and Curved Edge settings. The masked area was filled with 100% black fill and zoomed to 300%. The Average mask (left) has the greatest amount of blurring. Linear (middle)has a tendency to produce points at perpendicular intersections of straight mask lines. The Curved feather (right) doesn't spread out as much as the other two although the Width setting was the same.

A
Non-feathered
mask can
cause
problems

FIGURE 8-3

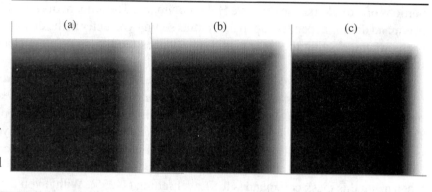

(a) (b) (c)

a) Average direction
b) Middle with Linear
c) Middle with Curved

FIGURE 8-4

The Shape Category Mask Commands

Some of the other mask commands you may have occasion to work with are located in the Shape category in the Mask menu. These commands are Border, Remove Holes, Smooth, Threshold, Expand and Reduce.

The Border mask command subtracts a portion of an existing mask to produce a border whose width is determined by the setting in the Border dialog box that opens when this command is selected. It offers the option of three different Edges-hard, medium and soft. The resulting mask frames protected pixels in the image. Borders only move outward from the mask regardless of the Mask Mode setting. Be careful when applying this command to circles, it tends to degrade the general shape of the circle

TIP: *For a creative effect try applying the Border command to a square or rectangle mask multiple times.*

Remove Holes is a real timesaver -sometimes. This command removes of the those nasty little mask fragments that tend to be left when using the color-sensitive masks. Unfortunately, it may also remove any isolated portions of masks that you may not want to remove. That said, when it works it works great. It has no adjustable settings it will either work or not work for what you want to use it for. Keep the old faithful Undo command (CTRL-Z) handy and give it a try.

The Smooth mask command creates a more fluid mask boundary by smoothing out sharp bends (jaggies) in the mask that occur when creating color-sensitive masks. Some pixels that are not in the selection before smoothing will become part of the selection after smoothing, and some pixels that are currently in the selection will no longer be included in it. The Smooth command can sometimes eliminates entire portions of a mask like the Remove Holes command. The amount of smoothing this command does is dependent upon the Radius setting you enter in the dialog box that opens when selecting the command. Large values tend to completely change the shape of the mask.

The Threshold mask command is the opposite of the Smooth command. When you have a mask that has too indefinite of an edge, as you would see in a feathered mask, this command makes it into a binary (black-and-white) mask by applying a Threshold function to it. If you do the hands-on exercises in Chapter 18, you will get to use this filter. Oddly enough, this is one of my favorite filters in the category because it allows me to make the edges of masks more distinct. The only setting when using this mask command is the Level setting (1-255). With it you determine the point in the mask at which any grayscale value in the mask below the threshold becomes white and above it becomes black.

Expand and Reduce mask commands do just what they say they do. Use them to make masks larger or smaller. Like the Border mask command these commands tend to degrade shapes if large values are used or they are applied multiple times.

Creating Distressed Text

In this little hands-on exercise we are going to create the illusion of text that was stenciled on a wooden crate. We will be using some tools that you may not be familiar with but have no fear. Follow the directions and you will be fine.

1. Create a new image by selecting New from the File menu. The size is 4 x 4 inches at 96 dpi, and 24-bit color.

   From the Edit menu choose Fill. This action opens the Edit Fill & Transparency dialog box. Select the Bitmap Fill button (the one with the checkerboard icon on it) and click the Edit button in the lower right corner of the dialog box. When the Bitmap fill dialog box opens click the Load Button. From the Import dialog box locate the file on the CD-ROM: EXERCISE\TILES\WOOD07L.CPT. Click the Open button to select the file. Click the OK button to close the Bitmap Fill dialog box and OK to apply the fill.

2. Click the Text tool button in the Toolbox. Click on the image an type the word DANGER. Change the Font to Stencil at a size of 96. Part of the word will be off of the image area at this point. Click the Object Picker tool in the Toolbox.

3. In the Object menu select Rotate and choose Free causing rotation handles to appear on the text. Holding down the constrain (CTRL) key drag one of the corner handles until the text is at an angle of 45 degree as shown in Figure 8-5. Also move the text so all of it is inside the image if necessary. Double-click on the text to apply the Transformation.

4. Create a Mask from the object (text) using CTRL-M. From the Object menu select Delete. The text disappears leaving only the mask.

5. From the Mask menu select Save and then Save As Channel. You will receive another dialog box asking you to name the mask channel. Name it Original Mask and select Channels by clicking on the tab.

6. From the Mask menu select Shape and then Expand. When the dialog box opens enter a Width value of 4 (pixels). Click OK. Click on the Paint on Mask button to see that the mask has become almost unreadable as shown new. Click the Paint on Mask button again to return it to its normal mode. Now it time for some mask magic.

The rotated
text shown
with the
mask from
next step

FIGURE 8-5

7. From the Mask menu choose Mode, then XOR. This is the Exclusive OR mode of the mask tool that, if you were honest, you had serious doubts had any function whatsoever. From the Mask menu choose Load and select Original Mask. Click the Paint On Mask button again and you will see we now have an outline of the text as shown below. Disable the Paint on Mask button.

8. Click the red color swatch in the on-screen palette to change the Paint color to red. Select the Paint tool button in the Toolbox. Open the Tool-Settings Roll-Up (CTRL-F8) and choose the Spray Can. Change the Type to Power Sprayer. Change the Paint setting to Subtract. This will cause the Type to change to Custom Spray Can as shown in Figure 8-6. If the Spray Can is not in the top four icons on your Tool Settings Roll-Up click the small button to the right of the buttons and select it from the list that appears.

9. Drag the cursor over the masked area. When you are finished turn off the mask marquee by clicking the button. The Subtract Paint mode prevent the red from painting over the dark shadow areas which would have made it look unreal. Your finished image should look like Figure 8-7.

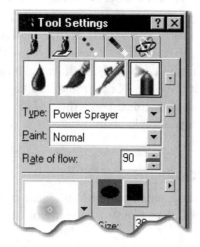

The Tool
Settings
roll-up for
the Paint
tools

FIGURE 8-6

The
completed
exercise
looks like
we really
painted it
on the wood

FIGURE 8-7

The Color Mask and Similar Command

The Color Mask changes with each new release of PHOTO-PAINT more than any other tool in the program and the release of PHOTO-PAINT 8 is no different. All of this change has produced a lot of improvement. All of the color-sensitive masks we have discussed until now could only include colors that were connected to the original sampled color. With the Color Mask and the Similar command pixels are selected based on their color content regardless of the position of the selected pixels in relation to the original sample point.

The Color Mask

Selecting the Color Mask, located in the Mask menu opens a dialog box (Figure 8-8) that may, at first appearance, appear a little intimidating. Actually, the principal of

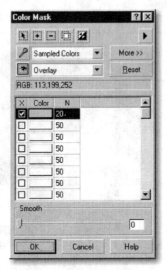

The Color
Mask
dialog box

FIGURE 8-8

its operation is quite simple. Use the eyedropper to select colors in the image that you want masked. If you don't like the result of one of the color selections, remove the checkmark from its box. Use one of the many preview options to determine how successful the color selection process has been and click the OK button when you have chosen all of the colors to create a mask. Really simple stuff – right?

If you used the Color Mask in with versions of PHOTO-PAINT prior to PHOTO-PAINT 7 you might find the Color Mask a little confusing so I have included some handy tips to help you get up to speed quickly.

- The Color Mask is no longer a roll-up so you must complete the selection of the mask and apply the mask before you can do any other operation.

- The Color Mask command no longer creates color masks. It creates regular masks. Color Masks, which were a different type of mask in PHOTO-PAINT 5, no longer exist.

- You can save and load your Color Mask dialog box settings as a Color Mask file.

- Preview of the mask made by the Color Mask tool is done on the actual image.

The best way to learn how to use this jewel is to take it for a test ride which is what we are going to do in the next exercise.

Replacing a Background Using the Color Mask

Replacing a background in a complex image can take time, even with the Color Mask. In this case we have a photograph of the ruins of a cathedral. The client's art director wants the photo to have a "gothic motif" and after he has spent the last half-hour explaining it to you are wondering why you didn't buy the extra-large size bottle of aspirin. The challenge is to replace the blue-sky background with something "gothic" looking. The first step is to mask the ruins. We could use the Magic Wand mask tool if we were being paid by the hour. Unfortunately it is a piece job so we need to finish the job as soon possible. Let's get started.

1. Open the image EXERCISE\PHOTOS\555083.WI. Select Resample in the Image menu, change the Width to 6 inches and click the OK button. The result is shown below.

2. From the Mask menu select the Color Mask. When the dialog box opens it will look like the one shown in Figure 8-8. If you have the room on your display I recommend positioning the Color Mask dialog box so you can see the parts of the image we are masking. Click the Reset button to clear any previous settings.

3. Click the Eyedropper button and the cursor becomes an eyedropper. Now place the cursor on the image. As you move the eyedropper around notice that the color swatch in the Color column of the dialog box changes to reflect the color currently under the eyedropper cursor. Click on the image

at a darker portion of the blue sky. I choose the point under the archway between the four towers on the right side.

4. Click the Preview button (it looks like an eye) and the image in the Preview shows masked (protected) areas in a red tint. The areas that are not protected are clear allowing the original color to be viewed. Change the Tolerance value (the N column) to 20 (%) by clicking on the number 28 and changing the value. Notice that the preview automatically updates the image. How did I come up with the number 28 you ask? The same way you will –experimentation. Click the OK button.

5. Turn off the Mask marquee. To view the mask, use the Mask Overlay button. It is more accurate and much less disconcerting to watch. If the mask still had some final touch-up work that needed to be completed we would do it at this point with the Mask Brush tool. Turn off the Mask overlay by clicking the Mask Overlay button again.

6. From the File menu choose Save As and in a place you can remember where you parked it save the file as RUINS.CPT.

7. From the Mask menu choose Create and then Object: Cut selection. Look at the thumbnail of the object in the Objects Docker window (CTRL-F7). The ruins should be an object. If the thumbnail is blue with a white background. Undo (CTRL-Z) the last action, click the Invert Mask button and create the object again.

8. With the Object Picker tool from the Toolbox, click on the Background in the Objects Docker window.

9. From the Edit menu choose Fill. When the Edit Fill & Transparency dialog box opens choose the Texture fill (last button on the right) and click Edit.

Choose Samples 7 for the Texture library and choose Contour Map from the Texture list. You can use the texture that comes up as default or enter the number 25044 in the Texture # box that is part of the Style Name section. Click OK and then OK again to apply the fill the result is shown next. Ok, so it doesn't look "Gothic" but it will later on.

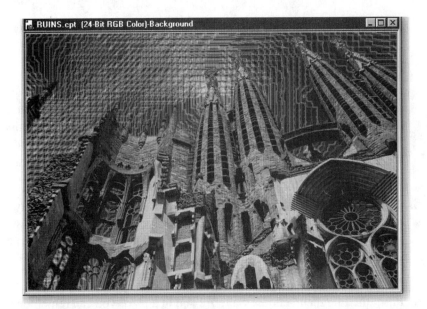

10. From the Effects menu choose Fancy and then Alchemy. From the Saved Styles list select the Style Cubist and click OK. The image below is getting more gothic, right?

11. From the Effects menu choose 2D Effects. Select Whirlpool and select the Super Warpo style. Click OK. The results are shown below. Close the file and save any changes.

Well, we have a great background, but we need to change the lighting on the ruins. We will learn how to do that in Chapter 20. Until then, remember where you parked RUINS.CPT.

What All of the Buttons and Controls on Color Mask Do

Back to the Color Mask. Overall the Color Mask tool contains many buttons and dialogs which are new with the PHOTO-PAINT 8 release but none the less are ones to which you have already been introduced. For example, across the top are the four Mask Mode and the Invert Mask buttons. The Mask Mode buttons control how the mask you make with the Color Mask tool reacts with an existing mask. The Invert Mask is a nice feature that allows you to either protect or select the sampled colors. In the previous exercise we started a project that was essentially easy. Let's be honest, a nearly uniform blue sky is nothing like the backgrounds that make up the bread-and-butter jobs of photo editing. So, the next exercise is a working guided tour of the Color Mask, when we are finished you will know how to use this powerful selection tool.

The Working Tour of the Color Mask Tool

The photograph we will be working on is tricky since to our eyes it appears to be a flower against a solid background. In a moment we will discover that it contains some surprises.

1. Open the file EXERCISE\PHOTOS\586050.WI. From the Edit menu resample it to 6 inches wide and click OK.

2. The most important step with any masking procedure is to examine the image. The photograph looks dull. In this case we can enhance the image by selecting Adjust from the Image menu and choosing Auto Equalize. Wow, that made quite a difference. Notice that the uniform dull gray background is actually composed of different shades of gray and green.

3. From the Mask menu choose Color Mask. When the dialog box opens click the Reset button to clear out any previous settings. Ensure the Mask Mode is in Normal mode (first button on the left).

4. Click the Eyedropper tool and move the cursor over the image. On the right side of the flower click on one of the lighter areas of green. Notice the Color Mask dialog box displays a color swatch of the sampled color and the RGB value of the selected color is displayed as well.

5. Change the Numerical (N) value of the color we have selected to 15. The N value is a percentage (0-100) that states the range of included colors in relation to the sampled color. In other words, every color in the image whose value is within 15 percent of the sampled color is included. Now let's see what we preview what we have selected.

6. Click the Preview icon (eye button) and the flower is covered with a mask overlay, just as if we had clicked the Mask Overlay button in the Toolbar. There are several preview modes and it is a wise PHOTO-PAINT user who learns to look at alternative previews (which is exactly like alternative lifestyles but completely different).

7. Click the Preview mode (next to the Preview button) and select Grayscale. The result, shown below, produces an image identical to the Paint on Mask mode.

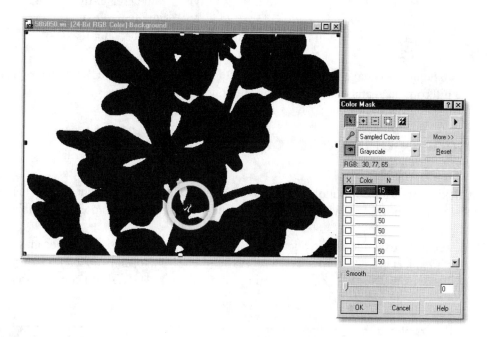

NOTE: *Grayscale preview, quickly alerts you to any part of the mask that didn't get picked up by our color selection. I have placed a circle over the portion of the image shown above that was not selected. While we are here look at the White and Black Matte. Each creates an overlay either in White or Black. In this case the White Matte is much more revealing. Had it been a very light picture, the Black Matte would have been more helpful. If your Mask Marquee is enabled it will appear as an option in the list as well.*

8. At this point we have the background selected. Click the Mask Invert button and then click OK.

9. Select the Mask Brush tool from the Mask tool flyout, click the Mask Overlay button and using either the Subtractive or Additive mask modes, add or subtract from the mask to complete the selection process.

10. With the Mask Overlay still enabled look at the petals of the flowers. Do they have a slight fringe of the old background? You can select Feather in the Mask menu and choose a Width of 1 with a setting of Inside and curved but I advise caution in using any Width value greater than 2. This is because you end up with a fuzzy edge when you attempt to create an object which we will learn about in Chapter 13 (objects –not fuzzies).

In Figure 8-9 I have shown the flower with a new background. In this case I used the Fill command and chosen a bitmap fill - one of the wood tiles.

Additional Information about the Color Mask

Clicking the More>> button on the Color Mask dialog box opens the rest of the dialog box, shown below, containing a few additional settings that modify how this Mask Tool operates.

From the expanded dialog box you can determine what criteria the Color mask uses to select its color. You can use HSB instead of Normal mode. For most applications the Normal setting (default) will do the job. HSB uses a combination

The Color
Mask tool
allows easy
background
replacement

FIGURE 8-9

of Hue Saturation and Brightness to make its selection of colors. You can also select to use the HSB components individually to determine which colors are selected.

You can save all of the settings as a color mask (.CMK) file. This file can be opened and used at a later time. The color mask can also be saved to a Mask Channel through this option. Remember if you choose to use this, that the Mask Channel is a temporary storage area that disappears when the image is closed.

The default settings for the Color Mask tool is to create a mask in Sampled Colors mode. In this mode everything that is not selected is protected.

Choosing Edit Color opens the Select Color dialog box from which you can specify a specific color to select. For example, if you only wanted to select every place in the image that the color Pantone CV742 was used. This is where you would make the selection.

At the top of the Color Mask (next to the Eyedropper icon) is a large list of preset settings that allows you to quickly select at type or range of colors or shades. Some of the selections are not what they appear to be. For example, the setting Blues does not select everything blue in an image rather it is set to the color Blue in the palette at a high value (50). If we had selected this as the starting point in the previous exercise, it would not have initially selected any colors in the sky. You can choose Blues and then change the blue that is used as the reference by clicking on the sky with the Eyedropper tool.

Using the Color Mask More Productively

The following are suggestions that may help you when using the Color Mask:

If you are attempting to mask a narrow range of colors, like the blue in a sky, use multiple samples or take a single sample and increase the Tolerance setting for it. Many times when selecting a color or range of colors you end up with parts of the image selected that you didn't want selected. Rather than waste time trying to balance the color/tolerance settings to get the "perfect" mask, focus on getting the area selected that was the original objective. Any areas that are also included in the mask can be easily deleted with one of the mask tools after the mask is applied. It is always easier to remove a portion of a mask than it is to create one that has a boundary along a ragged or irregular boundary.

When changing the color tolerance, value the Preview window won't reflect the changes until you hit the ENTER key or click on another color.

If you must edit photographs a lot to select and modify backgrounds this tool will serve you well. If the background is very well defined and non-contiguous you may want to consider the Similar command, which happens to be the next subject.

Similar Command

The Similar and Grow commands in the Mask menu share a common selection process. Both of these commands the use the color content of the pixels making up the marquee boundary as their reference (or starting) point. They both expand by comparing the reference value with the color value of adjacent pixels to see if they fall within the Color Tolerance value that was set either in the Tools Settings Roll-Up, or the Property Bar. All pixels that fall within that range are included, those that fall outside of the range are not included. Where the two commands differ in the adjacent part. The Grow command continues to grow until there are no more adjacent pixels. The Similar command continues to evaluate every pixel in the image.

The difficulty you may encounter with the operation of either of these commands happens when working with a mask boundary containing pixels with many different colors. All of the colors in the mask boundary (plus or minus the Color Tolerance setting) will be included. When you run into a situation like this, lower the Color Tolerance to either a very low number or change from Normal to HSB.

Stroke Mask Command

This command is used to automatically apply brush strokes along a path defined by the mask. From the Stroke Mask dialog box you can select any brush or effect tool. Any parameter that can be selected from the Tool Settings Roll-Up for a Brush or Effect tool can be selected and used with the Stroke command.

Applying the Stroke Command

In this hands-on exercise we are going to create a small poster for a small organization that is trying to abolish the use of stamps. Our Mask Stroke command will make the job really simple.

1. Create a new image that is 4 x 4 inches at 96 dpi, 24-bit color with white Paper color.

2. From the Tools menu select Grid & Ruler Setup. Select Show grid and Snap to grid. Change the Spacing to .5 in both Horizontal and Vertical. Click OK.

3. Select the Circle Mask tool from the Toolbox. Starting at a point that is two squares in and down from the upper-left corner click and drag a 4 x 4 circle.

4. Select the Image Sprayer tool from the Toolbox. When the Image Sprayer Tool Settings Property Bar appears click the Load button and select EXERCISE\IMGLIST\STAMPS.

 NOTE: *In previous releases of PHOTO-PAINT you made your choice of brushes, settings etc. after launching the Stroke Mask dialog. In PHOTO-PAINT 8, all of these settings are controlled through the Tool Settings before selecting Stroke Mask.*

5. From the Edit menu select Stroke and choose Stroke Mask. When the Choose Stroke Position dialog box opens, leave it at Middle of the Mask border and click OK. It will take a few moments depending on the speed of your computer. Figure 8-10 shows the results I got. Your will be different because the Image Sprayer applies its stamps randomly.

6. Remove the mask by clicking the Remove Mask button. Turn off Snap to Grid by pressing (CTRL-Y) and from the View menu uncheck Grid.

7. With the Paint color set to Black, click the Text tool in the Toolbox. Change the Font to Stencil and the size to 72. Change the Interline spacing to 82. Click on the image and enter the text **STAMP OUT**

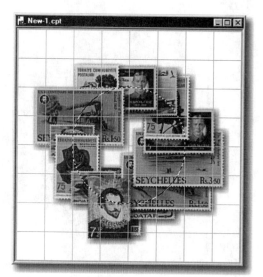

The stamps are applied with the Stroke Mask command

FIGURE 8-10

STAMPS. Click the Object Picker button in the Toolbox. Open the Align dialog box (CTRL-A) and select Align to Center of Page. Click OK. The problem we now face is the black text blends in with the stamps as shown in Figure 8-11.

Click the white color swatch in the on-screen palette. Open the Objects Docker window (CTRL-F7). With the text selected click the Create Mask buton (CTRL-M). Our text is now masked. Click on the background. The text is now protected.

From the Paint tool flyout select the Airbrush tool from the Brush tab and choose the Medium Cover.

8. From the Mask menu select Stroke Mask. When the Choose Stroke Position dialog box opens, leave it at Middle of the Mask border and click OK.Click the OK button. The final result is shown in Figure 8-12.

9. Close the file and don't save any changes.

TIP: *If you ever get an assignment from a group that wants to stamp out stamps, get paid in advance—in cash.*

The text is
hard to read
over the
darker
portions of
the stamps

FIGURE 8-11

The
completed
exercise

FIGURE 8-12

There is one remaining subject that comes under the topic heading Advanced Masks—Paths.

Paths

What are paths? Paths are line and curve segments connected by square endpoints called nodes. If you work with CorelDRAW the paths will be familiar to you. Masks and Paths share some common characteristics. A mask is created from a bitmap image. A Path on the other hand is a vector drawing that exists on a layer above the image and is independent of the image resolution. A path that completely encloses an area, as a mask would, is referred to as closed. A path with start and end nodes that are not connected, something that a mask cannot do, is called open.

The advantage of the path over the mask is in the word precision. You can only adjust a bitmap mask by adding or subtracting from it with a brush tool or something similar. With a path you have full Bezier level control over the points and nodes, just as you have in Corel DRAW. When you need to make accurate masks then you will want to create a path using the Path Node Edit Tool. The advantage offered by paths is as vector images they can be precisely edited. When the path is exactly the shape you want, you can either save the path, convert it to a mask or more likely do both. Masks can be converted to Paths, edited as paths and converted back to mask.

Paths offer powerful and precise editing tools that allow you to modify isolated segments of the outline you create.

New paths can be created using the Path Node Edit tool or existing masks can be converted to Paths. Double-clicking on the Path Node edit tool opens the Node Edit Tool shown in Figure 8-13.

You can save the path if you wish to work on it later, use it in another image, or export its contents as a bitmap. You can save a path as a path or convert it to a mask. If you export a mask as a part of an encapsulated postscript (EPS) image the mask is converted to a path. You can stroke a path in the same manner that we learned to Stroke a Mask earlier.

Corel has produced a large volume of material on paths, how to manipulate them and apply them so in the interest of saving space, I refer you to either the PHOTO-PAINT User's Manual or the extensive on-line help. With the on-line help I recommend opening the index and entering the word Path. You will find a large amount of material on the subject.

The Node Edit Tool Settings roll-up offers a large number of controls to create and manipulate paths

FIGURE 8-13

Correcting
Existing Images

247

Sometimes the most important operations we perform in PHOTO-PAINT are not found in the dazzling special effects we create or in the fantastic surrealistic images produced using our vast array of filters. Some of the most important work done with PHOTO-PAINT is the correction and enhancement of existing images. In other words, making poor or bad photographs look good.

In this chapter you will be introduced to some basic PHOTO-PAINT commands in the Image menu used to make an image look better on a computer screen, look better when it is printed, or both. This is what photo-editing is about. It is not glamorous work but it more often than not pays the bills. We will also mention other color correction tools included with PHOTO-PAINT: PhotoLab, Intellihance, and the new Lens feature. First we begin by covering some basic terms and concepts.

It's Not A Perfect World

The challenge facing anyone working with digital photo-editing that is destined to be printed is based on one fundamental fact. What you see on the screen is not, and will never be, what you will get. The monitor that you stare at all day long has a greater range of color and shades than any output device can reproduce. Therefore all of the tools that we will be looking at in this chapter essentially do one thing. They shuffle existing pixels around inside an image so that they will look their best on the media (ink-jet, laser, or web offset) on which you will be doing your final output.

Understanding Image Correction and Targeting

The adjustment of lightness and darkness in an image is called *tonal manipulation*. We adjust the tones in an image for two reasons. The first is to correct flaws that are either inherent in the image or are introduced during the scanning process. This is image correction. The second reason for applying tonal manipulation to an image is to compensate for the limitations of the output device. This is called targeting. You can do both at once or one at a time, either way it is important to keep the distinction between the image correction and targeting -at least for the remainder of the chapter. We will be concentrating on image correction in this chapter.

With few exceptions, if all you need to do is perform image correction on grayscale images, it can be accomplished using only two PHOTO-PAINT tools: Histogram and Level Equalization. The other tools are either for color and will be discussed later in this chapter or their effects can be found in these tools

Stop Before You Start

The most important step in image correction is to stop and examine the image you want to correct. For example, a photograph with debris (dust and hairs) that is painfully obvious can be fixed in Photo-Paint. Does the photograph have detail in the shadows you want to recover? Is it over-exposed? Decide first what you want to do, and then plan out a strategy to accomplish it. All of the stretching and squeezing of bits done by PHOTO-PAINT (or any photo-editing program) causes loss of image information. The loss is made worse by multiple applications tonal corrections. It may not be obvious, but it is there. The damage may appear as posterization in areas of tonal shading, noise that begins to appear, or general loss of detail. For this reason your general rule should be to make only as many tonal corrections as are necessary.

Shades, Shadows, Highlights and Histograms

Every digital image contains pixels that have a maximum range of 256 levels of brightness numbered 0-255. At this point, for sake of simplicity, we are going to restrict our discussions to grayscale images. These levels of brightness or shades range in value from black (0) to white (255). These values can be visually charted on a terribly complicated looking graph called a histogram. Figure 9-1 shows a portion of the histogram that is displayed by PHOTO-PAINT. It is divided into three regions: shadows, highlights and midtones.

A histogram is a simple bar chart that plots the number of pixels at each brightness level in an image. The histogram can tell you a good many things about an image before you begin to work on it. In Corel PHOTO-PAINT 8 you can see the histogram of an image by selecting Histogram in the Image menu.

How to Read a Histogram

The following examples will shown the relationship between different types of photographs and their respective histograms. Only the actual histogram is displayed. The numerical information that is displayed with this histogram is not shown.

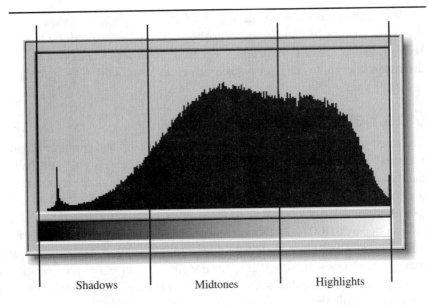

The three major regions of a histogram

Shadows   Midtones   Highlights

FIGURE 9-1

In the photograph shown below, the histogram tells us things that are not apparent from looking the image. Because the image is of a white subject taken against a dark background, almost all of the pixels are in the shadows area (far left). There are no midtones and the highlights is the area that contains the detail information. The purpose of the histogram is to provide a general overview of the image contents. From this one we learn there is no detail in the shadow area that can be recovered through image correction because it is all one shade of black and no mid-tones. Even thought the photograph is predominately dark, this is referred to as a *high key* image because the details (the part we want to actually see) are in the highlights. This information in the highlights is very close to the high end of the spectrum (approaching paper white) so when adjusting the picture it would be necessary to move that range down so as to get all of the detail in the flower.

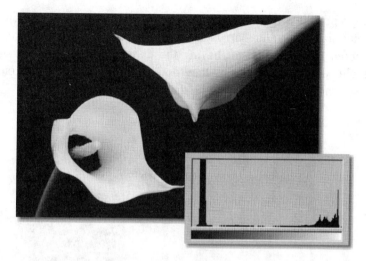

The next photograph and its histogram show that most of the information in the image is concentrated in the highlights. The reason the histogram doesn't show any midtones or shadows is because the display is adjusted so as to see most of the image content displayed. Since there is so much in the highlights, the midtones and shadows are there but in such small quantities as to not shown up on this scale of graph. When planning a strategy for this type of image you will have a problem. If we make the wall dark enough to pick up the detail in it, we will push everything in the shadows into solid black. Any image with extreme contrasts is a challenge.

This photograph is a well-balanced image. Notice the histogram shows lots of midtones and highlights, and there is detail information in the shadow region. The best part about the image is not having the extreme ends of the shadows and highlights clipped. In other words, they don't concentrate on either end of the histogram so that they are clipped off by the end points.

Other things we can see with histograms is the quality of a scan. If the shadows or highlights are badly clipped, it was either a poor scan or a cheap scanner. We can also see if an image has already been manipulated. The histogram shown below is the same histogram that was displayed above after the output range was compressed using the Level Equalization tool. The spikes you see are normal after such a compression because when the image is compressed the adjacent shades of pixels are pushed one on top of another. This increases the number of pixels in certain shades which are represented by the spikes. The truth is after you have applied tonal correction to an image, the histogram can begin to look downright ugly which is fine. The histogram is only a guide.

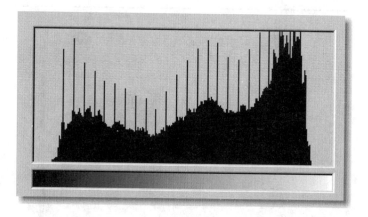

The Numerical Side of Histograms

Before we leave the subject of histograms, it is time to show you the entire display. I have not do it until now because I find most people are a little overwhelmed by the vast array of numbers that are associated with it. Figure 9-2 shows the entire display. Not many of them will benefit you in the area of image correction but here are a few you might find helpful or at least interesting.

In the range section, the Start and End points are shown. These values are related to the Percent setting in the clipping section. You can click and drag your cursor over the histogram display to view the percentage value (percentage of the histogram selected) and the tonal range of the selected area. The Mean value is the average brightness of the image. The first photograph of the two flowers against the black background has a Mean value of 67 out of 255 (because it is a predominately dark photograph). Std Dev. is standard deviation, which represents numerically how widely the brightness values vary. The Pixels value in the Range section is the total number of pixels in the image. Aren't you glad you know that?

The Individual section reads the value of the cursor when it is positioned in the histogram and reflects the brightness value as indicated by the Level figure and the total number of pixels at that brightness value. For example, in Figure 9-2 the cursor was last at the shade value of 198 and there were a total of 1,695 pixels of that brightness throughout the image.

9

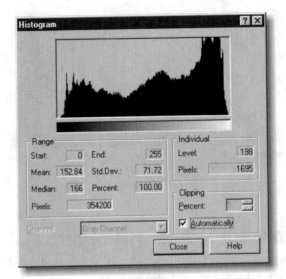

The entire histogram dialog box with all of its amazing numbers

Clipping reminds me of judging at sports events where they throw out the high and low scores. Clipping removes a percentage of the extreme shadows and highlights.

Tools for Image Correction

PHOTO-PAINT provides two different types of image correction tools. Linear and non-linear. Don't go looking for them under that title because you won't find them listed as such.

Linear Correction Tools

The linear correction tools are probably familiar to you, they are Brightness-Contrast-Intensity located in the Image menu under Adjust. They are called linear tools because they do exactly the same thing to every pixel in the image. This means that pixels are lost at one or both ends of the tonal range. For example, the Brightness control (-100 to 100) shifts all of the pixel values up or down the tonal range. If you were to increase the brightness by 10, PHOTO-PAINT adds 10 to the brightness value of every pixel. The pixels at 150 become 160, those at 200 become 210. Those at 245 become 255 and those at 250 become 255 because you can't go above 255. This produces clipping of the highlights. The Contrast control stretches the tonal range when you increase contrast which effectively throws away image information. Does this mean these controls are bad? Not really, but I strongly recommend very moderate use of them. Once you learn how to use the non-linear tools, Level Equalization and Tone Curves, also found in the Adjust flyout, I doubt you will ever use Brightness-Contrast-Intensity again.

Non-Linear Correction Tools

These are the tools that you may have opened up, taken a good look at the dialog box and immediately closed it thinking that someday you would learn how to use them. We are going to learn how to use some of them in this book. It takes an entire book to learn all about what these and the other tools do. In fact, if you want to learn all of the things you can do with these tools, I highly recommend the book *Real World Photoshop 3* by David Blatner and Bruce Fraser. Even though it covers Photoshop, the tools in PHOTO-PAINT are almost identical and the principles are the same.

The two non-linear tools we use for grayscale and color image correction are Level Equalization and Tone Curve. Both are found in the Adjust category of the Image menu. Both of these tools change the distribution of pixels throughout the tonal range in an image. Rather than describe them in great detail, we are going to use them in a hands-on exercise to correct an image which Corel was kind enough to include on the CD.

Correcting an Image

In this hands-on exercise we are going to take an overexposed, dirty photo and make it ready for publication.

1. Open the image EXERCISE\PHOTOS\570033.WI. Resample the image to a width of 6 inches. Figure 9-3 shows the starting photo. Using the Save As command, save the file as MODEL.CPT.

2. From the Image menu, select Histogram, opening the display shown in Figure 9-4. Looking at the histogram we see there are three areas of concentration. In the shadow region are the dark colors of the sweater vest. The upper-end of the midtones contain most of the colors of the model and the large number of pixels in the highlight area are the very bright background. Although we will eventually remove the background our need is to shift the center of the curve that contains the details of the model more toward the middle. Since such a shift will shove all of the detail information in the sweater into black we must first isolate it.

Corel PHOTO-PAINT 8: The Official Guide

The Original photo is in need of image correction

FIGURE 9-3

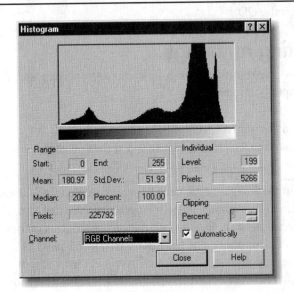

The Histogram of the original photograph

FIGURE 9-4

3. Close the Histogram dialog box and select the Magic Wand Mask tool from the Mask Tool flyout in the Toolbox. Ensure the Tolerance setting is 10 in the Property Bar and the Normal button is selected. Click the Additive button in the Property Bar.

4. Place the cursor in the image and click inside on one side of the sweater vest. Click on the other side of the vest. Click the Grow button in the Property Bar. The mask should cover the entire vest. Click the Invert Mask button. At this point the vest is protected.

5. From the Image menu select Adjust and choose Level Equalization. A rather intimidating dialog box opens. Notice the histogram displayed in the dialog box is different from the one shown in Figure 9-4. This is because the sweater vest has been isolated from the image by the mask and its pixels are no longer included in the histogram. Move the Gamma Adjustment slider to the left until it reads .72. The histogram displays an approximation of what the new histogram will look like after the Gamma adjustment is applied. The dialog box shown in Figure 9-5. Click OK to apply.

The Level Equalization dialog box shown after the Gamma adjustment is made

FIGURE 9-5

6. The image now looks much less underexposed but the model has a bluish cast about him. From the Image menu choose Adjust and select Color Tone. When the dialog box opens (Figure 9-6), move the position of the model in the Preview window so you can see his face. Change the Step value to 6 and click Saturate one time. By increasing the saturation by a small percentage we increase the overall color in his face. These changes are subtle but necessary. Click OK to apply. Next we will apply a hue shift to the one of the individual channels.

7. From the Image menu choose Adjust and select Color Hue. When the dialog box opens (Figure 9-7), move the position of the model in the Preview window so you can see his face. Since most of his features are in the Midtones and Highlight region, we will only apply the hue adjustment to that region, so uncheck the Shadows box. Uncheck the Preserve luminance box too. Click the More yellow box one time and click the OK button. The result is shown in Figure 9-8.

8. Save the file as MODEL1.cpt.

The Color Tone dialog box provides a highly visual interactive have to adjust color in an image

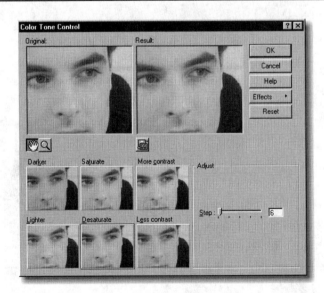

FIGURE 9-6

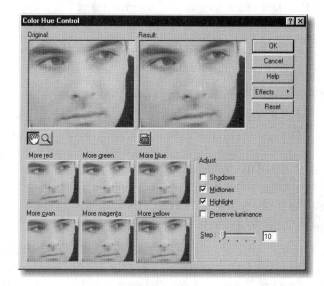

The Color Hue dialog box allows for the fine tuning of each color channel

FIGURE 9-7

Our overexposed photograph now looks a little more normal

FIGURE 9-8

TIP: *Did you notice that Color Tone and Color Hue didn't have Undo buttons? By clicking the opposite function you can undo it. For example, to undo a click of the Saturate click the Desaturate.*

To Complete the Job...

There are some things that should be done to this photograph that are not tonal correction. At this point our photograph no longer looks like an over-exposed image of a well-dressed cadaver. We have preserved the detail in the sweater vest. To finish the job I recommend the following:

1. Use the Clone tool to remove all of the debris on the photograph. The use of the Clone tool is explored in Chapter 11.

2. Add to the existing mask to include the rest of the model (excluding the background). I recommend clicking the Magic Wand tool around his head but when you get to his shirt, change the Tolerance to 5. There is a real tendency for the mask to break out into the background on the left side of the image.

   After you have finished masking the model, apply Smooth at a Radius of 5 located in the Mask menu in the Shape flyout.

3. Invert the mask so only the background is selected. Select Fill from the Edit menu and from the Fountain Fill choose a fill like a Circular Green or Blue preset. Make sure it is a light color and apply it to the background.

4. Invert the mask again and only the model is selected again. From the Effects menu select Sharpen and choose Directional Sharpen. Apply at 100 percent.

The Tone Curve Exercise

The Tone Curve command performs the same image correction that we accomplished with the previous exercise. The difference between the two is the degree of control that the Tone Curve offers. With the Tone Curve you can map individual tonal ranges that remap small portions of the tonal range. The following is a brief demonstration of the Tone Curve and an effect mentioned earlier.

1. Open the file Model.CPT (the one we saved in Step 1).

Select Adjust from the Image menu and choose Tone Curve. When the Tone Curve dialog box opens, shown in Figure 9-9, click the Open button in the Curves section. When the dialog box opens, select Neggamma.map (change Files of Type, if necessary) and click Open. Move the slider to the right until you get to the value of .72. Click the OK button.

2. This applies the same gamma value as we did in the previous exercise. Look at the sweater. All of the detail has been lost and the sweater has turned nearly solid black.

3. Undo (CTRL-Z) the last command. Open the Tone Curve dialog box again (CTRL-T). This time experiment by loading different settings. You can modify the curve by placing the cursor at a place on the curve, clicking and dragging it. You will see the result immediately (well, nearly immediately) if the Auto preview button (looks like a lock next to the Preview button) is enabled. To reset the curve to a straight line, click the Null button. Class is over, click Cancel, close the file and don't save any changes.

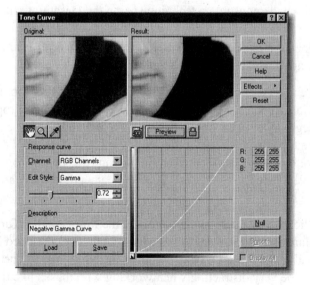

The Tone
Curve
dialog box

FIGURE 9-9

Other Tools

One of the other tools available under Adjust includes Gamma, which quickly allows you to only adjust the Gamma without any other options. Color Balance offers the same capability as Color Hue. The only advantage of this dialog box is you can apply all three effects without the delay of the automatic preview. Between the two, I like the interactive preview of the Color Hue. Likewise Hue-Saturation-Lightness does the same as Color Tone.

Auto Equalize, which is applied immediately and has no dialog box, stretches the image's tonal information and spreads it across the entire tonal range of 256 shades. The results are sometimes interesting. I recommend applying it at the beginning of work on an image, because you can never tell what the effect will be on any particular image. There have been several occasions when the application of Auto Equalize did the trick and no other correction was necessary.

Desaturate takes all of the colors in the pixels to a -100% setting; in this state the image looks like a grayscale. A popular way to emphasize an area or a subject in a photo is to leave the object you want to emphasize in color and apply Desaturate to the rest of the image.

Using the Desaturate Filter

Although this is a chapter about Image Correction, this hands-on exercise will allow you to quickly demonstrate a technique using the Desaturate file.

1. Open the file EXERCISE\PHOTOS\677061.WI. Resample to a Width of 7 inches and click the OK button.

2. We want to mask the bottle. Select the Lasso Mask tool from the Mask Tools flyout in the Toolbox. Set the Tolerance in the Property Bar to 20. Begin by clicking on the background and make a shape that includes the top portion of the bottle. With the Lasso Mask tool drag the horizontal bottom of the mask between the "S" and "h" of the word Shampoo. The object is to use the Lasso Mask to create a tight mask around the top of the bottle.

   Click the Additive mode button on the Property Bar. Turn off the Mask Marquee. If you want to see what is and is not included in the mask, enable the Mask Overlay option in the Mask menu. The Mask Marquee can be very distracting when working with masks like these.

3. Select the Freehand Mask tool from the Mask flyout in the Toolbox. Click on the edge of the bottle and begin to click at every point that encloses the bottle. Continue until you have enclosed the rest of the bottle with a mask.

4. Click the Mask Invert button.

5. From the Image menu choose Adjust and select Desaturate.

PhotoLab

For more advanced image correction PHOTO-PAINT 8 offers the PhotoLab filters created by CSI. PhotoLab consists of eight filters which are located in the Effects menu under PhotoLab. These filters are designed for use by professional photographers and prepress professionals. These filters are designed to bring out the maximum potential in your image by controlling and manipulating exposure, contrast and color casts. Included are powerful controls for color negative reversal and special effects such as accurate Sepia tones, infrared simulations and flexible noise generation.

The operation of this software would take several chapters in of itself. Fortunately Corel has provided a copy of the CSI Photolab User's Manual on the PHOTO-PAINT CD-ROM in the DOCUMENT\PLUGINS\PHOTOLAB folder. It is in Envoy format so you will need to install the Envoy viewer that came with your Corel software to read it.

TIP: *If you cannot find the PhotoLab plug-in filters in the Effects menu, you will need to install them. Refer to Chapter 14 for instructions on how to do that.*

The Lens Objects

The Lens Objects were first made available in the PHOTO-PAINT Plus release. A lens is an object that covers the entire image or a section of the image. You use a lens to try out various color or tonal corrections on your images.

There are a large number of lenses to choose from; each type of lens corresponds to an Image menu command found in either the Adjust or Transform flyouts. In the previous hands-on exercise with the model we applied the Level Equalization filter to the image. With a lens we can apply the setting to the lens and see the effect of the equalization through the lens.

The difference between applying a lens and using the Level Equalization command in the Image menu is that the lens does not modify the pixels in the image, whereas using the Image menu command does. The lens is between you and the image pixels and shows you the result of the Equalization attributes you have selected. You can move the lens elsewhere in your image to see how the pixels in another area look with the correction applied. Lenses that you use on an image are listed in the Objects Roll-Up just like any other object.

Using the Lens

The following hands-on exercise will show you how to create, modify and apply a lens.

1. Open the file MODEL.CPT that was saved at the beginning of an earlier exercise in this chapter.

2. Select the Circle Mask tool. Holding down the CTRL key drag a circle mask over the image that covers the model's head.

3. From the Object menu, choose Create and then Lens: From Mask. This opens the New Lens dialog box, shown in Figure 9-10. Select Level Equalization and click OK.

4. When the dialog box opens, you will notice that it is slightly different from the first Level Equalization dialog box we opened. All of the controls are present except for the Preview window because the image becomes the preview. Move the dialog box off of the image, if it is covering it, and move the Gamma Adjustment slider to .72. Watch the image change interactively as you move the slider. Click the OK button.

5. Use the Object Picker tool to move the lens around the image. As you do, the area viewed through the lens reflects the Gamma changes made by the filter.

6. Duplicate the Lens (CTRL-D). From the Objects Docker window select the top lens. Ensure the bottom lens is deselected. From the Object menu, select Lens Properties.

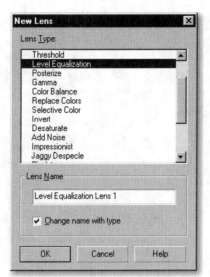

PHOTO-
PAINT
offers
different
lenses to
work with

FIGURE 9-10

7. When the Level Equalization dialog box opens, click the Lens button. This opens the New Lens dialog box. Choose Color Balance. In the Range portion, deselect the Shadows and Highlights. Enter **6** in the Magenta-Green channel. Click OK.

8. Now the two Lenses act together. From the Objects Roll-Up, select both lenses and click the Group button in the Property Bar. The action of the resulting Lens is shown in Figure 9-11.

9. Close the file and don't save any changes.

Creating Lenses

From the previous exercise we learned we can create a Lens from a mask. Actually, Lenses can be created in two ways; from scratch using the New Lens command also located in the Object menu. The New Lens command creates a lens object which covers the entire image. However, you can edit the size and shape of the lens like you would any other object.

Using the
Lens
feature
allows
selective
preview and
application
of 12
different
Adjust and
Transform
actions

FIGURE 9-11

The type of your image you apply the Lens to determines which lens types are available. For example, if you are working with a grayscale image, the Replace Color lens type is not available because the image consists only of different shades of gray.

The Create Lens:From Mask command creates a lens that has the precise shape and size of the mask in the Image Window. When you create a new lens, you can assign a descriptive name to it in the New Lens dialog box.

You can create as many lenses as you need in an image. When you create a lens, it appears in the Objects Docker window at the top of the stacking order because it is on top of the image background. The name assigned to the lens in the Roll- Up is either the name you have assigned it in the New Lens dialog box, or the lens type. A number appears at the end of the lens's name in the event you create more than one lens of the same type in a single image.

You can use the Objects Docker window to change the position of lenses in the stacking order, to hide or delete them, and to change their name. You can change the properties of a Lens by selecting the Object Properties option from the right-facing arrow in the Objects Roll-Up.

When you are satisfied with result of the selected Lens you can apply it by selecting the Lens and choosing Combine in the Objects Roll-Up. If the Lens is not combined with the background, it will not have any affect on the output of the file. Only those Lenses that are combined will cause changes in the printed output.

NOTE: *Lenses can be* grouped *together but they cannot be* combined *together as objects can.*

In all, Lenses can be used both for previewing and applying a large variety of different PHOTO-PAINT effects and functions.

9

10

Exploring Corel PHOTO-PAINT's Brush Tools

Brush tools are PHOTO-PAINT's tools that you apply with a brush and paint mode. The Paint, Clone, Image Sprayer, Effect, Local Undo, Mask Brush, and Object Transparency tools are all brush tools in the Toolbox. In this chapter, we will explore the Paint and Effect tools and their variations, some of which you have already seen in other chapters. While the purpose of each tool differs, all of the tools can be customized using the Property Bars and Tools Settings. Before discussing individual types of brushes we will look first at the common features.

The Paint tool paints an area characteristic of the type of brush selected using the current Paint color. The Paint tool's brushes replace (not cover) pixels with the currently selected Paint (foreground) color.

Selecting and Configuring Brush Tools

Once you've chosen one of these tools from the toolbox, selection of a tool is accomplished by clicking on its icon button from the Property Bar or selecting it from the Tool Settings roll-up. You can vary the effect any tool has by changing the brush settings and using different paint modes found on the Tool Settings roll-up. Many, but not all, of the same tool settings can be changed through the Property Bar. The Tool Settings roll-up for most of the brush tools contain five tabs, each dealing with different qualities of the brush. The first tab offers a selection of preset brush types. You can customize any preset brush or create an entirely new brush that specifically suits your needs.

Parts of a Brush

Each brush type is a combination of different settings in the Tool Settings roll-up or Property Bar. The size and shape of the brush stroke is determined by the size and shape of the selected nib. A nib is the tip of the brush you use to apply effects with any of the brush tools. Brush nibs can be selected from several different locations. Clicking the Nib Shape button, shown next, on the Tool Settings roll-up opens a smaller selection initially displaying 16 nibs (displayed on the left of the illustration). The size of the selection of nibs is fixed at 16. You can access all of the nibs by using the scroll bars. You can also customize any existing nib in the Tool Settings roll-up or create one from a mask for any of the brush tools. Any nib that has been created or customized can be saved. Once a nib has been saved, it appears at the bottom of the nib selection list. Displayed to the right of the Tool Settings roll-up is the dropdown selection of Brush tool styles which will be explored later in this chapter.

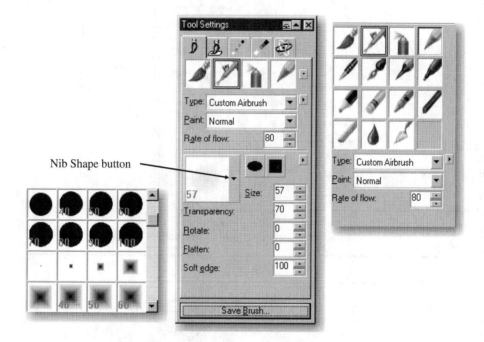

Nib Shape button

Tool Settings Roll-up

There are five tabs on the Tool Settings roll-up which can be opened by selecting roll-ups in the View menu and choosing Tool Settings, pressing CTRL-F8 or by double-clicking one of the tool buttons. With the roll-up open, you can select the brush preset and the Type of selected brush you want. For example Figure 10-1 shows the Airbrush selected and the six presets from the Type list.

Tool Selection

On the first tab, shown next, the top of the Tool Settings Roll-up displays the last four brushes used. To view all available tools, click the down arrow and icons representing all of the available choices are displayed as shown in Figure 10-2. To select a brush, click its icon. You can achieve different effects with each brush by

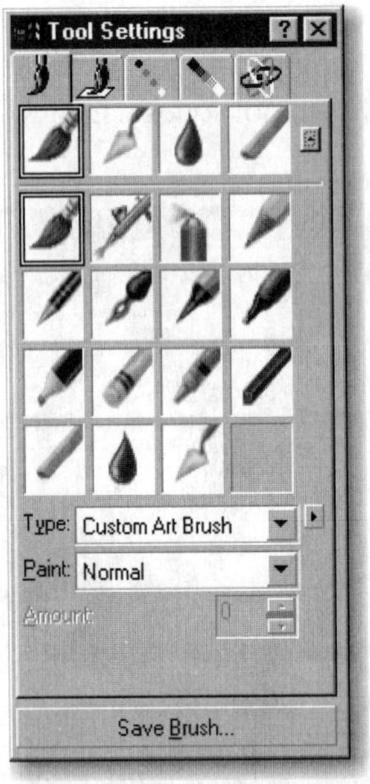

The
available
Type
settings
with
Airbrush
selected

FIGURE 10-1

Each
selected
tool offers
several
different
types from
which to
choose

FIGURE 10-2

using different types (available in the Types box), or by customizing different brush settings. The icon at the far left on the Property Bar opens the same menu.

Type

This setting contains all of the saved brush styles for the selected tool. Many of these preset styles have names that indicate how they operate examples of which are shown in Figure 10-2.

Brush Reset /Symmetry Options

Figure 10-3 shows the arrow (pointing outward) to the right of the Type: box that opens a menu that allows you to reset the brushes to their default values. You can reset a single brush, i.e. a brush type or all of the brush types. This is really handy when you have been making all kinds of changes to the tools and need to return them to their original values. You can open a similar menu by clicking the Brush Reset Option button on the Property Bar.

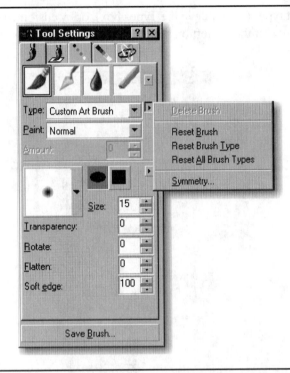

The Brush
Reset
Option
button
selected
from the
Tool
Settings
roll-up

FIGURE 10-3

Paint

This setting determines the way the paint pixels are applied to the image. There are up to 25 different modes, as shown in Figure 10-4. The Paint Mode button on the Property Bar offers the same selection of Paint modes. How these modes work is discussed in detail in the user's manual.

Rate of Flow

This setting is only available on the Airbrush and Spray Can category of brush tools. Rate of Flow controls the rate at which the effect or paint is applied to the image, ranging from 1 to 100. A higher value results in a more pronounced effect or heavier application. It controls the amount of the paint applied over time. If you have a low setting and place the tool over a spot and hold it there without moving the brush, the area will continue to have the effect applied at the rate set by this setting. This setting is called Amount in the Property Bar and replaces the Transparency setting on the Property Bar when either the Airbrush or Spray Can tool is selected.

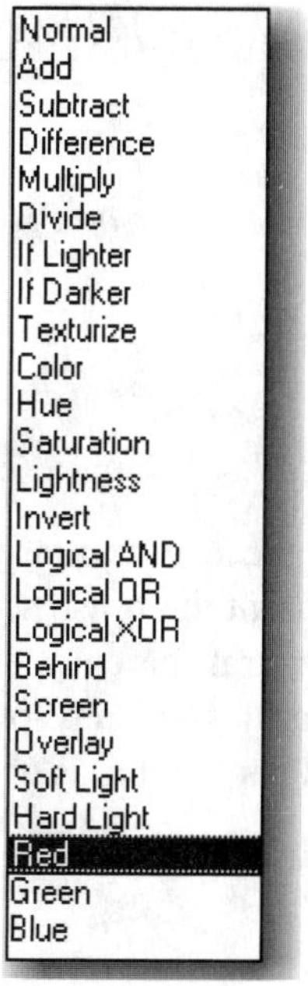

Normal
Add
Subtract
Difference
Multiply
Divide
If Lighter
If Darker
Texturize
Color
Hue
Saturation
Lightness
Invert
Logical AND
Logical OR
Logical XOR
Behind
Screen
Overlay
Soft Light
Hard Light
Red
Green
Blue

PHOTO-
PAINT 8
has a large
selection of
Paint Merge
modes

FIGURE 10-4

Shape Buttons

These determine the shape of the nib. The two basic shapes selectable by buttons are Oval and Square. In addition to the two basic shapes, you can choose an existing Nib from the Nib Shape box, which offers a large selection of different sizes and shapes. In addition to the size and shape of the selected nib, the custom preview area in the Tool Settings roll-up shows other characteristics of the nib. For example, if a nib has a high transparency setting or a soft edge, the preview area will reflect it in the nib that is displayed.

Size

This setting allows adjustment of Round or Square paintbrush sizes from 0 to 999 pixels. The size of nib selected is shown by red text in the corner of the display for nibs whose size is greater than 30 pixels. The nib size can also be adjusted by moving the nib size slider or entering in a value in the nib size box on the Property Bar .

10

TIP: *New to PHOTO-PAINT 8 is the ability to adjust the nib size interactively on the image by holding down the SHIFT key and dragging the brush.*

 NOTE: *In earlier versions of PHOTO-PAINT, the size of the Custom brush was not adjustable. Now all of the brushes can have their size changed.*

Transparency

This setting (range 0-99) sets the level of transparency of the brush stroke. The higher the setting, the more transparent the brush stroke. At a high setting, the color acts like a tint. A setting of 0 has no transparency, whereas a setting of 99 makes the brush stroke almost invisible regardless of any other settings. The availability of the Transparency setting in the Property bar is dependent upon the tool selected.

Rotate

This setting (range 0-360 degrees) rotates the nib by the amount entered. You can see the effect of the rotating in the preview window as the change is being applied. The Rotate setting is not available in the default configuration of the Property Bar for all tools.

Flatten

The Flatten setting (range 0-99 %) controls the height of the nibs. Flatten values are in percentage of height nib height. You can see the effect of the flattening in the preview window as the change is being applied. Using combinations of the Rotation and Flatten settings allow you to create nibs for creating calligraphic strokes among other things.

Soft edge

This determines the amount of transparency at the edges of the nib. Large settings produce soft edges which make the brush stroke the least dense at the edges. Low settings produce hard edges that are dense up to the edge, with little to no softening, depending on the nib size and other brush settings. The preview box displays the softness of the nib selected.

Save Brush

This saves any customization made to a brush setting. Clicking the Save Brush button opens the Save Brush dialog box as shown below. Entering a name and clicking the OK button saves all of the current brush's settings in the Type list for the currently selected tool. The name will only appear in the Type: box for the Tool under which it was saved. This command is available as Save Brush in the Brush Reset Options button in the Property Bar with some tools.

Controlling Texture, Water Colors and Brush Strokes Settings

The second tab, shown in Figure 10-5, controls the Texture and Watercolors settings. This tab has the greatest effect on any painterly effects produced by the brushstrokes. Painterly effects are brushstrokes that appear to be made by natural media tools like pastels, oils, etc. The controls on this tab are not available for the Image Sprayer, Mask Brush, Local UnDo and Object Transparency Brush tool.

Brush Texture

Brush texture uses a bitmap texture to cause the paint color or effect to be applied in an uneven pattern so that it simulates the patterning exhibited by application of materials, like pastels or chalk over rough media. The setting has a range of 0-100. A setting of zero produces no effect regardless of the texture pattern that is loaded. A setting of 100 produces a rough texture when the brush tool is applied. Figure 10-6 shows a sample of 6 different textures of the 10 that are provided with Corel PHOTO-PAINT.

To load a different texture, click the left-pointing arrow and select Load A Texture from the menu. By default, COREL\DRAW80\PHOTOPNT\BRUSHTXR folder contains ten texture files. Select a drive and folder in the Look in list box, and double-click the texture file name to load it.

10

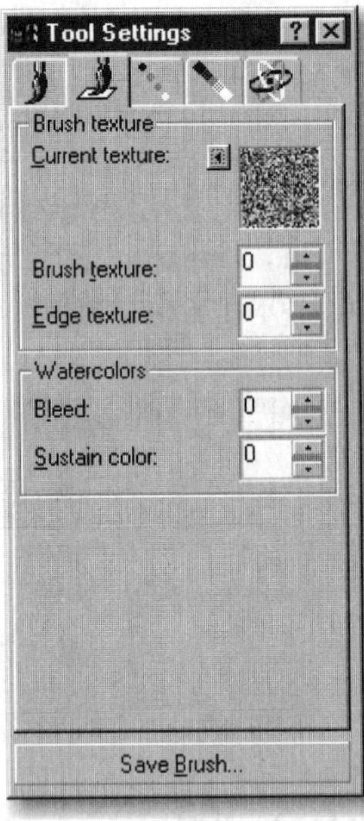

The second
tab of the
Tool
Settings
roll-up.

FIGURE 10-5

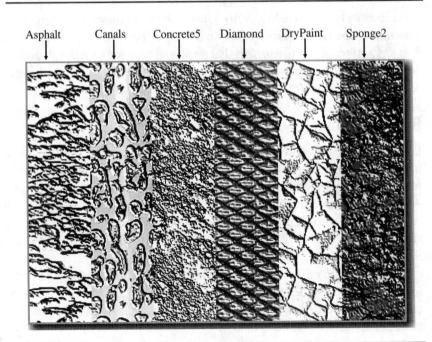

Asphalt   Canals   Concrete5   Diamond   DryPaint   Sponge2

Samples of
several of
the
available
brush
textures .

FIGURE 10-6

TIP: *The best images to use for brush textures possess high contrast. The dark area paints and the light area doesn't.*

Edge Texture

This works like Brush Texture, except it controls the amount of "texture" (0-100) that is applied to the edge of the stroke. Edge texture is only apparent if the nib has a soft edge. To adjust this setting, type a new value or adjust the existing one using the scroll arrows. A higher value will result in a more pronounced effect.

Bleed

In the Watercolors section, the Bleed setting determines how much pixels in the image are affected when the brush is dragged across them. The Bleed setting controls the application of color throughout the brushstroke in conjunction with the Sustain Color control. With a range from 0-100, the greatest effect is seen when set to 100 and no effect is seen when it is set to zero.

Sustain Color

This setting controls the application of color throughout the brushstroke in conjunction with the Bleed control. A brushstroke with a bleed value will, during the course of an extended brushstroke, run out of paint and simply smear the background colors (as though you were painting with a wet brush). With Sustain Color, traces of the paint color remain throughout the brushstroke.

Dab Attributes and Dab Color Variation

The third tab is divided into two parts, Dab Attributes and Dab Color variation, as shown in Figure 10-7. This tab controls the number of dabs as well as the spacing, spread, and fade-out effects applied when any of the brush tools are applied.

Number of dabs

A brushstroke is composed of a number of dabs as determined by the Number of dabs setting. This value, and the Spacing value, can have a significant effect on the speed at which your computer creates a brushstroke. It is recommended that you keep the number of dabs low and the spacing as high as practical to achieve the effect

10

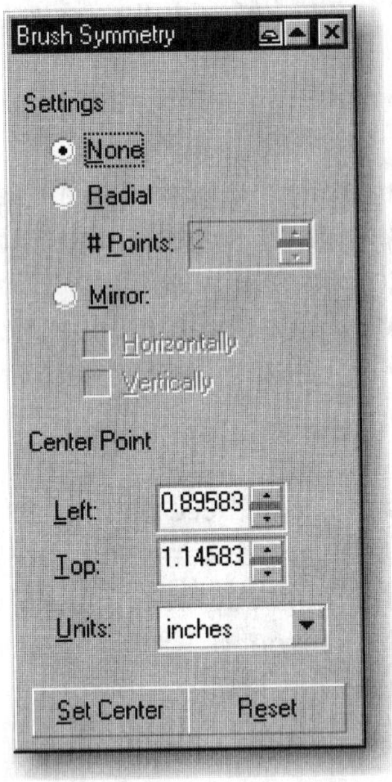

The
Attributes
and Dab
Color
variation tab

FIGURE 10-7

you require. The Spread and Spacing controls let you specify the layout of the dabs along the brushstroke.

Spacing

This sets the distance, in pixels, between applications of the brush. To create a brush stroke, the pointing device draws a line across the image. At a frequency determined by the Spacing setting, the brush is applied to the line. For example, if a brush stroke is made with a Spacing setting of 5 (pixels), Corel PHOTO-PAINT will produce the selected brush on the image area at a spacing of every 5 pixels. While it may seem that a setting of 1 would be desired, a lower setting slows down the generation of the brush stroke considerably. It can be really slow on some systems, especially when using a large nib (>70). When a large brush is being used, the Spacing setting can be larger (and this is recommended) because of the overlap caused by the larger brush. A number of brushstrokes are illustrated at different Spacing settings to show these effects next.

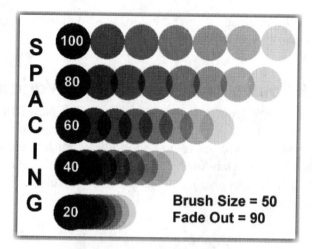

Spread

As the brushstroke moves along a line this setting controls the distance between dabs along the line of the brushstroke. The setting is a measure of how many pixels each dab can be off of the stroke centerline. Higher values mean the dabs can appear greater distances from the centerline of the brushstroke. A setting of zero means each dab will be placed on the line of the brushstroke. For example, if a setting of 5 is used each dab of the brushstroke will be placed within a 5 pixel radius of the brushstroke.

Constraining and Automating the Brush Tools

With a steady hand, it is theoretically possible to maintain a straight line with a brush tool, but it is very difficult. Fortunately, Corel provides some features that allow you to create straight lines with any of the brush tools. Use the CTRL key to constrain the tool to a vertical or horizontal direction. Pressing the SHIFT key changes the direction of constraint. You can automatically apply the Paint tool along a straight line between two points by clicking the brush at the beginning of a line and holding down the ALT key and clicking at the end of the line. The Paint tool will be applied between the two points automatically.

Dab Color Variation

These three sliders control the amount, if any, of variation applied to the color of the individual dabs on a brushstroke. If Hue is set to zero, then the hue of the stroke will not change. If it is set to the maximum (100%) then each dab of the brushstroke can

10

be literally any color in the spectrum. Likewise the Saturation and Lightness sliders control the how much color and lightness is in each dab.

Stroke Attributes and Stroke Color Variation

The fourth tab, shown below, is also divided into two parts. They are Stroke Attributes and Stroke Color Variations. Stroke Attributes controls fade and other parameters to make a mouse movement look like a brush made it. The Stroke Attributes differs from the Dab Attributes in that it controls the amount of variation applied to the entire stroke rather than individual dabs. Stroke Color allows you to create multi-colored brushstrokes.

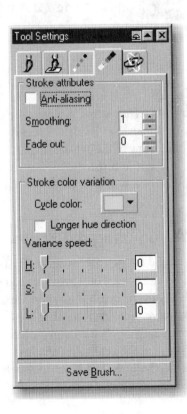

Anti-aliasing and Smoothing

Enabling the Anti-aliasing option produces smooth-looking curved or diagonal edges and prevents jagged edges from appearing. In combination with the anti-aliasing check box, the Smoothing setting determines how smooth the brush stroke of the tools are. Both of these controls determine how faithfully the brushstrokes follow the mouse/stylus movements. Without Anti-aliasing and Smoothing enabled, the lines made with a mouse will appear to be very jagged. Apply too much smoothness and any sharp corners in the line become smoothed out to the point you can no longer recognize the original variations that were applied.

Cumulative

This option is only available when using the Clone Tool or the Effects Tools. When enabled, the effects of brushstrokes are cumulative. When using the Clone tool to repair an area, this setting can catch you by surprise. Depending on whether it is enabled or not determines if the source point of the Clone tool reads the original image or the newly cloned image. Confused? Just remember this: If you are restoring an area of an image and suddenly you notice that an area you have already cloned out of existence is reappearing as the source point passes over it, change the Cumulative setting. When using Effect tools you may want to disabled it to prevent the cumulative effect of each brushstroke from adding to one another. For example, if you are applying a tint to an area that you want to appear uniform, you must disable the Cumulative option.

Fade Out

This setting determines the length of the brush stroke before it fades entirely by adjusting the rate at which the brush stroke disappears. This is similar to adjusting the pressure of the brush against the canvas as the paint is applied. The greater the Fade Out value, the quicker the fade-out of the brush stroke occurs as shown in the illustration below. As the Fade out value decreases, the amount of fade-out applied to the brush stroke diminishes; a value of 0 turns off the Fade Out function completely.

Fade Out works by counting the number of brush applications to determine when to begin applying the gradual fade-out function. This is important for the following reason. Since spacing controls the distance between brush applications, increasing spacing increases the distance that the brush stroke will go before Fade Out begins.

Stroke Color Variation

This set of controls is new with the release of PHOTO-PAINT 8. With it you can control the variation of hue, saturation and lightness along the length of the brushstroke. With the three sliders set to zero, the controls are turned off. By experimenting with the settings of the sliders and the selection of the Cycle color, you can produce everything from brushstrokes that shift gradually from one color to another to multi-colored lines that repeatedly cycle through a set color combination.

Orbits

The fifth tab is the Orbit tab. Based on the appearance of the icon on the tab you may have thought it to be the atomic tab. Orbits is an exciting new feature to

PHOTO-PAINT that creates wild and crazy brushstrokes. It's like an old Spirograph on steroids. Figure 10-8, which you thought was a page from a 1890 biology book, shows a few brushstrokes produced by presets included in the Orbits tab.

Rather than try to explain each control in detail, here is the big picture. The most important control is Enable Orbits. When it is not checked, the Orbits feature is disabled. Like all of the other tab settings, if you save a brush with the Orbits enabled, the orbits will be enabled anytime the saved brush is selected.

Number of orbits is similar to dabs. In the preset Rings, increasing the number of orbits makes the rings darker because the are applied to the same spot many times. The Radius isn't the size of the brush but the size of the orbits produced. Rotation speed can be thought of as how many times per brushstroke the orbit is going to cycle through its pattern. Grow Speed and Grow Amount control the overall amplitude and duration of the cycle. For more detailed (and accurate) descriptions of how each tool works place your cursor on the item in question and click your right mouse button. When the "What's this?" box appears, click and the context-sensitive description will appear.

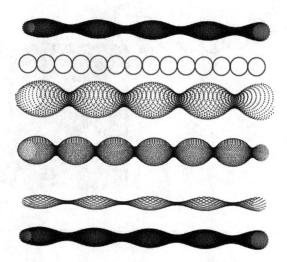

Orbits
brush
stokes
produce
fantastic
results

FIGURE 10-8

What Can You Do with Orbits?

Let your imagination run wild. I recommend playing with the existing presets first before you begin rolling your own variations. While you are playing (sorry—experimenting), use the orbits in concert with other PHOTO-PAINT features. For example, you can create an elliptical mask and then apply Stroke to Mask using the Preset Rings with the result shown in Figure 10-9a. From there, I made it into an object, filled each ring with a radial fill, and then applied a perspective transform to the object. After adding a drop shadow and a background, I had—in less than 5 minutes-faux pearls as shown in Figure 10-9b.

Brush Symmetry

Brush Symmetry is the other new paint feature in PHOTO-PAINT 8. The engineers who designed it really like it a lot. The Brush Symmetry roll-up (CTRL-F10) can also be found on the Tool Settings roll-up and in the Property Bar in the Reset Brush

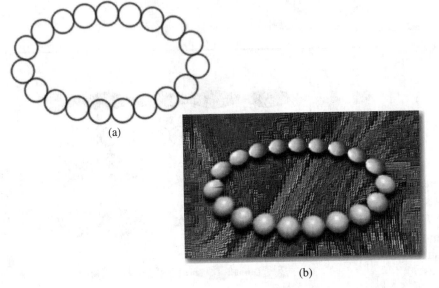

a) Applying the Rings Orbit to an ellipse using Stroke to Mask. b) The image served as the foundation for the completed work

(a)

(b)

FIGURE 10-9

options—you remember, it is opened with the little button to the right of the Type settings—or the reset Reset Brush Options button on the Property Bar. The Brush Symmetry roll-up is shown next.

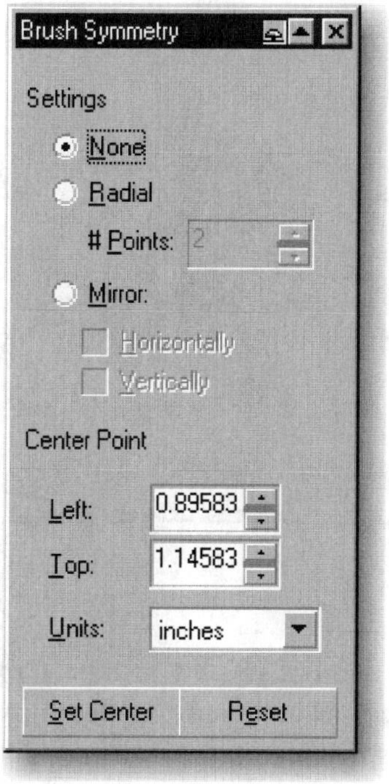

The Brush Symmetry roll-up, shown above, allows you to choose one of two symmetry modes, Radial and Mirror. The Radial option allows you to define the number of points (2-100) that will simultaneously be drawn about the center point as you drag your mouse or stylus. Mirror just mirrors whatever brushstroke you apply either Horizontally, Vertically or both. After choosing a Mode, you must may select a center point in the image or use the one the program maintains, which is the geometric center of the image. Selecting a point on the image is simple. When you move the cursor over the image, a crosshair appears and the cursor becomes a hand. At this point, click the cursor at the location that you want to be the center point. If you are numerically oriented, you can also enter the Center Point's position in the dialog box.

10

The samples of the two basic Brush Symmetries Radial and Mirror are shown below. The interior star was made with the Radial setting (63 points) and the area outside was made using the Mirror brush.

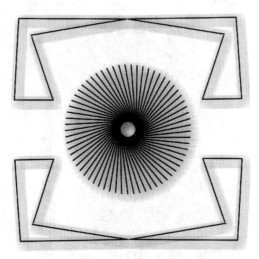

Making Doilies

Here is a simple exercise that has you use both the Orbits and Symmetry together. If the idea of making doilies is not manly enough for you, think of it as designing telescopic sight crosshairs for large caliber weapons like the ones in Eraser.

1. Create a new image that is 3 x 3 inches at 150 dpi with Blue paper color.

2. Select the Paint tools and open the Tools Setting roll-up (CTRL-F7). Select the paintbrush icon and, from the Type drop-down list, choose Sm. Hard. Click on the Orbits tab and check Enable Orbits. Select Rings from the Presets list.

3. Open the Brush Symmetry dialog box. Check Radial and enter 18 for the number of points. By default, the center will be the center of the image, so click OK.

4. Left-click the White color swatch to change the Paint color. Click the Create New Object button at the bottom of the Objects Docker.

5. Place the cursor on the image and you will notice the cursor changes. One of the tiny shapes is a square and the others are x's. The square is in charge. Move you mouse up and down and you will notice our circle

rotates. Place the circle about 1/2 an inch in from the right edge and about equidistant from the top and bottom. Click and drag you cursor toward the middle. The result is shown below.

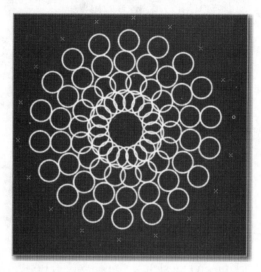

6. Now start again at the same spot and drag you mouse down to make the cursors rotate. Roate just enough so the circle cursor is half way between the two spokes of the doily (gun sight) we made in Step 5. The resulting image is shown below.

10

7. Repeat Step 6. The image is shown below.

8. For those working on gun sights, you are done. For those of us working on doilies, there is an additional step. With the Object Picker tool, select the doily and from the Effects menu choose 3D Effects. Select Emboss. Click the reset button and change color to the Original color. Click OK. Add a Drop shadow that tickles your fancy and there you have it.

 TIP: *Go back and turn off the Symmetry or you will get really confused the next time you go to use a brush tool.*

So, what can you do with a doily? Since it is an object I could apply a perspective transform to it so it would appear I was viewing it at an angle. I could place an object like BOOKWIG.CPT on top of it and it would probably look like Figure 10-10. Yeah, I could do all that, but I don't think I will.

The Paint Tools

 The Paint tools are virtual equivalent of a fully-stocked artist's studio, but with the advantages of being able to work around things like the law of gravity. Choose from a wide selection of brush tools, such as water color, oil pastel, felt markers, chalk,

With the Radial and Orbits we were able to make the intricately designed object under the book.

FIGURE 10-10

crayons, several types of pen, pencils, spraypaint, and an artistic brush with a wide variety of settings. Each of the preset paint tools has a number of variations built in, and you can customize any aspect to suit your specific needs. Many of the tools are very similar in their appearance and purpose. For example, the Air brush and the Spray Can are different brush tools but are very similar in the brushstrokes they produce. In the following section is a brief description of the Paint tools and examples of the brushstrokes they produce. For some of the Paint tools, I have included some hands-on exercises.

NOTE: *The names of some of the brushes may seem, at times, inconsistent. For example, if you select the Pastel tool, it will say Oil Pastel. That is the first of several choices. I have named each tool according to its overall description rather than the name associated with the default brush type.*

Paintbrush Tool

The Paintbrush tool offers a wide selection of Types. These types are also available with some of the other tools. I am not an artist, so I do very little original work with this tool. It is a great way to add texture to objects. The following hands-on exercise teaches how to create a wood texture using the Paintbrush tool.

Creating A Wood Texture

Even with the addition of Corel TEXTURE this technique offers a quick way to make a texture that looks remarkably like real wood.

1. Create a new file that is 6 x 4 inches, 24-bit color at 72 dpi, with a White Paper color.

2. Click the color gold in the on-screen palette with the left mouse button, changing the Paint color. Click the Text tool button on the Toolbox and click inside the image area. Change the font to Kabel Ult BT, the Size to 96, and inter-line spacing to 70. Select the Center Text button.

3. Enter the text CUSTOM WOOD WORKING as shown in Figure 10-11. Click the Object Picker tool. Move the text to the center of the image. Open the Objects Docker and select the text object.

4. Double-click the Paint tool in the Toolbox. In the Tool Settings roll-up, choose the Paintbrush and in Type: select Medium Fine Streaks. In Paint: choose Logical AND. The Type: setting will change to Custom Art Brush. Click on the color brown in the on-screen palette.

5. Click inside the image at the point to the upper-left of the word CUSTOM as indicated by the left arrow in Figure 10-11. Hold down the ALT key and click at the point indicated by the right arrow. Holding down the ALT key causes a straight line to be applied between the two points. Click again on the left size moving the position of the cursor down approximately the width of the cursor and repeat the procedure. Continue to do this until the brushstrokes cover all of the text.

6. Click the Object Picker tool and select the text. In the Objects Docker window, make sure the Lock Transparency is not checked.

7. From the Effects menu select 3D Effects and choose Emboss. When the Emboss dialog box opens, click the Reset button and then change the Emboss color to Original color. Click the OK button. The resulting image should look like Figure 10-12.

8. In the Objects Docker window check the Lock Transparency. In the Objects menu, choose Drop Shadow and change the Offset direction to 225, Distance to 0.05, Direction to Average, Feather to 10 and Opacity to 75. Click the OK button.

Text
showing
Paint brush
tool start
and ending
points.

FIGURE 10-11

10

It almost
looks like
wood after
embossing

FIGURE 10-12

9. In Objects Dockers window, select the background. From the Edit menu choose Fill. When the Edit Fill & Transparency dialog box opens, click the Bitmap Fill button and then click the Edit button. From the Bitmap Fill dialog box click the Load button. On the Corel CD-ROM locate and select the file EXERCISE\TILES\ WOOD27L.CPT. Click the OK button three times to close all of the dialog boxes. The result is shown in Figure 10-13.

10. Close the file and do not save any changes when asked.

The Airbrush Tool

The Airbrush tool is one of the most often used Brush tools to create shadows and highlights on images. It produce a very soft diffuse edge. The following exercise depends on the Airbrush tool for the shadows.

Making A Flag

My editor for the first PHOTO-PAINT book, Chris Denny, is a race car buff. I was thinking about making something that would spruce up his Web page when I came

The
finished
project

FIGURE 10-13

up with this hands-on exercise. Our objective is to make a checkered flag, the kind that is associated with the finish of a race. During this exercise we will be using some Effects filters that you will read about later in the book. Since there isn't a checker pattern in PHOTO-PAINT we must first make one. So, that will be our first task.

1. Create a New image that is 2 x 2 inch, 24-bit color at 72 dpi. When the image is open, enable Snap to Grid (CTRL-Y) and from the View menu select Grid. If your Paint color is not black, click the color black in the on-screen palette with the left mouse button.

2. Select the Rectangle Shape tool from the Toolbox (F6). Click at the top-left corner of the image and create a black square that covers the upper-left corner of the image. Repeat this procedure to fill the bottom-right corner with Black.

3. Save the file as CHECKER.CPT. Remember where you saved the file. Close the file and open a new file that is 6 x 5 inches, 24-bit color at 72 dpi.

4. Select the Rectangle tool (F6). Open the Tool Settings roll-up (CTRL-F8), click the Bitmap fill icon and click the Edit button. When the Bitmap Fill dialog box opens, click the Load button. Locate and select the file CHECKERS.CPT. Click the Open button. In the Bitmap Fill dialog box, uncheck Use original size in the Tile section. Click OK.

5. In the Tools menu ensure Snap to Grid is enabled. Enable the Rulers (CTRL-R). Ensure Render to object is enabled either by checking the option in the Rectangle tool's Tool Settings roll-up or by clicking the Render to Object button in the Property bar. Beginning about an inch from the top and left side, click and drag a rectangle that is 4 x 3 inches. Disable Snap to Grid and the Rulers. The result is shown in Figure 10-14.

6. Select the Object Picker tool. With the object selected in the Objects Dockers window and Lock Transparency unchecked, open the Effects menu and choose 2D Effects and then Ripple. Change the settings to Ripple mode: Single wave; Period: 50; Amplitude: 15; Direction angle: 90. Click the OK button. The resulting image is shown in Figure 10-15.

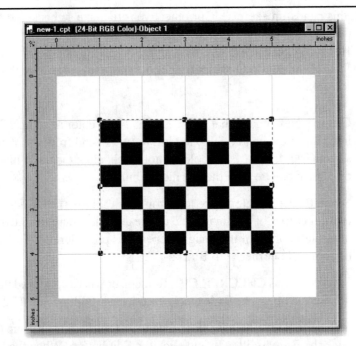

The
checkered
flag made
from the
bitmap
pattern we
created

FIGURE 10-14

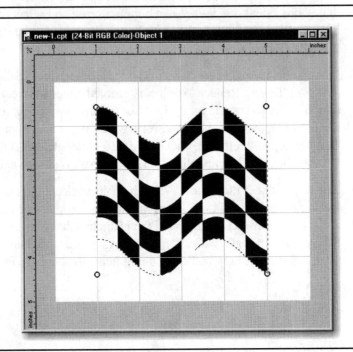

The result
of the
Ripple filter
applied to
the pattern

FIGURE 10-15

Enable the Lock Transparency by checking the option in the Objects Manager.

7. Disable the Snap to Grid (CTRL-Y). Double-click the Paint Tool button in the Toolbox. From the Tool Settings roll-up select the Airbrush. If it is not one of the top four icons, click the button to the right of the icons and select it from the list, then close the list again. Change the Type: setting to Wide Cover. Change the Size to 60 and the Transparency setting to 60.

8. Place the cursor at the point indicated as A on Figure 10-16. Click once and let go of the mouse button. Place (don't drag) the cursor at the point marked B. Hold down the ALT key and click the mouse button again. Now repeat that procedure at the other points beginning with the point marked C. Feel free to apply the Airbrush tool to any area more than once - I did. Especially areas where the white of the flag disappears in the white of the

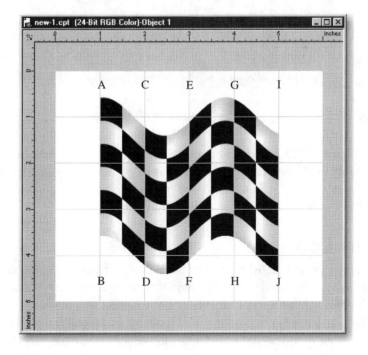

The addition of airbrush strokes at the points shown adds shadows.

FIGURE 10-16

background. Always use the edge of the airbrush when possible to get the smoothest efects.

9. From the Effects menu choose 3D Effects and select Mesh Warp filter. Click on the control nodes in the filter dialog box and move them as shown below.

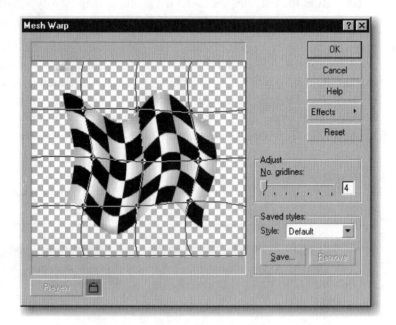

10. Close the image and don't save any of the changes.

In Figure 10-17 I have taken a flag like the one we just created and used the Draw tools to place what appears to be a rope holding it against the wind and then placed a sky background to finish the image. Figure 10-18 shows an example of what you can do with the flags once you have created them.

Spray Can

The Spray Can and the Airbrush tools share the same controls, but the brushstokes produced by each is noticeably different. Where the Airbrush produces soft diffused patterns of paint, the Spray Can creates a brushstroke that tends to appear spattered. This tool is used for creating a textured look to a surface. It is especially good when working with fonts that are associated with stencils—like the Stencil BT font.

A flag the
brickyard
would use

FIGURE 10-17

The Finish
Line was
created
using two
copies of
the flag
made in this
exercise

FIGURE 10-18

10

Pencil Brush

 The Pencil brush offers different types that produce a brushstroke that looks like it was created with a pencil. If you are artistically gifted you can actually create images that appear to be pencil drawings using the pencil brush in conjunction with a stylus and digitizer pad. The recommendation for the stylus and pad is based on the well-known fact that most people on this planet cannot write, much less draw, with a mouse. If you are one of the few that can write and draw with a mouse, you are fortunate and you need to get out more.

Making Tracing Paper

Along with the Pencil brush, the other pen -related tools require some artistic ability and a stylus to take advantage of their potential. However, there is a way to work around the lack of artistic gifting -use tracing paper. PHOTO-PAINT doesn't have any tracing paper commands but it is easy to create. Ensuring the Lock Transparency is not enabled and with help from the Grid, it is possible to make excellent tracing paper. It is accomplished with the following steps:

1. Load the image you want to trace.

2. In the Objects Docker window (CTRL-F7), ensure Lock Transparency is not enabled and that the New Object button appears to the left of the Delete button with the trashcan icon. You now have a transparent layer over the original and can trace to your heart's delight without affecting the original image.

3. You may find it helpful to display the grid by selecting the Grids and Ruler Setup in the Tools menu.

 TIP: *If you are used to working with pencil and charcoal, you may find yourself looking for a smudge stick. Corel provided it. It is called Light Rub and is described later in this chapter.*

Ball Point Brush

 This brush tool makes brushstrokes that mimic a ball point pen. You may be wondering why you would use a computer costing several thousand dollars to make brush strokes that look like they were made with a 20-cent disposable pen. Actually, I was wondering the same thing.

Calligraphy Brush

This pen can be used to add some real "non-computer-looking" touches to images created in PHOTO-PAINT. One of the benefits of PHOTO-PAINT over a vector program like DRAW is this ability to look "real." The Calligraphy brush, like the Pencil brush, is best used with a stylus and digitizer pad. The shape of the nibs with this brush tool makes possible many of the strokes associated with calligraphy. If you are using a pressure sensitive stylus you can achieve even more "realistic" appearing pen strokes.

In the illustration below is a treble clef that was made using the Calligraphy brush.

Fine Felt Pen brush

This Brush tool operates like a real felt pen right down to the part where it makes darker spots when you keep it in one place too long. For drawing line art and cartoons in general this one is my favorite. You really need a stylus to use this tool effectively.

Felt Marker brush

This tool replicates the brushstroke of those felt markers we all get to make out garage sale signs. Included in the different Type settings is one called Dry Tip which drags out colors irregularly just like a felt marker that is running out of ink does.

Hi-Liter Tool

This is a fantastic tool. It acts just like the highlighter pens you buy at office supply stores. One of the things you can do with it is to scan the text you want to highlight with a scanner. Bring in the image of the scanned paper and use the highlight tool

10

to highlight the text and then print it out on your color printer or you could just use a real highlighter pen that costs less than a dollar and highlight the original. All kidding aside, it is good for a quick tint or shadow.

Chalk Brush

 This Brush tool requires two things to look correct: the background should be a dark color and the Paint color should be light; a small nib is more effective. The large nib that is the default for the brush is too large and it ends up looking like the Pastel brush.

Wax Crayon Brush

 The Chalk, Crayon and Pastel tools share similar properties. The Wax Crayon tool has a hard texture that makes the distinctive waxy look. For a more realistic appearance you may want to apply it as a new object in Layer mode and then Emboss it.

Light Rub Brush

 This is the tool you use with the Pencil and other pen-related tools to smear the pencil/pen strokes. It also contains the Custom Charcoal Type setting. Just as the Chalk brush needs to be on a dark background, the Charcoal brush needs to be on a light background with a dark Paint color. The viewer's mind expects charcoal to be dark.

Oil Pastel Brush

 If you are working in grayscale, this will look a lot like the Charcoal. There are a lot of choices for different pastel textures, making this a versatile Brush tool.

Watercolor Brush

 This brush mixes all of the adjoining colors as it is dragged on the image. It can produce a brushstroke similar to watercolors and is good for making part of an image look like someone spilled water on it.

Pointillism Brush

 The Pointillism brush offers the greatest variety of settings, not in number of settings but in how different the types are from each other.

The Effect Tools

The Effect tools discussed in this chapter are located on the brush tools flyout in PHOTO-PAINT, hence the terms tools and brushes are used interchangeably throughout the chapters. The Effect tools are accessed by clicking the Effect Tools button in the Brush Tools flyout of the Toolbox. Selection and configuration of the tools is via the Tool Settings roll-up. Effect tools offer a rich assortment of different effects, many of which can be found in the Effects and Image menus. Unlike their menu-based counterparts, the Effect tools can be applied selectively in small areas, sometimes without the necessity of creating a mask. Although the effects provided by many of the tools can also be achieved through various menu commands, others are unique to the Effect Tools and not available elsewhere in Corel PHOTO-PAINT. In Corel PHOTO-PAINT 8, they can be accessed from the Property Bar and the Tool Settings roll-up. There are twelve different tools that constitute the Effects tools. Like the Paint tools, the Effects tools offer multiple Types for each tool. We will begin our exploration of the Effect Tools with the Smear Tool.

NOTE: *The names of some of the Effect tools may seem, at times, inconsistent. For example, if you select the Smear tool, it will say Pointy Smear. That is the default Type setting. I have named each tool according to its overall description rather than the name associated with the default type setting.*

The Smear Tool

The Smear tool smears colors. The same tool in Adobe Photoshop is called the Smudge tool (which can get confusing, because there is a Smudge tool in Corel PHOTO-PAINT). The Smear tool spreads colors in a picture, producing an effect similar to dragging your finger through wet oil paint. The size and shape of the Smear tool is set from either the Property Bar or the Tool Settings roll-up.

10

For Corel PHOTO-PAINT 5 Users

In Corel PHOTO-PAINT 5, these tools are called the Freehand Editing tools, and they are all located on a flyout. The Freehand Editing tools are no longer located on a flyout. They are now accessed through the Tool Settings roll-up.

Using the Smear Tool

The purpose of this tool is to smear colors. I know I said that before, but it's worth repeating, because many first-time users of Corel PHOTO-PAINT misuse the Smear tool. That is, they use it to soften color transitions. That is the purpose of the Blur tool. Think of it this way: The results of using the Smear tool are not that much different from finger painting (except you don't have to wash your hands after you're done). Blending an area causes the distinction between colors to become less pronounced. Choosing a blending amount of 0% in the Tool Settings roll-up causes no blending to occur although it stills smears existing pixels, while an amount of 100% will give you the maximum amount of blending possible. Adjacent pixels must be different colors for the effect to work correctly.

 TIP: *Make a practice of using the Checkpoint command (which makes a temporary copy of the image that can be quickly restored) before you begin application of the Smear tool or any other freehand editing tool.*

Have the Smear Tool Settings roll-up open when you work with this tool. For retouching, the Soft Edge and Transparency settings should be adjusted to produce the greatest effect without being obvious. A higher Soft Edge setting causes the edges of the Smear tool to appear more feathered, which is desirable for most Smear tool applications. Fade Out and Spacing, on the third tab, are not the critical settings. That said, you might want to play with the Fade Out settings for applications where you do not want the effect to end abruptly. The effect of the Smear tool is additive. Every time you apply it to the image, it will smear the pixels, no matter how many times you apply it.

For retouching, you may end up "scrubbing" the area with the tool to get the effect desired. When retouching a photo, you do not want a solid color after you are done—you need to have texture for the subject to look real.

 TIP: *If you start the Smear tool well off of the image, it pulls the pixels (Paper color) onto the image. This can be used to give the brush-stroke effect on the edge.*

The last application of the tool can be removed with the Undo command (CTRL-Z), provided it was applied with one continuous stroke without letting go of the mouse button.

Creating Paper Letters or Numbers with the Smear Tool

The Smear tool is not limited to retouching photographs. The following hands-on exercise shows a little of what you can do with the Smear tool if you only apply a little imagination.

1. Create a new file that is 3 x 3 inches at 96 dpi.

2. Click the Text tool and place the numeral 8 in the middle of the image. Change the font to Futura XBlk BT at a size of 300.

3. Open the Objects Docker window (CTRL-F7) and insure the Lock Transparency is not checked.

4. Select the Effect Tools and from the Tool Settings roll-up (CTRL-F8) select the Smear tool. Click on the Nib tool preview window to the left of the shape buttons. When the Nibs appear scroll down the list until you find the nib that looks like the one shown below. After you have selected the nib change the Transparency setting from 0 to 50.

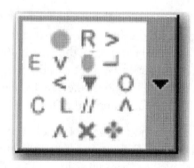

5. On the 8 click on the inside of the character and drag outward. This creates a ragged edge. Continue to do it until it looks something like the illustration below.

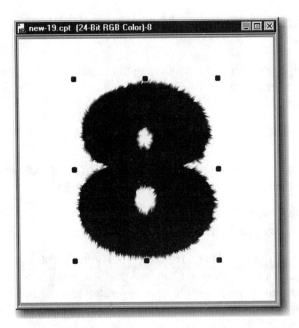

6. In the Objects Docker window check Lock Transparency. From the Edit menu select Fill. When the Edit Fill & Transparency dialog box opens, click the Bitmap Fill button and click the Edit button. From the drop-down list in the upper-left corner scroll down the list until you find the beige colored pattern that looks like canvas. Click OK to close the dialog box. Click OK again to apply the fill.

7. In the Objects Docker window uncheck Lock Transparency. From the Effects menu, choose 3-D Effects and choose Emboss. Click the Reset button, change the color to Original color and the Depth to 4. Click OK, the result is shown below.

8. I picked a darker wood background from the Bitmap Fill drop-down list. From the Object menu, choose Drop Shadow and change the settings of the dialog box to match the dark side of the image created by the Emboss filter. The finished project is shown below.

TIP: *If you are doing touchup work with the Effect tools, never count on an image being small enough to cover the sins of sloppy touch-up. With all of the fancy equipment in the world today, it is too easy for people to get a photo blown up to poster size, and that is when they might get real ugly about your touch-up work.*

The Smudge Tool

 Maybe it is just me, but the first time I began exploring the freehand editing tools, I thought Smear and Smudge sounded like they did the same thing. The Smudge tool in Corel PHOTO-PAINT is different from the tool with the same name in Adobe Photoshop. As it turns out, the Smudge tool adds texture by randomly mixing pixels in a selected area. It is like a can of spray paint that sucks up color from the area that it is currently over and then sprays it back onto the subject. Technically, it acts like a local color noise filter. I am not aware of any equivalent of this tool in Photoshop.

The Smudge Tool Settings

All of the controls are identical to those shown for the Smear tool with one exception. The Rate of Flow setting determines how fast the noise (texture) is placed on the image. A rate of flow of 1 causes the noise texture to flow very slowly; therefore, to create a noticeable change, the tool has to be held at the same location for a longer period.

Using the Smudge Tool

The Smudge tool adds texture. It is really color noise. The effect of the Smudge tool is additive. As long as you hold the button down, the effect is being applied, *even if the brush is not moving*.

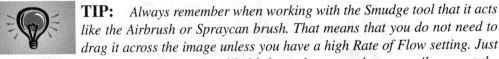 **TIP:** *Always remember when working with the Smudge tool that it acts like the Airbrush or Spraycan brush. That means that you do not need to drag it across the image unless you have a high Rate of Flow setting. Just put it over the area you want and hold down the mouse button until you get the desired effect.*

Thoughts about Retouching Photographs

While the Smudge tool removes highlights very well, it must be used with caution. When the bright highlights are removed, the image appears to be "flatter" than before. This is a drawback as we seek perfection in a photograph. Too many highlights may distract, but they also add contrast to the photograph, which deceives the human eye into thinking the image looks sharper. Another consideration when you are touching up photographs is whether what you are removing or modifying is necessary for the overall effect the photograph is trying to convey. Ultimately, you must make the call, but consider what you are changing before you change it. The only photographs that are digitally manipulated to perfection without regard to the original subject generally are the type that fold out of magazines.

The Brightness Tool

Brightness is the degree of light reflected from an image or transmitted through it. The Brightness tool can be used to both lighten and darken areas of the image. This tool is similar to the Dodge-and-Burn tool in Photoshop. These tools are simulations of traditional darkroom techniques. Photographers can improve their work by using the dodge and burn technique to block out or add light from a negative in order to enhance an image. In photography, dodging is used to lighten shadow areas (the darkest portions of an image), and burning is used to darken the highlights (the brightest portions of an image). Both dodging and burning can increase the detail in a photograph. The Brightness/Darkness tools produce the same effect in a digital image.

Using the Brightness Tool

The Brightness brush brightens or darkens areas in an image. Choosing an Amount of 100 in the Tool Settings roll-up causes all the black to be removed from the affected area, resulting in a much lighter color. Conversely, choosing -100, turns the affected area black.

Using the Brighten Tool

When using this tool, remember that you want the changes to be subtle, so make them in small increments using a Brighten tool with a round shape unless you are working near straight lines, as in a geometric figure. The effect of the tool is not additive. It will apply the effect at the level set in the Tool Setting dialog box each time it is applied.

To achieve any subtle effects in areas that have no naturally occurring visual boundaries, you must be prepared to apply the brush in several stages to reduce the sharp transition of the contrast effect.

The Contrast Tool

Contrast is the difference between the lightest and the darkest parts of an image. The Contrast tool intensifies the distinction between light and dark. It operates in the same manner as the Contrast filter, except that it can be applied to small areas without the need to create masks. The size, shape, and level of the Contrast tool is set from the Tool Settings roll-up. The Contrast Tool Presets are Custom Contrast, Increase Contrast and Decrease Contrast, plus small, medium, and large Soft and small, medium, and large Flat.

Using the Contrast Tool

Use the Contrast tool to bring out color in scanned photographs that appear dull or flat. Don't increase the contrast too much or the picture might appear overexposed. Some scanners have a tendency to darken the photographs when they are scanned, which causes them to lose contrast. Video images that are obtained through a frame grabber also tend to be dark. Both of these applications can benefit from the selective application of contrast.

Be careful not to overuse the Contrast tool, which can result in exaggerated white and dark areas. At the maximum Amount setting for Increase Contrast, highlights and shadows are blown out. That is, the areas that are lighter become white and almost all shades are lost. It is as if the image were converted to *bi-level*, which means the image is composed of only black and white pixels.

The effect of the Contrast tool is additive. It will apply the effect at the level set by the Tool Setting dialog box the first time it is applied. After the mouse button is released, progressive applications add to the effect already applied.

The Hue Tool

There are two hue tools, the Hue tool and the Hue Replacer tool, that at first seem to do the same thing. I found their names to be especially confusing. The Hue tool shifts the pixels of the image the number of degrees specified in the roll-up. The Hue Replacer is used to replace the hue of pixels in the image with the hue of the selected Paint (foreground) color.

How the Hue Tool Works

The Hue tool actually changes the color of the pixels it touches by the amount of the setting. The number of degrees entered in the Amount setting relates to the color wheel. The maximum setting is halfway around the color wheel (180 degrees), which represents the complementary color of the changed pixel.

TIP: *The best way to get the most realistic color change is to experiment with the transparency settings for the Hue tool. I have found that the default setting has insufficient transparency.*

Limiting the Effect of the Hue Tool

The Hue tool is like using the tint control on your color TV. The difficulty with using this tool is that it will shift every pixel you paint with the tool. To prevent unwanted hue shifts, it is best to mask the area first. By using the Color Mask, you can create a mask that is limited to the colors that you want to change. The best part about this combination of Color Mask and Hue tools is that you need not concern yourself if the Color Mask exists in an unwanted portion of the image, since you will limit the application of the Hue shift by where you place the Hue tool.

TIP: *Use the Hue brush to create interesting shifts in color within your image.*

10

The effect of the Hue brush tool is additive if the Cumulative option on the third tab of the Tool Settings roll-up is selected. It will apply the effect at the level set by the Tool Setting dialog box the first time it is applied then progressive applications after the mouse button is released will shift the hue of the pixels that much again.

The Hue Replacer Tool

The Hue Replacer tool replaces the hue of pixels in the image with the hue of the selected Paint (foreground) color. By changing the Hue, the color changes but the other two components (saturation and brightness) remain unchanged. The same considerations exist with the tool's masking and other settings, as mentioned with the Hue tool. The Hue Replacer brush changes the colors of pixels by the value set in the Amount value box. The color values relate to the degrees on the HSB Color Wheel.

Mixing Colors and Other Confusion

The amount of the original hue that remains is determined by the Amount setting in the Tool Settings roll-up or the Property Bar. All of the traditional rules of color you learned, like yellow + blue = green, do not apply with digital color. To complicate matters further with regard to predicting the color outcome the default color model of Corel PHOTO-PAINT is RGB. To accomplish the Hue mix, Corel PHOTO-PAINT must temporarily convert the model to HSB. This text is not here to discourage you, only to help you understand that predicting the color outcome is very difficult, and the best method I am aware of is experimentation.

 TIP: *Use this Hue Replacer effect tool to replace the color of an object without removing its shading and highlights. For instance, you can change the color of a red dress to yellow, while still retaining the shading that distinguishes the folds in the skirt.*

The Sponge (Saturation) Tool

The Sponge tool acts in the same manner as the Saturation filter, discussed in Chapter 9. The Sponge tool is used to increase the saturation or intensity of a color. When saturation is added to a color, the gray level of a color diminishes; thus it becomes less neutral. The Sponge tool can also be used to desaturate or diminish the intensity of a color. When Saturation is reduced to -100 percent, the result is a grayscale image. The size, shape, and level of the Saturation tool is set from the Tool Settings roll-up.

 TIP: *Also use the Sponge brush to make colors more vibrant. For the amount, select a low negative value (-5, for example) and brush over the desired area. Nonessential colors that cause dullness are stripped away, leaving pure, vivid colors.*

Using the Sponge Tool

The Sponge tool actually removes the color of the pixels it touches by the amount of the setting. The effect of the tool is not additive. It will apply the effect at the level set by the Tool Setting dialog box the first time it is applied. Progressive applications will not make any changes to the previously affected area unless the tool settings are changed.

The Tint Tool

The Tint tool tints an area in the current paint color. This may seem the same as painting with a high-transparency paintbrush, but it is not. The paintbrush is additive. That is, when the same area continues to have the brush applied to it, the paint builds up until it reaches 100 percent. The Tint tool will apply the paint color as specified by the Tint setting, regardless of how many times it is applied. The amount of tint set in the Tool Settings roll-up is the maximum level of the paint color that can be applied to the pixels in the image.

Using the Tint Tool

The first thing to remember with the Tint tool is that 100 percent tint is a solid color without any transparency. The Tint tool provides a way to highlight a selected area with a color. The same effect can also be achieved over larger areas by using the Rectangle, Ellipse, or Polygon Draw tools and controlling the Transparency setting through the Tool Settings roll-up.

Another use of the Tint tool is for touching up an image. The technique is simple. When you have a discoloration to cover, pick an area of the image that is the desired color. Using the Eyedropper tool, select a large enough sample to get the average color that is needed to match the adjoining areas. Now apply the tint to the area with progressively larger percentage settings until the discolored areas disappear into the surrounding area. If the resulting tint application looks too smooth, use the Smudge Effect tool to add texture. You can also use the Blend tool to reduce spots where there are large differences in the shades.

The Blend Tool

This is a better tool to use for some types of retouching than the Smear tool. The Blend tool enables you to blend colors in your picture. Blending is the mixing of different colors to cause less distinction among them. For example, if you have two areas of different colors and they overlap, it is possible to blend the two different colors so that the separation of the two areas is indistinct. You can use the Blend tool to soften hard edges in an image and to correct any pixelation caused by oversharpening.

TIP: *You could use this effect to blend the edges of a pasted object with the background to make it appear more natural.*

Blending an area causes the distinction between colors to become less pronounced. Choosing an Amount of 1 in the Tool Settings roll-up causes no blending to occur, while an amount of 100% will give you the maximum amount of blending possible. Adjacent pixels must be different colors for the effect to work.

Using the Blend Tool

The Blend tool acts like applying water to a watercolor. The effect of the tool is additive. It will apply the effect at the level set by the Tool Setting dialog box the first time it is applied.

The Sharpen Tool

The Sharpen tool sharpens selected areas of the image by increasing the contrast between neighboring pixels. It operates in the same manner as the Sharpen filter except that it can be applied without the need to create masks. The size and shape of the Sharpen tool is set from the Tool Settings roll-up.

Using the Sharpen Tool

Avoid overusing the Sharpen tool, which results in exaggerated white spots (pixelation) wherever the white component of the image approaches its maximum value. The effect of this tool is additive. It will apply the Sharpen effect to the Sharpen level set in the Tool Settings dialog box every time it is applied. Progressive applications intensify the changes. Any application of the tool can be removed with the Undo command (CTRL-Z) as long as it was applied with one continuous stroke without letting go of the mouse button. If you must be zoomed in at great magnification to do your work, keep a duplicate window open to a lower zoom value so you can see the effect in perspective.

Undither Tool

This brush, introduced in PHOTO-PAINT 7, allows you to create a smooth transition between adjacent pixels of different colors or brightness levels. It works by adding intermediate pixels whose values are between those of the adjacent pixels. Use this tool to remove dust and scratches and to smooth jagged edges. Its effect is similar to that of the Smear tool except is has a more pronounced effect.

Dodge and Burn Tool

New to PHOTO-PAINT 8 is the Dodge and Burn tool. It has several modes of operation and I will do my best to describe them to you. These modes selectively affect pixels in an image dependent on where in the tonal spectrum they exist. Clear as mud? The tonal range of an image, we learned in Chapter 9, is divided into Shadows, Midtones, and Highlights. The Dodge and Burn tool will make pixels in one of these three regions either darker or lighter. It is an excellent retouching tool because you can darken (burn) or lighten (dodge) pixels in an area without affecting pixels that are adjacent to it. For example, you can lighten an area that is close to a shadow with the midtone or highlight setting without concern about affecting the shadow area.

Creating A Custom Nib from A Mask

You can create a custom nib for any of the tools discussed in this chapter using a mask. The following hands-on exercise uses some of the newer features in Corel PHOTO-PAINT 7 to create a custom nib.

1. Create a new image that is 6 x 4 inches at 96 dpi.

2. Open the Objects Docker window (CTRL-F7). Ensure the Lock Transparency is not selected and then select the New Layer button in the lower portion of the roll-up.

3. Select the Image Sprayer Tool and from the far left button on the Property Bar ensure it is set to butrfly.cpt. If it's not, click the file folder to open the list and select it.

4. Open the Tools Setting roll-up (CTRL-F8). Click the middle tab and change the Image Choice setting so it reads From: 2 To: 2. Click once on the image area and a single butterfly appears.

5. Click the Create Mask button in the Toolbar and then click the Combine button at the bottom of the Objects Docker window. The butterfly is now part of the background.

6. Select the Paint tool from the Toolbox and, from the Tool Settings roll-up, click the small button on the right side of the roll-up to the right of the two shape buttons. Select the Create from Contents of Mask option to open the Create a Custom Brush dialog box. Change the size of the brush to 97 and click OK. Congratulations, you have created a custom nib as shown below. Now before we apply it let's clean up the image. From the Mask menu select Remove. From the Edit menu select Clear.

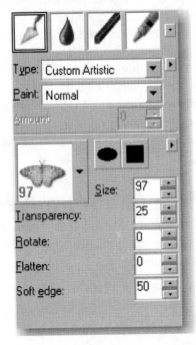

7. From the Tools menu, choose Grid and Ruler Setup. On the Grid tab, select Snap to Grid and Show Grid, and change the Spacing to .5 in both Horizontal and Vertical. Click OK.

8. Because our nib is large we need to change the spacing of the dabs or all of the butterflies will overlap one another. Click on the third tab in the Paint Tool Settings roll-up and change the Spacing setting to 90. In the Dab color variation section change the Hue setting to 100. This will make each butterfly a different color. Ensure the Orbits (fifth tab) is not enabled.

9. Click on the color Red in the on-screen color palette to change the Paint color. lick in the image window in the upper-left corner one time and then, while holding down the ALT key, click on the upper-right end of the image. A single row of butterflies is applied on the image. Continue to produce more rows. The illustration shown below has been cropped and is displayed without grid lines.

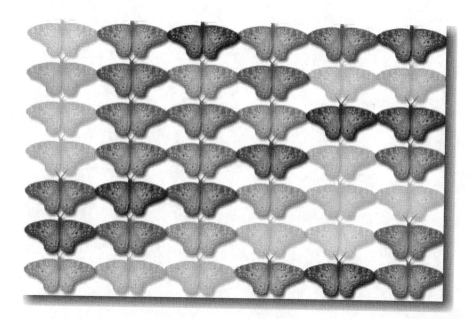

Just a few thoughts to leave you with concerning the creation of nibs from masks. The mask must contain something. You cannot make a nib from an empty mask. If you used a previous version of PHOTO-PAINT the nibs used to be limited to 100 pixels. That is no longer true. You can make them up to 999 pixels. Of course you system may throw a hairball, but hey no one said it would ever be easy.

10

(1)

(2)

What happens when you mix this (1) with this (2)? In Chapter 4 you will learn to use them to make this (3).

(3)

Using the power of grids allows the creation of complex and fantastic images like this one.

A cutout filter in PHOTO-PAINT 8? No, but in Chapter 21 you will learn how to use the Vignette filter as one.

Need some text to really stand out from the herd? You will learn how to make it in Chapter 18.

*Got some dirty pictures?
You will learn how to repair
them and make them
presentable.*

Grids, masks, and filters allow the PHOTO-PAINT user to create complex tiles in a matter of minutes.

In Chapter 6, you will learn to make a single graffiti eye into a pair of watchful eyes.

Another use for the parchment effect you will learn how to create.

Using a variety of techniques taught in this book allows you to create photo montages like this one that was a finalist in the 1997 Corel World Design contest.

In Chapter 19, you will learn how to use a multitude of 3D-effect filters to create this very large box of crayons.

In Chapter 15, you will learn how easy it is to enhance the subject of an image using the Radial Blur filter.

Here are 3 different images you will make using the improved Psychedelic filter.

Here is the new improved version of the checkered flag you will learn to make in Chapter 10.

What do you do with a checkered flag we made in Chapter 10? You make a finish line of course.

In Chapter 18, you will learn how to make
chrome that really dazzles.

This is what happens when you take the chrome
you learned to make in Chapter 18 and combine it
with flowers — now that's flower power.

In Chapter 24, you will
learn how simple it is to
make objects like these to
dress up your publications,
or even your Web site.

If you ever wanted to make a fashion statement, in Chapter 24 you will learn how simple it is to create this garish but fashionably correct magazine cover.

Using the Boss filter you will learn how to make these 3D-looking buttons in Chapter 24.

Want to make your clip art look like it came from the latest comic book? In Chapter 23, we will show you how to do it with the Half-Tone filter.

The page-curl filter still has some life left in it.

In Chapter 10, using only the Orbits and Symmetry brushes, you will create this doily in a matter of seconds.

In Chapter 12, you will learn how to change a dull photograph of diskettes into something a little more exciting.

In Chapter 19, you will discover the power of the Map-to-Object filter as you learn to make the glass sphere shown here.

A traditional use for the Glass-Block filter.

In Chapter 20, you will learn to use the Lens-Flare filter to add the "professional" touch to this photograph.

Using the new Clip to Parent capability of PHOTO-PAINT 8, you will find how simple it is to produce the effect shown here in Chapter 13.

Be it for a Web page, brochure, or newsletter, you will have fun learning to make this rope border in Chapter 24.

The same Glass-Block filter can transform the large wood poles in the background into smaller ones.

Learn how to create powerful multimedia titles that don't look like everyone else's when you make this one in Chapter 22.

They're weird, even ugly, but when you combine the power of the new Orbit Brushstrokes and the Image Sprayer, you can get some fantastic results.

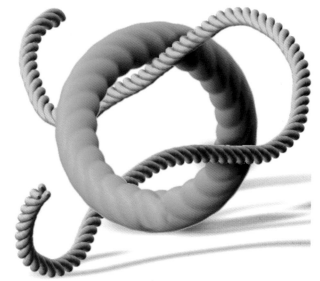

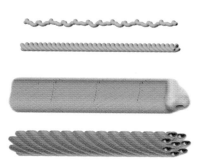

Before PHOTO-PAINT 8 this type of image would have taken a long time to create, but with Clip Masks and the new Perspective Drop Shadow it is easy.

555083.wi (24-Bit RGB Color)-Background

In Chapter 8, we learn how simple it is to change ruins on a sunny day into a gothic night scene.

This chapter is called the Power Tool chapter because the two sets of tools described are the kind that have lots of horsepower! These are the Clone tool and the Image Sprayer. The Clone tool has been around for some time, although it has had a new feature added with the PHOTO-PAINT 8 release. The Image Sprayer first appeared in PHOTO-PAINT 7 but remains one of the fun tools. Let's begin our tour through POWER land with the Clone tool.

The Clone Tool

This used to be the last button at the bottom of the Toolbox. Its new location is just a short distance away, on the Brush Tools flyout at the bottom of the Toolbox. The ability to clone images is one of Corel PHOTO-PAINT's more valuable features. Many people assume that the primary use of the Clone tool, shown at left, is to duplicate people or things in an image. Actually, while the Clone tool is used to replicate images or portions of them for effect, it's more often used in photo-editing for repair and restoration. If you thought it was Clone tools that created the dinosaurs in *Lost World,* I hope you won't be too disappointed.

In the world of Corel PHOTO-PAINT, Clone tools are used to take part of an image and apply it to another part of the image. The cloned area can be on the same image or in a different image window. This is important when part of an image has to be removed and something is needed to replace the removed section. The Clone tool has a mode that lets it operate as the world's best Undo tool.

The Clone Tool Settings Roll-up

There are several ways to open the Clone Tool Settings roll-up shown in the next illustration. With the Clone Tool button selected, choose Roll-ups and Tool Settings from the View menu, use the keyboard combination of CTRL-F8, or double-click the Clone Tool button on the Toolbox. The Clone Tool Settings roll-up is identical to the Brush Tool Settings roll-up except for the Clone selections. To see the entire set, click the down arrow in the Tool Settings roll-up. The category headings are

- Normal Clone
- Impressionism Clone

11

The Power Tools

- Pointillism Clone
- Clone From Saved
- Clone From Fill

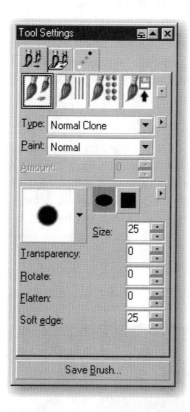

Normal Clone

In Normal mode, shown at left, the Clone tool does not modify the pixels. The pixels from the source are painted precisely as they appear in the source. The process of cloning one object to another to create something that is missing is commonly used both in still photography and motion pictures. In the movie *Forrest Gump,* the actor who played Lt. Dan had special blue socks on when they shot the scenes that showed his legs. By using a blue screen process, anywhere his blue socks appeared would not record on film. They used a clone tool similar to the one in Corel PHOTO-PAINT 8 to clone other parts of the background to replace the areas covered by his feet—one frame at a time. In Figure 11-1, I used the Normal Clone tool to remove the man from the image. Other parts of the image were cloned over the area occupied by him until he was gone.

How the Clone Tool Works

 When the button is selected, the cursor icon becomes a circle with a blinking plus sign in it. The first time you click the mouse button, a plus sign (the source point shown at left) remains at the point where you clicked it. The circle part of the cursor continues to follow your mouse or stylus movement until you click it again, at which time the Clone tool paints the pixels from the source point on the image. As you move the Clone tool, the source point moves, operating in what is called *aligned mode*. The source point and the tool can be on the same image or on different images. To reset the source point, click the right mouse button, and the Clone tool is set to where your circle cursor was. The source point in now anchored at the new location. The plus and circle cursor momentarily line up and it starts all over again.

Holding down the CTRL key constrains the Clone tool to horizontal/vertical movements. To draw a straight line in any direction with the Clone tool, click to establish a starting point, hold down the ALT key, move to where you wish the line to end, and click again to create the line.

The Normal Clone tool provides a quick way to remove an old boyfriend

FIGURE 11-1

Aligned and Non-Aligned Clone Modes

The clone has two modes in which it can operate: aligned and non-aligned. In aligned mode, the source point moves in relation to the Clone tool. This mode is used to clone whole images. In non-aligned mode, the Clone tool can move about, but the position of the source is restricted by the user. This mode is generally used to clone nondetailed areas like clouds or abstract backgrounds.

To use non-aligned mode, click the cursor on a point in the background that contains the colors we want to clone. Next, while holding down the SHIFT-ALT key, drag the Clone tool and release the mouse button without releasing the SHIFT-ALT key. When the mouse button is released, the source crosshair jumps back to the original anchor point. This is what non-aligned mode is all about. It operates, like the mouse, in relative mode. As long as you hold down the SHIFT-ALT key, each time you release the mouse button, the source point will return to its previous (not the anchor) point. This allows us to "paint" an area using clones of the pixels under the source.

 TIP: *Give the Clone tool a soft edge with greater than normal transparency if you want to ensure the cloning will not be evident.*

How to Use the Clone Tools to Clone an Area

- Double-click the Clone tool on the Toolbox to open the Tool Settings roll-up.

- Select the type of clone tool desired.

- Set a clone point on the area you want reproduced, and then move the Clone tool to the new location. The cloned area can be on the same image or in a different image window.

- To re-anchor the clone point, place the cursor over the area you want to clone, hold down the SHIFT key, and click.

11

 TIP: *You can use the Normal Clone tool to retouch photographs that contain scratches or other defects. Clone an area containing similar color and copy over the damaged section of the photograph.*

Removing Defects from a Photograph with the Clone Tool

Probably the most common use for the Clone tool is removing defects from a photograph. In 1993, the film *My Fair Lady* was restored. Even though it is only 20 years old, it was in very poor condition. In the opening credits, several pieces of film had broken off, leaving black spots on the screen. Technicians used clone tools to clone part of another background to cover the spots. The result was that the black spots were gone without a trace.

Corel was considerate enough to provide an image for use in demonstrating this technique of using cloning to remove or repair damage.

Restoring a Photograph with the Clone Tool

In the following hands-on exercise, we are going to remove some dust and debris that was left on a negative when it was scanned.

1. Locate and open the file EXERCISE\PHOTOS\651017.WI on the Corel CD. Resample the Width to 7 inches using the Resample command in the Image menu.

2. Near the couch on the right side of the image, there is a large black spot and some other debris. Click the "Z" key (the cursor becomes a magnifying glass) and enclose the area around that spot.

3. Double-click on the Clone tool to open the Tool Settings roll-up. Select the Normal Clone Tool button (it should be selected by default) and Normal Clone from the Type drop-down list. The cursor should be a large circle (my image is zoomed at 600%) with a small plus in it. The size of the source point cursor never changes, but the clone brush cursor reflects the size of the clone tool brush.

4. From the Property Bar, change the brush size to about 7. The cursor and source point should still be together. Click on a spot to the left of the debris. Move the clone brush so it is over the ugly spot. The source point (plus sign) should remain where you clicked it. Click the left mouse button once. The debris should be gone.

5. Try this on the other debris on the shades in the background (a lot was left for you to practice on). Remember to reset the clone brush when you

move to a new area. The key to good clone repair is to locate source points that are the same general shade and texture as the area where you are cloning to prevent the cloning from being noticed. When you have finished here, hold down the "N" key. This opens the Pop-Up Navigator. In the small picture that just appeared on your screen, click and drag the rectangle over the smaller girl's nose and click the left mouse button.

6. The object in this area is to remove the dark spot at the tip of her nose. Change the Type to Small Soft Clone. Place the cursor just under and to the right of the spot. Click the right mouse button. Now place the cursor over the dark spot and click the left mouse button. If it doesn't look right, click Undo (CTRL-Z).

7. Save the file as GIRLS.CPT.

Figure 11-2 shows some of the debris that remained when the original film negative was scanned. Figure 11-3 shows the result when the Clone tool is used to remove the imperfections on both the young girl's face and the background.

A close-up of a dirty picture

FIGURE 11-2

With PHOTO-PAINT anything is possible

FIGURE 11-3

Removing scratches, dust, and other debris is fun at first, but after the 100th time, it gets a little old. Still, I still never cease to be amazed at what can be done with the Clone tool.

Making an Oil Painting with the Clone Tool

As stated earlier, you can clone between two points on an image, which we did in the previous exercise, or clone from one image to another. In the following exercise we will clone the image of the smaller child to another image, in a unique way.

1. Open the file GIRLS.CPT.

2. Create a new file that is 4 x 5 inches at 96 dpi.

3. Save the new file as HATGIRL.CPT.

4. Select the Clone tool and double-click on the button to open the Tool Settings roll-up.

5. Click on the title bar of GIRLS.CPT (to bring it forward). From the Tool Settings roll-up, select Fine Streaks as the Type. This changes the nib shape so the cloned area resembles the fine brush strokes of a paintbrush.

6. Place the cursor on the little girl's nose and click the left mouse button.

7. Click on the title bar of HATGIRL.CPT or select HATGIRL.CPT from the Window menu. Place the clone brush in about the middle of the image area, click the mouse button, and begin to drag the brush. The girl under the source is cloned in the new image to look a little like a painting, as shown in Figure 11-4.

Using the Clone tool we are able to make a painterly copy of her in another image

FIGURE 11-4

11

8. To remove any portion of the material you have just cloned, click the last button on the Tool Settings roll-up, choose either Custom From Saved, Eraser, or Light Eraser, and paint it away. This is the reason I had you save the blank image in step 3. The Clone From Saved mode requires a saved version to operate.

9. When you have finished, close the file and don't save any changes.

Impressionism Clone

In this mode, the pixels from the source are modified using the Impressionist effect. This effect applies brush strokes to the image, causing it to look like an Impressionist painting. Impressionist paintings are marked by the use of unmixed primary colors and small brush strokes to simulate reflected light. Notable Impressionist painters include Monet, Cezanne, and Degas.

This tool wins the big prize: I have been unable to find any practical use for it whatsoever. Think about it for a moment. A clone is an exact copy of the original, right? The Impressionist Clone tool makes randomly distorted copies of the original. Am I missing something here?

In using the tool, remember that by keeping your brush size and number of line settings small, your result will more closely approximate the original. At least the outcome will be recognizable. The results with this tool are unpredictable, so be sure to use the Checkpoint command before beginning your work.

Pointillism Clone

In Pointillism mode, a dotlike appearance is added to the image. The brush stroke made with the Clone tool incorporates a selected number of dots in colors that are similar (e.g., eight shades of red). The size, shape, and qualities of the Pointillist Clone tool are set from the Variation Tab in the Tool Settings roll-up. The effect can be subtle, retaining the overall appearance of the original image, or you can vary the dots and the colors to create very unusual special effects. The Pointillism Clone tool selects colors in an image and paints with them in a pointillist style. It does not reproduce areas in an image as does the Normal Clone tool.

Experiment with this tool when you have lots of time on your hands and no deadlines. Use it to create special effects. Keeping the brush size very small (a setting between 2 and 5) enables the creation of a clone that looks vaguely similar to the original. As with the Impressionism filter, use objects that have definite shapes, making them easily recognizable as the Clone tool distorts their appearance. The results with this tool can be unpredictable, so use the Checkpoint command before beginning your work.

Clone From Saved

 This is the ultimate Undo tool, shown at left. Called Clone From Saved and Custom From Saved, Eraser, whatever the name, it uses the last saved version of the image file as a source, allowing you to selectively remove any changes that had been made since the last time the file was saved. It has three presets that are unique to it, each producing a different effect. They are

- Light Eraser
- Eraser
- Scrambler

The Eraser and Light Eraser Presets

This is a wonderful feature for you to use when cloning images. After you have cloned a portion of an image, you may end up with cloned material that you do not want. The Eraser and the Light Eraser allow you to restore the original pixels from the last saved version of the image. This restores areas to their saved states. The Light Eraser allows you to control how much of the changes you want to remove, requiring multiple passes to achieve the full restoration. The Eraser removes all of the cloned pixels. The Scrambler option is a pointillism version of the Clone From Saved, so it allows you to distort the current image from a saved version. (What were they thinking?)

 TIP: *To restore background with the Clone From Saved feature, I recommend you use the Eraser setting with a soft edge setting of 60-80. This way the transition is gradual and you won't need to go over the area later with a Smear or Blend tool.*

Clone From Fill

 This feature is new to PHOTO-PAINT 8. The Clone From Fill tool, uses the current Fill as the source and applies the fill as the brush is applied to the image. The relationship between the source (Fill) and the image is the same as if the fill was applied to the image. In other words, when Clone From Fill is selected, PHOTO-PAINT internally creates an image the same size as the one to which you are applying the clone. This is why you might notice a slight delay. If the current fill is a Texture fill, then PHOTO-PAINT must first generate an internal source file that is the size of the image on which you are working. This is an important point to remember, since unlike a Bitmap fill, the size of the image determines the size and shape of the Texture fill and the Fountain fill.

The advantage of the Clone From Fill is in its ability to selectively apply fills with a brush tool without the necessity of a mask. In prior releases of PHOTO-PAINT, it was only possible to apply the various fills using either the Shape or the Flood tools.

All of the settings in the Tool Settings roll-up for the Clone tool operate in the same fashion as the Brush Tools described in Chapter 10. Now let's look at the Image Sprayer tool.

The Image Sprayer Tool

Here is a tool that has both changed its address with the PHOTO-PAINT 8 release and has some new exciting presets as well. The Image Sprayer tool can be found next to the Clone tool on the Brush Tools flyout. The Image Sprayer allows you to load one or more images, and then spray them across your image. We have already used this tool in several hands-on exercises in this book. The Image Sprayer tool makes it possible to paint with multiple images instead of simply a paint color. The images you paint with are contained within a special file called an *image list,* which you can create from selected objects; or you can use any of the image lists available in the ImgLists folder on the PHOTO-PAINT CD. You can adjust the size, transparency, and spraying sequence of the images by adjusting the brush settings on the Property Bar or from the Tool Settings roll-up as shown in Figure 11-5.

The Presets located at the bottom of the Tool Settings roll-up are the newest addition to the Image Sprayer tool. These presets change the settings of the parameters in all three tabs of the roll-up. Of special note is the new Orbits tab. This applies the powerful orbits engine to control the application of the Image Sprayer. The best effects are achieved with the Orbits enabled if the image list only contains one object. When multiple object lists are selected, the effect is diminished if not lost altogether. Figure 11-6 shows an example of several of the presets. In Chapter 24 you will see some neat Web page objects that can be made with these.

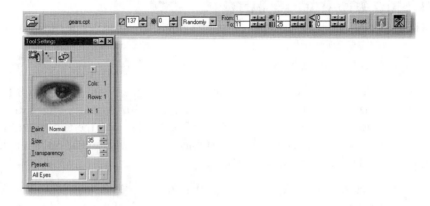

The Property Bar and Tool Settings roll-up offer complete control over the Image Sprayer tool

FIGURE 11-5

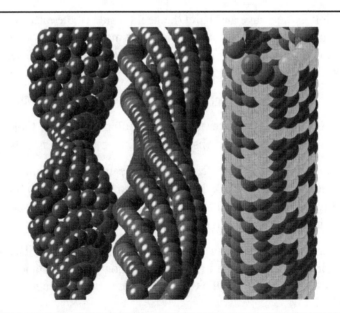

Using presets with the Image Sprayer tool produces powerful brushstrokes

FIGURE 11-6

11

Using the Image Sprayer Tool

Here is a fast hands-on exercise to make a quick logo for a company.

1. Create a new file that is 6 x 3 inches at 96 dpi.

2. Click the Text tool in the Toolbox. Change the Font to Futura XBlt BT at a size of 96 and the interline spacing set to 70. Type **GEARS Unlimited**. Click the Object picker tool in the Toolbox. Center the text (CTRL-A), choose the Create Mask (from Object) in the Msk menu, and then delete the text, leaving only the mask.

3. Click the Image Sprayer tool in the Toolbox. By default it is set to Butterfly. Click on the Load Image Sprayer List button on the far left of the Property Bar. When the dialog box opens, select Gears from the Presets list. Click the Open button.

4. The current size of the gears that would be painted are so large that they would lose their effect, so change the size of the image in the Property Bar from 137 to 100.

5. Click in the image and paint the gears inside of the masked area. The result is shown in Figure 11-7 with the mask marquee off. Because the gears are applied in a random fashion, yours will look different than the one shown.

6. Click the Create Object: Cut Selection button in the Toolbar.

7. Select the Object Picker tool in the Toolbox. Open the Objects Docker window (CTRL-F7) and ensure Lock Transparency is not checked.

8. From the Effects menu, choose 3D Effects and then Emboss. When the dialog box opens, click the Reset button. Change the Emboss color to Original and the Level to 150. Click the OK button. Check the Lock Transparency option in Objects Docker window.

9. From the Objects menu, select Drop Shadow. From the Drop Shadow dialog box, choose the lower-left direction with a Distance value of 0.1. Set the Feather to 12, the Opacity to 60, and the direction to Average. Click OK.

10. In the Objects Docker window, deselect the text by clicking on the Background. From the Edit menu, choose Fill. From the Edit Fill &

The Image
Sprayer
applied to
the masked
text creates
a power
visual

FIGURE 11-7

Transparency dialog box, click the Fountain Fill button and choose Edit.
From the Fountain Fill dialog box, change the preset value to Gold Plated.
Click OK to close the box, and click the OK button again to apply the fill.
The finished logo is shown in Figure 11-8.

11. Close the file and don't save the changes.

The
finished
company
logo

FIGURE 11-8

More Image Sprayer Information

There are many more image lists that are included with PHOTO-PAINT 8 than the ones in the Presets list of the Tool Settings dialog box. To see a lot more of these jewels, open the ImgLists folder on the PHOTO-PAINT CD by clicking the Load Image Sprayer List button at the far left of the Property Bar. To learn how to make your own image lists, click the F1 button in PHOTO-PAINT. Select Index and enter "Image Sprayer tool, using." Click the Display button and choose "Creating and editing image lists for the image Sprayer tool."

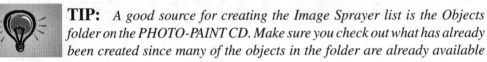 **TIP:** *A good source for creating the Image Sprayer list is the Objects folder on the PHOTO-PAINT CD. Make sure you check out what has already been created since many of the objects in the folder are already available as image lists.*

12

Working With Fills and the Shape Tools

Until now we have looked at fill tools only as far as necessary. In this chapter, we will learn everything there is to know about the subject of fills. All of the technical details are here, so if you are having trouble sleeping at night, start reading the definition of Pantone colors. That should put you out pretty quick. We will also be looking at the Shape tools. Since the addition of the Fill command, the Shape tools aren't used as much as they used to be, but they still remain an important part of the PHOTO-PAINT Toolbox.

The Fill Command

This command is a real time saver in that from this dialog box you can access any of the individual roll-ups, like Fountain Fill or Bitmap Fill, and you can directly apply the fill to the image. Located in the Edit menu, the Fill command opens the Edit Fill & Transparency dialog box, shown in Figure 12-1. In releases prior to PHOTO-PAINT 7 these required the use of the Fill tool or the Shape tools which are both still available and necessary.

The Edit Fill & Transparency dialog box is like a jumping off point for all of the fills within PHOTO-PAINT. The dialog box contains two tabs—Fill Color and Transparency. The Fill Color is used to set the color of the fill and the Transparency tab controls all of the different transparency options that are possible with the fill.

Controlling the Fill

Prior to PHOTO-PAINT 7 the Fill roll-up was one of the roll-ups that you used the most. While it is still there, you may find yourself using it less and less. In PHOTO-PAINT 8 there are 3 different ways to control the different Fill tools – the Select Fill dialog box, the Tool Settings roll-up for the Fill tool and the Tool Settings Roll-Up for the Shape tool. Although all three are basically identical in operation, they do exhibit minor differences.

The Select Fill tool dialog box, shown below, is used to select the current fill. It is accessed by double clicking on the Fill swatch in the Status bar.

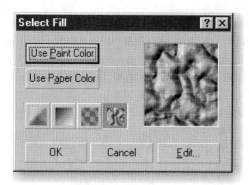

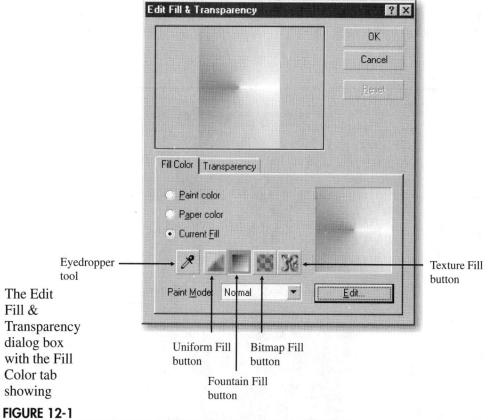

Eyedropper tool

Texture Fill button

Uniform Fill button

Bitmap Fill button

Fountain Fill button

The Edit Fill & Transparency dialog box with the Fill Color tab showing

FIGURE 12-1

12

The Tool Settings roll-up (CTRL-F8) for the Fill tools (Figure 12-2) offers more control of the Fills than the Select Fill dialog box and the roll-up for the Shape tools (Figure 12-3) while looking similar offers controls that are specific to the Shape tools which are explored later in this chapter.

Fill roll-up controls what fill is applied when you use the Fill tool, or the Shape tools. It provides access to a wide variety of preset and custom fills, ranging from simple spot colors to complex custom bitmap fills.

The Fill roll-up can be accessed many ways, as follows:

- Double-clicking the Fill tool in the Toolbox.

- Double-clicking the Fill swatch in the Status bar opens the Select Fill dialog box

- Double-clicking the Rectangle, Ellipse, or Polygon Shape tool in the Toolbox.

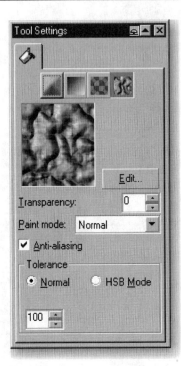

The Tool
Settings
roll-up for
the Fill tool

FIGURE 12-2

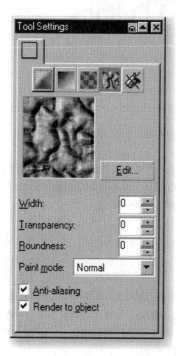

The Tool
Settings
roll-up for
the Shape
tools

FIGURE 12-3

- If any of the Tools mentioned above are selected, you can also open the Tool Settings roll-up where fill can be edited.

- With a Shape tool selected, access the Fill roll-up by using CTRL-F8 or selecting Roll-Ups and then Tool Settings from the View menu's Roll-Ups flyout.

When you open the Fill roll-up, you will notice that there are four buttons near the top of the roll-up. Each of the buttons in the Fill roll-up are identical in appearance and operation to the ones shown in Figure 12-1. The icon on the buttons indicates the operational mode they activate.

NOTE: *If you open the Fill roll-up feature of the Tool Settings roll-up by double-clicking either the Rectangle, Ellipse, or Polygon tool, there will be five buttons at the top. The fifth button is the No Fill button.*

The Mode Select Buttons

Before going into detailed descriptions, let's summarize the functions of the buttons in Figure 12-1.

The first button selects the Eyedropper tool (only on the Edit Fill & Transparency dialog box). Enabling this button actives the Eyedropper tool. In this mode you place the cursor on the image and click on the desired color and it becomes the Current Fill color.

NOTE: *If the Edit Fill and Transparency dialog box is not open, you can also set the Fill color by clicking the "E" key (the cursor becomes an eyedropper) and right-clicking the desired color in the image.*

The next button enables Uniform Color fill. From this mode, choosing Edit allows you to select any solid (non-gradient) color from the existing palette or from a custom palette.

In the middle is the Fountain fill button. Choosing Edit opens the Fountain fill dialog box to produce Linear, Radial, Conical, Rectangular and Square fills. This fill comes with a large selection of presets. All of the fountain fills can be customized.

The next button is the Bitmap fill, indicated by the checkerboard icon on the button. Like its CorelDRAW counterpart, it can provide bitmap fills either from its existing library of fills or from custom fills that are created with Corel PHOTO-PAINT or other graphics programs. This is a powerful tiling engine. By choosing Edit, you can select any bitmap file to be used for Bitmap fill patterns (tiles).

The last button is the Texture fill, the most unique in the Fill roll-up. This mode does not use existing tiles or patterns. Instead, it creates them at the time of use through a powerful fractal generator. You can produce some unusual and exotic textures (or patterns) with this fill.

NOTE: *The No Fill button that was available on releases prior to PHOTO-PAINT 7 has been removed. Use the Transparency control to prevent fills from being applied.*

Fill Status Line

You can see the currently selected fill color/pattern by viewing the Status bar. You will notice that there are three small rectangles located on the status line as shown below. The Paint color is the foreground color, the Paper color is the background color, and the Fill can be a color or pattern. Because the area is small, it is sometimes difficult to accurately determine the selected type of fill.

The Uniform Color Fill Mode

Uniform Color Fill is the simplest fill mode and is used to select and apply solid (uniform) colors to an image. When Uniform Color fill is selected, the Fill Color Swatch in the Status Bar reflects the current fill color that is selected.

Selecting a Uniform Color Fill

The currently selected color is shown as a color swatch on the roll-up. There are several ways to change the color. The quickest is to click on the desired color in the on-screen color palette with the right mouse button. If the color you want is not available in the onscreen palette, then from either the Edit Fill & Transparency or the Fill roll-up, select the Uniform Fill button and click the Edit button. This action opens the Uniform Fill dialog box, as shown in Figure 12-4. From this dialog box you can just about do anything that you can think of in regards to solid color.

The Uniform Fill Dialog Box

The Uniform Fill dialog box is where you can literally pick any color in the universe. The operation of this dialog box can intimidate the faint of heart. The dialog box is an essential tool for defining and correcting colors for those doing pre-press work.

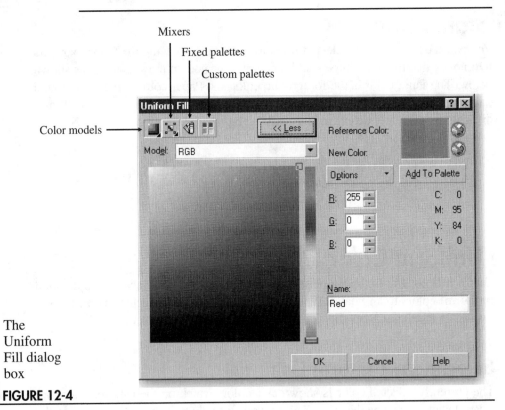

The
Uniform
Fill dialog
box

FIGURE 12-4

If you only want to make a simple modification to a color so it will look better in an image, you can do that as well.

Just so you know, the Uniform Fill dialog box is common throughout Corel PHOTO-PAINT as well as all of the CorelDRAW suite of applications. Changes made to the palette in this dialog box are global. That means that they apply to all of the CorelDRAW suite of applications. The Uniform Fill dialog box allows you to choose colors from various color models and custom palettes. You can also import and select individual colors from existing image files.

How to Approach the Uniform Fill Dialog Box

There are several general approaches to using the Uniform Fill dialog box. When the dialog box opens the default setting for the four buttons on top is Color Model. The simplest way to select the color you want is to pick the color closest to the desired color from the vertical spectrum in the middle of the dialog box which changes the preview window to display all of the colors available in that part of the spectrum. You can then pick a spot in the preview window that most closely matches the one you want. The New Color is shown in the upper-right corner. Clicking OK returns to the Fill roll-up or to Edit Fill & Transparency. The advantage of this approach is speed. The disadvantage of this method is that you will be using an undefined color that may be difficult, if not impossible, for someone at a different location (like a service bureau) to duplicate.

If the final image is going to be printed using an established color matching system, like Pantone, click the Fixed Palettes button in the dialog box and choose the palette and specific color you want.

A third approach is to create one or several colors, name them, and save them on a custom palette. This way you can use the colors in another image because the colors have been named and saved. Another site can duplicate your work since you can send the palette along with the image. The disadvantage is that it takes longer to do. That said, let's examine this cornucopia.

Setting the Mood—Models, Palettes, or Mixers?

The operation of the dialog box is controlled by which of the four mode buttons on the top of the dialog box are selected. These affect not only the operation but also the appearance of the dialog box. You have four choices, as follows.

■ **Color Models Mode**   This method of choosing a color allows you to select one of 10 color models from the Model: drop-down list to establish the color you want. This is the mode shown in Figure 12-4. The reason for selecting a specific color model to use when choosing colors is based on the type of work you are doing. For example, if you are color-correcting a photograph that will be printed using the four-color printing process (CMYK), you should choose the CMYK or CMY? color model.

■ **Mixers Mode**   It slices, it dices, it's the Color Blender. This is a very handy tool for selecting colors from RGB, CMYK, or HSB models. Shown in Figure 12-5, you select four colors and it produces a range of colors for the colors selected using gradations between four colors across a square grid.

■ **Fixed Palettes Mode**   Selecting this button changes the color selection to one based not on color model but on a predefined palette as shown in Figure 12-6. From the Type: drop-down list, pick one of 13 predefined

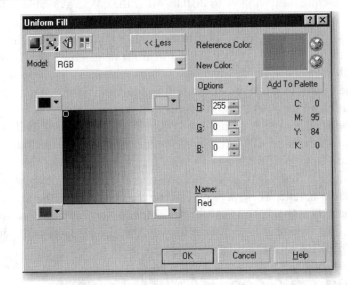

The
Uniform
Color
dialog box
in Mixers
mode

FIGURE 12-5

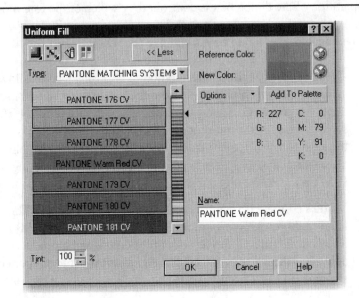

The
Uniform
Color
dialog box
in Fixed
Palettes
mode

FIGURE 12-6

systems, such as Pantone or Netscape navigator. Use Fixed Palettes if you are using spot colors or working with a Web site.

■ **Custom Palettes Mode**   This is the mode of choice, as shown in Figure 12-7, if you need to use a specific set of colors that are not part of a known palette or color matching system. Both the Corel PHOTO-PAINT and the CorelDRAW custom palettes are in this category.

Color Models

Color models are a method for representing color, usually by their components as specified along at least three dimensions. The first button allows you to select one of ten color models. As you change color models, the numerical value system on the right and the 3D color model displayed below the model name change.

The color model options available are as follows.

The
Uniform
Color
dialog box
in Custom
Palettes
mode

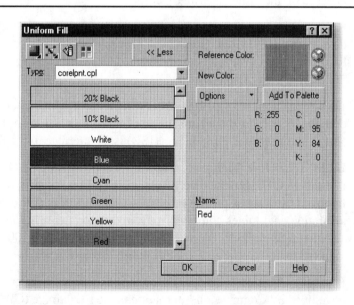

■ **FIGURE 12-7**

Color Model Options

- **CMY**   This color model contains only Cyan, Magenta, and Yellow. You should only select this if the final output will be done on a CMY device, such as a three-ink printer. The C, M, and Y values range between 0 and 255.

- **CMYK**   This shows the CMYK model and list value boxes for each of the components in percentages. Cyan, Magenta, Yellow, and Black (CMYK) is the model used for the four-color printing process. *A note about CMYK:* When this model is selected, there may be some display irregularities if you are using blended colors. When blended colors are displayed on the monitor, they show up as banding. The printed output itself is unaffected, but the display may be banded.

- **CMYK 255**   This is like the previous CMYK model, except the values are listed according to a computer-based scale (0 to 255) rather than percentages. As in the previous model, the letters represent Cyan, Magenta, Yellow, Black ("K" is used to indicate black). This color model is based on the printer's primary colors.

- **RGB**   This is the standard of monitor color models. All computer displays are RGB (Red, Green, and Blue) —the same as your eyes. The RGB model is the default color model of Corel PHOTO-PAINT. This is the ground zero of all color models.

- **HSB**   The popularity of HSB isn't what it used to be, although components of this model are still used when working with the filters. Hue, Saturation, and Brightness (HSB) is an alternate to the RGB model.

- **HLS**   HLS (Hue, Lightness, Saturation) is a variation on HSB and an alternative to RGB. Hue determines color (yellow, orange, red, etc.), lightness determines perceived intensity (lighter or darker color), and saturation determines color depth (from dull to intense). The visual selector defines the H value (0 to 360), the S value (0 to 100), and the L value (0 to 100).

- **L*A*B***   This color model is becoming more and more popular. It was developed by Commission Internationale de l'Eclairage (CIE) based on three parameters: lightness (L*), green-to-red chromaticity (a*), and blue-to-yellow chromaticity (b*). The rectangular two-dimensional visual selector defines the a* and b* coordinates from -60 to 60, and the L* value from 0 to 100. This model is device-independent, meaning that it does not need to have information about the devices it is working with to operate correctly. For the prepress industry, it encompasses the color gamuts of both the CMYK and the RGB color models.

■ **YIQ** The preferred model when working with video is YIQ, which is used in television broadcast systems (North American video standard: NTSC). Colors are split into a luminance value (Y) and two chromaticity values (I and Q). On a color monitor, all three components are visible; on a monochrome monitor, only the Y component is visible. All values are scaled from 0 to 255. In Corel PHOTO-PAINT, the Y component of the splitting process produces a grayscale image that is often superior to results obtained with a grayscale conversion using the Convert To command from the Image menu.

■ **Grayscale** This is your basic plain vanilla 256 shades of gray color model. No, that's not a typo—gray is a color. The visual selector contains 255 levels of grayscale, with 255 being the lightest and 0 the darkest.

■ **Registration color** The Registration color model consists of a single color in the CMYK color space, for which C, M, Y, and K are at 100 percent. You can use this color on any object that you want to appear on all separation plates. It is ideal for company logos, job numbers, or any other identifying marks that you may need for the job. This color cannot be added to the custom palette.

TIP: *If the project you are working on is not going to an offset printer, select the RGB or Grayscale color model.*

How to Select or Create a Color Using Color Models Mode

The following is a general procedure to create a specific color in the Uniform Fill dialog box.

■ The first step is to remember what color it was that you were working on to begin with. That is found in the upper-right corner. It is labeled Reference Color. This was the color originally selected in the on-screen palette or on the palette in the Uniform Fill dialog box.

- Select a color model. This step is easy: use RGB unless you have good reason to use another model. If you are working with 32-bit color, use CMYK or CMYK-255.

- If the only change you want is to make the Reference color darker or lighter, click and drag the small square in the color model display moving it to make the selected color darker or lighter. The color of the area under the square is shown in the New Color box under the Reference Color in the upper-right corner of the dialog box.

- If you want a completely different color, you can click on any point in the color model display area on a color on the vertical spectrum on the right side of the color display area. You can then adjust the shade of the color in the color model display area. You can also enter values numerically. For example, with the RGB model, entering a value of **0,0,0** will produce Black and **255,255,255** will produce the white.

- New Color is useful when you are matching colors and wish to update your reference point. To swap the Reference and New Colors, use the Options flyout, and choose Swap Color.

Using the Non-Printable Color Icon

If you are new to color printing, you may not be aware that there are ranges of colors that cannot be reproduced by your printer. The Non-Printable Color icon warns you when the color you are selecting is outside of the capability of your printer.

As you adjust the square in the color model display area, an icon of a printer within the universal red circle with slash sign will appear (and sometimes disappear) to the right of the New Colorand Reference Color. This is an ingenious device that warns you of colors that cannot be printed using SWOP (Standard Web Offset Press).

There are also symbols shown in all of the dialog box figures that indicate the selected color is out of gamut. If you are not having it printed on an offset press, don't be too concerned about this feature. The swatch continually displays an approximation of what the color will actually look like. To try it out find a vivid blue or green and you will see that the swatch will only display the closest color that can be reproduced.

Once you are satisfied with the color displayed in the New Color swatch, click the OK button and you will return to the Edit Fill & Transparency dialog box or the Fill roll-up with the New Color selected.

Color Options Drop-down List

The Options buttons opens a drop-down list that provides a list of 8 options of which the last one, Postscript is always grayed out. The Value 1 and Value 2 selections allow you to set and display color values based on different color models. For example, by default the model for value 1 is RGB and CMYK for Value 2. This allows the user to see the value of the selected color in both RGB and CMYK values.

Add Color to Palette adds the New Color, if it is not already available, to the custom palette. Swap Colors, when selected, will swap the New Color and the Reference color. Gamut Alarm is causes the Color Model Display area to display areas that contain colors that are outside of the color gamut for the printer selected in Corel Color manager. The color of the Gamut Alarm is selected in the Color Manager.

Measure From opens a selection menu of several industry standard measuring devices. If you have not used one of these before and think it might be a neat idea to hop down to your local computer super center and check them out, think again. The least expensive ones I have seen cost over one thousand dollars.

Saving a New Color on a Palette

Now that you have created that special color you wanted, you need to save it. Colors are saved on palettes. Before I show you how to save a color to a palette, you need to understand a few things about palettes. Palettes, like the original artist's palette, are files that store colors. Palette files have a .CPL extension. The only way to display the palette is to open the Palette Editor in the Tools menu. This will be dealt with in more detail in the next section, which concerns Palettes mode.

The Corelpnt.cpl palette is the default Corel PHOTO-PAINT palette. The palettes discussed in this chapter store a large selection of colors. You can use a special palette to keep all of the colors used in a particular project or painting. Some people like to keep a palette that contains all of their favorite colors. The choice is yours. Here is how to save a color you have created.

1. After you are satisfied with the new color enter in a name for the new color in the Name value box. Naming colors is not necessary, but it is recommended.

2. Click the Add to Palette button and the new color will be added to the current palette. You cannot remove a color from the palette with this dialog box.

TIP: *When creating new colors, especially for company logos, be sure to give the new color a specific name. This can be critical when the job needs to be modified and you are trying to guess which color that you used out of a possible ten billion combinations.*

The Mixers Mode

The Mixer mode in the Uniform Fill dialog box allows creation of colors by mixing one or more colors together.

Color Mixer

The color mixer box provides a method of picking four colors, and the computer automatically generates all of the intermediate colors. It is from these intermediate colors that you can pick the color you want. Use the Color Blender to create a four-way blend of color and choose from the range of color variations. The Grid size, ranging in size from 3x3 to 25x25 (smaller grids produce more distinct colors while larger grids produce more subtle color variations), can be changed in the Options menu Colors are selected from the custom palette and can be mapped to the CMYK, RGB, and HSB color models.

USING THE MIXER MODE The operation is simple enough. There are four colors at the four corners of a color square. Each of the four colors is selected by clicking on the color square in the corner, which opens a palette. From the palette, select a color. Clicking the Options button gives a great degree of control over the operation of Color Blend. The options are the same as with the Color Models mode with two additions:

- **Add All Grid Colors to Palette** This option applies all of the colors in the Color Blend area to the custom palette, which is very handy when you want to place a large range of colors in a palette.

- **Grid Size** This allows selection of one of ten different grid sizes ranging from 3X3 to 25X25.

Fixed and Custom Palettes Mode

Enabling either the Fixed Palettes or Custom Palettes button of the Uniform Fill dialog box opens the Palette mode. This offers a collection of different color-matching-system palettes available to the Corel PHOTO-PAINT user. The number of colors or shades available in each palette is dependent on the color mode of the image. The different palettes are provided when you have projects that work with Spot or color process systems like Pantone, TOYO and Trumatch. The palettes contain industry-standard colors that are essential for color-matching accuracy when the project is to be output to offset printing.

NOTE: *When using the Pantone color-matching system in Palettes Mode, be aware that the colors cannot be changed. Only the percentage of Tint can be modified. This is because the ability of a system like Pantone to match the colors printed on the swatch (which you must buy from them) is based on the combination of inks that make up the color and do not change.*

Viewing Palette Selections by Name

Click the Options button and you will immediately notice some of the selections have changed. Selecting Show Color Names will cause the currently selected palette to change to an alphabetical listing of all of the color names for the color system selected as shown below. Each name is displayed on a color rectangle displaying a sample of the named color. Regarding the displayed colors, please remember that what you see is only a good approximation of what that actual color looks like, even when you are using a very expensive monitor and graphics card and even when you have done all of the calibration voodoo. When using color samples from a color-matching system, always trust the swatches provided by the manufacturer over the screen.

Searching for Colors by Name

The Search provides a quick way to locate a specific, named color in a color system. As each character is typed in, the computer begins its search. As subsequent characters are entered, the search field is narrowed. Here is a quick exercise to find the spot color blue.

1. In the Type: area, click the down arrow button and select Pantone Matching System®.

2. Type **BL** in the area labeled Name:. As the letters "BL" are entered, the computer goes to the first BL in the system, which is "black."

3. Then type in **U**, and Pantone Process Blue CV is selected.

Exploring the Palettes

When the Fixed Palettes mode is enabled, the Type choices change as well. The 13 different palette choices available when you click the arrow in the Type box are as follows.

PANTONE MATCHING SYSTEM PALETTE   This is one of 3 available Pantone palettes. This palette offers colors that are available through the Pantone Matching System (known as Pantone Spot Colors in previous releases of PHOTO-PAINT). In this system, you define tint through the Tint percentage box, ranging from 0 (lightest) to 100 (darkest) to control saturation. This system also allows you to define PostScript options.

Since spot colors correspond to solid inks and are not CMYK-based, each unique color applied to an object results in an additional color separation plate. In Corel PHOTO-PAINT, you can use spot colors only in CMYK images to affect duotones. Colors can be displayed by name or swatch through the Options menu.

The Name box is used to search for specific Pantone Spot Color names. Spot colors are specific colors that are applied to an area and are not the result of multiple applications of inks. Pantone is one of the more popular color-matching systems. As with FOCOLTONE, when using Pantone, you pick out a specific color from a sample and then pick out the color name or number from the Pantone list. When it goes to the service bureau to be made into film, the computer then knows what particular Pantone color was specified.

PANTONE® HEXACHROME   Displays the PANTONE® Hexachrome colors which are based on the CMYK color model but adds two additional inks for a total of six inks and a broader range of colors. While this system is gaining popularity, it still is more expensive to reproduce because it requires 6 printing stages instead of the tradition 4-step process.

PANTONE PROCESS PALETTE   This operates like the Pantone Matching System model except that it shows Process colors. Process colors are colors created by multiple applications of ink. Pantone specifies all the information that is necessary for the printer to be able to duplicate the color. When Pantone Process is selected, it shows the Process Color model, based on the CMYK color model, and the Name box. Tint is not an option with Pantone Process. The first 2,000 colors are two-color combinations; the remainder are three- and four-color combinations. Colors are based on CMYK and therefore do not add additional color separation plates. Use the scroll bar on the right to display other areas of the palette. Colors can be displayed by name or swatch through the Options menu.

UNIFORM COLORS PALETTE   This is the default palette for Corel PHOTO-PAINT. The Uniform Color palette offers 255 standard RGB colors for quick selection. Colors are expressed as RGB values for all images and drawings. Use the scroll bar on the right to display other areas of the palette. Colors can be displayed by name through the Show Color Names option in the Options drop-down menu (the color names correspond to the R, G, and B values). It is a sampling of the entire visible spectrum at 100 percent saturation.

FOCOLTONE PALETTE   This palette offers colors that are available through the FOCOLTONE color system. Because the colors are based on CMYK, there is no need to add additional color separation plates. When FOCOLTONE is selected, the dialog box shows the FOCOLTONE model and a Name box for finding specific FOCOLTONE color names. Like all other color-matching systems, FOCOLTONE provides a specimen swatch to printers and designers so there is a point of agreement as to what the color specified is supposed to look like.

TRUMATCH PALETTE   This is a competing color-matching system for Pantone. Like Pantone, the Trumatch palette allows specification of colors according to specific samples, but it offers colors that are available through the TRUMATCH color system. This system is based on the CMYK color model and therefore colors do not add additional color separation plates. Colors are organized by hue (red to violet), saturation (deep to pastel), and brightness (adding or removing black). Use the scroll bar on the right to display other areas of the palette. Colors can be displayed by name or swatch through the Options menu.

NETSCAPE NAVIGATOR™   Displays the 8-bit palette of 256 colors used by the web browser Netscape Navigator. By limiting your choices to the colors found on this palette, you ensure that your image colors will display clearly on systems using the Netscape Navigator browser.

MICROSOFT® INTERNET EXPLORER   Same as the Netscape Navigator except the palette is for the Microsoft Internet Explorer.

12

SPECTRAMASTER R COLORS   This is a specialized color-matching system. The palette offers colors that are available through the DuPont Spectramaster solid color library. This library was developed to provide a paint color selection and matching tool for industrial coatings and colorants. Colors are based on L*a*b* and are converted to RGB for display and CMYK for printing. Colors can be displayed by name or swatch through the Color Options menu.

TOYO COLOR FINDER   If you have a printer who uses only TOYO inks, this is the palette that you will need to use. The TOYO palette offers colors that are available through the TOYO 88 Color Finder system. The range of colors offered here includes those created using TOYO process inks and those that are reproduced using TOYO standard inks. These colors are defined using the Lab color space and are converted to RGB for display and CMYK for printing. Colors can be displayed by name or swatch through the Options menu.

DIC COLORS   This palette offers colors that are available through the DIC Color Guide, DIC Color Guide Part II, and DIC Traditional Colors of Japan. Colors in these palettes are created by mixing DIC brand inks. Reproduction through Corel applications is achieved through the CMYK color space. Colors can be displayed by name or swatch through the Options menu.

 NOTE: *The custom palette in the Fixed Palettes mode displays the contents of the currently selected custom palette and does not reflect the colors of the color-matching system in use.*

The Fountain Fill Tool

Now it's on to the next icon on the Fill Tool's Tool Settings roll-up. Next to the Effect filters, the Fountain fill tools represent the greatest tools for creating stunning backgrounds and fills. A fountain fill is a fill that fades gradually from one color to another. This type of fill is also called a "gradient" or "graduated" fill. When you click the Edit button, Corel PHOTO-PAINT lets you create linear, radial, conical, square and rectangular fountains fills in the Fountain Fill dialog box, shown in Figure 12-8.

From this dialog box, it is easy to select and configure one of four types of fountain fills.

Advanced Features of the Fountain Fill Dialog Box

If you require greater control of the fills, there are more advanced control features in Fountain Fill dialog box. The Fountain Fill dialog box edits and creates fountain fills. It is laid out into four sections: Type, Options, Color Blend, and Presets.

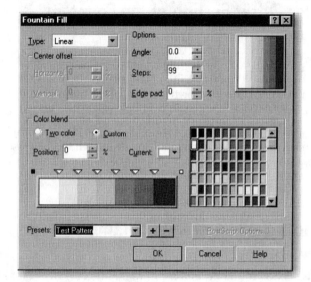

The
Fountain
Fill dialog
box

FIGURE 12-8

Fountain Fill Dialog Box Options

- **Preview Box** This shows you how the fountain fill will look with the colors you have chosen. The Type selects one of five types of fountain fills.

- **Linear** This selects a fountain fill that changes color in one direction.

- **Radial** This selects a fountain fill that changes color in concentric circles from the center of the object outwards.

- **Conical** This selects a fountain fill that radiates from the center of the object like rays of light.

- **Square** This selects a fountain fill that changes color in concentric squares from the center of the object outwards.

- **Rectangular** Same as square except it uniformly radiates to all corners of the rectangle.

12

The Center Offset Section of the Fountain Fill Roll-up

The Center Offset values reposition the center of a Radial, Conical, Square, or Rectalgular fountain fill so that it no longer coincides with the center of the object. Negative values shift the center down and to the left; positive values shift the center up and to the right. You can also use the mouse to drag the center to the desired position.

At first appearance this seems pointless. Why would anyone in their right mind waste the time to use a value system to determine where the offset is when you can move it with the cursor to the desired position? However, the Center Offset is necessary when you need to make several fills with exactly the same offset values.

The Options Section of the Fountain Fill Roll-up

The Options section of the Fountain Fill dialog box allows you to adjust any of the settings to customize the appearance of the fountain. The choices are described in the following paragraphs.

THE ANGLE BOX   The Angle box determines the angle of gradation in a Linear or Conical fountain fill. You can also change the angle by dragging the line that appears when you click in the preview box with the right mouse button. Holding down the CTRL key while dragging constrains the angle to multiples of 15 degrees.

THE STEPS BOX   The Steps value box displays the number of bands used to display and print the fountain. The preview display always shows 20 steps regardless of the Steps setting, so don't think that it is malfunctioning. The preview when you exit the Options section will correctly display the higher number of steps.

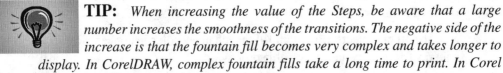

 TIP: *When increasing the value of the Steps, be aware that a large number increases the smoothness of the transitions. The negative side of the increase is that the fountain fill becomes very complex and takes longer to display. In CorelDRAW, complex fountain fills take a long time to print. In Corel PHOTO-PAINT, they take no longer than anything else because it is all bitmaps.*

TIP: *Beware of producing too narrow a range of colors over a large area, which produces banding. For example, if a range of six shades of colors is spread over an 11" x 17" area, banding will result.*

THE EDGE PAD   The Edge Pad increases the amount of start and end color in the fountain fill. It is used primarily with circles and irregularly-shaped objects in which the first and/or last few bands of color lie between the object and its highlighting box. The effect is to take away from the smooth transition between the starting and ending colors. The Edge Pad can be used when applying shading to an object such as text. Entering a large number into the Edge Pad box will cause a wide band to separate the top and bottom of a Linear fill. The Edge Pad option is not available for Conical fountain fills and therefore is grayed out.

The Color Blend Section of the Fountain Fill Roll-up

The Color Blend section of the Fountain Fill dialog box is where you select the colors you want to use in your fill. There are two modes of operation in the Color Blend area: Two Color (default) and Custom.

TWO COLOR BLEND   With the Two Color blend option, intermediate colors are created between the From color and the To color. This is best for appearances of shading and highlights. The operation of the Two Color Blend is controlled by one of the three buttons to the right of the From and To colors. These buttons are:

- **Direct**   When selected, it determines the intermediate fill colors from a straight line beginning at the From color and continuing across the color wheel to the To color. This option produces a color series composed of blends of the From and To colors.

- **Counter-Clockwise Color Path**   Determines the fill's intermediate colors by traveling counter-clockwise around the color wheel between the From and To colors.

- **Clockwise Color Path**   Determines the fill's intermediate colors by traveling clockwise around the color wheel between the From and To colors.

- **Mid-Point Slider**   This option is only available with Direct selected. It adjusts the midpoint between the From and To color. The Mid-point slider allows the user to control the distribution of color/shading of the fountain fills.

CUSTOM BLEND   The Custom Blend allows you to add more than two colors to a fill and in specific locations on the fill. In the Custom feature, even more incredible effects and backgrounds come to life. When the Custom button is clicked, the dialog box changes as shown in the following illustration. The Custom option allows you to select up to 99 intermediate colors from the palette at the right of the dialog box. Specify where you want the color to appear by adding markers with a double-click above the preview box. The markers look a lot like the tab markers on my word-processing program.

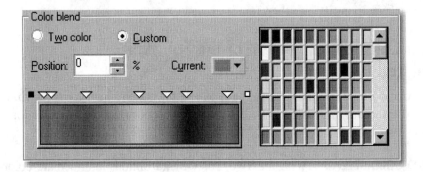

ADDING MARKERS   There are two ways to add markers. When you double-click just above the preview box in the color blend area, a black marker will appear. Apply a color from the palette and the preview box in the color blend area and in the upper-right corner of the Fountain Fill dialog box will reflect the change. Another way to add a marker is to select the To or From color squares at either end of the preview ribbon and specify a new value in the Position box and then click on the end color square again. (The first works the best.)

TIP: *Use the position box to enter precise positions for the markers. An easy way to do this is by double-clicking where you want the marker and then putting the exact position for it in the Position box. For example, by double-clicking near the middle of the fill you can get an approximate center position. To be exact, enter 50 percent in the Position box. The halfway point between the middle and the ends is 25 and 75 percent, and so on.*

After adding a marker, choose a color from the palette. To reposition a color, select its marker and drag it to the desired spot, or edit the value in the Position box. The preview box in the color blend area and in the upper-right corner of the Fountain Fill dialog box will reflect the change. To delete a color, double-click on the marker.

NOTE: *More than one color marker can be selected at a time by holding down the SHIFT key when selecting or deselecting.*

The Presets Area

The Presets area lets you save the fountain settings you specified so that you can apply them to other objects at a later time. It also contains over 100 predesigned fills that were installed with Corel PHOTO-PAINT.

SELECTING A PRESET   To select a preset, click on the down arrow to the right of the preset text box and a list appears. Click on a preset name and the preset appears in the preview window. If you want to browse through the list, just click on the first one you wish to view, and then each time you press the down or up arrow, the next preset will be selected and previewed. You might enjoy doing this if your cable TV is out and you are really bored.

SAVING A PRESET   To save a preset, type a name (up to 20 characters in length) in the Presets box, and then click the plus button. (Clicking the minus button removes the selected settings from the Preset list.)

Bitmap Fill

The Bitmap fill is enabled by selecting the Bitmap Fill button on the either the Edit Fill & Transparency dialog box or the Fill roll-up. It is the one that looks like a checkerboard. The Bitmap fill allows you to fill a selected area with a bitmap image. There are a large number of images in the Corel library (located in the \TILES folder on your Corel PHOTO-PAINT CD-ROM). In addition to the bitmap images provided, you can import almost any bitmap that can be read by your PC.

 NOTE: *Corel PHOTO-PAINT can import vector-based images for use as bitmap fills.*

12

Loading a Different Bitmap Image

When you invoke the Bitmap fill, you will see the currently selected image in the preview window. To change the image, you must click the Edit button. This will open the Bitmap Fill dialog box. The dialog box in the image below is shown with the bitmap selection palette open to the left so you can see all of the buttons. This is done with PHOTO-PAINT magic. In actuality, the palette opens on top of the dialog box.

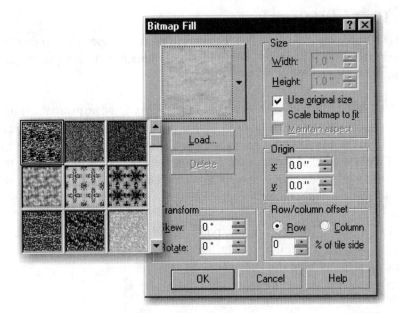

How the Bitmap Fill Operates

Here is a brief summary of how the Bitmap fill works. You have so much versatility when using bitmaps for fills that it is sometimes difficult to get a grip on all of it. Here are some pointers about using files for bitmap fills:

- Remember that if you use the Fill tool (the bucket), the fill will be calculated to the boundaries of the mask or the edges of the image. If the bitmap image is larger than the mask or the image, Corel PHOTO-PAINT will put as much as will fit, beginning with the lowers-left corner of the original image.

- You can control what appears in a flood-filled area by using the many tile/offset controls in the Bitmap Fill Dialog box.

- The Rectangle, Ellipse, and Polygon tools, on the other hand, will fill to the perimeter of the defined area. If there is a mask, the masked area that falls within the area will be filled.

TIP: *When using Corel Photo CDs as bitmap fills, make sure to crop them in the Import dialog box to get rid of any black film border. If you don't, the results can be really ugly.*

Controlling the Size and Position of the Bitmap Tiles

With the settings in the Bitmap Fill dialog box set to their default settings, if the bitmap that you import is too small to fill the area, it is tiled. If the image is too large, the fill does not resize the bitmap but rather, beginning in the lower-left corner of the original bitmap, it takes all of the bitmap that can fit in the area that is being filled. As a result, if you have a large file you have used for a bitmap fill and a small area to fill, you might find that a large portion of the bitmap didn't make it into the fill area.

In Corel PHOTO-PAINT, you can control the size, offset, and several other parameters of the bitmap fill.

Tile

The controls in this section allow you to set the size of your pattern tiles. You can choose one of the preset sizes or enter custom dimensions. By selecting Use original size, the bitmap file will not be scaled to a new size. If it is not checked, the bitmap will be scaled to the size set in the Width and Height settings. These settings are grayed-out if the Use original size option is enabled.

Scale Pattern to Fit

When enabled, it scales the tile pattern to fit entirely within the tile preview window. It also disables the entire dialog box when enabled.

First Tile Offset

Controls in this section set the offset of the first tile (and therefore the rest of the pattern) relative to the top right-hand corner of the object. If you want the pattern to start flush with the corner, set the X and Y values to zero percent.

Row/Column Offset

These controls shift either the rows or columns of tiles so that the pattern is staggered rather than continuous. The percentage of tile side setting shifts alternating rows or columns by the amount specified. This feature helps break up the repeating patterns, which would normally not allow many types of bitmap fills to be used.

Selecting Among Currently Loaded Bitmap Images

On the right side of the preview window in the Bitmap Pattern dialog box is a down arrow button. Clicking the button or anywhere in the preview window opens a color preview of the first nine bitmaps that have been imported into Corel PHOTO-PAINT. If there are more bitmaps than can be displayed, scroll bars appear on the right side of the preview window that allow the user to see the remainder of the bitmap fills in Corel PHOTO-PAINT.

Importing Bitmaps

Clicking the Load button opens the Import dialog box, where you can import a graphic to use as your bitmap pattern. The Import dialog box is the same one used to open a graphic file. There is a large selection of bitmap fills available on the CD-ROM containing the \TILES folder.

Now on to the next section of the Fill roll-up: Texture Fills.

The Texture Fills

This is the feature that makes Corel PHOTO-PAINT unique. I do not know of another package that can do the things that can be done with Texture fills. There are some tricks to using the fills effectively, but you will learn them here. The Texture Fill dialog box is used to select one of the 100-plus bitmap texture fills included in Corel PHOTO-PAINT. Each texture has a unique set of parameters that you can modify to create millions of variations.

The results depend on your printer, your taste, and your willingness to experiment.

What's in a Name?

As with the filters, don't let the names of the fills confuse your thinking. As an example, using the Rain Drops, Hard Texture fill, I was able to obtain the effect of a cut metal edge.

I came across this cut metal effect when I was writing the Corel PHOTO-PAINT 5 Plus manual for Corel. I found by filling each character individually, the size of the "raindrop" doesn't get too large. Too large? This leads to our first general rule regarding the texture fills. As in Boyle's law of expanding gases (gas expands to fit the volume of the container):

Rule of bitmap textures: A texture fill expands to fit the volume of the available area.

In the following illustration I have created squares of various sizes and filled them with the same texture fill. As you can see, as the squares increase in area, the size of the fill increases proportionally. While this can be used to create some unusual effects, it can also catch you by surprise, especially when working with a large image only to find that when it is applied, it looks nothing like the thumbnail preview.

 NOTE: *The fill size is calculated by creating a square that is determined by the greatest dimension of the mask. For example, if you made a mask that was 50 x 500 pixels, the resulting fill would be as if it was a 500 x 500 pixel square.*

Exploring the Texture Fill Dialog Box

When the Texture Bitmap mode of the Fill roll-up is selected, the currently selected fill is displayed in the preview window. The Edit button opens the Texture Fill dialog box, shown below. This dialog box allows you to edit and create an unlimited number of new texture fills from existing fills. Unlike bitmap fills, you cannot import files for use as texture fills. The texture fills are actually fractals that are created as they are applied. This goes a long way to explain why some textures can take a long time to apply.

If you cannot find the exact file that you want in the 160+ preset textures that were shipped with Corel PHOTO-PAINT, you can edit the existing textures in the Texture Fill dialog box.

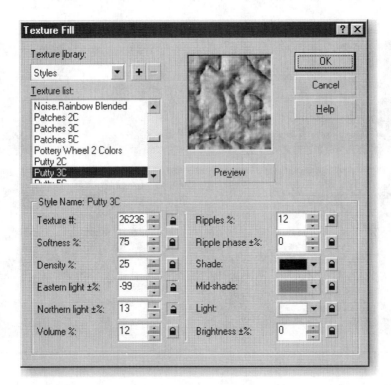

Texture Library

This list box displays the names of the texture libraries. Corel PHOTO-PAINT 8 ships with five libraries described in the following paragraphs: Samples, Samples

5, Samples 6, Samples 7 and Styles. There may even be a Samples 8, but it didn't exist in my beta copy.

SAMPLES   This is the original set of samples that were made with the Texture generator in the Styles library. For example, Clouds, Midday was created with Sky, 2 Colors. It is a quick way to get a texture without having to wade through all of the texture parameters to make it. The Samples library shipped with the original version of Corel 5.

SAMPLES 5/6/7   These libraries are like Samples except that there are more variations. Some of my personal favorites are in this library. I find that I use the Night Sky and Planets textures in the Samples 5 library more than almost any other texture. The Sample 5 library first shipped with the maintenance release of Corel PHOTO-PAINT 5. The Sample 6 shipped with Corel PHOTO-PAINT 6. Samples 7 is by far my favorite. Make sure you check it out.

STYLES   These are the building blocks of the bitmap texture fills. It is from the textures in this library that all of the other samples in the other three libraries are made. This library is a read-only library. If you modify a texture and want to save it, you will not be allowed to save it in this library. You must either create a new library or save it in one of the Samples libraries.

Texture List

This lists the texture fills available in the currently selected library. Clicking on a texture in the Textures list will select it, and the default setting for the texture will display in the preview window.

 TIP: *Each time a library is selected, the texture list returns to the default texture for that library. For example, if you were in Samples 5 and had been working with Night Sky and then you switched over to look at something in Styles, when you returned to Samples 5, it would have returned to the default texture.*

Preview and Locked/Unlocked Parameters

Each time the Preview button is depressed, Corel PHOTO-PAINT varies the appearance of the selected texture by randomly changing all unlocked parameters. This button does more than is apparent at first. There are over 15,000 textures with several million possible combinations for each one. Rather than requiring you to wade through a sea of permutations, Corel PHOTO-PAINT textures have certain variables that are either locked or unlocked by default.

You can lock and unlock a parameter by clicking the Lock button next to it. You can also use the Preview button to update a texture after changing the parameters yourself.

 TIP: *Until you get used to using a texture, I recommend using the default settings for the locks. They generally provide the best, quickest results.*

Save As (Plus Button)

After changing the parameters of a texture in the library (or a new library you created), click the Plus button in the upper-right corner to overwrite the original. This opens a dialog box for naming (or renaming) a texture you have created. The texture name can be up to 32 characters (including spaces). The Library Name option allows you to create a new library in which to store the textures. You can type up to 32 characters (including spaces). The Library List displays libraries where you can store the modified texture.

 NOTE: *You must save any modified Style textures in a library other than the Styles library, because Styles is a read-only library.*

Delete (Minus button)

This deletes the selected texture. You can only delete textures from libraries you created and added.

Style Name and Parameter Section

This part of the Texture Fill dialog box shows the name of the selected textures. Because each texture has different value assignments, methods, colors, and lights, it would take a separate book to list even a few of the combinations provided by the parameters. The value boxes in this area list parameters for the selected texture. Changing one or more of these parameters alters the appearance of the texture. The changes are displayed in the preview box whenever the Preview button is depressed.

The Style Name fields list numeric parameters. All textures have a texture number, which ranges from 0 to 32,767. The names of the other parameters vary with the texture selected and have ranges from 0 to 100 or -100 to 100.

To change a numeric parameter, enter a value in the text box or use the cursor and click on either the up or down arrow.

TIP: *If you are going to ascend or descend very far on the numeric list referenced above, you can use a speedup feature of the up and down arrows. Place the cursor between the up and down arrows. The cursor will change into a two-headed arrow cursor with a line between the two arrowheads. After the cursor changes, click and drag either up or down, and the selection list will move rapidly up or down the list (depending on which way you choose). To see the change entered, click the Preview button.*

The right side of the field lists up to six parameters, depending on the texture selected. To change a color, click on the color button and select a new color from the pop-up palette. If you desire a specific color or named color that is not on the color palette, click on the Other button. The Other button opens the same dialog box (but it is called Select Color) as the Uniform Fill dialog box. (See the Uniform Fill section for specific details regarding the use of this dialog box.) After you have made the desired changes, click the Preview button to see the effect the new color has on the selected texture.

No Fill button

The No Fill button is not available with the Fill tool roll-up, but it is available with the Shape tool which is explained later in this chapter.

The Palette Editor

Located in the Tools menu, this dialog box offers all of the controls found in the Uniform Color dialog box except it has some additional palette display and control features. Figure 12-9 shows the Palette Editor for the Color Model mode. The major difference between the Palette Editor and the Uniform Color dialog box is that the palette in the Uniform Color dialog box can have colors added but not edited, moved or removed, as in the Palette Editor.

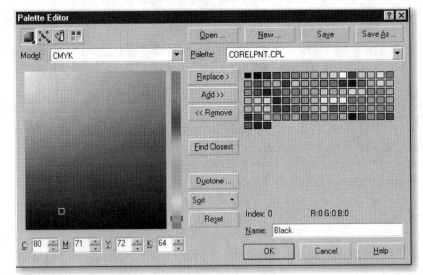

Palette
Editor in
the Color
Model mode

FIGURE 12-9

Removing a Color from the Palette

Fair is fair. If I am going to show you how to add a color to a palette, I should also
show you how to get rid of it.

1. In the Palette Editor, click on the swatch of the color you want to delete.

2. Click on the <<Remove button and a confirmation box appears, giving
   you one last chance before deleting the color.

3. If you click the Yes button, the color is history.

Renaming a Color in the Palette

Sometimes you don't want to remove the color, just rename it. Renaming colors is
simple as well.

1. Click on the color you want to rename, and type in a new name.

2. Click the Update button.

NOTE: *Don't rename existing industry-standard colors. For example, if you are using Pantone 1615V, don't call it Flaming Neon Ties. While you may find the nomenclature entertaining, it will not be understood by the service bureau or your printer. Another reason for sane color names is that human memory is frail, and if you give a color a cute name, there is a strong chance that when it comes time to look for it again, you may not be able to remember that specific shade of green that you created was called Aunt Fred's Toenail Clipping. Now that I've spoiled your fun, the good news is that Corel PHOTO-PAINT gives you 20 characters with which to name your new color creation. This is a vast improvement over the terse eight-character restriction of DOS naming conventions.*

Working with the Palettes

Now that you know how to get colors on and off the palettes as well as rename the colors, the only thing left is how to manage the palettes themselves.

OPENING AN EXISTING PALETTE The Open Palette option opens the Open Palette dialog box. The default palette is CORELPNT.CPL, an RGB color model palette. When opening an existing palette, you have the choice of opening one of three different types of palettes from the File of Type list:

- **Custom palette (.CPL)**
- **Spot Palette (.IPL)**
- **Process palette (.PAL)**

NEW PALETTE The New button opens up an empty palette that you can fill with any combination of colors. If you attempt to create a new palette without saving the current palette that you have modified, you will receive a warning message. To create a new palette, proceed as follows:

1. Select New.

2. When the New Palette dialog box opens, enter the name for the new palette.

3. After you enter a name, click the Save button. By default, it is placed in the Draw8\Custom folder.

12

4. Use the Add button to add colors from the palette on the left to the empty palette on the right.

 TIP: *Sometimes when you are working on a project that requires a number of exact reference colors (e.g., Pantone), you may find it is easier to create a palette specifically for the project with the required colors.*

SAVING A PALETTE   Selecting the Save option opens the Save Palette dialog box, which saves the current palette under the same name. This is used to save any changes made to a palette. If you do not save a palette, any change made it will be lost when Corel PHOTO-PAINT is closed or a new palette is selected.

SAVE PALETTE AS   Use the Save As option when you have modified an existing palette but do not want to apply the change to the original palette. This is the best way to build a custom palette of favorite colors. The basic palette has 99 colors. By adding colors to the existing palette and saving it under a unique name, you have all of the basic colors plus your personal favorites or specific colors made for a project or client.

 TIP: *Use the Save As command when you have made changes to the default palette. Many times, image files that you can get from various sources expect to find the default palette. If you have changed it, you may get unpredictable results.*

Find Closest

This is a neat little feature. After you find the color you like on the left palette, click the Find Closest option and PHOTO-PAINT determines the closest color that exists on the palette that is currently selected on the right.

Sort

Clicking this button opens a choice of methods to sort the palette displayed in the Palette Editor. You can sort by name, hue, brightness, etc.

Duotone

Selecting this opens the same dialog box you get if you were to select Convert to...
Duotones.

Mixing Area

New to PHOTO-PAINT 8 is an area whose sole purpose is to assist you in selecting
colors that either complement or are harmonious with the selected colors. Opened
by choosing the Mixer button on the Palette Editor, you have a full-featured selection
of colors. Alll you need to do to pick a color is to select on the one Hues settings
(default is Harmony 3) and pick the complementary or harmonious colors from the
palette below (see Figure 12-10). There are an endless number of combinations
possible by choosing from the Variations drop-down list. It gives you choices such
as cooler colors, warmer colors, etc. Once you have selected the color you can add

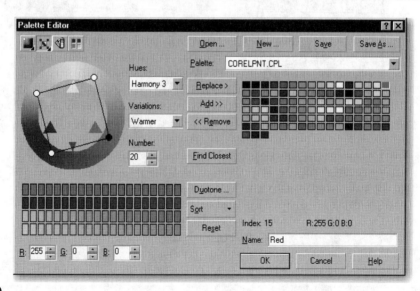

The Mixer
Mode of the
Palette
Editor

FIGURE 12-10

it to the currently selected palette. If you are like me and sometimes struggle with what color to pick to go with an existing color, this feature will make your life a lot easier. Now, if I can just get it to match my ties with my shirts.

The Transparency Tab

The Transparency tab of the Edit Fill & Transparency dialog box offers the ability to control the transparency of fills. With the Transparency tab you apply fills with one of eight transparency fills by selecting it in the Type box.

Choosing None (default) means there is no transparency applied to the fill. This is the way fills are normally applied. Choosing Flat creates a transparency that is uniform through out the fill. Because it is a uniform transparency it only has a starting value. The default setting for the Start Transparency is zero. If this setting isn't changed then the Flat setting operates like the None setting. The photograph shown below had a bitmap fill applied to it at a Flat transparency setting of 60.

The Linear setting applies a the fill beginning with the level of transparency specified in the Start Transparency value and ending with the level defined by the End Transparency. The beginning and ending point of the fill is determined by the starting and ending points placed in the preview window. Using a value of 0 to 100 the Linear fill was applied to the picture of the mask in the image. In the image below, the cursor in the Preview window (enlarged in the insert above the dialog box) indicates the starting and ending point of the transparency. The resulting image is displayed above and to the left of the dialog box.

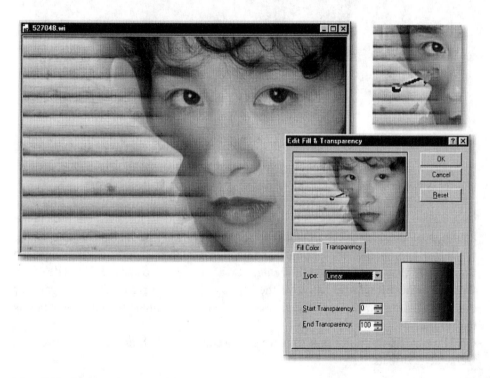

The Elliptical setting provides the greatest control in the creation of irregularly shaped fills. The original photograph has a solid black background. By applying a parchment fill through an elliptical transparency as shown in the dialog box below we are able to make the man appear to be part of the original paper. Believe me when I tell you it looked much better in color.

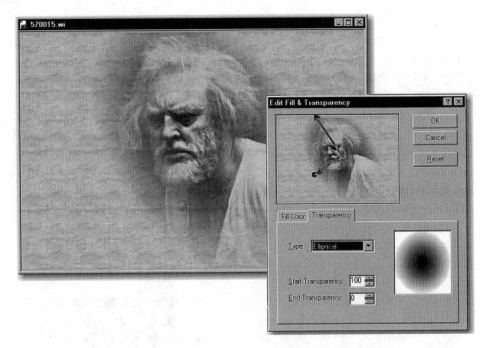

The Radial setting, like the Elliptical setting offers the advantage of circular lines which allows another image to be applied without straight lines which attracts the attention of the viewer. The Radial Type was selected and instead of one of the traditional fills another photograph was selected. Because the photograph being used for a fill also had the subject in the center, it was necessary to use the First Tile offset feature of the Bitmap fill to move the photograph to the right. The transparency direction is shown in the expanded preview window. The final result is shown below the original.

The other two choices are Square and Rectangle. Both are good for creating frame style effects.

The Shape Tools

The three Shape tools allow you to draw outlined or filled shapes on your image. The buttons along with the Line tool, shown below, are available in the Shape tools flyout in the Toolbox. If you want to create the shape as an object, enable the Render to Object check box in the Tool Settings roll-up for the Shape tools or the Property Bar. This allows you to reposition or edit your object before you merge it into your image. If you do not create the shape as an object, it will instantly merge into the background, so ensure you set the color, fill, and outline in the Tool Settings roll-up before you begin. Another unique feature of the Shape Tools is the No Fill tool. When enabled, the Shape tools create rectangles, circles and polygons borders without applying a fill.

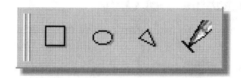

 TIP: *The Render To Object option in the Property Bar creates shapes as objects that can be moved and transformed without affecting the underlying image but the Render to Object feature is not enabled for all of the Shape tools. If you enable it on the Rectangle Tool it is not automatically enabled on all of the other tools. This is true of all of the Shape tool properties.*

Width and Roundness of Borders

With the Tool Settings roll-up or the Property bar, you can control the size and shape a border made by the Rectangle, Ellipse, or Polygon tools.

Width

This determines the thickness of the border in points (remember, a point is 1/72 of an inch).

Transparency

The Transparency setting determines how transparent the fill will be when applied to the image. This setting can be of great benefit when you need to apply a fill for an effect. It can also be a real pain.

TIP: *You must understand that when you change the transparency, it remains, and it is very easy to forget that you now have a transparency setting. What happens to me is that I will apply a color like red and I observe* *that it looks washed out. I sit there puzzled, wondering if I have left some sort of mask on the image, and then after a few moments I remember that I have a transparency setting. This transparency setting only works for the Rectangle, Ellipse, or Polygon tool. It does not affect the transparency setting for the Fill tool.*

Roundness (Rectangle Tool Only)

The "roundness" of the corners is determined by the Roundness settings. A rough representation of the rounded curve is continuously updated as the value of roundness is increased or decreased.

Joints (Polygon Tool Only)

This setting, available when the width value is at least 1, gives you three choices for how Paint is to treat the joints of multiple line figures. Use the drop-down list to select the type of joint. Choices are Butt, Filled, Round, and Point.

- **Butt**   The Joints are the squared ends of the lines where they meet and overlap.
- **Filled**   The open areas caused by the overlap are filled.
- **Round**   The corners are rounded.
- **Point**   The corners end in points.

Paint Mode

The Paint mode drop-down box lets you control the way paint colors and paper colors combine to create new colors and effects. With most paint tools, the paint color simply replaces the paper color (just as you would use a colored paint to paint a white wall). However, with the paint modes, it is the combination of paint colors and paper colors that produces the new color.

Anti-Aliasing

Anti-aliasing removes jagged edges from a mask, object, or image by adding duplicated pixels where the mask, object, or image edge contacts the background image.

Using the Rectangle Tool

The Rectangle tool is used to draw hollow or filled rectangles and rounded rectangles. Without the tools in this flyout, we wouldn't be able to control the fill of masked areas as well as we do.

Here are the facts for the Rectangle tool:

- F6 is the keyboard shortcut.

- If the CTRL key is held down while defining the shape, the rectangle is constrained to a square.

- Holding down the SHIFT key while creating a rectangle will cause the rectangle to shrink or grow (depending on the direction of the mouse movement) from the center.

- When the Rectangle is produced, it is filled with the current fill setting in the Fill roll-up.

- If the No Fill setting is selected, a hollow rectangle is created. It doesn't consume system resources; it doesn't do anything. Sounds Zen. Very good, Grasshopper.

To Draw a Rectangle or Rounded Rectangle

Here are some hints about drawing Rectangles or Rounded rectangles.

- Select the Rectangle tool and choose the border color by left-clicking the desired color on the onscreen palette and the Fill color by right-clicking on the desired color. The paint (background) color determines border color.

- Specify the width and roundness of the border in the Tool Settings roll-up.

- Press the left mouse button to anchor the rectangle and drag until you have achieved the desired size.

- The rectangle is filled with the current Fill color when the left mouse button is released. The rectangle is hollow if No Fill is selected in the Fill roll-up.

- If the rectangle is not what you desire, it can be erased by pressing the ESC key *before* releasing the mouse button.

12

The Ellipse Tool

The Ellipse tool draws hollow or filled ellipses. If the CTRL key is held down while defining the shape, the ellipse is constrained to a circle. Holding down the SHIFT key will shrink or grow the ellipse/circle from the center.

To Draw an Ellipse

The following are some general guidelines for drawing circles and ellipses with the Ellipse tool.

- F7 is the keyboard shortcut
- Click the Ellipse tool and choose the border color by clicking on the desired color in the onscreen palette with the left mouse button.
- The paint (background) color determines border color. The ellipse is filled with the current fill color unless the No Fill is selected in the Fill roll-up.
- Specify the width of the border in the Tool Settings roll-up.
- Press the left mouse button to anchor the ellipse, and drag until you have achieved the desired size.
- If the circle is not what you desire, it can be erased by pressing the ESC key *before* releasing the mouse button. Holding down the SHIFT key produces a circle.

The Polygon Tool

The Polygon tool produces closed multisided figures. By selecting different Joint settings in the Tools Settings roll-up, the Polygon tool can provide a wide variety of images.

To Draw a Polygon

The following are some procedural guides for using the Polygon tool:

- Select the Polygon tool. (There isn't a keyboard shortcut.)
- Choose Color, Width, type of joints, and Transparency of the border and fill.

- Click where the polygon is to begin in order to anchor the starting point. Move the cursor where the first side of the polygon is to end. As the cursor is moved, the closed shape of the polygon is continually redrawn on the screen to assist the user in what the final shape will look like.

- Click the left mouse button again to complete the first side. Continue moving the cursor to define the remaining sides.

- Double-clicking the end of the last line completes the polygon.

- Holding the CTRL key down while moving the cursor constrains the sides of the polygon vertically, horizontally, or at 45-degree angles.

The Line Tool

The last button on the Shape tools flyout is the Line Tool. There are times when working with any photo-editing package when you just need to make a line. This tool draws single or joined straight line segments using the Paint color. The Render To Object option in the Property Bar or Tool Settings roll-up creates new lines as objects that can be moved and transformed without affecting the underlying image which is very handy because it allows you to correct mistakes that were impossible before this feature was introduced.

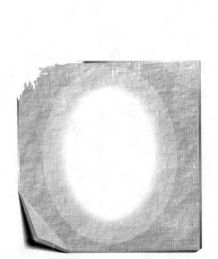

13

Understanding Objects

Up to now we have been manipulating images with the help of various types of masks. In this chapter, we will begin to work with one of the more powerful features of Corel PHOTO-PAINT, which is the ability to create and control objects. The use of objects falls into a category I call fun stuff. There is a tabloid sold in the United States called *The Sun*, which may be one of the leading forums for unique photo-editing. If you live in the United States, you have probably seen *The Sun* while standing in grocery lines. Last night, the headline was "Baby Born with Three Heads." The photograph showed a woman holding an infant who fit the headline's description. Someone on *The Sun* staff had masked the face of a small child, made it into an object, duplicated several copies, and placed them on the body of the baby. Like I said, this is fun stuff. If you are an avid reader of *The Sun*, do not take what I say as criticism of the tabloid. I love *The Sun*! I stand in a lot of grocery lines, and it provides entertainment during an otherwise boring wait.

In this chapter we will explore Objects, the Text tool and all that can be done with them.

Pixels and Crazy Glue

When an image is placed in a bitmap program like Corel PHOTO-PAINT, it becomes part of the background of the image. Traditionally with bitmap programs (like Microsoft PAINT), there is only the background. With such programs, if we were to take a brush from the Toolbox and draw a wide brush stroke across an image, every pixel the brush touches would change to the color assigned to the brush. If we then removed the brush color, the original image would have vanished, because the brush color did not go on *top* of the original color, it replaced it. It is as if every pixel that is applied has super glue on it. When an action is applied to an image, it "sticks" to the image and cannot be moved. Anyone who has spent hours and hours trying to achieve an effect with these older bitmap programs will testify that the process by which bitmaps merge into and become part of the background was the major drawback of photo-editing programs. And then along came objects.

Objects Defined

So what is an object? Here is one definition:

> *An object is an independent bitmap selection created with object tools and layered above the base image.*

Let's expand that definition. In Corel PHOTO-PAINT, an object is a bitmap that "floats" above the background, which is also called the *base image*. Because the object is not a part of the base image, but instead floats above it, an object can be moved as many times as needed without limit. Objects can also be scaled, resized, rotated, and distorted. We also have the ability to apply Perspective transform in addition to the ones already mentioned as well as new Modes of operation, which greatly increase the flexibility of many of the tools.

When the concept of objects was introduced in Corel PHOTO-PAINT 5, there were *simple* and *complex* objects. Now PHOTO-PAINT has only one kind of object. Here is the best part: objects are much easier to create in Corel PHOTO-PAINT 8 than they are with Corel PHOTO-PAINT 5. You are about to learn how to do some amazing things with objects. Most of the rules you learned in previous chapters regarding masks also apply to objects.

Expanding the Definition

When the Objects Roll-Up changed names and became one of four docking windows, some of the ways in which objects were previously managed changed. To help understand how the Objects Docker window works, it is necessary to expand on our previous definition of an object. When we look at the image in Figure 13-1, we see a phone against a green (if it's in color) background. Because in this particular

A picture
composed
of a
background
and an
object
(phone)

FIGURE 13-1

13

image the phone is an object, we visualize it as shown in Figure 13-2. The background is on the left and the telephone is an object whose visual edge is the edge of the object. The misconception that the object only exists to its visible edge is reinforced by the Object Marquee, which displays the "edge" of an object. In reality, an object may be composed of both opaque and transparent pixels. Although it appears the object stops at the edge of the phone the fact is, transparent pixels actually extend to the edge of the image. If Figure 13-1 were observed from the side, we would see that the object (the phone and its opaque surroundings) is actually the same size and dimensions as the background. I have made a visual representation of it in Figure 13-3. It may help to think of the object as on a large sheet of clear acetate, rather than as a cutout placed on the background.

The Objects Dialog

The Objects Docker window is the control center for all object manipulations. The following is only a partial list of the functions that can be accomplished through the Property Bar and the Objects Docker window:

- Render to Object
- Select object
- Lock or unlock object transparency
- Make objects visible or invisible
- Create objects from masks
- Create masks from objects
- Move objects between layers
- Change rate of the transparency/opacity of objects
- Apply transformations to individual objects
- Select merge modes for individual objects
- Label different objects
- Combine objects with the background
- Combine individual objects together
- Delete objects
- Get a babysitter on a Saturday night (OK, that might be pushing it)

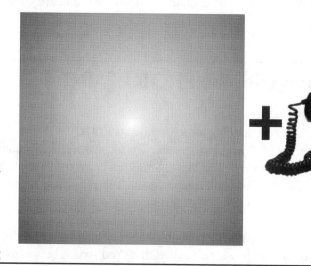

Background
and what
object
appears
to be

FIGURE 13-2

Exploring the Objects Dialog and Property Bar

The Objects Dialog, Figure 13-4, can be opened by double clicking on the Object Picker tool in the Toolbox, or with the keyboard combination CTRL-F7. The Property

Object
actually is
same size as
background

FIGURE 13-3

13

Bar that is associated with objects offers many more controls that are not available on the Objects Dialog.

A Moment with the PHOTO-PAINT 7 Veterans...

Probably the greatest amount of change in PHOTO-PAINT 8 has occurred in the area of object management. The Objects Roll-Up became an Objects Docker window. The Multi, Single and Layers mode are no longer there and the Preserve Image button has also been reported missing. Here is a synopsis of the changes and their equivalents.

- Multi mode has been removed and Single and Layer modes remain except they aren't called that. You switch between Single and Layer mode using the Lock Transparency checkbox in the Object Dialog. When this switch is off (default) you are in the equivalent to the old Layer Mode.

- With Multi mode gone, you may ask, how can I apply effects to several objects? There have been some new repeat commands that allow any action that is applied to one object to be applied to any and all other objects.

- The Preserve Image button is gone. Selecting Create Object: Copy Selection is the same as Create Object with the Preserve Image button on. Conversely, Create Object: Cut Selection is like Create Object with Preserve Image off.

If this is the first time you have run into this, it will take a little bit of adjustment. I have been working with this for over 5 months and I think it's great. For the record, I was staunchly opposed to the changes when they were originally presented to us. So, read how everything works and trust me, you will like the changes, you will like the changes. Now, keeping your eyes on the swinging watch, repeat after me, I will like the changes.

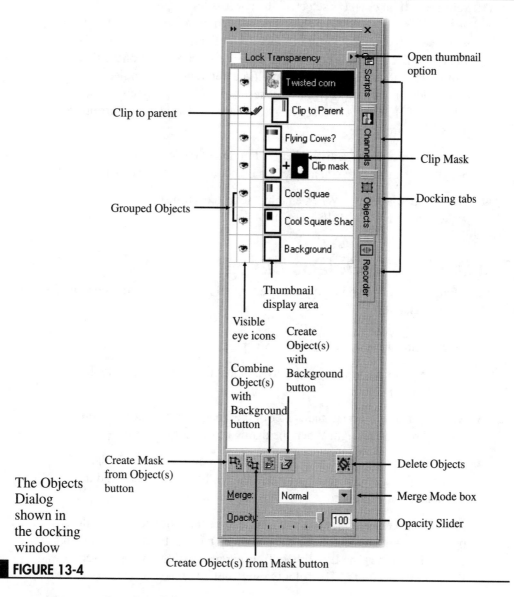

Open thumbnail option

Clip to parent

Flying Cows?

Clip Mask

Docking tabs

Grouped Objects

Thumbnail display area

Visible eye icons

Create Object(s) with Background button

Combine Object(s) with Background button

Create Mask from Object(s) button

Delete Objects

The Objects Dialog shown in the docking window

Merge Mode box

Opacity Slider

Create Object(s) from Mask button

FIGURE 13-4

Object Modes

New to PHOTO-PAINT 8 is the way that object editing is accomplished. There were 3 modes in PHOTO-PAINT 7 but now the interface has been simplified to make life a little simpler. Here are some definitions to describe states in the Object dialog.

13

- **Selected** If an object is selected, the name is highlighted. It can be moved, grouped with other objects or merged with the background or with other objects. An object is selected by clicking on its thumbnail or label. To select multiple contiguous objects, select the first one and SHIFT-click the last one. To select multiple non-contiguous objects CTRL-click on each object you want selected. Selected objects are not subject to PHOTO-PAINT actions (for example sharpening, blurring etc.) unless they are active.

- **Active** An object is active when its thumbnail has a red border. Only one object can be active at a time. An object that is active is also selected.

- **Lock Transparency** When enabled, it protects transparent areas of the object from PHOTO-PAINT actions.

Test Driving the Objects Dialog

This is a simple exercise to help you get a better feel for what the modes do and do not do—do-whackaa-do.

1. Create a new image 3 x 3 inches, 150 dpi.

2. In Futura Xblt BT at 72, type MODE. Select the Object Picker tool. The text is now an object.

3. Align the text (object) to the center of the image by right clicking on the text and selecting Align. When the dialog box opens click OK.

4. Select the text by clicking on it (if it is not already selected). In the Objects Dialog the object appears as MODE. It is highlighted and the thumbnail has a red border.

5. Click Lock Transparency to enable it. Change the Paint color to Yellow by left clicking on the color in the on-screen palette. From the Edit menu, choose Fill. When the Edit Fill & Transparency dialog box opens, choose Paint color. Click OK. The fill was only applied to the object.

6. Uncheck the Lock Transparency and apply the same fill again. The entire image is filled. Now the object consists entirely of opaque pixels (this term may be confusing: of pixels containing the same color.) Undo (CTRL-Z) this last action.

7. Select the Background by clicking on it in the Objects Dialog.

TIP: *You can select objects in an image by clicking them with the Objects picker tool. The background can only be selected in the Objects Dialog.*

8. From the Brush Tools flyout at the bottom of the Toolbox, select the Image Sprayer. From its Property bar, click the Load Image Sprayer List button (on the far left—looks like a file folder) and select foliage.cpt. Click Open.

9. Click in the image and drag the brush around until you have a nice patch of green like the one shown below.

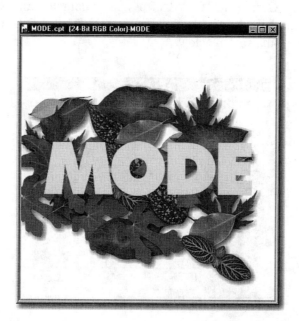

10. That's all for now. We are going to use this file again, so either keep it open or save the file as MODE.CPT. Don't forget where you parked it.

NOTE: *For purposes of clarification, the terms* object *and* layer *are used interchangeably. This is because each layer can contain only one object, and without an object there cannot be a layer. In this chapter, we will* use the term Object to avoid confusion.

Looking Deeper into the Objects Docker Window

The Objects Docker window is composed of the Thumbnail display area, the Dialog Display options, the Multi-function buttons and the Merge/Opacity controls. Let's find out a little more about these wonders.

Thumbnail Display Area

The Thumbnail display is divided into four columns. The column on the far right shows the thumbnail and the name of the object. The bottom object is automatically named Background. It cannot be renamed or moved. Unless it is text, each time an object is created, Corel PHOTO-PAINT assigns a default name to it. The object name can be edited by double-clicking on its name. This action opens the Object Properties dialog box, shown below.

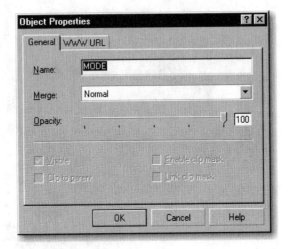

Using this dialog box allows you to give the object any old name your heart desires, as long as it is less than 39 characters. The display of the thumbnails is controlled by the Display Options box which is discussed in the next section.

The next column in the Objects Docker window can contain the Clip to Parent icon. This looks like a paper clip and can only be enabled when there are two or more objects. The "Eye" icon in the center column indicates the object is either visible (black) or invisible (grayed out). When an object is invisible, it is automatically protected from any PHOTO-PAINT actions. The narrow column to the far left is used to display any groupings of objects.

Objects Docker Display Options

To the right of the Lock Transparency option is a small right-arrow button. Pushing it opens a drop-down list, shown below, that determines the size of the thumbnails displayed. The choices are Object Properties (same one we met in the previous paragraph), No Thumbnails, Small, Medium, and Large and Update Thumbnails. Why is there a No Thumbnails option you ask? Turning off the thumbnails speeds up PHOTO-PAINT, especially on slower systems.

Multifunction Buttons

There are several buttons on the bottom of the Objects Dockers window. The availability of the buttons and the buttons that are displayed are dependent upon the mode you are in.

- **The Create Mask from Object and Create Object** Copy Selection buttons.These provide a quick method to convert masks into objects and visa versa. If you are a PHOTO-PAINT 7 user, you will be pleased to know that these actions no longer delete either the object or mask when used.

- **The Combine button** This merges all selected object(s) with the background. Objects that are not selected are unaffected.

- **The New Object button** This button creates an empty transparent object that covers the entire image. This button is not available when the Lock Object Transparency checkbox is enabled. It is the same as selecting New Object command in the Object menu.

■ **The Delete Objects button** You select the objects, click this little button and it hauls off the objects screaming into the night where they are never heard from again (unless you evoke the powers of the Undo).

Merge Mode and Opacity

The Merge box determines the way in which the colors of the object and the colors of the background image are combined when the object is merged with the background. You can preview the result of using each merge mode directly in the Image Window. The Opacity Slider determines the opacity or transparency of the selected object. Some people are confused by opacity and transparency. Remember the 100% opacity is zero transparency or 100% transparency is zero opacity. You can call it either opacity or transparency. It's a "Is the glass half empty or half-full?" kind of question.

Clip to Parent

Clip to Parent is one of the new object properties introduced in PHOTO-PAINT 8. Although it sounds like what happens to me when I get the phone bills my children have run up, when this property is enabled the object's shape gets clipped to the shape of the object below it in the object list. This feature is activated by clicking in the column to the right of the eye in the Object dialog. A paperclip icon appears to show Clip to Parent is active.

There are many uses to this feature, but let's try the following one:

Working with Clip to Parent

One of the fun things to do with this feature is to place a photo inside of a shape or text. We will start off learning to use the feature in this exercise and use it with a photograph later in the book.

1. Open MODE.CPT if you closed it.

2. Ensure the Lock Transparency is unchecked. Click the Create New Object button on the Objects Dialog.

3. From the Edit menu choose Fill. From the Edit Fill & Transparency dialog box, click the Fountain Fill button and then the Edit button. Change the Preset to Gold Plated. Click OK to return and OK again to apply the fill. The fill we just applied filled the entire image.

4. In the Objects Docker window, the new object is on top. Click the column between the thumbnail and eye icon. A small paper clip icon appears on the image window and the fill layer is only visible at the point where it is above the text. Let's check it out.

5. Click the Tab key on the keyboard once and the text object is selected.

 NOTE: *When there is a Clip to Parent object the same size as an image, you cannot select any objects below it by clicking directly on it in the image. You must either cycle through with the Tab key, click on the object in the Objects window or hold down the* ALT *key and marquee-select the object.*

6. With the Object Picker tool, click and drag the word MODE around the image. Notice that wherever the text is placed, the fill in the top object is clipped to it. Drag the text back to the center.

7. If we want to permanently apply the fill to the text we need to select both objects. The text is currently selected, so hold down the SHIFT key and click on the top object. Both of the objects should be highlighted as shown below.

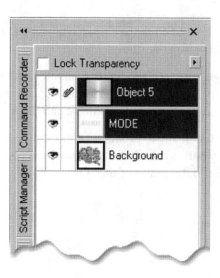

8. From the Object menu, choose Combine and select Combine Objects Together. The two objects have become a single object. The bottom object defined the edge and the top defined the fill.

9. Save the File, we'll be back.

Now let's move on to another new feature in PHOTO-PAINT 8, the Clip Mask.

Clip Masks

Clip Masks are masks that are attached to individual objects. As you may recall from Chapter 7, there can only be one mask on an image. Through the use of clip masks, you can apply a clip mask to every object. One of the primary uses of the clip mask is to provide a non-permanent transparency. Later in this chapter, we will learn about the Transparency tools that achieve the same effect as the Clip Mask except that when the transparency action is done with the clip mask, modifying the Clip Mask can modify the object's transparency at any time. Let's do a brief exercise and it will make more sense.

The Old Rope Through the O Trick— a Clip Mask Exercise

In this exercise we are going to take the Clip Mask for a spin and see what it can do.

1. Open MODE.CPT and click the Create New Object button. We now a have new object on top.

2. Select the Image Sprayer tool and then double-click it to open the Tools settings Roll-Up. At the bottom of the Roll-Up choose the Preset: Green Rope (you can also use Rope if you don't care for the color).

3. Click and drag the image to produce a rope somewhat like the one shown below. The only part that requires accuracy is to insure the rope goes through the hole in the center of the "O" in MODE.

4. From the Object menu, choose Add Clip Mask and select Show All. Notice there is now a Red square to the right of the new object in the Objects Docker. This is the clip mask and the red indicates it is active. Click the Reset Colors button in the Status Bar (to the left of the Paint color swatch).

5. Select the Interactive Fill tool from the Fill Tool's flyout. Click on a spot at the top of the rope and drag down to the word MODE. The transparency of the object is greatest at the origin point (black square) and least at the end point (white square). Let's change the transparency of the rope so only the starting point in the upper-left corner is faded. Position the origin and end points of the transparency so the rope looks like it is coming out of the white as shown. When you have it the way you want it, click the Object Picker tool.

13

6. Now let's do some real magic. Select the Paint Tool (F5) and then double click it to open the Tools Settings Roll-Up. Change the brush to Paintbrush and the Type: Quick Doodler. Because the Clip Mask is active, any brushstrokes we apply will modify the mask. Carefully apply the brush to the rope above the center of the letter O. Every place you apply the brush (with black) disappears. Continue to remove the rope around the letter until the rope looks like it is going through the letter as shown below. In my case I went crazy and made it look like it was going under the letter M as well.

7. In the Objects Dialog, right click on the Clip Mask. Several choices appear on a list. Select Disable and look at the image. All of the changes made to the rope object are hidden. Select the list again and notice it is from here, and the Objects menu, that we could remove the Clip Mask completely. For now, click the Disable again to turn it off.

8. Close the file and Save the changes.

More Stuff About Clip Masks

Everything we did to the green rope in the previous exercise we could have done with the Object Transparency tools. The big difference is that the changes made by the Object transparency tools are permanent, while the changes made with the Clip Mask are only there until you remove or change the mask. To make the changes permanent select Combine (which is now available as a choice from the Clip Mask part of the Objects menu) as shown below. This will permanently apply the mask effects to the object. If remove is selected, then the mask is discarded and the object returns to its pre-Clip Mask appearance.

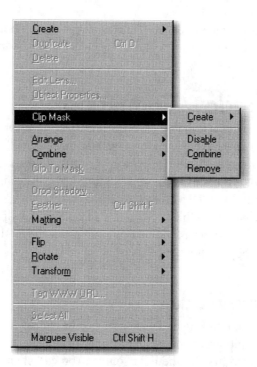

Editing Clip Masks

Remember that the Clip Mask is an extra mask that applies only to the object to which it is attached. Clip Masks have nothing to do with regular masks although you can view and edit them like regular masks although the procedure is a little tricky. In fact, I couldn't figure it out and had to ask the PHOTO-PAINT Product manager, Doug Chomyn and he provided the following procedure to view and edit Clip Masks:

1. Select the Channels docking dialog.

2. Click the eye icon beside the channel identified as "Object ## Clip Mask" while any of the color channels are visible; this will produce a Mask Overlay view.

3. If you hide all the color channels when the Clip Mask is selected in the Channels docking dialog, the Paint-on-Mask (grayscale) view will appear. In this mode, you can modify the mask just as if you were in Paint-on-Mask mode.

Now let's move on to the Object Transform modes. It's boring reading but great reference stuff when you get stuck and are wondering why something doesn't work.

The Drop Shadow Command

So what is this command doing in the objects chapter? The Drop Shadow command creates objects that look like shadows. While the Drop Shadow command was introduced with release of PHOTO-PAINT 7, it has been significantly enhanced in the PHOTO-PAINT 8 release. The major improvement lies in the ability to create perspective shadows as well as flat shadows.

Accessed through the Object menu, the Drop Shadow dialog box for both the Flat and Perspective modes is shown in Figure 13-5. While they may appear to be a little complex, they are not hard to use.

Flat Shadow Mode

The location of the controls in the Flat dialog box has changed from PHOTO-PAINT 7 but the functionality has remained unchanged. The Orientation portion shows the direction of the shadow –not the light source. You can change the direction either

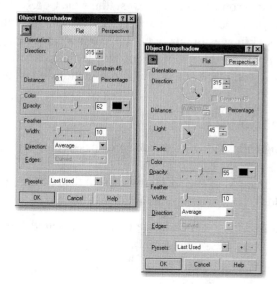

The two
modes of
the Drop
Shadow
Command,
Flat (left)
and
Perspective
(right)

FIGURE 13-5

by dragging the arrow dial indicator to the desired position, entering a numerical value, or changing the direction interactively on the image. You can also change the distance of the shadow interactively as well. Checkboxes allow restricting changes to 45 degree increments and displaying the distance as a percentage.

The Color section controls the color and the Opacity of the shadow created. The Color reminds me of Henry Ford's famous quote "You can get our car in any color you want as long as it's black." There are times while making a glow when you may want to change colors but shadows generally come in one color—black. Opacity is one of the two most important settings, the other is feathering. With it you control the very nature of the shadow—how soft it appears.

The Feather section offers several controls, Width (in pixels) determines the amount of feathering applied to the created shadow. This setting of how blurry the shadow is makes the difference between a shadow that looks fake and one that looks real. The Direction setting gives you four choices: Average, Middle, Inside and Outside. Inside places the feathered portion inside the shadow's edges; Outside adds pixels just outside the shadow's edges; Middle places approximately as many feathered pixels inside the edge as outside; and Average samples all pixels in the defined width and assigns a color value to each one individually. This results in some pixels being inside and some being outside, and creates a more gradual transition in color between the shadow object and the background, much like a gradient.

13

Presets contain some preset shadow settings the Corel artists have created. This is a wonderful new addition for someone like me who has settings for many of the different types of images in this book. Before this came along I had to get a paper list by the computer of the different standard settings. Operation is simple. Get the settings the way you like them, click the plus button and name the setting.

Dave's Shadowy Rules

When working with shadows here are some basic rules that may help you:

- If the object is to appear far away from the background, the shadow should be larger, very transparent, and blurred.

- If the object is to appear close to the background, the shadow should be much darker (less transparent), very close to the size of the object, and have only a small amount of blurring.

- To make some glow, set the Distance to zero, and increase the Feather width. The Opacity setting will determine how much go you put into your glow.

- Never ever forget the shadow is to fool the eye. It is not and never should be the center of attraction. If you apply a shadow, and someone viewing the picture makes a comment on how lovely the shadows are –you did something wrong.

Perspective Shadow Mode

This operates very similarly to the Flat shadow with a few exceptions. The Light section, unique to perspective, tells PHOTO-PAINT where the light source is in relation to the object. An angle of 90 degrees creates the longest shadows while zero degrees creates the shortest. The Fade adds a real touch of realism in making the shadow fade away as it gets further from the object. An example of both the Flat and Perspective shadows is shown in Figure 13-6.

When you click OK a shadow object is created. The new object is Grouped together with the original object. If you want to make any adjustments to the shadow you must first Ungroup it (CTRL-U). Before we finish the topic of shadows, we will apply it to finish up the file we have been working on in this chapter.

Flat as well as Perspective adds a professional touch to the Drop Shadow command

FIGURE 13-6

Final Touches Using the Drop Shadow Command

In this exercise we are going to put the finishing touches on the MODE.CPT we have been working on in this chapter.

1. Open MODE.CPT

2. With the Object Picker tool, select the green rope (not the Clip Mask) in the Objects Dialog.

3. From the Object menu, select the Drop Shadow command. When the dialog box opens choose Flat. Change the Direction to 325, Distance to 0, Opacity to 45 and Feather to Average with a width of 9. Click OK.

4. Now select the text. Choose the Drop Shadow again and keep the same Distance and Direction. Change the Opacity to 65 and the Feather width to 12. Click OK and we are done.

5. Save the file if you want; we won't be coming back to it. The final image is shown in Figure 13-7.

Transform Modes

There are seven different Transform Modes that provide all of the control that you could ever dream about when it comes to manipulating and transforming objects.

13

Final
version of
the MODE
exercise

FIGURE 13-7

All of these modes are available either through the Property Bar or by clicking on the object to cycle through the modes. With the Object Picker tool selected, press CTRL-F8 to open the Tool Settings roll-up, shown next. Here, five of the modes can be selected.

The Tool Settings roll-up for objects provides a very powerful and easy way to make precise manipulations to objects. There are five tabs that control the following:

- Object Position

- Object Rotation

- Object Scaling/Flip

- Object Resizing

- Object Skewing

Each of the Tabs within the Tool Settings dialog box for objects have three common functions. They are:

- **Apply To Duplicate button**   This button creates a copy of the selected object with the effects applied, while leaving the original object unchanged. For example, the Object Rotation tab was selected and a value of 15 degrees was entered. Clicking the Apply to Duplicate button would create a copy of the object that was rotated 15 degrees while leaving the original unchanged.

- **Transform button**   Clicking this button displays a preview of the transformation of the selected object in the Image Window. This is a preview only. You can either press ESC, or double-click outside the object or marquee in the Image Window to cancel the transformation and return to the original state.

- **Apply Button**   After clicking the Transform button, click Apply in the Tool Settings Roll-Up, press ENTER, or double-click inside the object to apply the transformation permanently. This control is available for both the Object Picker tool and the Mask Transform tool.

Object Position

Going from left to right, clicking on the first tab accesses the Object Position. These controls are used to reposition or move objects.

If you attempt to move an object with a setting that will place the object outside of the image area, the object will be placed outside of the image area. The object is still there, just not in the viewing area. When these controls are used in conjunction with the rulers, you can position objects very precisely and quickly anywhere within the image.

Absolute/Relative Positioning

When the Relative Position option is unchecked, the Horizontal listing displays the leftmost position of the object and the Vertical listing displays the topmost position of the object in relation to the 0,0 point of the image (upper-left corner). Moving the object is accomplished by changing these values. Objects of equal size can be positioned on top of one another by entering the same values for each object in these settings.

When the Relative Position option is checked, the Horizontal and Vertical Settings start out at zero pixels in both the horizontal and vertical axis in reference to the object.

 TIP: *You can quickly create a duplicate object that is precisely positioned over the original by pressing the Apply To Duplicate button without changing the Horizontal and Vertical settings.*

Object Rotate

The second tab provides access to the Object Rotation controls as shown below. While rotation of objects can be accomplished from the Objects menu or by dragging the Rotation handles, the Transform roll-up allows for precision rotation, which is very handy when you are applying it to multiple objects. Control of rotation is divided into two parts, angle and center of rotation.

Angle of Rotation

The first control determines the Angle of Rotation. There is nothing mystical here, the value is in degrees. The range of rotation is +360 degrees through - 360 degrees. You can enter a number for the Angle of Rotation as low as one one-thousandth of a degree. If you rotate an object 15 degrees, close the Object Tool Settings roll-up, and then reopen it three hours later after having worked on several other files, the setting will still be 15 degrees for the Angle of Rotation. If you close and reopen Corel PHOTO-PAINT, the setting will default back to 0 degrees. Regardless of what rotation values are entered into this setting, the Center of Rotation setting remains centered on the object.

Center of Rotation

The next set of controls is a little more interesting. With the Center of Rotation controls, you can precisely position the center of rotation. With the Relative Center option turned off, the controls for Center of Rotation report where the center of rotation is located on the currently selected object. Whenever you need to reposition the center of rotation, simply use the rulers to locate the new position and enter those values into the Center of Rotation controls. For example, if your currently selected object has a center of rotation at the Horizontal and Vertical position of 1 inch each, you could easily change that to, say, 2 inches Horizontal and 3 inches Vertical by simply entering those values in the Center of Rotation Controls.

Relative Center

When the Relative to Center option is turned on, the controls for Center of Rotation start off at 0. Units are controlled by the Preferences dialog box. Values entered in the Center of Rotation controls will move the center of rotation according to the values relative to its current position. For example, if you are working in inches and you enter a Center of Rotation value of 1 inch for both the Horizontal and Vertical settings, the center of rotation would be repositioned 1 inch down and to the right of the current center of rotation.

TIP: *A quick way to rotate an object is to select it with the object picker and then click on the object a second time. The control handles will change to indicate it is in rotation mode. By holding down the CTRL key on the keyboard while dragging the handles, you get rotation in 15-degree increments.*

13

Object Scale/Flip

The Object Scale tab, shown below, enables you to do exactly what its name suggests: scale objects. An object can be scaled by percentages of the object's size. You cannot enter negative numbers for the Object Scaling settings. Rather, numbers larger than 100 percent scale the object larger than its current size; numbers smaller than 100 percent scale the object smaller than its current size.

When Maintain Aspect is selected, the Horizontal and Vertical settings within the Object Scale remain the same. The Flip buttons flip the objects horizontally and vertically. The Object Scale settings and the Flip buttons can work in conjunction with one another. For example, if you have 50 percent Horizontal and Vertical settings for Object Scale with the Vertical Flip button on, the selected object will be flipped vertically at 50 percent of its original size when the Apply button is pressed.

 TIP: *You can create a duplicate object exactly over another by hitting the Apply To Duplicate button with 100 percent Horizontal and Vertical Object Scale settings and the Mirror buttons not selected.*

Object Size

The Object Size tab, shown below, offers settings that are a more accurate way to resize an object than Object Scale. The Object Size settings list the dimensions of the currently selected object. To change the dimensions of the currently selected object, simply enter in the new values and select Transform, and then Apply or Apply To Duplicate. Units are determined by the default setting in the Options dialog box. Negative numbers should not be entered for the Object Size settings.

Maintain Aspect

When the Maintain Aspect option is checked, the aspect of the object will be maintained when you enter a new value in one of the Horizontal or Vertical settings. For example, if you have an object that is 1 inch horizontal and 2 inches vertical, and you enter 2 inches in the Horizontal setting with the Maintain Aspect option checked, the Vertical option will automatically maintain the aspect ratio of the object by changing to 4 inches.

Object Skew

The Object Skew tab, shown below, allows you to numerically skew objects. Like all of the other settings in the Object Tool Settings roll-up, Object Skew simply provides a way to accurately enter in values for alterations that could otherwise be performed manually. Negative degree values can be used. Once new values are entered into this setting, the Object Skew settings will remain the same until they are changed, even if the file you are working on is closed and another is opened.

Perspective Mode

This mode, introduced in PHOTO-PAINT 7, is one of the most powerful for creating realistic-looking perspectives. Although this mode is not selectable from the Tool Settings Roll-Up, it can be selected from the drop-down menu at the far left of the Property Bar or by clicking on the object until the handles that look like to be small circles appear.

Perspective is the symmetrical distortion of an object that gives it a sense of depth, making it appear three-dimensional. The transformation is achieved by moving either of the two handles away from each other making the side of the object you moved longer, and this side now appears to be closer to you than the other side. You can also move the handles closer to one another to make a side of the object appear further away.

Additional Tips for Working with Objects

- Transform Options will be unavailable when anything other than the Object Picker tool is selected from the Toolbox.

- Objects do not have to be the same size as the image. You can paste or drag-and-drop an object into an image that is larger than the page size and not have the area outside the image boundaries clipped.

It is the ability to create, modify, and position objects that makes Corel PHOTO-PAINT 8 such a powerful photo-editing program. We have only covered the basics to this point.

How to Group Objects

To group objects, you must have two or more objects selected. There are several ways to select objects for grouping in an image.

- Using the Object Picker tool, you can drag a rectangle over (marquee select) the objects you want grouped together.

- From the Objects Dialog you can select the objects you want selected by clicking on them.

- If you want to select all of the objects in the image, you can choose Select All… from the Object menu.

- You can select the first object, and then, holding down the SHIFT key, select more objects. Each time you select an object, it is added to the number of Objects selected. The action is a toggle, so if you select an object you do not want, click it again to deselect it. (Did you know "deselect" is not a real word? Isn't it amazing what we learn from our spelling checkers?)

After you have selected the objects, depress the keyboard combination CTRL-G. All of the selected objects will become grouped together. How will you know the objects are grouped together? Looking at the Object roll-up gives a visual clue of what objects are grouped. When objects are grouped, they are joined together with a black bar in the far left column of the Objects Dialog. To ungroup the objects, select the group and depress CTRL-U or choose Ungroup from the Object menu. You may also use the Group and Ungroup buttons in the Property bar.

The Text Tool

 Although introduced in back in PHOTO-PAINT 6, the most powerful feature of the Text tool remains the editable text capability. In Corel PHOTO-PAINT 5, the text becomes a bitmap image after it is entered and becomes an object. In Corel PHOTO-PAINT 7 and 8, we can return to text and change the fonts, size, or other attributes at any time. Only when the text is combined with the background does it cease to be editable. When the Text tool is used in combination with the fill capabilities and layers/objects, stunning effects can be produced quickly.

Paragraph Text and Corel PHOTO-PAINT

As great as Corel PHOTO-PAINT's text capabilities are, if you are planning to add paragraph style text to a Corel PHOTO-PAINT image it is best to use another program like CorelDRAW. It is a simple procedure. Just finish whatever enhancements to the image are needed and save it as a CPT file. Next, import the file into CorelDRAW or a similar graphics program and add the text at that time. While I have mentioned this before, it bears repeating. When text is created in Corel PHOTO-PAINT, it is a bitmap image that is resolution-dependent. Text in a program like DRAW is resolution-independent. This means that text placed in Corel PHOTO-PAINT will be the resolution of the image. If it is 300 dpi (dots per inch), then the text will be a bitmap image that is 300 dpi regardless if it is printed to a 300 dpi laser printer or a 2450 dpi imagesetter. If the same text is placed in DRAW, it remains text. If it is output to a 2450 dpi imagesetter, then the resolution of the text will be 2450 dpi. The result is sharper text.

Basics of the Text Tool

You use the Text tool to add text to an image. Text is by default an object that floats above the image background. Text properties, the font, style, size, kerning, leading and other effects are determined through the Property Bar or the Tool Settings Roll-Up. You can manipulate, edit, format and transform the text object while it is still an object. Once you've combined the text object with the background, you can no longer edit it as text. Render Text To Mask, when selected converts the text automatically to a mask. It is a real time saver.

If you have worked with recent versions of word processors in Windows, everything on the Property Bar or Tool Settings should be familiar to you. The first box shows all of the available fonts that are installed in WIN'95 . The second box displays the selected font sizes in points (72 points = 1 inch). While the font size drop-down list shows a long list of available sizes, you can select any size you need by typing the desired font size (in points) in the Font Size box. Any change you make in the Text toolbar is instantly reflected in the text displayed in the image area. You can also move the rectangle containing the text by clicking on its edge and dragging it with the left mouse button.

There are no system default settings for the Text tool's font selection. The typeface is always the first element of the list of installed fonts. Since lists in WIN'95 are maintained alphabetically, the typeface whose name is first alphabetically (i.e., AARDVARK) will always appear as the default. The last settings of the text toolbar remain until changed again or Corel PHOTO-PAINT is shut down.

Here are the facts about the Corel PHOTO-PAINT Text Tool:

- The color of the text is determined by the setting of the Paint (foreground) color. It is very easy to change the color of the text in Corel PHOTO-PAINT. With the text selected with the Text tool, click on any color in the palette with the left mouse button and it will change the color of the text to match the color you just clicked.

- When you select existing text with the Text tool all transformations that have been applied to that text will be lost.

- To correct a text entry, use the BACKSPACE or DELETE key.

- To check the spelling of text, use a dictionary. Sorry no spell checker.

- There is no automatic line wrap (soft carriage returns) of text. This is because Corel PHOTO-PAINT has no idea where to wrap the line.

- Text always looks ragged until it becomes an object.

13

Note for Corel PHOTO-PAINT 5 Users

In Corel PHOTO-PAINT 5, the text is a bitmap after it becomes an object. In Corel PHOTO-PAINT 7 and 8, the text remains editable as text after it becomes an object until it is combined with the background or another object.

TIP: *When you go into text edit mode, the text will look pretty ugly (lots of jaggies). Don't worry! It will look fine once you exit text edit mode by selecting a different tool.*

Highlighted Text

Two features of PHOTO-PAINT 8 make this hands-on exercise very simple. They are Render to Mask and Lenses. When you have a dark background it is sometimes difficult to create text that doesn't stand out from the background but is still readable. In previous versions of PHOTO-PAINT this process took as many as 15 steps.

1. Locate and open the file EXERCISE\PHOTOS\345092.WI. After it is loaded Resample to a width of 6 inches.

2. Select the Text tool in the Toolbox and change the Font to Futura XBlk BT at a size of 72, Centered and Line Spacing of 70. Enable the Render to Mask button on the Property Bar. Click on the image and type SUNSET CRUISES.

3. Select the Object Picker from the Toolbox. The text has become a mask. From the Object menu select Create Lens From Mask. When the New Lens dialog box opens, double-click on Gamma. When the Gamma dialog box opens, change the slider to 2.2 and click OK. You are done. The result is shown below.

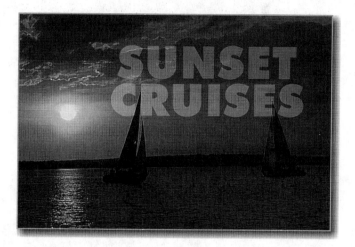

The beauty of using the Lens is two fold. You can move the Lens anywhere in the image that you want. Second, you can change the Gamma settings by selecting Lens Properties in the Object menu. The only limitation, if you can call it that, is any Lens must be combined with the image if the effect is to appear when it prints.

There are many other hands-on exercises involving text throughout the book. Check the Table of Contents or the Index for their location.

PART

IV

Filters—Using the WOW Stuff

14

Third-Party Filters

Given the power of filters, support for the plug-in standard provides even more power to PHOTO-PAINT's already strong feature set. In this chapter, we will explore how to enable the filters that are included in PHOTO-PAINT, how to install filters from other vendors, and some tips about the use of filters in general.

Understanding Plug-in Filters

The concept of plug-in filters is simple. A company (like Corel) provides an access that can be used by programmers to control parts of their program. These programs (known as plug-in filters) can be called from within an application (like PHOTO-PAINT) to provide a wide variety of functions and effects. The plug-in concept first appeared in photo-editing programs several years ago, and the concept is now being used in other applications, including page layout and vector drawing programs. In this chapter, and the ones that follow, we are going to explore the filters that were provided with PHOTO-PAINT 8 and find out some of the many things we can do with them.

Different Jobs, Different Filters

Just as there are many different tasks in photo-editing, there are also many different types of plug-in filters. For purposes of discussion, filters can be loosely classified as either utility or artistic. An example of a *utility* filter would be one that converts images to a format not normally supported by the application. Those that provide artistic or painterly effects represent an *artistic* type of filter. An example of an artistic filter would be the Kai's Power Tools 3.0 that are included in PHOTO-PAINT 8. Some of the filters do a little bit of both. Regardless of the type of filter, they must first be installed.

Installation of Filters

The first time that you launch PHOTO-PAINT after installation, you may notice that not all of the filters are available when you open the Effects menu as shown in Figure 14-1a. After you have installed all of the filter sets that came with PHOTO-PAINT, your drop-down list will look more like Figure 14-1b. Any filter that can be installed by the user appears in the list (alphabetically) under the dividing line that appears below the Sharpen category. Figure 14-1c shows the list that appears when some additional third-party filters are installed, which brings us to the subject of installing the filters.

Installing Plug-in Filters

Installing plug-in filters in Corel PHOTO-PAINT means you are making the filters available so that they appear on the Effects menu drop-down list. The procedure for doing this is a breeze. Simply select Options from the Tools menu (or CTRL-J) and click on the plus sign to the left of the Workspace. This action opens a series of selections including the Plug-In Filters page (Figure 14-2). The currently installed filters appear in the Plug-ins list. To add a filter click on the Add... button, which opens the Select a Plug-In Folder dialog box shown below, and locate the directory where the plug-in filters have been installed. PHOTO-PAINT keeps all of its plug-ins

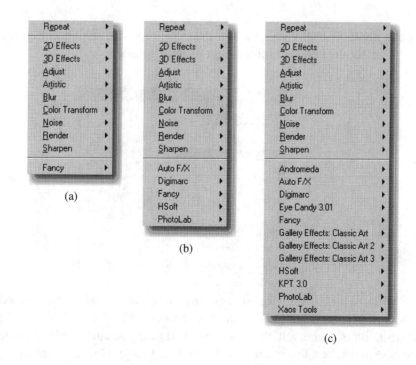

a) Default list of filters;
b) all supplied filters installed;
c) even more filters installed

FIGURE 14-1

14

The Plug-In
Filters page
of the
Options
dialog box

FIGURE 14-2

in a separate PLUGINS folder. For example, to install the PhotoLab filters, you would select the Photolab folder in the Plugins folder.

With the Initialize filter at start-up checkbox enabled, all of the selected Plug-In filters will be initialized when you launch Corel PHOTO-PAINT. When disabled, Plug-In filters are not initialized until the first time you click the Effects menu. This process may take a few minutes. I recommend that you leave it enabled.

When you install the filters, you may wonder if it is necessary to have them in their own subdirectory that was created by their installation program or if it would be possible to just copy the filters into the \COREL\COREL80\PLUGINS folder. While you can copy all of the filter files into the same PLUGINS directory, be aware that by installing them all in the same folder, you cannot selectively turn sets of filters on and off. This is because you cannot select individual filters within a folder. All of the filters in a folder are made available when the folder is selected. Corel PHOTO-PAINT can use filters installed in folders just about anywhere in the system. So while it may be more tidy to have all of the sets of filters in folders under PLUGINS, it is by no means necessary.

TIP: *You may find that some of the of filters give you a choice of automatically installing the filters for Corel PHOTO-PAINT. If this choice is offered, make sure of the location where the program will install them, since the location of the filters is different in PHOTO-PAINT 5–8, and it may load them in an unexpected area.*

While it is a matter of personal preference, it can be useful to only load those filters that you need during your PHOTO-PAINT session. Some filters take up system resources when they are loaded into PHOTO-PAINT. Making available a set of filters that won't be used during a particular PHOTO-PAINT session is a waste of system resources. New with Corel PHOTO-PAINT 8 is the ability to load and unload filters on the fly. Clicking the checkbox next to a highlighted filter determines if the filter will be available when the dialog box is closed. Filters that are checked are available. When you have a lot of filter sets loaded, it also takes a little longer to load each set initially.

If you really need to get rid of the filters and not just temporarily make them unavailable, you can use the Remove button. The Remove feature doesn't actually remove the filters from the system; it only makes them unavailable to enable or disable with the checkbox. Removing plug-in filters from your system is like installation in reverse: select the folder where the filters are located and hit the DEL button. Once you exit the dialog box by clicking on the OK button, PHOTO-PAINT automatically loads all of the remaining filters that are selected. It takes a moment for PHOTO-PAINT to find the plug-in filters and rebuild the Effects menu. You will have access to your filters without having to restart PHOTO-PAINT.

Some Technical Information About Plug-In Filters

Filter files for plug-ins are easily identified by an .8BF file extension. All of the noninstallable filter files provided with PHOTO-PAINT are contained in dynamic link libraries that have a .DLL extension. The reason they do not have an .8BF extension is twofold. First, DLLs provide a faster way for PAINT to access the filters. Second, this way you can only use the filters with Corel PHOTO-PAINT. The second point is worth mentioning in case you are wondering how to load Alchemy or one of the other Corel filters into another photo-editing program, such as Photoshop or Picture Publisher. It won't work.

Not All Filters Are Created Equal

All of the filters that are appearing on the market today are designed to work in a 32-bit environment like PHOTO-PAINT 8. These 32-bit versions offer the advantage of greater processing speed and functional capabilities. There are many older, 16-bit filters still available in the marketplace. Corel PHOTO-PAINT 8 allows the use of these filters in most cases, but I strongly recommend that you stick with the 32-bit versions. At the time I am writing this book, all of the vendors for third-party plug-ins are offering 32-bit versions. Some of the newest ones are only available in 32-bit versions.

Will plug-in filters designed for Adobe Photoshop work in PHOTO-PAINT 8? I get this question a lot. The answer is a definite maybe. Whether a filter works or not depends on whether the program was written as a general plug-in filter (it will probably work) or to control specific and unique Photoshop commands (it won't). The best way to find out is to call the vendor who wrote the program and ask.

Where Can I Get Additional Plug-Ins?

This isn't always easy since most of the plug-ins are not sold in the normal reseller channel. This is because with few exceptions, the companies that make these filters are very small. So where do you find out about them? Look in the magazines and catalogs that specialize in DTP. *Corel* magazine, *Adobe* magazine, and *Publish* are all periodicals that contain both articles and advertisements about plug-in filters.

A Note on Downloading Free Filters

If you are an avid user of the Internet or other online services, you will find a lot of plug-in filters available as freeware or shareware. Before you begin downloading all of these wonderful filters, carefully read the filter description. Many of the ones I have found in online services are only for use on a Mac, even though some of the descriptions don't specify this. The filter designers are not being deceptive. In most cases they don't know or can't imagine that anyone from the Windows world uses plug-in filters. There are several telltale signs that the filter is for a Mac. First, there won't be any mention of Windows in the description. I have found that if a filter is available for Windows, the designers tend to shout it from the rooftops. Second, look at the extension of the file to be downloaded. If it has an .SEA or any other extension that is not a standard IBM PC type compression extension like .ZIP, .ARC, etc., then it is for a Mac.

As long as we are discussing downloading of filters, I should point out that PHOTO-PAINT 8 now works with nearly all of the Filter Factory filters that are available on the Internet. The Filter Factory is a user-definable type of filter that many people have used to create unique effects. By downloading the filter files and reading a lot of text files, you can use the filters they have made or roll your own.

Introducing the Filter Dialog Box

The filter dialog box has changed somewhat since PHOTO-PAINT 7. We are going to take a quick look at how it works and what options it offers. Figures 14-3, 14-4 and 14-5 show the three different preview options available for one of the filters. Although the lower portion of the dialog box containing the sliders, checkboxes and number boxes changes to accommodate the different filter controls, the upper portion remains generally the same.

Clicking the Original/Results Preview button shows preview thumbnails of the original image as well as what the image will look like after application of the filter. The advantage of this approach is you can see and compare the result against the original.

The large result preview button is used to change the preview mode of the filter from Original/Result to Large Result. It is also the button that is used to return the filter dialog box from On-screen preview.

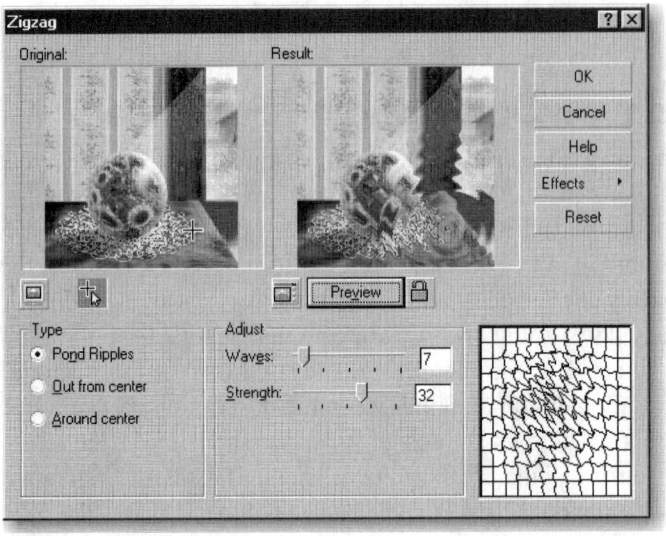

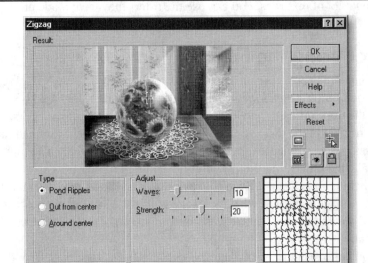

The Traditional Original/Result Preview style Filter dialog box

FIGURE 14-3

The Large Result Preview

FIGURE 14-4

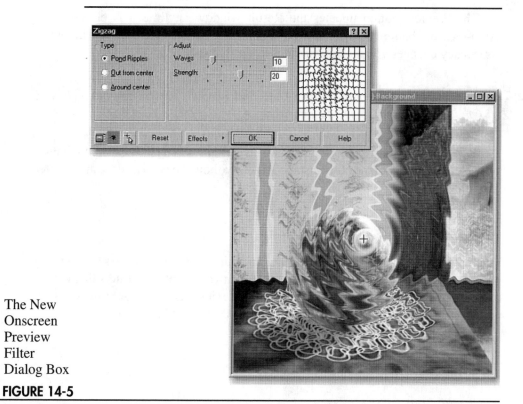

The New
Onscreen
Preview
Filter
Dialog Box

FIGURE 14-5

This is the newest, and some will say the best, way to preview filter actions. Using the actual image to preview the effects gives the most accurate possible form of preview. Clicking the Full Screen preview button changes the filter dialog box to full screen.

Panning and Zooming

The Hand (and Zoom) button on the left of the dialog box controls the positioning and zoom level of the preview window. The Hand tool is applied either in the Original window, the Large Result window or the actual image in On-screen preview mode and the Result or image pans accordingly. With the Hand tool selected, you can drag the image anywhere you want to get the best possible view of an effect. Clicking the Hand tool zooms in with left mouse clicks and zooms out with right mouse clicks.

14

The Preview button updates the Result window anytime it is clicked. The Auto-Preview button when enabled automatically updates the Result window to reflect any changes you make to settings in the dialog box.

 NOTE: *When in Single Result window mode, the Preview button has an icon on it that looks like an eye.*

The Reset button returns the filter to its default settings. The Effects button allows access to any of the other installed filters without the need to close and reenter the Effects menu.

Into Undiscovered Country

The fun of filters is that there seems to be something new every day. As I am writing this chapter I have received prerelease copies of two new plug-in filters that will be released by the time you read this. As you can see, it never stops. Our filter odyssey continues in the next chapter where we will look into the blur filters.

15

The Blur Filters

This is a fun chapter for me. There are so many things that you can do with the Blur filters, it's almost scary.

The Blur Filters

The Blur category in the Effects menu contains a collection of eight filters that produce a variety of blur effects. The type of blur filter you select is chiefly determined by the type of image you are working with and by the effect you want to obtain. While there were no new blur filters added with the release of PHOTO-PAINT 8, the controls for some of the filters have been enhanced. The filters in this chapter are not listed in order of their appearance in the menu, but in order of their day-to-day usefulness, which leads us to the Gaussian Blur filter.

The Gaussian Blur Filter

This filter, although deceptively simple, is used every day to make shadows, produce glows, diffuse backgrounds, and in many of the special effects that are created with Corel PHOTO-PAINT. The Gaussian Blur filter produces a hazy effect that gives the image a slightly out-of-focus look. The filter can also be used to improve the quality of images containing jaggies, although with some loss of detail.

The Gaussian Blur Filter Dialog Box

Selecting Blur in the Effects Menu and selecting Gaussian Blur... opens the dialog box shown below. For information on the operation of the common filter dialog box controls, see Chapter 14. The following information describes the Gaussian Blur controls in detail.

All Things Gaussian

In digital photo-editing, you often hear the term *Gaussian*. I am sometimes asked why Gaussian is capitalized and who is this person with a blur filter named after him. The term *Gaussian* comes from Dr. Carl Friedrich Gauss, a German mathematician who was born in 1777. Dr. Gauss did not invent the Gaussian Blur, but he did discover the mathematical principles that the programmers use to create it.

Dr. Gauss demonstrated the mathematical principle of normal distribution, which is the distribution of values described by what is called a *normal curve.* The few of you who actually stayed awake in Statistics 101 recognize normal distribution as one of the first things you were shown just before you dozed off. Because the shape resembles that of a bell, the curve is also known as a *bell-shaped curve* or *bell curve.*

When I was going to school (way back when) and everyone in the class was doing poorly, the teacher often graded "on the curve," meaning that all of the grades would have been distributed uniformly above and below the average of all the test scores. The result would have been a few "A"s, more "B"s, mostly "C"s, some "D"s, and a few "F"s. That is because the score necessary to get a grade of "C" would be the center of the curve (the average of all the scores), rather than an absolute, like 70 percent. This principle of Gaussian distribution is the basis for the Gaussian Blur filter and many other tools in Corel PHOTO-PAINT work.

In photo-editing, the Gaussian Blur filter distributes the blur effect based on a bell-shaped curve. This curve is generated by mapping the color values of the pixels in the selected area and then distributing the blurring around the center value. So what's so hot about Gaussian blurring? Good question. It provides a true blurring, not a smearing, of the pixels, resulting in the blurred area appearing to be out of focus. End of history and math lessons.

The Radius Slider

The Radius slider controls the amount of filter action. Adobe Photoshop users are accustomed to seeing three separate controls for Gaussian Blur. Corel PHOTO-

PAINT has combined the functionality of three controls so that a single percentage setting will allow you to determine the filter's effect. While it can be argued that three separate control settings gives the user a greater degree of control, I have found the single slider to be more than sufficient to produce the necessary blur.

To operate, set the Radius slider in the dialog box to a value between 1 and 250 percent to specify the degree to which you want to blur the selected image or masked area. Be aware that any value over 30 percent turns the image into a nicely colored cloud. Want to make some smoke?

For the technically minded, the percentage would be more accurately described as *pixel radius*. With a setting of 5, the blur will be averaged over a radius of five pixels around each pixel in the image. The greater the Radius slider setting, the greater the amount of blurring of the image. High percentage values (more than 30) can turn almost any image into fog. Use the preview window to see the effects of different slider settings before applying the filter. Click the OK button to apply the filter.

Subtle Emphasis by Creating a Depth of Field

Creation of a pseudo-depth of field by slightly blurring an area of the image is a good way to subtly emphasize a subject without making a big show of it. The hands-on exercise in Chapter 7 showed us how to use the Freehand mask tool to create a slightly blurred background with some buildings. That was easy since the buildings had nicely defined edges. In day-to-day type photo-editing you have edges that are more difficult to define. In this hands-on exercise you will learn some unique ways to create that blurred background with such subjects.

1. Open the image EXERCISE\PHOTOS\677043.WI on the CD-ROM. Then select Resample… from the Image menu that appears. When the dialog box opens, the width will be highlighted. Type in the number 5 (for five inches) and click the OK button.

2. Select the Path Node Edit tool in the Toolbox and click in the image at the points around the glass as shown in Figure 15-1. Don't spend a lot of time being exact about the position of the path nodes because the beauty of creating a path, instead of a mask, is the ability to adjust the position of the individual path nodes. Complete the path by clicking on the origin point. When you have completed the path, if you need to make adjustments to it, click on the Node Edit tool in the Property Bar and

move the nodes. The only portion of the path requiring some degree of accuracy are the points where the path is next to the stem of the left glass.

3. To adjust the nodes, select the Node Edit tool from the Path Node Edit mode Property Bar as shown in Figure 15-2 and click and move the nodes as necessary. When the path matches the one shown in Figure 15-1, click on the Path to Mask button on the right end of the Property Bar. Since there is no reason to save the path, click on the Delete Path button. Click on the Object Picker tool.

TIP: *When creating a mask to isolate a part of the image for blurring, you should consider feathering the mask so the transition isn't apparent to the viewer. In this exercise it isn't necessary because the background is uniform.*

4. Select Blur in the Effects Menu and choose Gaussian Blur…, opening the filter dialog box. Ensure that it is at the default setting of 5 and click the OK button. The result is shown in Figure 15-3.

5. Close the file when you're finished.

677043.wi (24-Bit RGB Color)-Background

The Path shown in the figure outlines the area to be blurred

FIGURE 15-1

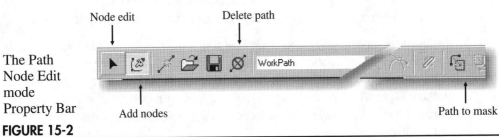

The Path
Node Edit
mode
Property Bar

Node edit   Delete path

Add nodes   Path to mask

FIGURE 15-2

The glass in Figure 15-3 now appears to be some distance away from the glass on the left. This exercise was easy because the area between the two of them consisted of uniform color. This type of background prevents the rough edges of this crude mask from making the transition areas between the blurred and nonblurred areas apparent to the viewer. In the next exercise it won't be as easy.

The second
glass now
appears
more distant

FIGURE 15-3

Subtle Emphasis by Creating a Depth of Field II (The Sequel)

In the following food shot, you want to make the background slightly blurred; however, a mask like you made in the previous exercise will not work. The blurring should occur gradually beginning near the front (bottom) of the image and moving back (up). In this exercise you want to emphasize that beautiful tomato in the center for an ad for a new restaurant: The Red Tomato. This requires that you isolate the tomato from the gradual blur you are going to apply to the background.

1. Open the file EXERCSE\PHOTOS\577054.WI. When the image opens, select Resample... from the Image menu. When the dialog box opens, the width will be highlighted. Type in the number 5 (for five inches) and click the OK button.

2. Select Paint on Mask in the Mask menu (CTRL-K). Next, choose Fill... in the Edit menu. When the Edit Fill & Transparency dialog box opens, select the Fountain fill button and click the Edit button. Change the values

in the Fountain Fill dialog box to match those shown here. The From color is black and the To color is white. Click the OK button to close the dialog box and click OK again to apply the fill.

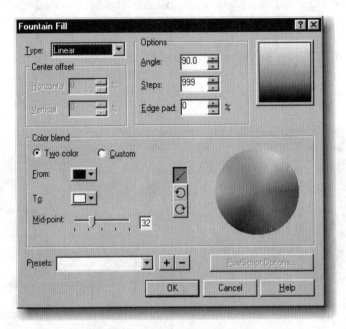

3. Switch off Paint on Mask mode (CTRL-K). You now have a mask that allows any effect you apply to be applied gradually from top (maximum) to bottom (minimum).

4. To isolate the tomato, click on the Circle Mask tool in the Toolbox. Change the Mask mode to Subtractive. Beginning above and to the left of the tomato, click and drag a circle that covers the tomato. This doesn't need to be exact. It is better if it is slightly inside of the tomato. If it doesn't work the first time, select Undo (CTRL-Z) and try, try again. It took me three attempts to get a mask that covered most of the tomato.

5. Switch on Paint on Mask mode (CTRL-K). The mask should look something like the one shown in Figure 15-4a. The edges of the circle you just made are too hard to use. Select the Gaussian Blur filter and change the Radius setting to 10. Click OK. The result is shown in Figure 15-4b.

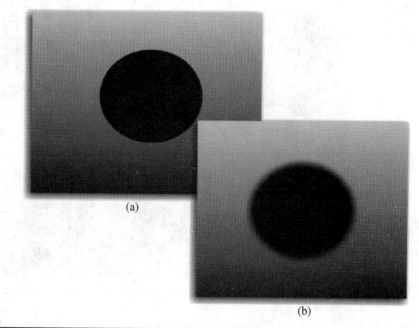

a) This mask exhibits hard edges. b) A little blurring softens the mask transitions

(a)

(b)

FIGURE 15-4

6. Switch off Paint on Mask mode (CTRL-K). Select the Gaussian Blur filter and change the Radius setting to 7. Click OK. The result is shown in Figure 15-5.

7. Before closing the file, select Adjust from the Image menu and select Hue/Saturation/Lightness. Move the Saturation slider to –70. This removes the color content of the image, creating what looks like the background for an expensive ad in some gourmet-cooking magazine. Notice the slight glow appearing around the tomato where the mask went out too far into the background. Close the file and don't save the changes.

When applying blurring to a background, you must remember how the human eye sees things. Objects near the viewer are usually slightly out of focus, while those further away are even more so. If you create effects that go against what the mind expects to see, it looks fake or artificial—even though the viewer in most cases cannot tell you why it looks fake.

The
finished
work ready
to be made
into an ad

FIGURE 15-5

Removal of Banding Using the Gaussian Blur Filter

The Gaussian Blur filter can also be used to diminish the effect of banding in a fountain fill. The text shown in Figure 15-6a contains a six-step fountain fill to make the banding apparent. The same image after it has had a Gaussian Blur filter applied to it (Figure 15-6b) shows no evidence of the original banding. Be careful not to set the amount of Gaussian Blur you apply too high. At very high settings you will turn the entire image into fog.

The Motion Blur Filter

The Motion Blur filter is designed to create the impression of movement in an image. It achieves this effect by determining the edges of the image for the direction selected and smearing them into the adjacent pixels. There are several issues to consider before using the Motion Blur filter. First, the selection of a subject for use of the filter is important. You need to find people, events, or things associated with speed. After all, it looks wrong to see a photograph of two chess players in Central Park with speed blurs coming off of them. Not only does the subject need to be associated

(a)

a) Original text has serious banding problems.
b) The Gaussian Blur filter removes the banding

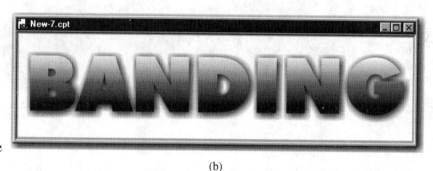

(b)

FIGURE 15-6

with movement, but the direction the subject is facing is also important. For instance, the photograph of a racing car like that shown in Figure 15-7 is a good choice because it appears to be traveling across the field of view. If it were coming directly at or away from the viewer, it would be more difficult to achieve the effect.

High-speed films can freeze the action so the subject in the photograph looks like it's standing still. In fact, there isn't any indication in this photo that there is movement. It looks look the vehicle is parked on the raceway. When using a photograph like this in an ad or brochure, you want to convey a sense of action to the viewer. While no one viewing the image would say the car is parked, it still doesn't "look" like it is moving. You can achieve this apparent motion using the Motion Blur filter.

There are two ways to approach the application of motion. You can blur the subject or blur the background. Blurring the subject makes it appear to be moving fast but has the drawback of making the subject blurred. The popular technique used

The original
photograph
of a race car

FIGURE 15-7

in the car advertisements these days is to blur the background. This is most effective since it conveys the sense of speed and keeps the product (car) in focus.

Regardless if you are blurring the subject or the background, you must begin by making a mask to limit the areas of application of the filter. If you apply the Motion Blur filter to the entire image, it will just appear to be an out-of-focus picture and you haven't accomplished your purpose. Creating a mask around the car and then inverting it limits the effect to just the background. A mask with hard edges will produce areas of transition where the blur begins and ends abruptly, which looks very strange. To eliminate this, the mask must be feathered. In Figure 15-8, the background had a large amount (70 pixels) of Motion Blur applied. It made the background unrecognizable, but since the subject is the car, it just adds to the effect. Notice how the Motion Blur filter created a faint halo around some of the car edges. This is the result of applying the filter to a feathered mask. This again helps convey the sense of motion to the viewer, and is more a result of perceptions we humans have regarding things in motion than of laws of physics.

Figure 15-9 shows what happens if you don't invert the mask and apply the motion blur directly to the subject. You can still make out details on the car because after applying the Motion Blur filter, the Local Undo tool was used to remove the effect on the front, top, and sides of the cars. Not wishing to remove all of the effect, I set the Transparency value of the Local Undo tool (in the Tools Setting roll-up) to

The
background
is a blur, but
the car no
longer
appears
parked

FIGURE 15-8

The car is
blurred, but
the Local
Undo tool
recovers
some detail

FIGURE 15-9

a moderate-to-high value. As a reminder, when the Local Undo tool is selected, you must use CTRL-F8 to open the Tool Settings roll-up. Double-clicking the Local Undo tool removes the entire application of the effect. I did it more than once myself, so learn from my mistakes.

TIP: *You can only Undo a Local Undo action once. If you try it a second time, you will get the error message "This tool requires an Undo Buffer."*

The Jaggy Despeckle Filter

The Jaggy Despeckle filter scatters colors in an image to create a soft, blurred effect with very little distortion. It also smoothes out jagged edges (*jaggies*) on images. It is most effective in removing jaggies on high-contrast images. If the image has this problem, the Jaggy Despeckle filter will probably work well for you.

Using the Jaggy Despeckle Filter

This filter will not work with line art, images composed of only black-and-white pixels. The image must be either grayscale or color. When applied to a photograph, it has a tendency to blur the image slightly, depending on your setting. Jaggy Despeckle operates by performing edge detection on the image. After the filter thinks it knows where all the hard edges are, it applies antialiasing to the edges to give them a smoother appearance.

Another application of the Jaggy Despeckle filter is to correct an individual color channel that has a lot of noise or areas that are exhibiting jaggies. If you use this approach to reduce noise in an image, you first must check each channel in the image to see which one exhibits the greatest amount of noise. Next, with a mask tool, select the area of the channel image to apply the Jaggy Despeckle filter to. Don't apply too large a setting to an individual channel or the image will show multicolored artifacts when the channels are all viewed together.

The Radial Blur Filter

The Radial Blur filter allows you to create a blurring effect that radiates outward from a central point. You can reposition the center point, set the intensity of the effect, and choose between two blur modes. Spin rotates the blur around the point. Zoom blurs outwards from the point. The crosshair button (below the Reset button) is used to set the center point of this effect. Click this button, and then click on the image either on the screen or in the preview window, to place the center point of the effect.

Like most of the filters, the key to using the Radial Blur filter effectively is controlling affected areas with masks. Without masks the Radial Blur effect causes sufficient distortion to make the original subject unrecognizable.

Here is a quick exercise to make a so-so picture into an attention-grabber.

1. Open the image EXERCISE\PHOTOS\3650030.WI. Select Resample... from the Image menu that appears. When the dialog box opens, the width will be highlighted. Type in the number 5 (for five inches) and click the OK button.

2. If you like, you can use the Crop tool and crop off the black edge of the image as shown in Figure 15-10.

3. Select the Freehand Mask tool and create a mask as shown in Figure 15-11. When you have completed the mask, select Feather from the Mask menu and set it to a Width of 15 and a setting of Average. Click OK and then Invert the mask (CTRL-I).

The original
photograph
is well
composed
and
uninteresting

FIGURE 15-10

The mask
selects the
area to be
protected
from the
effect filter

FIGURE 15-11

4. From the Effects menu, choose Blur and select Radial Blur. In the dialog box change the setting to 30; choose Mode: Zoom, and Quality: Best. Click the OK button and go get a cup of coffee. It is going to take a little while to process. Remove the mask to get the result shown in Figure 15-12.

Taking the Radial Blur filter out for a Spin

Here is another quick exercise to show what can be done with this very versatile filter. Again you will be using the filter to emphasize the subject without completely demolishing the background.

1. Open the image EXERCISE\PHOTOS\395018.WI. Select Resample... from the Image menu that appears. When the dialog box opens, the width will be highlighted. Type in the number 5 (for five inches) and click the OK button.

2. Select the Circle Mask tool from the Toolbox and drag an ellipse that roughly covers the boy's face as shown in Figure 15-13.

Add a little
Radial Blur
and you
have a real
winner

FIGURE 15-12

Cute young
boy in
photograph
is lost in the
bicycles

FIGURE 15-13

3. From the Mask menu, choose Feather. From the Feather dialog box, choose a Width of 15 and a Direction of Average. Click OK. Invert the mask (CTRL-I).

4. From the Effects menu, choose Blur and then Radial Blur. From the dialog box, choose an Amount setting of 5, Spin and Best. Click OK. The result is shown in Figure 15-14.

The Directional Smooth Filter

The Directional Smooth filter analyzes values of pixels of similar color shades to determine in which direction to apply the greatest amount of smoothing. Sounds great, right? Remember, this is a Blur filter. The Directional Smooth and the following two filters (Smooth and Soften filters) are nearly identical in operation, although the results obtained are slightly different.

The Smooth Filter

The Smooth filter tones down differences in adjacent pixels, resulting in only a slight loss of detail while smoothing the image or the selected area. The differences

Give it a spin with the Radial Blur filter and he's the focus of attention

FIGURE 15-14

between the effect of the Smooth and Soften filters is subtle and may only be apparent on a high-resolution display and sometimes not even then.

The Soften Filter

The Soften filter smoothes and tones down harshness without losing detail. The differences between the effect of the Smooth and Soften filters is subtle and may only be apparent on a high-resolution display or in the mind of the person who programmed this filter.

Getting It All Together—the Blur Control

The Blur option, found in the Effects menu, is available by selecting Adjust. This opens a very large dialog box called Blur Control, shown in the following illustration, that displays thumbnails side by side, showing the results of applying each of the five Blur filters—Gaussian Blur, Motion Blur, Smooth, Directional Smooth, and Soften—to the current image. Blur control should not be confused with government information agencies.

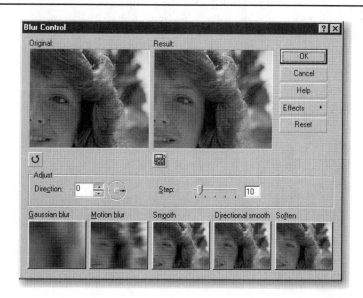

The Blur Control dialog box shows the comparative effects of all of the blur filters

FIGURE 15-15

The Blur Control Dialog Box

This provides a quick way to compare the results of different filters side by side. Clicking the thumbnail of the desired filter applies the filter to the image in the Result window. To Undo the last filter application, you can click the Undo button to the right of the Zoom button. Repeatedly clicking this button lets you step back through a group of effects applied. Different filters can be applied multiple times using the Blur Control dialog box.

The Low Pass Filter

Also found in the Blur drop-down list, the Low Pass filter is not a traditional Blur filter, which is why it has been mentioned only at the end of the chapter. This filter removes highlights and color from an image, leaving shadows and low-frequency detail. The dialog box contains two Slider bars, one for Percentage and the other for Radius. The Percentage value controls the intensity of the effect, and Radius controls the range of pixels that are affected. At higher settings, the Low Pass filter creates a blurring effect, which is why it is in the Blur filter section. This action erases much of the image's detail. If you need only to deemphasize (smooth) highlights, use a lower percentage setting.

Congratulations, you have made it through yet another chapter of filters. The next chapter introduces you to the exciting world of noise. Noise—not the kind that comes from a boom box—is a fact of life in digital imagery and these filters help create, remove, and control it.

16

Noise Filters

The Noise filters are very important to photo-editing. *Noise,* which is composed of random pixels, can be used to add an apparent sharpness to a soft image. It can be used to add "grit" to an otherwise smooth surface. Naturally occurring noise can result from poorly scanned images or from the film grain of certain film types. Whether noise needs to be removed or added, Corel PHOTO-PAINT provides the necessary filters. New to PHOTO-PAINT 8 is the Remove Moiré filter, which is used to remove the halftone patterns that can cause moiré patterns. The Noise subgroup in the Effects menu has the following eight filters: Add Noise, Diffuse, Dust & Scratch, Maximum, Median, Minimum, Remove Moiré, and Remove Noise.

Noise in digital images is normally a bad thing, akin to visual static. Like an uninvited guest at a party, noise seems to show up in the worst possible places in an image. For example, during scanning, it is difficult for the scanner elements to pick out detail in the darker (shadow) regions of a photograph. As a result, these areas will contain more than their fair share of noise. All of those ugly little specks on the faxes you receive are caused by noise. Because of the physical composition of noise, it tends to stand out and make itself known in a photograph, especially when you sharpen an image, as you will learn in the following chapter. Noise is everywhere and you cannot avoid it. However, you can control it, get rid of it, and even add it to your images. In fact, in this chapter you will learn that noise can be surprisingly useful to have around.

The Add Noise Filter

Why would you want to add noise? Actually, adding noise has more uses than you would first imagine. Noise (random pixels) can give the effect of grit and texture to a picture. It can add a dusting of pixels to an image in a way that emulates film grain. When the grain color is not quite compatible with the image, adding noise can be helpful in softening the look of stark image areas. When you are retouching photographs that have existing film-grain texture, it can be helpful to add noise so the blending is less apparent. If you are an old hand with PhotoShop, you probably know much of this already.

The Add Noise filter creates a granular effect that adds texture to a flat or overly blended image. There are several neat tricks that can be done with this filter. Let's begin with a description of how it operates.

The Add Noise Filter Dialog Box

Like the other filter dialog boxes, there are three possible preview modes for this filter: Onscreen, Original/Result, and Single Result preview. It controls the application of noise through selection of the level, the density, and the type of noise.

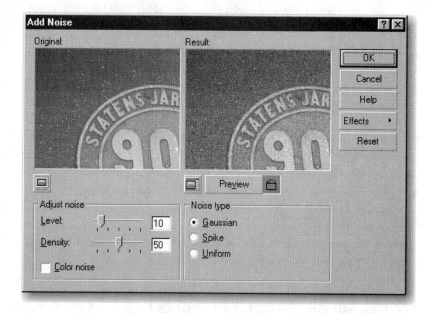

Understanding What the Controls Do

The Level slider, shown above in the Original/Result mode, controls the intensity of the noise pixels. The slider operates on a percentage scale of 0-100. A lower setting makes the noise barely visible; a higher setting produces higher-visibility noise pixels. The default setting of 50 for this slider is way too high for most applications. A Level setting of 10 is recommended as a starting point.

The Density slider controls the number of noise pixels added to the image. The slider also operates on a percentage scale of 0-100. A lower setting adds very few noise pixels; a higher setting produces a higher density of noise pixels. When Color

Noise is checked, the Noise filter creates noises that contain color values. When left unchecked, the noise that is introduced is grayscale.

TYPES OF NOISE Three types of noise are available: Gaussian, Spike, and Uniform. The difference between the Gaussian and Uniform noise is slight. The Spike noise appears as tiny speckles on the image.

- *Gaussian* This filter prioritizes shades or colors, if color noise is selected, of the image pixels along a Gaussian distribution curve (see Chapter 15 for a more detailed explanation of Gaussian curves). The results are more light and dark pixels than with the Uniform Noise option, thus producing a more dramatic effect.

- *Spike* This filter uses shades or colors, if color noise is selected, that are distributed around a narrow curve (spike). It produces a thinner, lighter-colored grain that looks like black-and-white specks. In fact, it is almost impossible to see unless you use a very high setting.

- *Uniform* This filter provides an overall grainy appearance that is not evenly dispersed like the Gaussian Noise. Use this option to apply colors in an absolutely random fashion.

Noise Filter Effects

The Noise filters are used to create a wide variety of effects, from creating textures to adding dramatic touches to an image.

Removing Banding from a Radial Fill

Many times, if a radial fill (or any gradient fill, for that matter) is applied to a large area, some banding occurs. *Banding* is the phenomenon wherein the changes of color or shades appear as bands in the image. This effect is more pronounced in low-resolution than in higher-resolution output. It is also more apparent in grayscale or 256-color fills than in 24-bit color. In Chapter 15 you learned that a blur could reduce or remove banding. The limitation of using the Gaussian Blur is that it blurs the subject matter. You can remove the effect of banding with noise. Figure 16-1 shows an eight-step fountain fill applied to some text (top). Next, a Gaussian Noise with a Level setting of 29 and a Density setting of 100 (bottom) was applied.

A little
noise
can hide
banding in
images

■ **FIGURE 16-1**

Making Metallic Effects

The Noise filter can not only remove banding from fountain fills, but also create
unusual textures as well. In the following hands-on exercise you will apply several
different filters to some applied noise to create gold metallic characters.

1. Create a new image that is 24-bit color, 7 x 4 inches at a resolution
   of 72 dpi.

2. Click the Text tool in the Toolbox. The font used is Futura XBlk BT at a
   size of 96. The line spacing is set to 80, so the two lines aren't too far
   apart, and the Center justification is enabled. Locate the gold color in the
   On-screen palette, click on it with the left mouse button to set the Paint
   color, and type the text **BRUSHED METAL**. Click the Object Picker
   button in the Toolbox.

3. Open the Objects Docker window (CTRL-F7) and, with the text selected,
   enable the Lock Object Transparency by clicking the checkbox.

4. From the Effects menu, select Noise. Choose Add Noise… from the list to open the dialog box. Click the Reset button and then OK. The result is shown in Figure 16-2.

5. From the Effects menu, select Blur and choose Motion Blur… from the list. In the filter dialog box, change the settings to Distance: 10; Direction: 120; Off-image sampling: and Ignore pixels outside image. Click the OK button. The pixels are blurred up and to the right as shown in Figure 16-3.

6. In the Effects menu, choose 3D Effects and select Emboss…. Change the settings in the Emboss filter dialog box as follows: Emboss color: Original color; Depth: 7; Level: 25; and Direction: 45. Click OK. The text now has a three-dimensional quality, as shown in Figure 16-4.

7. The texture of the text now looks smooth, so to roughen it up, use the Sharpen filter. From the Effects menu, choose Sharpen and then choose Sharpen…. Change the dialog box settings to Edge level (percent): 27, Threshold: 53. Click the OK button.

8. Select the Drop Shadow command in the Object menu to add a drop shadow as shown in Figure 16-5. While nearly any setting works with the Drop Shadow command, the settings shown are Flat, Direction: 315; Distance: 0.2; Opacity: 55; Black; Width: 10; Direction: Average.

Addition of Gaussian noise adds grit to the text

FIGURE 16-2

16

Motion blur
changes the
noise into
streaks

FIGURE 16-3

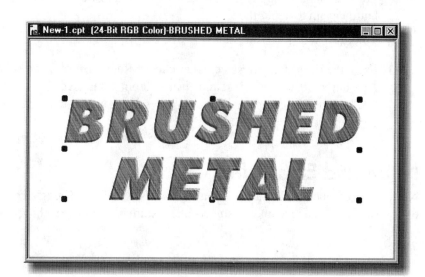

Embossing
adds depth
to the
texture

FIGURE 16-4

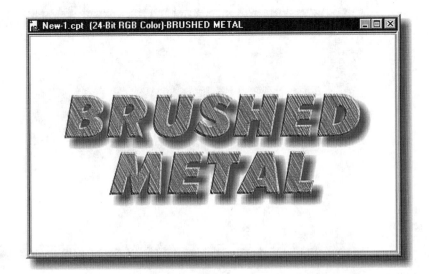

Sharpening
enhances
the brushed
metal effect

FIGURE 16-5

9. To put the finishing touch on the exercise, in the Objects Docker window, click on the Background. In the Edit menu, choose Fill…. In the Edit Fill & Transparency dialog box, select the Fountain Fill button and click the Edit button. Choose Preset: Circular - Green 02. Click OK and the OK button again to apply the fill.

10. Repeat Step 4.

11. From the Effects menu, select Blur, choose Radial Blur…, and set the Amount to 30. Choose Best and ensure Zoom is selected. Click the OK button. The complete image is shown in Figure 16-6 and in the color insert.

Noise and Embossing

Noise serves as the foundation for many textures and effects. Using a combination of noise and embossing to make a stucco-like texture is a favorite technique of mine.

The brushed metal effect is complete

FIGURE 16-6

Try this little hands-on exercise.

1. Create a new image that is 24-bit color, 6 x 2 inches, at a resolution of 72 dpi.

2. Click the Text tool in the Toolbox. The font used is Futura XBlk BT at a size of 120. Pick a light color in the On-screen palette with the left mouse button and type the text **NOISE**.

3. Select the Object Picker tool. In the Objects Docker window, enable Lock Transparency.

4. From the Add Noise dialog box, apply a Gaussian Noise at a Level of 50 percent and a Density of 100 percent.

5. Next, apply the Emboss filter under 3D Effects in the Effects menu. Click the Reset button, click OK, and add a Drop Shadow. The resulting image is shown here.

Noise and Focus

Noise can also make the focus of an image appear sharper than it actually is. This is because the human eye believes images are in sharper focus when it sees areas of higher contrast. So the viewer can be tricked into seeing an image as being in sharper focus by introducing a very small amount of Uniform noise onto a soft image. This process is often referred to as "dusting" the image. When you see the results, you may think at first that nothing was accomplished. In fact, to the operator, the image appears noisier. That's because (1) it does have more noise, and (2) you know what the original looked like before you added the noise. To a first-time viewer of the photograph, it will appear sharper.

The Diffuse Filter

Before the Gaussian Blur filter was added to Corel PHOTO-PAINT 5, the Diffuse filter was all that was available to blur an image. Corel's PAINT team received so many requests for Gaussian Blur that it was added to Corel PHOTO-PAINT 5 in the first Maintenance release. So where does that leave the Diffuse filter? It still has uses. First, it scatters colors in an image or a selected area, creating a smooth appearance. Unlike the Gaussian Blur, the Diffuse filter scatters the pixels in a way that produces a harsher or grittier blur. So why is it in the Noise section of Effects? Because its operation is based on noise.

The Diffuse Filter Dialog Box

The Level slider in the Diffuse Filter dialog box controls the amount of diffusion in the image. Set the Level slider in the dialog box to a value between 1 and 100. The number specifies how much adjoining pixels are shifted, which controls the amount of diffusion of the selected image. Higher values produce more pronounced effects. When selecting a level setting, watch the preview window for the appearance of an edge. When some objects are diffused at too high a setting, they develop an outline, which may be undesirable. To overcome this, do multiple applications of the diffuse filter at a lower setting. The important question is what do you do with the Diffuse filter? I have been writing about Corel PHOTO-PAINT since the PHOTO-PAINT 5 release and I still haven't figured out what to do with this filter. If you have any uses for it, my email address is dhuss@texas.net; let me know your ideas.

The Dust & Scratch Filter

The Dust & Scratch filter reduces image noise at areas of high contrast. Located in the Effects menu under Noise, the Dust & Scratch filter is not a magic cure-all, but it really is quite effective in the removal of garbage from an image that would take too long to manually remove. The best way to use this filter is to first mask an area that needs to be cleaned up with a mask before applying the filter. This method allows you to eliminate problem areas without affecting the rest of the image. The filter will give a softer appearance to the area to which it is applied. To prevent the areas affected from being visible when you create a mask, you should feather it before applying the filter.

Using the Dust & Scratch Filter

Most of your adjustment to this filter should be done with the Threshold slider (0-255). By setting Threshold low, you are telling the filter that all levels of contrast above the Threshold setting are considered noise. Adjust the Radius slider (1-20) to set the range of the effect. The Radius setting determines the number of pixels surrounding the noise that will be included in the removal process. Be advised that

A really
dirty picture

FIGURE 16-7

increasing the Radius setting dramatically increases the area affected. In almost all cases you should be using settings at or near 1. Figure 16-7 is a dirty picture (no, not that kind of dirty picture).

The best way to remove the dust and debris is to take the photograph (or negative in this case), clean it, and rescan it. This option is usually not available, so the second-best solution is to use the Dust & Scratch Filter. With an image this bad, I recommend a two-stage approach. First, use the Mask Brush Mask tool (in Additive mode) to select all of the worst areas. The resulting image shown in Figure 16-8 looks like someone has been putting calamine lotion on it. With these bad boys isolated, you can apply a very large setting of the Dust & Scratch filter that would, if applied to the entire image, be excessive. In this case, the Threshold is set to 0 and the Radius is set to 2. In other words, with the Threshold set to 0, the filter is going to be applied to every pixel selected by the mask. Even in this situation a Radius setting greater than 2 causes parts of the image to break down. The resulting image is shown in Figure 16-9.

To clean up the general noise, remove the mask and apply a milder setting. The best way to determine the optimum setting is to set the filter to operate in onscreen preview mode. From there you can adjust the Threshold slider until it looks right. The best setting is going to be a compromise between noise reduction and loss of image detail. The image shown in Figure 16-10 is the final result of using the Dust

Using the
Mask Brush
tool quickly
isolates the
worst areas

FIGURE 16-8

By using
a mask,
the worst
areas are
improved

FIGURE 16-9

& Scratch filter on the entire image. To correct for the loss of image detail, you can either apply a small amount of Unsharp Masking (Unsharp Mask filter in the Sharpen section of the Effects menu) or use the Contrast Effect tool in the Adjust menu and apply the contrast only in areas that require it. I did a little of both and the finished image is shown in Figure 16-11.

The Maximum Filter

The Maximum filter is not a traditional noise filter. Actually, it's a bit of a mystery why it's under Noise in the Effects menu. The Maximum filter lightens an image by adjusting the pixel values of the image, decreasing the number of colors. By using the Percentage slider (0-100 percent), you can control the percentage of filtering that is applied. This filter provides a method of lightening an image without washing it out (as would happen with brightness or intensity adjustments). With the Radius slider (1-20), move the slider to the right to increase the number of pixels that are successively selected and evaluated when you apply the effect. If you are an experienced PhotoShop user, the Maximum filter that you are already used to does something different.

The filter applied to the entire image now has reduced image detail

FIGURE 16-10

Localized
application
of the
Contrast
Effect tool
helps
recover
image detail

FIGURE 16-11

Fundamentally, Maximum as used in PhotoShop creates a spread trap. In layman's terms, the Maximum filter spreads the white areas and chokes the black areas. Spreading and choking are used to compensate for minute misalignments in the printing process. While the Maximum filter in Corel PHOTO-PAINT can be used as a traditional Maximum (Choke) filter, it doesn't do it as well as other programs. The effect is applied along a radius rather than on the pixel edge. (If you didn't understand the last sentence, don't bother rereading it. It will not become any clearer the second time around. If you live and breathe digital imaging and prepress, you understood it.)

The Median Filter

This filter reads the brightness of the pixels within a selection and averages them. Median simplifies an image by reducing noise (produced when pixels of different brightness levels adjoin one another) and by averaging the differences out of the selection.

The Median filter is used to smooth the rough areas in scanned images that have a grainy appearance. This filter uses a Radius slider to set the percentage of Noise removal that is applied. The filter looks for pixels that are isolated and, based on the percentage setting in the dialog box, removes them.

Notes on Using the Median Filter

There is nothing magic about the Median filter. Its ability to remove noise is dependent on the type of noise (sharp and high-contrast or blurred and low-contrast) that is in the image. The Median filter tends to blur the image if it is set too high. Use the Result window to experiment with various settings. If a particular area of the image has noise, mask it off and apply the filter to the noisy areas rather than to the entire image.

The Minimum Filter

The Minimum filter, like the Maximum filter, is not a traditional noise filter. This filter darkens an image by adjusting the pixel values of the image, decreasing the number of colors. By using the slider, the percentage of filtering applied can be controlled. This filter provides a method of lightening an image without washing it out (as would occur using brightness or intensity). Converse to the Maximum filter, this filter spreads out black or dark areas into the white or light areas of an image.

Notes on Using the Maximum, Median, and Minimum Filter

Besides the uses previously described, all three of the filters, when applied to a mask image, perform the same function as their counterparts in the Shape category of the Mask menu: Expand, Smooth, and Reduce. For example, if you create a mask, enable Paint on Mask mode, and apply the Maximum filter at 5 pixels, the result would be the same as if you had selected Mask, Shape, Enlarge by 5 pixels. Now, individuals on the PHOTO-PAINT development team have said that the three filters are not the same as the ones used for Expand, Smooth, and Reduce. My testing has shown there are very slight differences in the output of the Median filter but other than that, they operate identically. So, why say all of this? Because there are times when you will be manipulating a mask in Paint on Mask mode or working with a mask image and you will want to either enlarge, smooth, or reduce it. By knowing about this trio of filters, you can manipulate the mask directly.

Remove Moiré Filter

This newest addition to the Noise filter category is also known as a descreening filter in other scanning or photo-editing applications. Moiré patterns are nasty distortions that sometimes appear in images when they are resized or otherwise manipulated. You rarely see the moiré patterns in PHOTO-PAINT because the images are resampled when you change the size of an image. Other applications like word processors and page layout programs actually stretch and shrink the bitmap image, producing moiré. Moiré patterns usually originate during the scanning of a halftone image; they can also be caused by resizing an image that was dithered. As the pixels in the image are moved around, their proximity to other pixels causes patterns to develop. Internally, the Remove Moiré filter uses a two-stage process to break up the patterns that cause the moiré effect. First, the equivalent of a Jaggy Depeckle filter is applied to the image. This has the effect of producing an overall softening of the image. Next, the filter applies some sharpening to reduce the softening produced by the first step. This is the same filter that is applied if you select the Remove Moiré function while using Corel Scan.

Using the Remove Moiré Filter

The filter provides a Quality Level slider with a range of 0-10. This slider determines the amount of offset that is applied to the image. As the Level is increased, the shift applied to the pixels is increased. Larger amounts produce greater softness and loss of detail. The Better and Faster buttons are provided to allow the user to experiment. The output resolution of the filter can be controlled as well. This provides a method of scaling the final output so that the final image will appear sharper.

The Remove Noise Filter

This filter acts like a combination Jaggy Despeckle and Median filter. The Remove Noise filter softens edges and reduces the speckled effect created by the scanning process or from line noise in faxes. Each pixel is compared to surrounding pixels and an average value is computed. The pixels that exceed the threshold set with the slider control in the dialog box are removed. This operates in the same manner as the Jaggy Despeckle does on objects (reducing jaggies by softening edges), but, unlike Jaggy Despeckle, it also removes random pixels (noise) in the image.

Controlling the Remove Noise Filter

The operation of this filter is similar to the Remove Dust & Scratch filter described earlier. The most important setting on this dialog box is the Auto checkbox. Use it! The Auto checkbox, when enabled, automatically analyzes the image and determines the best Threshold setting for it. The Threshold setting is not available when Auto is set. The Threshold slider controls the amount of threshold the program uses to differentiate between noise and non-noise. Set the Level slider in the dialog box to a value between 0 and 255. Use the preview window to see the effects of different slider settings. While this slider can be set manually, I don't recommend it.

This filter is good for cleaning up faxes and poor scans. Like the other noise removal filters, it cannot take a real garbage scan and make it look pristine. It can, however, improve a poor scan or a scan of a fax.

Figure 16-12 shows a before-and-after type sample. The top image had Spike noise applied to it. This most closely resembles the noise one can expect in real life. Using the Auto setting, the Remove Noise filter lived up to its name and did an excellent job cleaning up the noise as shown in the lower image.

The Remove Noise filter is great for cleaning up faxes

FIGURE 16-12

TIP: *You can improve the performance of this filter on really trashy scans by masking the worst areas and applying the Remove Noise filter to them first. This speeds up the operation (because the area is smaller) and also keeps the filter from modifying areas that do not need to have any noise removed.*

This concludes the noisiest chapter in the book. Of all of the features in a photo-editing program, I use the filters in this category as much as the blur features. The next chapter, on the sharpening filters, covers some of the most valuable but generally misused filters in the lot. But after reading the chapter, you'll know how to carefully handle these very sharp tools.

17

The Sharpen Filters

No matter how crisp your original photograph and how great your scanner is, you will always lose some sharpness when any image is digitized. An image also loses sharpness when it is sent to an output device. As a result, most images will appear "soft" when printed unless some degree of sharpening is applied. Corel PHOTO-PAINT contains several sharpening filers that can help make your images as sharp as possible. The Sharpen subgroup of the Effects menu contains six filters that provide a wide range of sharpening effects that can be used to both improve image quality and create special effects.

The Sharpen Filters

The Sharpen subgroup of the Effects menu has the following filters:

- Adaptive Unsharp
- Directional Sharpen
- Find Edges
- High Pass
- Sharpen
- Unsharp Mask

Three of these filters, Adaptive Unsharp, Unsharp Mask, and Directional Sharpen, act in roughly the same manner, introducing small amounts of distortion to the image to reduce noise enhancement. The Sharpen filter is a true sharpen filter that sharpens both the image and its noise equally. The High Pass filter removes low-frequency detail and shading, while emphasizing highlights and luminous areas of an image. The Find Edges filter, which is not a traditional sharpening filter, is in this group because internally it uses the same sharpening techniques as the traditional sharpen filters to determine the edges in an image. Before we learn more about the individual filters, let's look at what happens when we sharpen an image.

What Is Sharpening?

Edges are what sharpening is all about. The human eye is influenced by the presence of edges in an image. Without edges, an image appears dull. By increasing the contrast between neighboring pixels, PHOTO-PAINT can enhance the edges, thus making the image appear to be sharper to the viewer, whether it is or not. Sharpening filters enable you to compensate for images or image elements that were photographed or scanned slightly out of focus. Sharpening cannot bring a blurred photograph into sharp focus. Figure 17-1 shows the original photograph before sharpening was applied; Figure 17-2 shows the result of selective application using one of the filters in the Sharpen group. In this example, the background was protected by a mask and the sharpening was applied to the architecture.

Before we discuss the various Sharpen filters, it would be beneficial to understand a little more about how sharpening affects different parts of an image. As s point of clarification, there is a group of filters called the Sharpen filters, and in that group there is a filter called the Sharpen filter. When I talk about the Sharpen filter, I am referring to the specific filter and not to a general type of filter. If you

This ancient
monument
lacks detail

FIGURE 17-1

Using one
of the
Sharpen
filters
brings out
the detail

FIGURE 17-2

find that confusing, wait until you learn that the best sharpening filter is called the Unsharp filter.

How Sharpening Affects Noise

In Chapter 16 we learned that all computer images include noise. Noise is unwanted pixels that may appear as a grainy pattern or as the odd dark or light spot. Images from photographs will always have noise. The noise associated with camera film is called *grain*. Actually, any image, including those captured with digital cameras, will have noise of some sort. The most pristine photo in your stock photo collection that was scanned on a ten-zillion dollar drum scanner will exhibit some noise. The only exception to this concept of universal noise is the Uniform color fill, which has no noise—or detail. Are you beginning to wonder if this chapter was supposed to be in another part of the book, maybe on noise? Not to worry. This really is the Sharpen chapter, and there is a reason for this noisy introduction.

So why do we care about noise in the Sharpen chapter? Because when we sharpen an image, we "sharpen" the noise as well. In fact, the noise generally sharpens up much better and faster than the rest of the image, which is undesirable. Why does noise sharpen up so well? Because noise pixels (like the tiny white specks in a black background) appear in sharper contrast to their background than the non-noise pixels in the image. These unwanted high-contrast visitors are usually so small as to not be noticed. But since they are high contrast, they contain the one component that sharpening filters look for, namely, the differences between adjoining pixels. The act of sharpening seeks out the differences (edges) and increases the contrast at those edges. The existing edges of the noise are enhanced and enlarged more than the rest of the pixels in the image. That is why they show up against the adjacent pixels so well, and that's what makes noise so noticeable after a Sharpen filter is applied.

A Noisy Demonstration

To illustrate how noise rears its ugly head, I have scanned and cropped a photograph of Sandy, a good friend of mine who has always wanted to have her picture in a nationally published book (not the kind with fold-out pages). Figure 17-3(a) shows a normal scan with no sharpening applied. It is one of those "glamour shots"—always (intentionally) a little out of focus—so popular these days at the shopping malls.

Next, I applied an excessive amount of the Sharpen filter to the masked area. The result, shown in Figure 17-3 (b), looks like she had dandruff and it got on the black curtain. The white specks in the background are the enhanced noise. The noise in the background was always there; the application of the Sharpen filter made it visible.

Specular Highlights and Dark Areas

The Sharpen filter increases the difference between adjoining pixels, eventually reaching the limits of the tonal spectrum. The white can only have a maximum value of 256, and the black can't be any lower than zero. The result is that in the image in Figure 17-3, shades that were nearly white are all pushed to the maximum, creating the white specks we see in the background and in Sandy's hair. These areas where light shades have been all pushed to the same value are known by several different names. They are called *blowouts, specular highlights,* or *tiny-white-blotches.* The effect is the same whether it is noise, dust specks on the original negative, or the small bright reflections you get from glass or highly polished metal. When the same effect happens on the dark side of the tonal spectrum (you thought I was going to say Force, didn't you?), the result is loss of detail in the shadow region as the darker shades all become the same shade of black. This is often referred to as plugging up the shadows.

a) Here is Sandy before Sharpening is applied; b) After Sharpening it looks like a dandruff commercial

FIGURE 17-3

The Sharpen filter can very easily create these unwanted bright and dark areas. It is not the filter of preference for sharpening an image. Does this mean you can't use the Sharpen filter? Not at all. It is useful for creating effects, just not for general sharpening. So if the Sharpen filter is not recommended for sharpening an image, what filter is? The Unsharp Mask filter, of course.

The Unsharp Mask filter

The Unsharp Mask filter can minimize the effect of the noise by distorting the image. Don't panic—when I say *distortion,* I mean in the technical sense, not the kind that produces a distorted image. The distortion I am referring to has the effect of toning down the sharp borders of noise while providing general sharpening of the other pixels in the image. The result is an overall sharpening of the image without enhancing the noise. This is how the Unsharp filters in Corel PHOTO-PAINT work. These filters have a strange name. In the trade they are generically referred to as *unsharp masking filters* (USM). The word *unsharping* is confusing to first-time users of photo-editing programs. Unsharping is named after a traditional film compositing technique that highlights the edges in an image by combining a blurred

film negative with the original film positive, which results in a sharper image without enhancing the noise.

The Unsharp Mask, like the Sharpen filter, compares each pixel in the image to its neighboring pixels. It then looks for amounts of contrast between adjacent pixels. PHOTO-PAINT assumes that a certain amount of contrast between adjoining pixels represents an edge. After it has found pixels that appear to be an edge, it creates a light corona around those pixels. USM can also produce an undesired effect by creating halos around detected edges if it is applied in excessive amounts. The best use of the Unsharp Mask (or any other filter in the Sharpen group) is to learn to apply the filter selectively.

The filter dialog box offers two control sliders, Radius and Percentage. Radius is the first control you should consider adjusting. It controls the width of the halo that is produced around each pixel. Start with an exaggerated amount and reduce it until you get the desired sharpening. The Percentage slider controls the amount of the halo created. Increasing the Percentage value creates big tonal shifts that push the shades that make up the edge into the black and white. If you are familiar with Photoshop's USM filter, the Percentage slider relates to the Amount.

Adaptive Unsharp and Directional Sharpen Filters

These filters produce similar effects to the Unsharp Mask filter. Because the Radius setting of these filters is fixed, the effects produced by them is more subtle than with the Unsharp Mask. It is not uncommon to make several applications of these filters, even at a setting of 100 percent. Beware of applying too much of any of the Unsharp filters, however. At some point, the image edges will begin to exhibit halos when too much Unsharp masking is applied.

It can be difficult to evaluate the effect of these filters using only the Original/Results window of the filter dialog box. I recommend using the On-screen preview mode and applying a relatively large setting. Evaluate the effect that this setting has and then adjust the filter setting to reduce the amount of the effect until it looks right. By now you will have lost an awareness of what the original looked like, so apply the filter and then use the Undo (CTRL-Z) and Redo (CTRL-SHIFT-Z) to see the before and after setting. At this point you can use the filter setting or just Undo and then apply the filter again. When applying any filter that sharpens the image, you must always be looking at the light or bright area of the image for blowouts (which is usually the first symptom of excessive sharpening).

Technical Notes About Adaptive Unsharp Filter

The Adaptive Unsharp filter uses a sharpening process with local control of the sharpening process around each pixel, rather than a global sharpening amount. It uses statistical differences (Adaptive) between adjacent pixels to determine the sharpening amount for each pixel. The effect of the Adaptive Unsharp filter is very similar to the other two Unsharp filters, Directional and Unsharp Masking. Testing done while writing the book has shown some subtle differences. Adaptive Unsharp seems to produce slightly less contrast than either the Unsharp Mask or Directional Sharpen filters.

Technical Notes About Directional Sharpen Filter

This is another sharpening filter with local sharpening control. In this filter, the sharpening amount for each pixel is computed for several compass directions, and the greatest amount of them will be used as the final sharpening amount for that pixel. In other words, the Directional Sharpen filter analyzes values of pixels of similar color shades to determine the direction in which to apply the greatest amount of sharpening. I have found that the Directional Sharpen filter usually increases the contrast of the image more than the Unsharp Mask filter does. The Directional Sharpen also produces good sharpening but with higher contrast than either the Unsharp Mask or Adaptive Unsharp filters. I prefer to use the Directional Sharpening for any image that contains lots of strong diagonals.

The Sharpen Filter

The most important thing to remember about sharpening an image is that the Sharpen filter is rarely the best filter to use. Use one of the three filters discussed in the previous paragraphs. Why? Because the Sharpen filter doesn't care about noise, it just sharpens everything in the photograph. It is a powerful filter that will blow the socks off of your image if you are not careful. The Sharpen filter sharpens the appearance of the image or a masked area by intensifying the contrast of neighboring pixels. There are times when this filter may be preferred over any of the previously described filters, but they are rare.

Using the Sharpen Filter

The Sharpen filter dialog box contains only two controls. The Edge Level (%) slider controls the amount of sharpening applied to the image. Use this filter at higher settings with some degree of caution. Higher values usually produce blowouts. The Threshold slider determines the level of contrast between adjoining pixels that is necessary for the filter action to occur. For example, if the Threshold value is set high, more pixels meet the minimum requirement and the sharpening effect will be applied to more of the image. If the Threshold is set low, only the high-contrast elements of the image will be affected.

TIP: *Unlike the previously discussed filters, the Sharpen filter has a much greater effect at 5 percent than the USM filter does at the 100 percent level or either of the USM filters do at the 100 percent level.*

When to Apply Sharpening

Some argue that the best time to apply sharpening is when an image is scanned. I have seen several comparisons between images that were sharpened during scanning and those done with Sharpen filters after the scan, and the sharpening on the scanned images was visibly sharper. In fairness, the scanner was a $500,000 drum scanner and the operator was an experienced professional. If your image is from a photo-CD or some other source, the decision to apply sharpening during the scanning process has already been made for you. If your image didn't have sharpening applied during the scan then to sharpen it, you will need to use one of the filters included with Corel PHOTO-PAINT.

TIP: *Sharpening is one of the last effects you should apply. Apply it after tonal and color correction, as it will affect the results of both.*

Let's Sharpen Our Sharpen Skills

After all this talk about the pros and cons of different Sharpen filters, wouldn't you like to see how they really work? I thought so. In this simple exercise, we are going to take a "soft" image and see just what the Sharpen filters can really do.

1. Open the image EXERCISE\PHOTOS\555016.WI. It is a photograph of the Coliseum, as shown in Figure 17-4. (Did you know it had a basement?). From the Image menu, choose Resample, enter 6 into the Width value, and click OK.

2. From the Image menu, choose Duplicate. When asked, name the file Sharper. Ensure that the Zoom level is 100% (even if it means the entire image doesn't fit on your display).

3. Our first and most important step in this process is to examine the image and see what the image needs. It is soft (meaning low contrast), but it is not out of focus. It has some areas of white (rectangular stones in the middle, the group of tourists waving at you near the back of the Coliseum), so we must watch these areas closely after we apply the sharpening. Don't make a big thing out of this. You are not looking for hidden mystical symbols in the image, just the presence of bright/light and dark/shadow areas. If there are large areas of either, we will be limited in the amount of sharpening we can apply. The other thing you should get into the practice of looking for is image detail. If this image had been out of focus, there wouldn't be any. How can you tell if there is any detail to recover with sharpening? In the next step, we are going to check out this image.

A soft image that can be recovered through the use of sharpening filters

FIGURE 17-4

17

4. Use the Zoom tool and zoom in on one of the tunnel-looking things in the Coliseum basement. Try 600% or until the pixels look like bricks. If the pixels look like different-colored bricks, then there is image detail that can be recovered in most cases. If the original image had been out of focus, all of the pixels would have been nearly the same color and would barely be distinguishable from one another. Of course, we've got bricks in this image—that's why I picked it. Return to 100% Zoom (CTRL-1).

5. From the Effects menu, choose Sharpen and then Directional Sharpen. Set the Percentage to 80. Click OK. The image shows marked improvement. Look carefully at the highlight and shadows area to see if there are any blowouts or large dark areas. In fact there are not. As described earlier, Directional Sharpen has a tendency to increase the contrast slightly more than Adaptive Unsharpen, making it a good choice for a secondary application of sharpening. Applying Sharpening twice is rarely recommended, but this image can benefit from it.

6. From the Effects menu, choose Sharpen and then Adaptive Unsharp. Set the Percentage to 80. Click OK.

7. To see the difference these filter applications have made, from the Windows menu, select Tile Horizontally or Vertically. If you do not see both of the images, you have minimized one of them. Figure 17-4 shows the original photograph. Figure 17-5 shows the result of the applications of the sharpen filters to it.

Find Edges

I love this filter; it kind of makes a colored pencil drawing. Find Edges is unlike any other filter in this chapter. Even though it is not a general image enhancement tool like the Sharpen filters, it allows you to obtain some effects that would not otherwise be possible.

Find Edges dialog box

The Find Edges dialog box contains a Level slider that controls the threshold that triggers the Find Edges filter. As the value increases, the threshold decreases, allowing the filter to include more of the edge. As the slider value decreases, less of the edge component is included, making the edges thinner and therefore lighter. Adjust the Level slider to define a sensitivity value. The higher the number, the more

What a difference a little bit of sharpening can make

FIGURE 17-5

edges are enhanced. The Edge Type options determine the type of outline produced. For dark bold lines, choose Solid. For lighter, more diffused outlines, choose Soft.

So What Can You Do with Find Edges?

The Find Edges filter can create an outline effect. The first step is to place some text over the photograph of leaves, as shown in Figure 17-6. The Find Edges filter determines the edges on everything in the image and removes everything that is not an edge, including the black fill of the letters. The Level Setting for the image shown in Figure 17-7 was 80, which produced darker lines.

Making Pencil Sketches with Find Edges

One of the unique things you can do with Find Edges is make fake pencil sketches. In this hands-on exercise we will make a thank-you card that will be reproduced on a photocopy machine. Our primary task will be to convert the photograph of a beautiful flower shot against a black background into something that is reproducible.

Placing text
on a
photograph
of leaves

FIGURE 17-6

Same
photograph
after
applying
the Find
Edges filter

FIGURE 17-7

Because Find Edges looks only for edges, the black background will disappear immediately when the filter is applied.

1. Open the image EXERCISE\PHOTOS\514081.WI on the Corel CD. Use the Resample command in the Image menu, change the Width to 6 inches, and click OK.

2. Select Convert To from the Image menu and choose Grayscale (8-bit).

3. From the Effects menu, choose Sharpen and then select Find Edges. From the dialog box, change the Level slider to 80 and the Edge type: to Soft. Click OK. The result is shown in Figure 17-8.

4. To clean up the background select the Magic Wand mask tool from the Toolbox and ensure that the Tolerance level in the Property Bar is 10. Click anywhere on the background outside of the flower.

The flower can now be reproduced on a photocopy machine

FIGURE 17-8

5. From the Edit menu, select Clear. Invert the mask. Click the Create Object: Cut Selection button. You may (and probably will) notice that a small outline of the original flower remains. From the Objects Docker (CTRL-F7), click on the Background to select it. From the Edit menu, choose Clear.

6. Select the Object Picker tool in the Toolbox. Click on the flower object to select it as indicated by the eight handles that appear. Duplicate the flower (CTRL-D). From the Objects Docker, make the original flower (bottom object) invisible by clicking on its eye icon.

7. Select the duplicate, drag one of the corner handles, and reduce the flower in size until it is a little less than one inch in diameter.

8. Duplicate the small flower (CTRL-D) three times. There are now four small flowers. Use the Object Picker tool to position them in the four corners as shown below. (Hint: You can use guidelines from the rulers to align the flowers.)

9. In the Objects Docker window, SHIFT-select the four small flowers. From the Object menu, choose Drop Shadow and create a shadow behind each of the four flowers. The Drop Shadow setting I used had a Direction of 0.0, a Feather setting: Average setting of 14, and an Opacity of 65 with the color set to black. It's all a matter of personal taste. Click OK. The result is shown below.

10. Make the original flower visible again by clicking its eye icon in the Objects Docker window. With only the large one selected, change its Opacity to 25. Now it looks like a watermark. Resize it by dragging a corner bounding box inward. Position as shown below.

11. Click on the Text button in the Toolbox, left-click on black in the color palette, and enter the text shown in the image above. The text is Dauphine at 48 points. I applied a drop shadow with an Opacity of 100 with the color set to black, Feather of 7, and a Distance of 0.333.

That's all there is to it. To be fair if you really are going to create something like this for reproduction on a copy machine, don't create the shadows. Copy machines are real shadow killers.

Another way to use the Find Edges filters with flowers is shown in Figure 17-9. The flower was imported into DRAW and then duplicated, aligned, and distributed to make the border. The text with the drop shadow and the scalloped lower border were created in PHOTO-PAINT.

High Pass Filter

I placed this filter last because it is unique. Officially, the High Pass filter removes low-frequency detail and shading, and emphasizes highlights and luminous areas of an image. This filter enables you to isolate high-contrast image areas from their low-contrast counterparts. The action of the filter makes a high-contrast image into a murky gray one. Now you may rightly ask why you would ever want a filter to do something like that. The answer is that this filter is best used as preparatory to other filter actions.

The High Pass Filter Controls

The Percentage value controls the intensity of the effect. The default setting is 100 percent, which is far too high for many applications. Low Percentage values distinguish areas of high and low contrast only slightly. Large values change all

Using a single photograph of a flower and the Find Edges filter, I was able to make an attractive banner for a menu

FIGURE 17-9

high-contrast areas to dark gray and low-contrast areas to a slightly lighter shade of gray. At higher settings, the High Pass effect removes most of the image detail, leaving only the edge details clearly visible. If you only want to emphasize highlights, use lower percentage settings. The Radius slider determines how many pixels near the edge (areas of high contrast) are included in the effect. The result is, the higher the setting, the more contrast is preserved.

So What Can You Do with the High Pass Filter?

The High Pass filter is especially useful as a precursor to the application of the Threshold filter. By first applying different levels of High Pass to an image, you can produce a wider variety of effects with the Threshold filter. You can also use it to help differentiate objects in an image when creating a mask. This is because the High Pass filter sees an image in terms of contrast levels, which is one of the ways your eyes perceive images in real life. Using the High Pass filter as the first step helps in the creation of a mask of an image element that is visually unique but proves difficult to isolate with a mask. By applying the High Pass filter set to a Percentage level of 50 percent and a Radius of 20, you can often create an outline around the object you want to isolate. After the mask is created, save it and use the Revert command to restore the image to its last saved state. Then reload the mask.

Sharpen Adjust

Now that you know what all of the Sharpen filters do, you can see them all (except High Pass) at once with the Sharpness Control dialog box, which is accessed by choosing Sharpness in the Adjust portion of the Effects menu.

The Sharpen Adjust dialog box provides a quick way to compare the results of different filters side by side. The preview operation is limited to the Before/After format and Large Result Preview as there is no onscreen preview. The windows, called Original/Result, are at the top of the dialog box. Clicking the thumbnail of the desired filter applies the filter to the image in the Result window. To Undo the last filter application, click the Undo button to the right of the Zoom button. Repeatedly clicking this button lets you step back through a group of effects applied. Different filters can be applied multiple times using the Sharpness Control dialog box.

Now you know a lot more about the sharpen filters. There are a few more ways to sharpen an image by sharpening individual channels. This is explored in Chapter 24. The next chapter deals with the wild and wooly world of the 2D Effect filters.

18

The 2D Effect Filters

This group of 15 filters comprises some of the most unusual and complex in Corel PHOTO-PAINT 8. Many of the 2D filters are not needed for day-to-day photo-editing but can be genuine lifesavers in some situations. Many of these filters first appeared in Corel PHOTO-PAINT 6. The listing of the filters in this chapter is in the order of their appearance in the drop-down list.

The Band Pass Filter

Leading off the lineup in the 2D Effect category of the Effects menu is the Band Pass filter. While the operation of this filter is a little difficult to comprehend, it does have some uses. In the Band Pass dialog box, shown below, you can adjust the balance of high contrast and smooth areas in an image. The Frequency plot displays a graph that shows the occurrence of sharp (high contrast) and smooth (low contrast) areas in the image. Smooth areas are located toward the center of the graph, while sharp areas are distributed toward the outer edges. By adjusting the radius and weightings of the bands, you can screen out unwanted tonal characteristics in an image. A low weighting for the center of the plot emphasizes image detail; a low weighting for the outside of the plot reduces image detail.

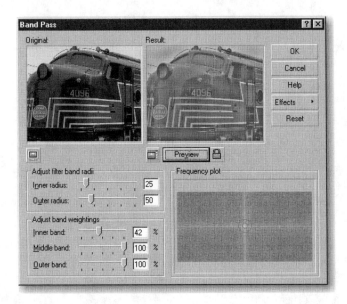

Reading the Frequency plot can be a little tricky. The area outside of the larger red circle is the Outer band; the area outside of the smaller red circle but inside the larger one is the Middle band. Everything inside of the smaller red circle is the Inner band. Use the Inner/Outer radius slider to determine which areas of the image (by frequency content) are in the Inner, Outer, and Middle bands. Then adjust the Inner, Outer, and Middle band sliders to set the intensity of each band. To eliminate either the sharp or smooth areas within a band, set its weighting to 0. To emphasize them, set the desired slider to the maximum of 100%.

Experiment with different weightings to see which provide the best results. For example, you can use the bands to eliminate unwanted noise by isolating the frequency of the noise within the middle band and reducing its weighting to 0. The only challenge you may experience with this experimentation method of using the filter is that its internal operation is very complex and therefore very, very slow in its operation. I thought it was slow and I am using a the AMD K6 chip at 233 MHz!

Using The Band Pass Filter

One of the only uses I have found for the Band Pass filter is to apply it to an image before applying the Threshold. Figure 18-1 is the photograph of a train after it has had the Threshold filter (set to bi-level) applied to it. Figure 18-2 is the result of applying the Band Pass filter before the Threshold filter. Notice the difference between the two resulting images. The application of the Band Pass filter brings a balance between the high and low contrast areas. This means that the Threshold effect will be able to produce more detail. Note that in Figure 18-2 you can read the "New York Central" on the nose plate of the train. You can also see much more detail in the wheel carriage assembly. I confess that setting up the Band Pass filter was done by experimentation, but the results are worth it if you must reduce an image to bi-level and need to preserve as much image information as possible.

The Displace Filter

The Displace filter enables you to distort or add texture to an image by moving individual pixels. The direction and distance that the pixels move is determined by an image in the dialog box called a *displacement map*. The Displace filter evaluates the color value of pixels in the image and the displacement map, and then shifts the image based on the values in the displacement map. Clear as mud, right? A visual demonstration may help. Note the grid has been added to help show the effect.

Threshold
filter
applied to
photograph

FIGURE 18-1

Threshold
filter
applied to
an image
after
application
of Band
Pass filter

FIGURE 18-2

Figure 18-3 is an illustration of how a displacement map works. While the Displacement filter uses both color value and brightness to determine displacement we need only be concerned about brightness. The displacement map at the top goes from 70% Black to 30% Black in 12 steps. The original image (middle) has the map applied to it and the result of applying our displacement map to the image appears at the bottom. Notice at the left end (70% Black) the image is pushed (offset) down and at the right end of the image (30% Black) the image is pushed upward. The image in the middle at the 50% gray point is unaffected. Sound boring? Wait until you see what we can do with this little jewel as you are about to find out when we make chrome.

Making Chrome

Maybe it was because I was raised in the '50s or I watched *Grease* once too often, but I love making chrome objects in PHOTO-PAINT. In this exercise, we are going to create some chrome letters and learn how to use the displacement filter at the same time.

Any image can be used for a Displacement map but we are going to create one from scratch.

Using File> New create an 8-bit Grayscale file that is 6 x 2 inches at a Resolution of 96 dpi with White for the Paper color.

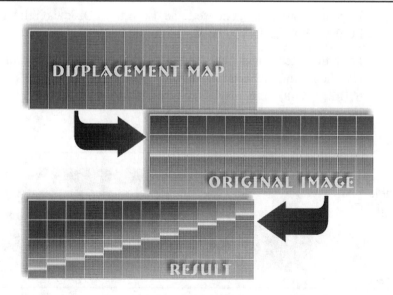

How
displacement
maps affect
an image

FIGURE 18-3

1. Select the Font Tool in the Toolbox and click inside of the image. Change the Font size to 96. In this example I used the SerpentineD Bol typeface, but any sans serif face will work.

 TIP: *Avoid fonts that are skinny or are complex as they don't make good chrome.*

Type the word **POWER**.

2. Click on the Object Picker (makes the text into an object). Align the Mask to the center of the image using the Align dialog box (CTRL-A).

3. Create a Mask from the Object (CTRL-M). From the Mask menu, choose Save and select Save to Disk. Name the mask POWER MASK.CPT. Select the Remove Mask button on the Property Bar. Combine the text with the background (CTRL-DOWN ARROW).

4. From the Effects menu choose 3D Effects and select Emboss. The settings for the Emboss menu are Emboss Color: Gray; Direction: 180; Depth: 5; Level 100. Click OK and the result should look like Figure 18-4. Ugly stuff, right?

5. From the Mask menu, choose Load, Load from Disk and reload the POWER MASK. Invert the Mask (CTRL-I).

6. From the Effects menu, choose 3D Effects and select Glass from the list. Use the Default Style setting and click OK. Remove the mask (CTRL-SHIFT-R). The image is too dark to use, it would offset the entire image, so we need to lighten it up a little.

The humble
beginnings
of a
displacement
map

FIGURE 18-4

7. From the Image menu, choose Adjust and the select Gamma. Change the Gamma setting to 1.8 and click OK. Save the file as POWER DISPLACEMENT MAP.CPT (Don't you love the new long file names?).

Creating the Reflection

Next we need a bitmap image to distort with our map. This will create the reflection. We must first understand the viewer's mind expects a particular placement of colors in the reflection. The top of the bitmap needs to be cool colors (like the sky) and the bottom warm or dark colors (like the earth). It is the fills that ultimately determine what the final reflections look like.

8. Using File> New create a 24-bit color file that is 6×2 inches at a Resolution of 96 dpi with White for the Paper color.

9. From the Edit menu, choose Fill. When the Edit Fill & Transparency dialog box opens, choose Fountain Fill (middle button) and then click the Edit button.

10. Set the Type to Linear, the Steps to 999, and the Angle to 90.0. In the Color Blend section change from Two Color to Custom. Click on the left color marker and click on the 60% Black color in the palette. Change the far right color to Pastel Blue in the palette at the right side of the dialog box.

11. We need to add 3 more colors. Double-click on the top edge of the color bar and a triangle appears. Set it to Pastel Blue and drag it until it reads 37% in the Position box. To the right of this color double-click again. Change its color to White and drag its Position to 41%. Repeat with Twilight Blue at 77%. Click OK twice to apply this fill to the image.

Making Chrome

This is the fun part. Where we put all of the parts together and make chrome.

12. From the Effects menu, select 2D Effects and then Displace. When the dialog box opens, click the Load button and locate the POWER DISPLACEMENT MAP. Change the Vertical scale setting to 100. The Horizontal setting doesn't affect anything with this displacement map.

Click the OK button. The result is shown below. WOW! Chrome. Wait, there's more.

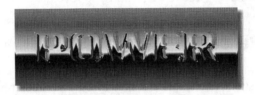

13. From the Mask menu, select Load and load from the disk the POWER MASK.CPT. Don't load the displacement map. Invert the mask (CTRL-I).

14. Open the Effects menu again and select Fancy and choose The Boss. The Boss filter provides the final touch. Change the Style setting to Wet and then change the Width setting to 3. Click the OK button.

NOTE: *The Width setting is the most important setting in this filter when working with inverted masks. Experiment with it to see how much difference the different width settings have on the final output. The wider the Width the more rounded the characters appear.*

15. Invert the mask again and select Create an Object from the Mask menu. The chrome is complete.

16. You can now select the Object with the Object Picker and add a drop shadow. The result, with the background removed, is shown below.

More Technical Information about Displacement Maps

The brightness values of the pixels in the displacement map tell Corel PHOTO-PAINT which pixels to move and how far to move them. It is important to remember that we are talking about Brightness values, so the following three values apply to grayscale and color images. The three determining brightness values are:

- **Black** Areas in the displacement map that contain black will move the corresponding pixels in an image being affected to the right and/or down by the maximum amount defined by the Scale settings in the Displace dialog box. Values between black and 50 percent gray move pixels a shorter distance.

- **White** Areas in the displacement map that contain white will move the corresponding pixels in an image being affected to the left and/or up by the maximum amount defined by the Scale settings in the Displace dialog box. Values between white and 50 percent gray move pixels a shorter distance.

- **Middle gray** Areas in the displacement map that are composed of gray with a brightness of 50 percent cause the pixels to remain unmoved.

Before we take leave of this very versatile filter, I have included one more exercise that shows another use for this filter.

Creating a Watercolor Effect

In this hands-on exercise we are going to make a displacement map and apply it to an existing image to change its overall appearance, making it look like a watercolor painting. I encourage you to do this exercise because the resulting image looks much better in color than the grayscale printed next.

Our first step is to make a displacement map. When making maps we have a choice of either making them the same size as the image or making them small so that they can be tiled. To achieve the effect we desire we will make a small one.

1. Select File, New. From the Create a New Image dialog box choose 24-bit color mode, Width/Height: 150 × 150 pixels; Resolution of 144 dpi.

2. To make the displacement map, we will use the Texture Fill feature of PHOTO-PAINT. Select Fill from the Edit menu to open the Edit Fill & Transparency dialog box. On the Fill Color tab, select the Texture Fill button (it is the button on the far right) and click the Edit button. This action opens the Texture Fill dialog box.

3. Select Styles in the Texture Library and from the Texture list choose Surface-Rainbow. We will use the pattern without modification. Click OK to return to Edit Fill & Transparency and click OK to apply the fill. Save the image using the File, Save to the \COREL\ DRAW80\CUSTOM\ DISPLACE folder. Select the "PaintBrush (*.PCX)" setting for the Save as type and name the file WATERCOLOR.PCX. Close the file after it has been saved.

4. Using the File Open command in the File menu, find the image EXERCISE\PHOTOS\ 514075.WI. Because this is a large file, use the Resample option. When the Resample dialog box opens, change the Width to 500 pixels and click the OK button. The image opens as shown below.

5. Under 2D Effects in the Effects menu, select Displace.... opening the filter's dialog box. Locate and click the Load button on the right side of the dialog box. This opens the Load Displacement Map dialog box. It should be at COREL\DRAW80\CUSTOM \DISPLACE, which is the default location for the displacement maps provided with Corel PHOTO-PAINT.

6. Locate the file WATERCOLOR.PCX and either double-click on it or select it and click the Open button. On the left side of the dialog box under Scale Mode keep the Tile option selected and change both of the Scale Values to 8. Click the OK button and the image becomes displaced giving the effect of a watercolor painting as shown below.

Suggestions for Creating Displacement Maps

This filter is a virtual storehouse of effects and I speak from experience when I tell you that it is possible to waste many hours working (playing) with it. Here are some practical suggestions for creating displacement maps to work with the Displace filter.

Remember that 50 percent gray is the neutral color that keeps the pixels from moving; therefore, it is a good background color when creating a displacement map. Next, when making displacement maps, keep the image area small. Some of the most effective displacement maps that Corel provides are smaller than 20 x 20 pixels. Keep the Horizontal and Vertical displacement settings small for the best effects. Also, you will find that the some of the more effective displacement maps are those that contain smooth transitions between the bright and dark components. Resolution and file formats are not critical factors. PHOTO-PAINT is not restricted to PCX format.

Some other Texture fills that make interesting Displacement maps follow using the format of LIBRARY/Texture name: STYLES/Surface1 2C; SAMPLES 5/Bacteria, SAMPLES 5/Beads, SAMPLES 5/Block Rainbow.

The Edge Detect Filter

There are many times it is necessary to create images that will be reproduced on a photocopier rather than a printing press. Because a photocopier doesn't faithfully reproduce grayscale images, you can use the Edge Detect filter to convert images into lines on a single colored background. Best results are obtained with high contrast images. This filter is similar to the Find Edges filter in the Sharpen group of the Effects menu, which is described in Chapter 17.

The operation of the Edge Detect filter is extremely simple. The Edge Detect filter dialog box has only two areas in which to make a choice. The first involves choosing the Background Color. This color will replace every part of the image that doesn't have a line in it. The other is setting the Sensitivity slider (1-10), which determines the intensity of edge detection.

Using the Edge Detect Filter

Move the slider to the right to increase the effect, which means that more of the original area surrounding the edges is included. A large sensitivity value can create the appearance of noise in the finished image. When this happens, and it will, use the Eraser tool to remove the noise from the image. Figure 18-5 is a photograph of a nautilus shell that is great for use in offset printing but suffers greatly when

This
photograph
will not
reproduce
well on a
photocopy
machine

FIGURE 18-5

reproduced on a photocopy machine. Applying the Edge Detect filter makes the photograph into something that can be used to advertise an upcoming shell exhibit. In Figure 18-6 the process of using the Edge Detect filter created a lot of noise that was removed with the Eraser tool.

The Edge Detect filter can work with both color and grayscale images. When used on a color image it will generally produce lightly multicolored lines. To make

The Edge
Detect filter
creates an
outline of
the shell

FIGURE 18-6

all of the lines black convert the image to a grayscale. Be aware that some images, especially low contrast photographs, really look ugly after having this filter applied. If that happens, another alternative is to use the Band Pass filter discussed earlier in the chapter and then apply the Threshold filter.

TIP: *An application of contrast or equalization before applying the Edge Detect filter improves the resulting effect in most photographs.*

The Offset Filter

18

The Offset filter moves an image according to a specified number of pixels or a percentage of image size. We are not talking about moving an object, this filter actually moves pixels in an image. It is a favorite of those Photoshop users who were heavily involved in channel operations (called CHOPS). This filter remains critical to many techniques described in many Photoshop books. Most of these techniques involving the Offset filter were developed before the advent of objects and layers. It allowed you to create an image, save it to a channel, and offset the duplicate to create highlights and shadows. Today it is easier to do that by creating objects and positioning the objects. Still, the Offset filter can be used to create effects that no other filter can create as shown in the hands-on project that follows.

Creating a Web Page Graphic Using the Offset Filter

This is a hands-on exercise using the Offset Filter to create a Web Page graphic for a coming shell exhibit at the museum. It seems our little shell exhibit has done so well we need to design a cover for it.

1. Find the file EXERCISE\PHOTOS\594011.WI, select the Resample option from the Open an Image dialog box, and click the Open button. When the Resample Image dialog box opens ensure the Units is set to inches and change the Width to a value of 5 inches. Click the OK button and the original image appears as shown in Figure 18-5.

2. Select the Offset... from the 2D Effects in the Effects menu, opening the 2D Effects dialog box. Click the button to enable Wrap around in the Fill empty area with: section. In the Shift section set the Horizontal to 30 and the Vertical to 25. Ensure the Shift Value as % of Dimensions box is checked. The result of the offset is shown next.

3. For the Book title, select the Text tool in the Tool box and click somewhere in the image. In the Property bar change the font to Futura XBlk BT at a size of 72 and click the Render Text to Mask button to enable it. You may want to ensure the Mask Marquee button is enabled so you can see the mask we are going to make. Click somewhere in the image and type the word "SHELLS" in all caps, then grab the edge of the text and move it as shown below. Create a mask from the object (CTRL-M) and then select Delete from the Object menu.

4. With only the mask of the text remaining, open the Object menu and choose Create and then Lens: from Mask. From the list, choose Gamma and then OK.

5. When the Gamma dialog box opens, set the Gamma to a value of 5.0 and click the OK button. If you used Gamma in versions of PAINT prior to PHOTO-PAINT 7, the value of 6.0 corresponds to a value of 600 in the previous versions. The lens applies the Gamma effect to any part of the image it happens to be positioned above and the lens can be moved anywhere in the image. This is an improvement over what was necessary in previous releases when the Gamma effect was applied and could be moved.

 NOTE: *Lenses are temporary things and while they will be saved if the image is saved as a PHOTO-PAINT (CPT) file they must be combined with the background when saved in other file formats.*

18

6. Select the Text tool again and change the Font to Bank Gothic Md BT, size to 20, and the Character/Line Spacing to –2. Click on white in the onscreen palette, if your Paint color is not white. Type in the words **OF THE SOUTH PACIFIC**. Click the Object Picker tool and move the text as shown below. Disable both the Show Object Marquee and Show Mask Marquee buttons.

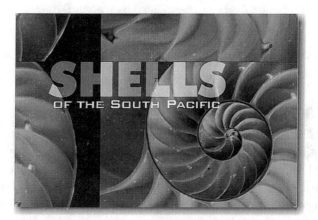

7. The image is too large to use on a Web page so we must either convert it to a JPEG or a GIF file. To convert to a JPEG, select Export and choose JPEG and give the file a descriptive name. I recommend a file name not longer than 8 characters—not everyone on the Internet has the latest equipment. If you choose to save as a GIF file, then you must first use the Convert to command in the Image menu to change it into a Paletted (8-bit) image. Optimized or Adaptive palettes will give you the best results.

Controlling the Offset Filter

The Offset filter dialog box controls are divided into two areas: the Shift controls and the Fill empty area options. Horizontal and Vertical Shift sliders determine the amount of shift in the Horizontal and Vertical. The values in the boxes to the right of the sliders represent either the number of pixels shifted or the percentage, depending on whether the Shift Value box is checked. When the Shift Value as % of Dimensions checkbox is enabled, it causes the coordinates of the horizontal and vertical shift values to be calculated as a percentage of the size of the object. Enabling this check box with the Vertical shift set to 50 and the Horizontal shift set to zero causes the image to shift along the vertical plane a distance corresponding to exactly one-half the size of the image.

Fill Empty Area Options

The keys to the operation of this filter are determined by the following options:

- **Wrap around** wraps another part of the image around the edges of the window when shifted.

- **Repeat edges** fills the space vacated by the shifted image with the color(s) currently appearing along the edge of the image.

- **Paint color** fills the space vacated by the shifted image with the current paint color.

Using the Offset Filter

There are a few things to consider when using this filter. First, the filter will shift either the entire image or an area enclosed by a mask. None of the pixels in the image being shifted will shift outside of the mask. Therefore, depending on the Fill Empty space option chosen, all of the effects will happen inside the mask. If the object being masked is a solid color and Wrap around is chosen as the option, it will appear as though nothing had happened.

The Pixelate Filter

The Pixelate filter gives a block like appearance to the selected area of an image. You have seen the effect many times before on newscasts where they pixelated their features to prevent viewers from seeing the face of the person talking. Because the pixelation was done on a frame-by-frame basis, the boundaries of the pixelation varied from frame to frame, which produced an apparent movement around the edges.

You can control the Pixelate effect by selecting either rectangular or circular mode and changing the size and opacity of the blocks. This filter can be used to create backgrounds that have the appearance of mosaic tiles.

Width and Height values (1-100 pixels) for the size of the pixel blocks can be entered independently. The effects of pixel block size are dependent on the image size. A value of 10 in a small image will create large pixel blocks. A value of 10 in a very large image will produce small pixel blocks. Use the Opacity % slider (range is 1-100) to control the transparency of the pixel blocks. Lower values are more transparent. The shape of the blocks of pixels is controlled with the Pixelate mode buttons. Square and Rectangular modes arrange the pixel blocks on horizontal lines. The Circular mode bends the blocks of pixels and arranges them on concentric circles beginning at the center of the image or the masked area.

Using the Pixelate Filter

Since Corel PHOTO-PAINT 8 can import and work on video files (if you have a video capture board), the most obvious use for the Pixelate filter is to pixelate the faces of key witnesses to gangland murders for the local news station. If that opportunity is not readily available, Pixelate is very handy for creating unusual backdrops or converting background into something akin to mosaic tile. When working with backgrounds, remember that the best effects occur when there are contrasts in the image that is being pixelated. For example, if you pixelate a solid blue sky, you will hardly see any effect on the image.

Making a Wild Thing with the Pixelate Filter

Using the Pixelate filter in concert with a few other filters can quickly make something wild that will spruce up any Web site. With this exercise we will learn to use the Pixelate filter with the several other filters including learning about the KPT Video Feedback filter. One of the unfortunate about writing a book using the beta version of software is that things change. At the last minute I was made aware that the KPT 3.0 SE filters were not being included in the PHOTO-PAINT 8 release. If you have PHOTO-PAINT 7 you can use the KPT 3.0 SE filters that were installed with that program. If not, you will need to skip the steps using the KPT Video Feedback filter.

1. Locate and open the image EXERCISE\PHOTOS\593002.WI. From the Image menu select Resample and change the image to 6 inches wide and click OK.

2. Select the Freehand Mask tool from the Toolbox and create a mask around the middle green diskette at the bottom of the image. Just click on each of the four corners, it doesn't need to be exact. Remember to double-click the last point to complete the mask.

3. Create an object from the mask selection using the Create Object: Copy Selection (CTRL-UP ARROW) from the Standard toolbar. In the Objects Docker window hide the object by selecting the background and then clicking on the object's Eye icon.

4. From the Effects menu choose 2D Effects and then Pixelate. Choose Circular, with a Width of 24 and a Height of 12. Click OK. The result is shown below. Not very exciting but it is a start.

5. From the Effects menu choose KPT 3.0 SE and select KPT Video Feedback 3.0 SE. A small, (very non-Corel looking) dialog box appears, as shown below. Place the cursor in the Mode area. Click and hold down the left mouse button and from the menu that appears, select Telescope feedback. Now click and hold down the left mouse button inside of the Feedback Intensity checkbox. While still holding the button down move the mouse and you will notice changing numbers next to Intensity appear on the bottom edge. Keep moving the mouse until the intensity is somewhere near 90. Click inside of the preview window. This action

controls the origin point of the effect. Click and drag the point until it is near X: 23 and Y: -145. Anything close will do. Click the green ball in the lower-right corner to apply the effect.

6. From the Effects menu choose 3D Effects and select Emboss. Check Original color, Depth: 4, Level:100, and Direction of 90. Click OK.

7. Now for the cartoon effect. From the Image menu, select Adjust and then choose Hue/ Saturation/Lightness. When the dialog box opens set Hue to -10, Saturation to 50, and Lightness to 5. Click OK.

8. Now we have what appears to be a tunnel. Every tunnel needs a light at the end of it. So, from the Effects menu choose Render and select Lens Flare. Change the Lens Type to 35mm prime and click at the vanishing point (where everything meets). Click OK and the result is shown below.

9. In the Objects menu make the floppy selected and visible by clicking on its name. The diskette is dark so to correct it (in this case) from the Image menu choose Adjust and Auto Equalize.

10. Because your diskette might have a jagged edge to it, select Feather from the Object menu. Pick a setting that smoothes the edge of the diskette (I used 6). You can use either Linear or Curved. Click OK.

11. We will add a little glow to our diskette using the Drop Shadow command. From the Object menu, choose Drop Shadow. Make the settings: Flat, Direction: 270, Distance: 0.1; Color: White, Opacity:100, Feather: Average, Width: 35. Click OK. The result is shown below and in the color insert.

12. If you were going to print this, you would have chosen a higher resolution during the initial Resample (like 150-200 dpi). If the destination of this image were a Web page you would follow the suggestions given in Step 7 of the "shells" exercise. For now, close the file and don't save any changes.

 TIP: *Always make sure the light at the end of the tunnel is not the headlamp of an onrushing train.*

The Puzzle Filter

The Puzzle filter lets you break down the image into "puzzle-like pieces, or blocks, resembling a jigsaw puzzle." The preceding quotation is from the definition in the help file. Now, maybe the puzzles look different in Canada, but I have worked with puzzles most of my life, and the results of this filter look like several things, but a puzzle is not one of them. It does change images or the selected portions of them into nice blocks that can give the effect of mosaic tile.

Using the Puzzle Filter

Just a few notes about the operation of the Puzzle dialog box. Adjust Block Width and Height sliders control the width and height of the blocks created by the filter. The range is 1-100 pixels meaning it will create blocks of a size determined by these settings. If the Square Blocks check box is enabled, these two controls are locked together. The Max Offset (Percentage) slider controls the offsetting, or shifting, of puzzle blocks. It is important to note that the offset is a percentage of the Block size. For example, if the Block size is set to a width of 50 pixels and the Max offset % slider is set to 10, the Offset will have a maximum shift of 5 pixels (10% of 50 = 5). Therefore, increasing or decreasing block size changes the effect the Maximum amount of Offset has, even though the numbers don't change. To make the effect look more like blocks, the actual amount of offset for each block is random. This setting only determines the maximum amount of offset that can be applied. Fill Empty Area with setting is the remaining option. When the blocks are offset, something must take its place unless PHOTO-PAINT is in Layer mode. Choose from one of the following five options from the Fill empty areas with settings to fill the empty spaces.

- **Black** Applies a black background.

- **White** Applies a white background.

- **Paint Color** Applies the current Paint color.

- **Original image** Uses the colors from the original image as a background.

- **Inverse image** Inverts the image adjacent to the shifted blocks and applies it as the background.

Stressful Text with the Puzzle Filter

Here is a quick effect using the Puzzle filter.

1. Create a new image that is 6 x 2 inches, 24-bit color at 96 dpi.

2. Select the Text button in the Toolbox. Change the Font to Futura XBlk BT at a size of 120. Click inside the image and type **STRESS**. Click the Object Picker to make the text an object. In the Objects Docker window ensure the Lock Object Transparency box is not checked.

3. From the Effects menu choose 2D Effect and choose Puzzle. When the dialog box opens, notice that only the Black is enabled when an unlocked object is selected. Click the Reset button and then click OK. Pretty simple. The results are shown below.

Adding a simple drop shadow and adding texture to the text results in the image shown below.

The Ripple Filter

The Ripple filter is one of the "fun" filters. There is just so much you can do with it. While it is of little use in the day-to-day work of photo-editing, when it comes to photo-composition, it is a very powerful tool. The Ripple filter creates vertical and/or horizontal rippled wave lengths through the image. This filter first appeared in Corel PHOTO-PAINT 5 and has been improved since.

Controlling the Ripple Filter

The Ripple dialog box provides control over the amount and direction of the Ripple effect. The Period slider controls the distance in between each cycle of waves. A value of 100 creates the greatest distance between each wave, resulting in the fewest number of waves. The Period setting works on a percentage basis of image size, the larger the image, the larger the number of waves created. The Amplitude slider determines how big the ripples (amount of distortion) are. The Directional Angle slider (0-180) determines the angle of the Ripple effect.

Enabling the Distort Ripple option causes the ripple produced by the filter to be distorted by placing a ripple on the ripple. One part of the dialog box has changed quite a bit with the release of PHOTO-PAINT 8. The Horizontal, Vertical, and Custom directions have been replaced with a slider called Direction Angle. The other additions are Dual:1 to 1, which allows the ripple effect to be applied in 2 directions at the same time, and Dual: 2 to 1, which controls the amount of ripple applied to one side versus the other side.

Doing Something with the Ripple

I don't know, maybe it's because I was raised in California, maybe it was the '60s, but just thinking about Ripple gives me a headache. Back to work. So what can you do with this filter? Like I told you before, have fun.

Note for Corel PHOTO-PAINT 5 Users

You probably noticed that one of the options for the Ripple filter, the one that applied both Horizontal and Vertical ripple effect simultaneously, did not make it into the current Corel PHOTO-PAINT release. I am sure the three people who used it are really disappointed.

A Simple Ripple Border Exercise

Here is a quick hands-on exercise to create a ripple shaped border which has become very popular with Web sites these days.

1. Create a new file (CTRL-N) with the settings of 24-bit, 4 x 6 inches and a resolution of 72 dpi.

2. Select the Rectangle tool in the Toolbox (F6) and choose Create, New Object from the Object menu . Enable the Render to Object button in the Property bar. Click and drag a vertical rectangle that is the height of the image covering the left third of the width.

3. Click the Object Picker tool in the Toolbox. Open the Objects Docker window (CTRL-F7) and ensure Lock Transparency is unchecked.

4. From the Effects menu choose 2D Effects and from the drop-down list select Ripple.... Set the filter to these settings: Period: 20, Amplitude: 9, Direction angle: 180. Click the OK button. The object has the ripple effect applied to both top and bottom.

5. To trim off one side of the object click and drag it so the rippled portion on the left side is off the paper (outside of the image area). When we convert it to a non-PHOTO-PAINT file format the left edge will be clipped off.

6. Enable the Lock Transparency in the Objects Docker window Choose Fill from the Edit menu and choose a fill you like. I selected the Fountain Fill and used the preset Cylinder -Blue 03. Click the OK button.

7. To finish the border select Drop Shadow... from the Object menu and use the preview area of the dialog box to make the drop shadow look like you want. Click OK and you have a border that looks like the one shown in Figure 18-7.

The Shear Filter

Here is another distortion filter that is lots of fun—a real time waster. The Shear filter distorts an image, or the masked portion of it, along a path known as a Shear map.

Using the Shear Filter

Figure 18-8 shows a good action photograph. By using the Shear filter with the Tilt preset, we add more energy to the photograph as well as create space to add a short banner under the motorcycle if desired. The results are shown in Figure 18-9.

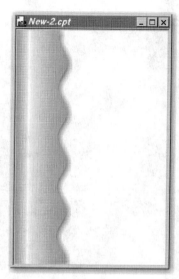

A professional looking edge border

FIGURE 18-7

The original photo of a racer

FIGURE 18-8

The Shear filter adds a little lift to the photograph

FIGURE 18-9

As I said, this is a fun filter. Applying the Wave preset to a rectangle of ducks I was able to quickly create a flag for the land of Duck (where Howard sought asylum after his movie bombed). The flagpole is an object I created from a photograph of a flag and placed in the image, shown in Figure 18-10.

The Swirl Filter

The Swirl filter rotates the center of the image or masked area while leaving the sides fixed. The direction of the movement is determined by Clockwise or Counter-Clockwise options. The angle set with the Whole rotations slider (0-10) and the Additional Degrees slider (0-359). Multiple applications produce a more pronounced effect.

Using the Swirl Filter

In the next illustration I created a 200 x 200 file and filled it with a simple conical fill. Next I applied the Swirl filter set to 360°. Using the CTRL-F keyboard shortcut, I applied the Swirl filter twice more. The last image shows the application a total of

The official flag of "Rubber Ducky Land" courtesy of the Shear filter

FIGURE 18-10

18

six times. By using the Swirl filter, you can make excellent ornaments and effects for your desktop publishing projects.

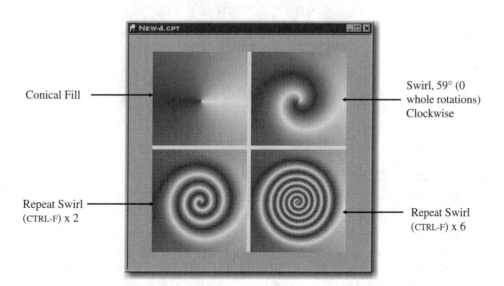

The Tile Filter

This is a very simple and therefore quite useful filter. The Tile filter creates blocks of a selected image in a grid. You can adjust the width and height of the tiles using the Horizontal and Vertical sliders in the dialog box. The values entered represent the number of images duplicated on each axis. So what can you do with it? The Tile effect can be used in combination with flood fills to create backgrounds as well as making wallpaper for Windows. Just remember that the Tile filter does not produce seamless tiles. The best effects are achieved when the number of tiles in relation to the original image is small. If you have a large number, then the original subject becomes so small as to be unrecognizable. The image shown below was created using the Tile filter to create the background.

The Trace Contour Filter

The Trace Contour filter lets you outline the edges of an image. This is one of those filters that is difficult to find uses for. It is similar in operation to the Edge Detect except it detects edges by their brightness values instead of their contrast component. Use the Level slider in the dialog box to set the edge threshold level. The Level slider in the dialog box ranges from 1 to 255. A lower setting leaves more of the image; a higher setting reduces the amount of the original image remaining after the effect is applied. Choose an edge type from the Edge Type settings. The Lower setting will trace the inside edges of an image, and Upper will trace the outside edges. The best effects are achieved when the subject matter is easily recognizable.

The User Defined Filter

The User Defined effect lets you "roll your own." Yes, you can make your own filters. The User Defined filter enables you to design your own *convolution kernel,* which is a type of filter in which adjacent pixels get mixed together. The filter that you make can be a variation on sharpening, embossing, blurring, or almost any other effect you can name.

The dialog box, shown in the next illustration, displays a matrix that represents a single pixel of the image shown at the center and 24 of its adjacent pixels. The values you enter into the matrix determine the type of effect you create. You can enter positive or negative values. The range of the effect is determined by the number of the values you enter into the matrix. The more boxes you give values to, the more pixels are affected.

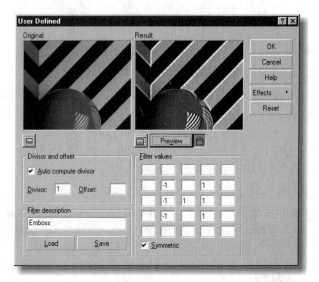

This filter is not for the faint of heart. To understand the operation of this filter would take a chapter in itself. So that you can see what the filter does, Corel has provided several sample user-defined effects. Use the Load button for this. These effects have been provided to help you determine what values to enter into the matrix.

NOTE: *For more information about User Defined filters: In PHOTO-PAINT depress the F1 function key, select the Index tab. Type in **User**, select User Defined Filters, Using. Click the Display button.*

The Wet Paint Filter

This filter can quickly create some neat effects. You can set the percentage and the degree of wetness. Percentage refers to the depth to which the wet paint look is applied. For example, if you set low percentages, the amount of wetness appears to affect only the surface of the image.

Technically, Percent controls the amount (how far down) the drip travels. The Wetness values determine which colors drip. Negative (-) wetness values cause the dark colors to drip. Positive (+) wetness values cause light colors to drip. The magnitude of the wetness values determines how large a range of colors drip. Maximum values are +/-50 percent.

Prior to the release of PHOTO-PAINT 7 the Wet Paint filter could not be applied to objects. Now it can be used to provide many different effects. Several combinations of positive and negative wetness can be applied to the same object to produce drop shadows, giving a 3D appearance to rounded text.

Frosty Text with the Wet Paint Filter

Here is a hands-on exercise that shows how to use the Wet Paint filter to make icicles hanging from text.

1. Create a new file (CTRL-N) with the settings of 24-bit color, paper color: a light blue, 6 x 4 inches and a resolution of 72 dpi.

2. Click on the Text tool and in the Property Bar set the font to Times New Roman and the size to 150. Click in the image and type **COLD**. Left click on the color blue on the onscreen palette to change the text color to a darker blue than the paper color. Click on the Object Picker tool in the Toolbox and the text becomes an object. You can center the text on the page using the Align command (CTRL-A).

3. Duplicate the text (CTRL-D). Open the Object Docker Windows (CTRL-F7) select the object closest to the background labeled COLD and enable Lock Transparency. Hold down the CTRL key and click on the color white in the onscreen palette to return the paper color to white. From the Edit menu choose Fill... and click the Paper color button in the dialog box and click OK. This makes the duplicate text, which may be hidden behind the original text, white.

4. Object Docker Windows Ensure the Lock Transparency is unchecked in the Objects Docker window Select Effects, 2D Effects, Wet Paint... and using the default settings click OK. Hide the Object marquee. The result is shown in Figure 18-11

5. For the finishing touches, select Effects, 3D Effects, Emboss.... From the Emboss filter dialog box use the default settings with one exception—change Emboss to the original color. Click the OK button. In the Objects Docker window ensure Lock Transparency is checked, Object Docker Windows select the top object and from the Object menu choose Feather.... Enter a Width value of 5 and Curved Edges. Click OK and we are finished, as shown below.

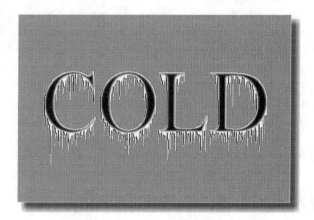

The Wind Filter

The Wind filter is described as creating the effect of wind blowing on the objects in the image. This filter is normally ignored by most PHOTO-PAINT users because

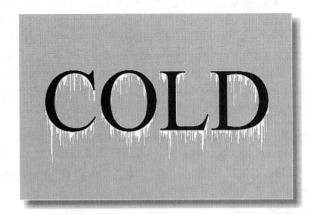

Icicles
made with
the Wet
Paint filter

FIGURE 18-11

they rarely have a desire to put wind into their image. The problem is not with the
filter or the description of it. It is important to learn what and how the filters do what
they do. Then you can use them effectively. It can be used to create some artistic
effects with objects and masks.

The Wind filter smears pixels as a function of their brightness. The brighter the
pixel, the more it gets smeared. Click and drag the Opacity slider (1-100) to
determine the visibility of the wind effect. Higher values make the effect more visible
and lower values make the effect more subtle. The amount of the wind effect (distortion)
applied is controlled by the Strength slider. The direction of the smearing can be entered
numerically or by clicking on the direction compass in the dialog box.

There are a few things to know about the operation of this filter when working
with objects. It needs to have a source for the pixels it is "blowing" across the image.
This means if you apply the Wind filter to an object it will not work unless the
background is unlocked or there is some unlocked object behind it.

Fuzzy Masks with the Wind Filter

One of the best things you can do with the Wind filter is to make masks with ragged
edges, which I call fuzzy masks. Because this effect involves multiple applications
of the Wind filter I strongly recommend that you make a custom toolbar with the
Wind filter button in it. The creation of Custom toolbars is discussed in Chapter 3.
Using a mask with a fuzzy edge allows you to produce realistic looking edges. First,
let's make the mask.

1. Create a new file: 24-bit color, 6 x 4 inches at 72 dpi. From the View menu, enable Rulers (CTRL-R).

2. Select the Rectangle Mask tool and create about a 5 x 3-inch rectangle. Use the Mask menu's Align feature to place it in the middle of the image.

3. Choose Paint on Mask (CTRL-K) to make the mask into an image.

4. Select the 2D effects in the Effects menu and choose Wind.... Change the settings to an Opacity of 90, Strength of 50 and a Direction of 90 degrees. Click the OK button.

 TIP: *Using the Command Recorder you can quickly make a script that will automatically apply the Wind filter in multiple directions.*

5. Repeat Step 4 seven more times, but change the Direction setting to 135, 180, 225, 270, 315, 0 and 45. The result is a feathered fuzzy edge as shown in Figure 18-12. Disable the Paint on Mask button to return to normal mask mode.

6. The feathering needs to be removed for this exercise. From the Mask menu select Shape and choose Threshold.... Enter a value of 90 and click OK. This will covert any part of the mask image with a brightness value of 90 or less to white. Clicking the Paint on Mask button shows the resulting mask (Figure 18-13). Click the button again to return.

With the Wind filter we can create a fuzzy edge on a mask

FIGURE 18-12

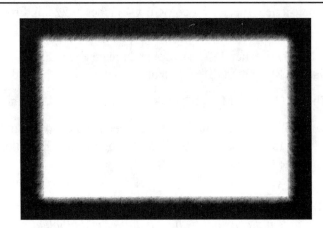

Using the
Threshold
command
we can
make a
firmer edge
to the mask

FIGURE 18-13

So What Can You Do with It?

From this point the limit is your imagination. With a fuzzy mask anything you apply
will have very realistic torn edges to it. Here are some things to try.

1. To make parchment: Select Fill… in the Edit menu. Choose the Bitmap
   Fill, Edit and Load. From the CD, choose EXERCISE\TILES\\
   PAPER06l.CPT. Click the OK button twice to apply the fill.

2. Select Create Object: Cut Selection from the Toolbar. The parchment is
   now an object.

3. You can give the parchment a raised appearance by applying a small
   amount of the Emboss filter. Use the default settings (Reset) and change
   the color to Original Color.

4. Next locate and install the font Calligraph421 BT and type in your
   message. I thought a Christmas card would be nice, but you can enter
   whatever you like.

5. Combine the text and the parchment together (CTRL-ALT-DOWN ARROW).

6. Open the Ripple filter and make the settings as follows: Ripple Mode:
   Single, Distort ripple: enabled, Period: 50, Amplitude: 1, Direction angle:
   90. Click OK. The result is shown below.

18

7. Save the mask as FUZZYMASK.CPT using the Save, Save to Disk in the Mask menu.

8. For the finishing touches we need to make it look like real parchment so enable Lock Transparency in the Object Roll-Up. Next select the Paint tool (F5). From the Tool Settings Roll-Up choose the Airbrush (second icon)and select Wide Cover and change the Transparency setting to 90. Now apply light shadows along the edge. When you are done, select parchment object and apply a drop shadow and the result will be like that shown below.

Using the same technique described above, I created figure 18-14. I imported the flower design clipart from the CorelDRAW clipart library and the background is one of the many Corel tiles.

The fuzzy mask was used to make the parchment in the sign

FIGURE 18-14

To make a photograph with rough edges either Paste or clone a photograph into the masked area and do steps 2 and 3 described above. An example is shown in Figure 18-15.

The fuzzy mask makes a good textured edge for photographs

FIGURE 18-15

The Whirlpool Filter

I used to refer to the Whirlpool filter as a poor man's Terrazzo. (I have also called it the "Smear tool on Steroids," which may be a more accurate description.) Since Terrazzo is now part of Corel PHOTO-PAINT, one would assume that there is no need for this filter. This is not true. Instead of making tiles, the Whirlpool filter does a blender operation on the selected area and creates some nice textures for use as backgrounds. Jeff Butterworth of Alien Skin Software, the original creator of the filter, states, "We just couldn't resist throwing in something fun. Swirl uses state-of-the-art scientific visualization techniques for examining complex fluid simulations. This technique smears the image along artificial fluid streamlines." This also may be one of the most CPU-intensive filters in the bunch. Be prepared for this filter to take a little time to complete its action. By clicking on Whirlpool in the 2D Effects category of the Effects menu, you open the Whirlpool Filter dialog box. This filter, unlike The Boss and Glass, does not require a mask to operate.

Note for Corel PHOTO-PAINT 5 Users

This filter is called Swirl in Corel PHOTO-PAINT 5.

The Whirlpool Filter Dialog Box

The Whirlpool filter has several options that are unique to this type of filter. These controls are described below.

SPACING SLIDER   All you really need to understand about spacing (of Whirlpools) is that it randomly places whirlpools in the selection and then smears the selected area with them. The Spacing slider controls approximately how far apart these whirlpools are from one another. A large spacing setting creates more of a "painterly" effect. Smaller settings make the whirlpools close together and create effects that are reminiscent of 1960s design.

SMEAR LENGTH SLIDER   Smear Length controls how much the underlying image (background) is blurred. Low values create noisy results, while large settings create smoother results. This is the one setting that has the greatest effect on how long the filter will take to process the image. A longer (higher) Smear Length setting results in longer processing time.

TWIST SLIDER   The Twist slider controls whether the flows flow *around* or *out* of the whirlpools. Twist angles near 0 degrees make the whirlpools act more like fountains, because the fluid flows outward in a starlike pattern. Twist angles approaching 90 degrees flow around in rings.

STREAK DETAIL SLIDER   Whirlpool is a form of blurring, so it can remove detail from your image or make your image altogether unrecognizable. To recover some of the image detail, increase the setting of Streak Detail.

WARP   When the Warp check box is checked, the simulated fluid stretches the image "downstream" along the stream lines. Warping makes the Whirlpool effect more striking, but it may not be desirable if you want the original image to remain recognizable. Turning Warp off causes smearing without moving the underlying image.

STYLE   The Style drop-down list box lists several whirlpool effect presets. When you choose a preset, dialog box values change to reflect its settings.

Making Distorted Text

While this filter is always useful for making blended backgrounds, the addition of the ability to move pixels around in objects greatly expands the use of this filter as we will see in the following hands-on exercise. Note that several times during this exercise you will receive warnings before applying one of the filters. Just click OK and move on.

1. Create a new file: 24-bit color, 4 x 2 inches at 150 dpi.

2. Click the Text tool button in the Toolbox and after clicking on the image type the word **TEXAS**. Change the font to Kabel Ult BT at a size of 96 (points). Select the Object picker tool. You may want to turn off the object marquee.

3. Open the Objects Docker window (CTRL-F7), enable Lock Transparency and select the Text object in the Objects Docker window. Select Fill… in the Edit menu.

18

4. From the Edit Fill & Transparency dialog box, select the Fountain Fill and click the Edit button. Change the Preset in the Fountain Fill dialog box to Sunset 2. Click OK and click OK again to apply the fill to the letters.

5. Uncheck Lock Transparency in the Objects Docker window

6. Create a mask from the text (CTRL-M) and Invert the mask (CTRL-I).

7. From the Effects menu choose 3D Effects and select The Boss filter. Choose the Wet Style and then change the Width to 3. Click OK. We now have nice-looking shiny letters as shown below.

8. Remove the mask (CTRL-D)

9. Select the 2D effects in the Effects menu and choose Whirlpool…. Select the Rings setting from the Style drop-down menu and click the OK button. The text is distorted but we now need to trim the text.

10. Select the Create Mask command (CTRL-M). We now have a mask that roughly corresponds to the shape of the letters.

11. From the Mask menu, select Shape and choose Threshold…. Enter a value of 170 and click OK. Now select Clip to Mask from the Object menu. Remove the mask (CTRL-D).

12. Create a suitable shadow with the Drop Shadow command in the Object menu. The result is shown in Figure 18-16.

I hope this chapter stirs your imagination a little. Always remember not to let the name given a filter dictate what you use that filter for. I know the original designer of the Wind filter didn't think "Boy, this would be great for making textures and

The
Whirlpool
filter
provides an
interesting
effect when
applied to
text outlines

FIGURE 18-16

other stuff." Now that we understand the 2D side of the world, let's prepare to move from the 2D filters to the world of 3D filters, which should be called pseudo-3D. Why you ask? Read on and find out.

19

3D Effect Filters

Corel PHOTO-PAINT has a rich collection of filters that can be loosely grouped under the 3D category. This can be confusing since there is a 3D program in the Corel 8 Suite. Some of the filters in this group give effects that appear to be 3D, but none are true 3D filters. Please note that all ten filters are available with grayscale, duotone, 24-bit, and 32-bit color images. You can use 3D Rotate, Map to Object, Perspective, Pinch/Punch, and Zigzag filters with Paletted (256 color) images. While no new 3D Effect filters were added to PHOTO-PAINT 8, two filters have been added to this category, Glass and The Boss, which used to be located under the Fancy category. The big news is not that these filters have moved but that they are now fully integrated into PHOTO-PAINT. In previous releases the filter either didn't have preview or zoom and pan capability. Now in PHOTO-PAINT 8 we have the whole enchilada, and speaking as one who uses The Boss everyday, it is wonderful.

3D Rotate Filter

The 3D Rotate filter rotates the image according to the horizontal and vertical limits set in the 3D Rotate dialog box. The rotation is applied as if the image were one side of a 3D box.

The 3D Rotate Filter Dialog Box

The dialog box is shown a little later, in Figure 19-1. The preview window shows the perspective of the image with the current slider settings. The plane of the box in the preview window that is shaded represents the image. By moving the vertical and horizontal sliders, the preview box can be oriented into the correct position. The preview window shows an approximation of the resulting application of the 3D Rotate filter.

If the Best Fit checkbox is checked, the 3D image will not exceed the image window borders.

Using the 3D Rotate Filter

The 3D Rotate filter may be applied to the background or to objects, although the Lock Transparency option should not be enabled, as the results may be unpredictable. The basic problem is that while the rotation of the image occurs within the object, the object retains the same shape.

There are a few limitations to this filter. Although you can apply rotation to both the horizontal and vertical axes simultaneously, it is not recommended. The resulting image loses varying degrees of perspective. Also note that the preview doesn't always display the 3D perspective correctly.

Now that I have told you the bad news, let's make a box of crayons with this filter—and a few others.

Making a Big Box of Crayons

In this hand-on exercise, we are going to create a box of crayons. In this super-turbo-extra-large world, it is only a matter of time before someone comes up with the idea for a box of crayons the size of a car, so why not design it now and beat the rush? It will require a little preliminary work to make the crayon art we will use for the box.

1. Open the file EXERCISE\PHOTOS\593029.WI using the Resample option. Click the OK button. When the Resample dialog box opens, change the Width to 6 inches. Click OK.

2. From the Image menu, select Paper Size and disable the Maintain aspect ratio checkbox. Change the Width to 4.0 inches. Click the OK button.

3. Mask the entire image using the Select All button in the Toolbar, and then click the Create Object: Cut Selection button to make the masked image into an object.

4. Select the Object Picker tool in the Toolbox. Open the Objects Docker window (CTRL-F7) and ensure that Lock Transparency is not enabled.

5. From the Effects menu, choose 3D Effects and then 3D Rotate. When the dialog box opens, enter a value of -45 next to the horizontal slider. Check the Best Fit box. Click OK. The resulting image is shown in Figure 19-1.

6. Duplicate the object (CTRL-D). From the Object menu, select Flip and choose Horizontally. Use the Object Picker tool to move the objects so they look like the ones shown below. Use the arrow keys to make minor adjustments to the position of either object.

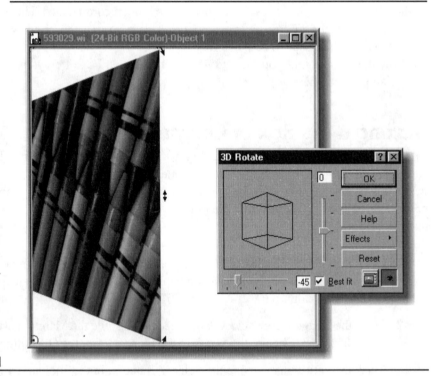

The 3D Rotate filter dialog box shown with onscreen preview

FIGURE 19-1

TIP: *A good method for aligning the objects is to SHIFT-select both of them in the Objects Docker window Manager and use the Align command (CTRL-A) to align them vertically—not horizontally.*

7. Select both of the objects and group them together (CTRL-G). Even though they are grouped together, they can still be selected separately. Use Align (CTRL-A) to align the two grouped objects in the center of the image.

8. It looks like a 3D box now, but really it doesn't. There are no shadows to fool the eyes. So, let's make some. In the Object window, select Object 1 (closest to the background) and enable Lock Transparency.

9. Select the Paint tool (F5) and from the Tools Settings roll-up (CTRL-F8), choose Custom Airbrush. Change the Type to Wide Cover. Make sure the Paint color is Black. Change the Transparency to 80. Place the brush so

that it is in the middle of the vertical line in the middle where the two objects join together. Click and drag the cursor up and down the line. The paint will only be applied to the left side. By only using half of the brush, we get a better edge.

10. Repeat the technique of placing half of the brush off of the box and make shadows along the remaining three edges on the left. When complete, make a few diagonal passes across the middle of Object 1. The finished version should look like the image below.

11. Repeat steps 8–10 but select Object 2 (top object) and use White for the Paint color. The result is shown below. Please note that I have put too much of both black and white to emphasize the shadows and highlights. If this were a production job, I would spend quite a bit of time determining where the shadows and highlights should appear. I just want you to get accustomed to using the airbrush.

12. SHIFT-select the other object (both should now be selected). Combine the objects (CTRL-ALT-DOWN ARROW).

13. With the Paint color still set to White, select the Text tool from the Toolbox. Change the Font to Kabel Ult BT at a size of 48 centered. Change the Interline spacing to 90. Click inside the image and type **BIG BOX OF COLOR**. Align the text box so the right side is in line with the middle line where the two sides join.

14. Select the Object Picker tool to convert the text into an object and position the text as shown next. Click on the object until the handles turn into circles (indicating it is in perspective mode). Click and drag the lower-right handle and drag it down and to the left until the rectangle bounding the text is approximately parallel with the edges of the box. When you are satisfied with it, double-click on the text to apply the

transform. Use the Object Picker to position the text on the box as shown below.

15. So how big is this big box? Let's add something to show the size. From the Edit menu, choose Paste From File and select EXERCISE\OBJECTS\ BRUSH2.CPT. The brush and its white background appear in the image. In the Object Manager, select the background (not the brush) and delete it by clicking the Delete Object icon at the bottom of the Objects Docker window.

16. Great, now we have a brush floating in the air. Click on the brush until Rotation handles appear. Turn one of the four corner rotation handles until it looks like the image shown next. Don't forget to double-click the image to apply the transform we just did.

17. From the Objects menu select a Drop Shadow for the brush. I couldn't resist applying some paint on the end of the brush with the Paint tool at a high transparency. The result is shown below.

The Boss (Emboss) Filter

Corel PHOTO-PAINT has two emboss filters: Emboss and The Boss. The Boss filter makes the selected area look as if it is pushed out of the image. The big difference between these two filters is that The Boss can be used to create some exciting 3D effects. The Boss filter effect is achieved by putting what appears to be a slanted bevel around the selected area. It is called The Boss to avoid confusion with the original Emboss filter. You must have a mask in place to be able to use this filter. If you are going to apply the filter to the entire image, select All from the Mask menu to quickly mask the image, and then create the mask from it.

 NOTE: *Are the Glass and The Boss filters grayed out? That's because they are not available unless there is a mask present in the image on which you are working.*

The Boss Dialog Box

The Boss filter and the Glass filter are very similar in operation. This is because they use the same filter engine (program) internally. This is not an uncommon practice. I only mention it in case later in this chapter when you are reading about the Glass filter you experience a feeling of deja vu. The programs at work here do have a commonality—you don't need to call the psychic hotline. The controls will be covered in order not of appearance but of use.

The Adjust Controls

The Adjust controls of The Boss dialog box affect the shape of the bevel around the selection. The Height slider controls how far the selection pushes out of the screen toward the viewer. The Width slider controls how much of the image is taken up by the bevel. This is the primary way to control the amount of the 3D effect and in most of the exercises it is the Width that will determine what effect is achieved with this filter. Be aware that the bevel grows around the area selected by the mask. Therefore, if it gets too wide or the objects selected are too close together, they will begin to merge into one another. Thin bevels appear steeper than wide ones, so this setting also controls the strength of the 3D effect. Drop-off controls the general shape of the bevel. The basis of the trade-offs with the Smoothness settings are that if there were no "jaggies," there would also be no sharp lines. So instead of deciding how much The Boss filter would "melt" the bevel, they added a Smoothness slider, so you can make the decision yourself. When Smoothness is set low, the edges will be sharper, but little steps in the bevel will be more noticeable. When Smoothness is high, the edges will be more rounded, and it will look like your objects are floating on marshmallows.

The Adjust Lighting Settings

Part of the realism of 3D is in how reflections of light are displayed. These controls determine the source point and brightness of the light source.

Brightness is the bright reflection of the light off of the 3D surface. The Brightness slider can make the highlight disappear at the lower settings, or it can wash out part of the image at the higher settings. The Sharpness slider lets you control how small and crisp the highlight is. Sharper highlights tend to make the surface look shinier or even wet. Dull highlights are more spread out and make the surface look chalky.

The shape of the bevel interacts with the highlights. Sharper bevel corners (low width, high height, low smoothing) will make sharper highlights, so you will have to experiment to see how all these parameters combine to make the final 3D effect.

You can control the direction that the sun or light source comes from using the Direction and Angle controls. High light angles light the selection from directly above the surface, which tends to cause bright and even lighting. Low light angles tend to make shadows stronger, thus accentuating the 3D effect.

Creating a License Plate

Here is a basic hands-on exercise that uses The Boss filter to create a very realistic license plate. You can make almost anything look like a license plate, embossing tape or almost anything your imagination can dream up. In this exercise we are not going to make an entire plate, but rather concentrate on the technique for a portion of the plate. You can use any state you want, but since I live in Texas, we are going to make something very similar to our plates in the Lone Star State.

1. Create a new file with the following settings: 7 x 3 inches, 72 dpi, 24-bit color, and white for the Paper color.

2. Select Noise from the Effects menu, and choose Add Noise from the drop-down list. When the filter dialog box opens, click Gaussian in the Noise Type section. Set the Density to 10 and the Level to 30. Check Color Noise. Click the OK button.

3. Change the Paint color by clicking on a blue in the onscreen palette.

4. Click the Text tool in the Toolbox. Place the cursor in the image area, and click with the left mouse button. Type in the word **TEXAS**. In the Toolbar, change the Font name to VAGRounded BT with a size of 150 and an intercharacter spacing of 8.

5. Select the Object Picker tool. Open the Align command (CTRL-A), and center the text to the page.

6. Click the Create Mask button. Select Shape and then Feather from the Mask menu. In the Feather dialog box, enter a Width of 5, Direction: Inside; Edges: Curved. Click the OK button.

7. In the Objects Docker window click the Combine with Background button at the bottom of the window.

8. From the Effects menu, select 3D Effects and choose The Boss… from the drop-down list. This opens The Boss dialog box. In the Style drop-down, select Dry. We are going to make a few changes to this preset. Reduce the Width to 12. Change the Smoothness setting to 60. Set the Height to 45. You can save this setting by clicking on the icon of a plus sign and naming the new setting License Plate. Click the OK button. The result is shown below. Close the file and don't save any changes.

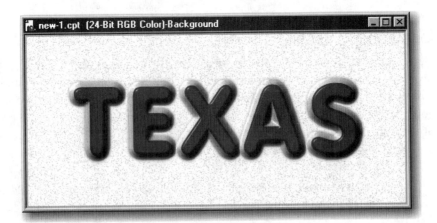

There are many other things that can be done with The Boss filter that are demonstrated in exercises throughout this book.

The Emboss Filter

This is the other emboss filter. Embossing creates a 3D relief effect. Directional arrows point to the location of the light source and determine the angle of the highlights and shadows. The Emboss filter has its most dramatic effect on medium-to high-contrast images. Several filters can be used in combination with the Emboss filter to produce photo-realistic effects.

The Emboss Filter Dialog Box

The Emboss Filter dialog box, shown here, provides all of the controls necessary to produce a wide variety of embossing effects.

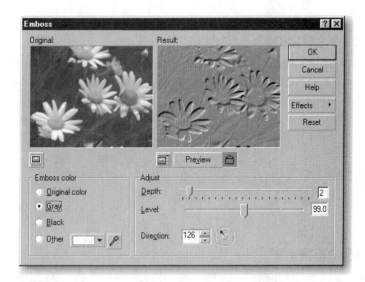

The Emboss Color determines the color of the embossed image. When Original color is selected, the Emboss filter uses the colors of the image to simulate the relief effect. When Black or Gray is selected, the entire image becomes filled with that color. Oddly enough, Gray is the default color and the one all of the PHOTO-PAINT wannabe programs display when showing their emboss filters. Maybe I spent too many years in the canoe club (Navy), but I have never had a desire to see something embossed in battleship gray. To select another solid color, other than black or gray, you must change the Paper Color (background color) to the desired color and select the Paper Color button.

The Depth slider sets the intensity of the embossing effect. Care should be taken not to use an excessive value (read greater than 5) since it can cause enough image displacement to make you think you need to schedule an eye appointment. The Level slider controls the radius of the effect. The effect on the image is that the white offset appears to be whiter. You can use a larger amount of Depth without distorting the image. Direction specifies the location of the light source. Light direction is very important since it is direction that determines if the image looks like it has either a raised or sunken surface.

TIP: *To reduce the "jaggies" when applying the Emboss filter to high-contrast images (like text), apply a Gaussian Blur filter at a setting of 1 before applying the Emboss filter.*

Using the Emboss Filter

The Emboss filter is used in many of the hands-on exercises throughout this book. There are very few tricks to using it effectively. One of the standard uses of the Emboss filter is to produce textures. You can try this one yourself. Mask an area and apply the default setting of Add noise in the Effects menu. Apply the default setting of the Emboss filter—instant sandpaper.

TIP: *To make 3D text, just apply the Emboss filter to the text object with the Lock Object Transparency unchecked.*

The Glass Filter

The Glass filter creates the effect of a layer of glass on top of the image. Keep in mind that the sheet of glass is the 3D part, while the image remains flat. By adjusting the combination of light filtering, refraction, and highlights, you can achieve some striking effects with this filter.

The Glass filter requires a mask to do its job. The shape of the glass sheet is controlled by the shape of the mask. The top edge of the glass bevel occurs along the mask. Feathering the mask has no effect on this filter's operation.

The Glass Filter Dialog Box

The Glass filter dialog box is opened by selecting Glass in the 3D Effects category of the Effects menu.

STYLE   This contains a drop-down list of presets that are provided with the Glass filter. Choosing any of them changes the controls in the dialog box for the selected presets. Custom settings are also saved in the Style area by changing the controls to the desired settings and clicking the plus button to the right of the Style name. Another dialog box opens that allows you to name the new style. The minus button is used to remove a saved style.

THE BEVEL WIDTH SLIDER   The Bevel Width slider is used to set the width of the bevel. The bevel is the area around a masked object that is slanted to produce that glassy 3D look.

THE SMOOTHNESS SLIDER   The Smoothness slider is used to set the sharpness of the edges of the bevel. A low-level smoothness produces sharper edges but may also display the steps used to create the embossed look. A higher smoothness level removes the jagged edges and makes for rounded edges.

THE REFRACTION SLIDER   The most striking 3D effect of the Glass filter is *refraction,* which occurs when the direction of light rays is changed (bent) as a result of passing through a material such as glass or water. Since we are looking directly at the glass sheet, refraction only occurs at the beveled edges. The Refraction slider sets the angle at which the light is to be bent at the bevel. This distorts the image at the bevel location, which is the most striking effect of the Glass filter.

TIP: *To make the refraction effect more noticeable, try using a wider bevel. This will increase the area of glass that does not directly face the viewer.*

THE OPACITY SLIDER   Colored glass affects light, and it affects it more where the material (the glass) is thicker. The Opacity slider is used to set the transparency level of the glass sheet. The more opaque you make the glass, the stronger the underlying image will be tinted to look like the glass color.

DROP-OFF TYPE   The *drop-off* is the area adjacent to the bevel effect and is selected from a drop-down list. The following choices are available.

- *Gaussian*   Use the Gaussian drop-off when you want a very subtle effect. On a complex image, it gives a wet appearance to the masked area edge. The Gaussian drop-off has an "S" shape; it starts and ends with a round and gradual slope that becomes steep in between. It results in a smooth and less noticeable transition between the bevel and the rest of the image.

■ *Flat*   Because the Flat drop-off produces a sharp drop-off bevel, the areas around the edges are very sharp. The effect on text with dark colors may not even be noticeable. This effect works best with objects that have smooth, rounded edges. The Flat drop-off is a straight diagonal line starting at the bevel area and ending on the image. The transition is not as smooth as a rounded bevel, but the slope of the bevel is less steep.

■ *Mesa*   This drop-off style probably gives the best overall glass effect of the three. The Mesa drop-off is a curve that begins abruptly (almost a 90-degree angle) and ends with a rounded gradual slope.

THE BRIGHTNESS SLIDER   The Brightness slider in the Adjust Lighting section controls the intensity of the highlights in the glass. A higher setting produces more highlights on the glass.

THE SHARPNESS SLIDER   The Sharpness slider controls the sharpness of the light striking the edges of the bevel. So what is "Sharpness of light"? This setting actually controls the amount of sharpness that occurs as a function of light striking the affected area.

COLOR   The glass can be any color that you choose. You can click the color swatch opening a color palette or use the eyedropper button to select the color from the image. Dark glass colors the underlying image more strongly than light glass does, so if you are experiencing difficulty in getting a noticeable glass effect, try darkening the glass color.

DIRECTION AND ANGLE CONTROLS   You can control the direction that the sun comes by using the Direction and Angle controls. High light angle values illuminate the selection from directly above the surface, which tends to cause lighting that is bright and even. Low light angle values tend to make shadows stronger, accentuating the 3D effect. The angles are referenced to the horizon. High angle (90°) is similar to the sun being directly overhead, whereas low angle (0°) is like the sun sitting on the horizon.

■ *Direction Dial and Value Box*   The Direction dial controls the direction of the light striking the bevel. The bevel is the area around a masked object that is slanted to produce the 3D look. You can drag the dial to point toward the light source, or you can enter a value directly in the value box.

■ *Angle Dial and Value Box* The Angle dial controls the angle at which the light is to be bent at the bevel. This distorts the image at the bevel location, which is the most striking effect of the Glass filter.

TIP: *You get better effects with Glass if you have a textured or high-contrast background to accentuate the glass effect.*

Glass Raised Text Using the Glass Filter

The Glass filter is an excellent filter, but it takes some practice to get the hang of how and where to apply it. The following hands-on exercise will give you some experience using the Glass filter, and you will learn some of the tricks to make it work better for you. We are going to make text that looks like it is composed of raised glass.

1. Create a new image that is 7 x 3 inches, 72-dpi, 24-bit color. Click the OK button.

2. The glass effect looks better when there is a high-contrast content in the background. From the Edit menu, select Fill. From the Edit Fill & Transparency dialog box click the Bitmap Fill button and click the Edit menu opening the Bitmap Fill dialog box. Open the preview palette of fills in the upper-left corner. Scroll down until you find a light colored wood down near the bottom. Click on it to select it and then click OK. Click OK again to apply the fill.

3. Click the Text button on the Toolbox. Click inside the image and type the word **GLASS**. Change the Font to Times New Roman at a size of 150 and select Bold. Insure the intercharacter spacing is at zero.

4. Click the Object Picker tool. Open the Align dialog box (CTRL-A), and select To center of Document. Click OK.

5. Click the Create Mask button on the Toolbar. Open the Objects Docker window (CTRL-F7) and select the background by clicking on it.

6. From the Effects menu, select 3D Effects and choose Glass. When the Glass dialog box opens, select the Wet Style setting. Click the OK button.

7. For the final touch, use the Object Picker and select the text object. Change the Merge mode at the bottom of the Objects Docker window to Overlay. This lets the highlights created on the background text by the Glass filter appear through the text. Click the Combine button on the Objects Docker window to merge the object to the background. The result is shown in Figure 19-2.

The important issue to remember when working with this filter is that it tends to make the image darker. We worked around that in the previous exercise by placing a copy of the original object on top of the background.

The Map To Object Filter

The Map To Object filter creates the impression that the image has been wrapped around a sphere, vertical cylinder, or horizontal cylinder. The sphere is easy to work with. The vertical and horizontal cylinders require the addition of extensive highlights and shadows to make them look like cylinders.

The Glass filter makes the text looks like it is on embossed glass

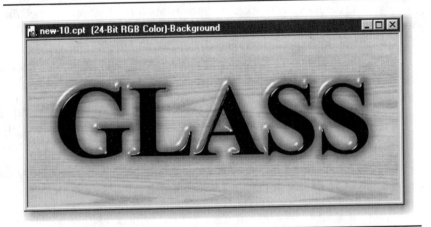

FIGURE 19-2

The Map To Object Dialog Box

The Map To Object dialog box, shown below, has controls that are common to many other dialog boxes. In addition, there are two unique areas: Mapping mode and Adjust.

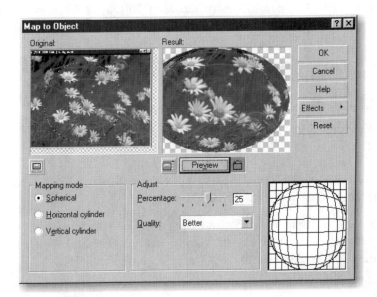

Clicking Spherical, Horizontal Cylinder, or Vertical Cylinder allows selection of the model used for wrapping. In the Adjust section, the Percentage slider is used to choose the amount of wrapping. Negative values wrap the image toward the back, and positive values wrap the image toward the front. The default setting for the

Note For Corel
PHOTO-PAINT 5 Users

The Map To Object filter is called Map To Sphere in Corel PHOTO-PAINT 5.

dialog box is a good setting for Spherical. The amount needed to achieve a noticeable effect with the Vertical Cylinder or Horizontal Cylinder is generally the maximum.

While the filter can be applied to the entire image, some of the most dramatic effects are achieved by applying it to a smaller area of the image that has been defined by a mask. The effect is more pronounced and successful if the object has horizontal and vertical lines. Almost all uses of the Map To Object filter will require the application of highlights and shadows with an airbrush to enhance their appearance.

Making Glass Spheres with Map To Object Filter

This is one of those exercises that have little or no practical use, but make up for it in fun.

1. Load the image EXERCISE\PHOTOS\586019.WI and Resample it to 4 inches wide at a Resolution of 150 dpi.

2. Select the Circle Mask tool, and drag a circle in the middle of the image. Remember to use the Constrain tool; you must click the mouse button and then hold down the CTRL key. The result is shown below.

3. From the Effects menu, choose 3D Effects and choose Map To Object. Click the Reset button and then click OK. The glass ball we created is shown.

4. Just like the "Big Box of Color" in the 3D rotate exercise, this one doesn't look much like a glass ball—yet. This is the fun part. Select the Paint tool (F5) and from the Tools Settings roll-up, choose Custom Airbrush. Change the Type to Wide Cover. Make sure the Paint color is White. Change the Transparency to 70.

5. The effect we are attempting to create is that of opacity. As the glass gets thicker at the edges it becomes lightly opaque. Using the edge of the airbrush tool apply a small amount of color around the edges (except for the bottom). Change the Paint color to Black, and put a little shade on the bottom.

6. For a final touch, apply the Lens Flare filter from the Render category in the Effects menu. The result is shown below.

The Mesh Warp Filter

The Mesh Warp filter distorts the image according to the movement of the nodes on a grid in the Mesh Warp dialog box. The user, through the dialog box, determines the number of gridlines positioned over the grid using the No. gridlines slider bar. (Generally, the greater the number of nodes selected, the smoother the Mesh Warp distortion.) Each node can be moved by clicking on it with a mouse and dragging it to a new position. Each node moves independently and can be positioned anywhere in the Preview window.

The Mesh Warp effect can be a little tricky to use at first. Use the Preview button to view the effects of a Mesh Warp transformation to ensure that it is acceptable before applying it to your entire image.

The Mesh Warp Filter Dialog Box

When the Mesh Warp dialog box opens click and drag the No. gridlines slider to determine the number of gridlines that will appear on the image. Use the Preview button to see the results of the node placement.

The No. gridlines slider controls the number of gridlines on the grid. The first horizontal gridline lies along the top, and the first vertical gridline is on the left. Be aware that they can be hard to see, depending on your display. At each point where a horizontal and a vertical gridline intersects, a node is positioned. It is the manipulation of the nodes along the grid that creates the effect. Each node moves independently of one another. Generally, the more nodes you use in the Mesh Warp operation, the smoother the effect will be.

So... What Do You Do with It?

From a practical day-to-day standpoint, not very much. You can use the selective distortion capability to distort people and places. While this can be cute, it isn't particularly useful. It does allow you to distort or "morph" images or photos with some interesting results. Figure 19-3 shows the original photograph of an owl, looking curious. After the application of the Warp Mesh filter, he looks mad enough to start a fight.

People and owls aren't the only things to which you can apply the Mesh Warp filter. In Figure 19-4, we improved the shape of a beer glass. The wrench and nut in Figure 19-5 were definitely given an attitude.

With a little
help from
Mesh Warp,
a curious-
looking owl
becomes an
owl with
attitude

■ FIGURE 19-3

Mesh Warp
can really
improve a
glass of beer

■ FIGURE 19-4

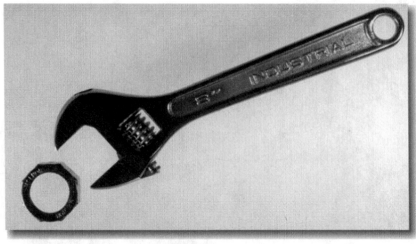

(a)

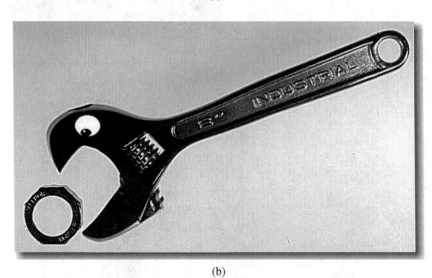

(b)

a) The wrench is less than interesting until b) we apply the Mesh Warp and make it hungry for a nut

FIGURE 19-5

Giving a Wall Some Attitude

If you completed the exercise in Chapter 6 you have a file called WALLEYES.CPT. While the eyes on the wall looked interesting, in this session we are going to find out how simple it is to give the wall some serious attitude.

1. Open the file WALLEYES.CPT . This is the one created back in Chapter 6 and is shown in Figure 19-6.

2. Anyone who has ever drawn cartoons (I confess I have done it) knows that to make a character appear mad, you need to arch the eyebrows. From the 3D Effects category in the Effects menu, select Mesh Warp.

3. When the dialog box opens ensure that the No. gridlines is set to 4. Click and drag the top-center control node straight down until it is on top of the middle node as shown in Figure 19-7. Click OK. The resulting image is shown below. As an alternative, you can move the top right and left node straight down so that they coincide with the center of the eye. The result is a sleepy wall like the one shown in Figure 19-8.

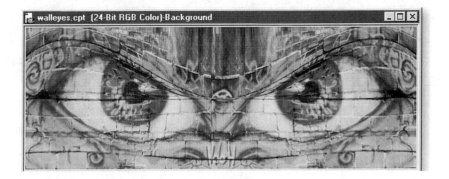

The walls have eyes but no attitude

FIGURE 19-6

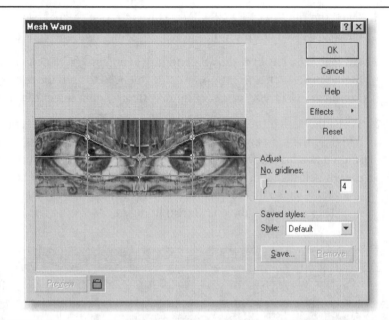

The Mesh
Warp dialog
box

FIGURE 19-7

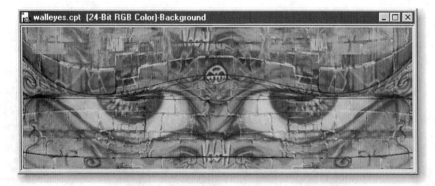

A different
MeshWarp
filter effect
and we
have a
sleepy wall

FIGURE 19-8

Notes About Using the Mesh Warp Filter

As I said before, the greater the number of nodes, the smoother the transitions on the image. Because each node is independent, each must be individually moved. There is a trade-off between the smoothness of the transition and the time required to move all of the nodes. Since there are no constrain keys to keep the gridlines on the horizontal or vertical planes, use the gridlines themselves as your guide. As long as the line in the preview window appears straight, the line is still in line with its respective plane. The Mesh Grid value represents the number of nodes on each line of the grid. (The two end nodes on each gridline are out of view and not adjustable.)

 NOTE: *There is no zoom or pan function in the preview window of the dialog box. There is also no onscreen preview or Original/Results preview.*

In previous versions of PHOTO-PAINT, applying the Mesh Warp filter to objects was not recommended, as the results could be unpredictable. In the current version it is not only possible but it is recommended. In the illustration shown below, I applied the Mesh Warp to some text that I had filled with a wood bitmap fill. The shadow was created using the Drop Shadow command.

The SQUIZZ Filter

The SQUIZZ filter made its first appearance in the PHOTO-PAINT 7 Plus package. Located in the plug-in portion of the Effects menu under HSOFT, selecting this filter opens the splash screen below. Although it is not in the 3D filters category, its actions and end effects are so close to the Mesh Warp filter, it needed to be included in this chapter.

What can you do with this filter? Well… you could use it to distort images much like we demonstrated with the Mesh Warp filter. I like to think of this filter as Super Mesh Warp. When the SQUIZZ splash screen opens, you are presented with two possible options—Brush and Grid.

Grid Warping

Selecting Grid opens the Grid Warping screen shown next. Although it looks like the grid in Mesh Warp filter, the operation of this filter is somewhat different. Apply

Grid warping effects is a two-step process. The first step is to click the Select button in the Grid Action section. Marquee select the nodes that you want to be included in the preview screen. Once the nodes are selected, choose the action that you want to apply. If you use the Move action, click inside the selected nodes (not on the nodes) and drag them in the desired direction. For the other actions, click inside of the selected area and click. Each time you click the mouse all of the selected nodes move in the direction indicated by the selected action. Multiple effects can be selected and applied to the image before the Apply button is clicked to apply the SQUIZZ effect to the image.

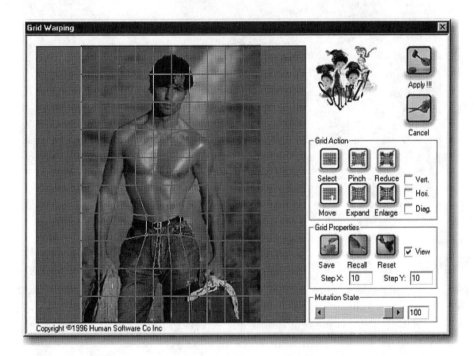

Brush Warping

Choosing the Brush opens the Brush Warping screen shown next. This mode applies the distortion using a brush stoke. Like the Grid Warping you can create multiple effects on the image before clicking the Apply button. One of the unique settings is the Undo mode which acts like the Local Undo command and is used to remove an action that was applied before the Apply button is clicked. The PHOTO-PAINT Undo command does not work while working in the SQUIZZ filter.

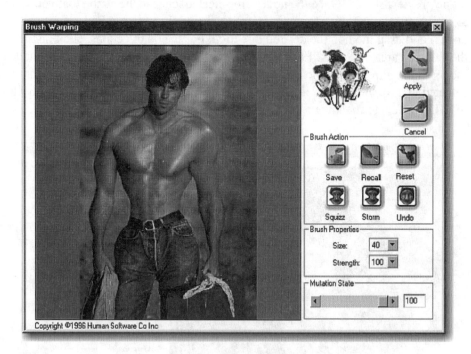

What Can you Do with SQUIZZ?

While surrealistic distortions are OK, I love using it to mess with images so that the viewer is not immediately aware that the image has been distorted. The advantage of the SQUIZZ! filter is the ability to apply effects in localized area using a brush style tool. There is also a Grid format tool that acts very much like the Mesh Warp filter. The interface for the filter is mildly intuitive, but you are advised to use the Envoy viewer provided with PHOTO-PAINT to look at the user's manual located on the CD-ROM disk.

Page Curl

This is a really superior filter. Its only drawback is that when it first came out, it was overused. I've seen a lot of flyers that have used the Page Curl filter, but its popularity has begun to wane. (I'm just warning you in case your client seems less than enthusiastic when you show them something with the Page Curl filter.) Page Curl simulates the effect of a page being peeled back, with a highlight running along the center of the curl and a shadow being thrown from beneath the image (if your image is light enough to contrast with a shadow). The area behind the image, revealed by the page curl, is filled with the current paper color. An example is shown below.

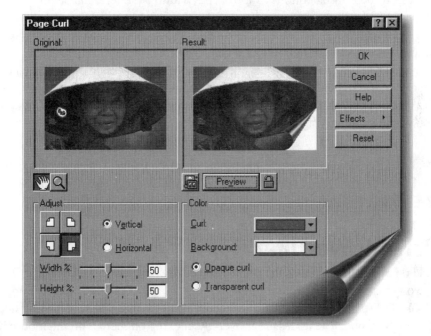

The Page Curl Dialog Box

The Page Curl dialog box is shown here with a curled edge that I added. The curl effect begins in one corner of your selection and follows a diagonal line to the opposite corner. You also may notice a slight transparency to the curl if there is any pattern or texture in the selected portion of your image.

The origination point of the curl is controlled by using one of the four keys in the Page Curl dialog box. The Vertical button creates a vertically oriented page curl, which curls the page across the image (from left to right or right to left). Experiment with this setting to achieve the effect you want. The buttons are mutually exclusive; that is, selecting one deselects the other. The Horizontal button creates a horizontally oriented page curl, which curls the page upward or downward through the image (from top to bottom or bottom to top). The Width % slider controls the vertical component of the page curl, regardless of whether it is a vertical or horizontal page curl. The Height slider controls the horizontal component of the page curl regardless of whether it is a vertical or horizontal curl.

Opaque Curl or Transparent Curl determines if the underside of the curled page is opaque or transparent. Choose the Opaque option if you want the curl to be filled with a blend of gray and white to simulate a highlight. Choose the Transparent option if you want the underlying image to be displayed through the curled paper.

 TIP: *To apply the effect to a portion of the image, select an area using a mask before you choose the effect. The page will only curl inside the masked area.*

The Perspective Filter

The Perspective filter creates the impression of 3D perspective to an image. There are two types in the Perspective filter: *Perspective* and *Shear*. Perspective applies the look of 3D perspective to the image according to the movement of the four nodes in the preview box. The nodes are moved by clicking on them with the mouse and dragging them to the desired location. Shear also applies perspective, but it holds the original size and shape, similar to skewing.

The Pinch/Punch Filter

The Pinch/Punch filter either squeezes the image so that the center appears to come forward (pinch) or depresses the image so that the center appears to be sunken (punch). The results make the image look as if it has been either pulled out or pushed in from the center.

The Pinch/Punch Dialog Box

This filter reminds me of the house of mirrors in the amusement park near where I grew up. They had all of these mirrors that distorted your features. This filter does the same thing. The Pinch/Punch dialog box lets you set the distortion effect attribute. In the dialog box, moving the slider in a positive (+) direction applies a Pinch effect, and moving it in a negative direction (-) produces a Punch effect. While the filter can be applied to the entire image, some of the most dramatic effects are achieved by applying the effect to a smaller area of the image that has been defined by a mask. The effect is more pronounced and effective if the object has horizontal and vertical lines.

The photograph in Figure 19-9 shows one of the sillier things you can do to a photograph.

Using the Pinch/Punch Filter

Besides distorting people's faces and bodies beyond recognition, there are actually some productive things that you can do with this filter. It's best to limit the effects to small manageable areas. Next, make applications in small amounts. In Figure 19-10, I have made a very loose-fitting mask around the head of the Statue of Liberty. Next, I applied a small amount of Punch to it, which gives it a different perspective without the obvious distortion that attracts attention. In the "punched" photograph shown in Figure 19-11, the only indication that the photo has been manipulated is

The Pinch/Punch filter can radically change the appearance of people, places, and things

FIGURE 19-9

The original
photograph

FIGURE 19-10

A different
look after
applying the
Pinch/Punch
filter

FIGURE 19-11

one of the rays protruding from the crown. Even this telltale sign could have been eliminated if I had invested the time.

The Zigzag Filter

The Zigzag filter is a distortion filter that will most likely render your original image unrecognizable. This filter distorts an image by bending the lines that run from the center of the image to the edge of the masked area or the circumference. This produces a wavelike action that changes curves to straight lines and creates angles that seem to twist the image from its center outwards. The Zigzag filter is great for simulating ripples and reflections in water. While the effect is slick, its uses are limited.

The Zigzag Filter Dialog Box

The dialog box for the Zigzag filter, shown here, has three controls that allow you many options in using the filter's effects. The preview for this filter has been improved greatly with the PHOTO-PAINT 8 release. The newest addition to this filter is the mesh/grid to visually display the effect that the filter will impose upon the image.

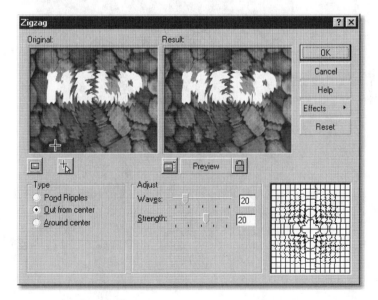

The Type settings control the direction and overall effect of the distortion. The Waves slider controls the distance between each cycle in the wave. Using larger values creates greater distances between each wave, resulting in a minimal number of waves. Smaller values create so many waves that it almost looks like a Fresnel lens. The Strength slider is used to control the intensity of the zigzag distortion. Keeping this value low helps most when trying to imitate the effect of ripples in the water. With the Around center option, an additional Adjust option, Damping, becomes available.

To create Figure 19-12, I applied the Stone Bitmap fill to an empty image. Next the Zigzag filter with Pond Ripples was applied. The clock is an object (which Corel calls a *watch*) that was placed in the center using the Paste From File command.

We have seen that while the 3D Effect filters are not true 3D, the variety of effects give the viewer the impression that they are. In the next chapter we will discover a filter that produces real 3D (stereograms) and others that act as the lighting directors for PHOTO-PAINT.

Ripples in time were easy to create with the Zigzag filter

FIGURE 19-12

20

The Render Filters

Render filters are used to produce special effects, backgrounds, and novelty images. Two of the filters, Lens Flare and Lighting Effects, were introduced in Corel PHOTO-PAINT 6. The Lighting Effects filter has been enhanced with this release of PHOTO-PAINT.

In case you were looking in here for the Julia Set Explorer 2.0, it has long since moved to the Fancy category. The Render filters are:

- 3D Stereo Noise
- Lens Flare
- Lighting Effects

3D Stereo Noise

This filter (originally from the Kai Power Tools 2.0 collection) is my least favorite because it has become such a fad. The 3D Stereo Noise filter takes a perfectly good image and converts it to something akin to a printer failure all over your paper. By staring at the paper, you can see the original image with depth effect. (It's rumored that if you can stare at it for over an hour, just before the onset of a migraine, you can see Elvis.) The 3D Stereo Noise filter, or a program just like it, is what is used to produce those stereogram posters that have gained such popularity at suburban shopping malls in recent seasons. If you stare at them, you can actually see an embedded image with depth perception.

3D Stereo Noise was discovered a long time ago at Bell Laboratories. The researchers observed that when certain points on an image were shifted, it gave the appearance of depth. As used here, the term "stereo" should not be confused with music. Human beings were designed with stereoscopic sight—two eyes that render a single image from two slightly different angles, thus producing depth perception.

The images that produce the best results with the 3D Stereo Noise effect use gray levels, are slightly blurred, and do not have extreme contrast. Don't waste precious system resources by using 24-bit color; the result will be grayscale. The 3D Stereo Noise filter generates a pixelated noise pattern that has horizontal frequencies that correspond to the gray levels of the initial image. This means that white will map to the highest frequency and appear closest to the viewer; black will map to the lowest frequency and appear furthest away.

Making an Image

First, create a grayscale image that uses text and simple objects. Although the filter will apply in all modes, the best images initially use gray levels. The smaller and more detailed the image you choose, the harder it will be to focus the stereo image. Apply a standard Gaussian Blur filter to the objects. This will soften the edges of the image for easier viewing. First, make sure there are no masks, and then open the Effects menu. Under the Render subgroup, click on the 3D Stereo Noise filter. This opens the preview dialog box. There are only two options with this dialog box: a Depth slider with a relative depth range of 1–9 and a Show Dots checkbox, which enables the creation of two dots in a box near the bottom of the image to help the user focus on the 3D image. The two dots that appear in the Result window are used to guide you in focusing correctly on the image; adjust your focus so that the dots fuse into one and a 3D effect is achieved. Apply the filter to the entire image. The result, shown below, will appear to be a random array of black-and-white noise.

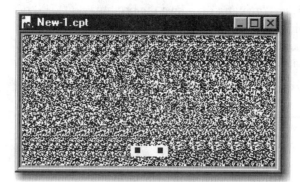

Viewing 3D Stereo Noise Pictures

After you have created a stereo noise picture, it is time to focus your eyes and energies to see the image. I was never able to view the depth onscreen. Maybe you can do better here than I did. Don't feel bad if you don't see the image right away; it may take a few tries. In fact, there are some people who just cannot see it at all. There are several ways to view the image in-depth. Try enabling the Show Dots checkbox to produce black dots about a half-inch apart at the bottom of the image. Defocus your eyes and gaze through the image as if you were looking into the distance. The dots you placed at the bottom will separate into four. If you focus so that the middle two dots fuse, depth should pop in or out. Another way is to try crossing your eyes to fuse the four dots into three. You may also try holding the edge of a thin object such as a floppy disk or your hand between your eyes in order to separate each eye's vision.

Lens Flare

The Lens Flare effect has controls in its dialog box, shown in Figure 20-1, that produce a spot of light resembling a reflection within an optical system. In photography, lenses of different focal lengths produce different lens flare effects. Photographers work very hard to make sure the effects added by this filter do not occur. With Lens Flare, you can add what they try to get out of a photograph. New to PHOTO-PAINT 8 is the addition of an eyedropper to the dialog box to allow the user to select the flare color from the image.

When you first open the dialog box, it will immediately render and provide a preview of the selected image. Choose from three lens types to produce the type of lens flare you want. You can also adjust the brightness (1–200 percent) of the lens flare with the slider bar. To change the position of the "flare," click on the preview window at the point where you want the flare to be. You cannot "drag" the existing point in the preview window to the new location. With the lock enabled, the preview

The Lens Flare dialog box provides a selection of different lenses and levels of brightness

FIGURE 20-1

function is automatic. This means that changing the lens type will start a preview cycle.

Applying the Lens Flare to an Existing Image

Many times you need to add some effect to an image to give it something extra. In this hands-on exercise, we are going to use the Lens Flare filter to add a final touch to what is an excellent picture.

1. Open the file EXERCISE\PHOTOS\511009.WI. Resample the file to 6 inches in width.

2. From the Effects menu, select Render and choose Lens Flare.

3. Change the Lens type to 50-300 mm zoom and click on the point indicated by the plus sign in Figure 20-1. Click the OK button. The Lens Flare gives the photograph a dynamic quality. The image is now ready to be a background in a sports magazine. Figure 20-2 shows the results of the Lens Flare.

The effect of Lens Flare applied to the final image

FIGURE 20-2

4. Close the file and do not save any changes.

 TIP: *The Lens Flare filter only works with 24-bit color images. To apply this effect to a grayscale, convert the grayscale to a 24-bit color image, apply the Lens Flare filter, and then convert it back to grayscale.*

One of my favorite uses of the Lens Flare filter is to apply it to an item that we expect to have a reflection. For example, the glass sphere we learned to make in Chapter 19 gets an added touch of realism by putting a slight lens flare on it as shown in Figure 20-3. Another use for the Lens Flare filter that we have already used (in Chapter 18) is the light-at-the-end-of-the-tunnel effect. An example of this is shown in Figure 20-4.

Lighting Effects Filter

The Lighting Effects filter lets you add one or more light sources to your image. Choose from a list of presets or create your own customized lights using the controls in the dialog box shown in Figure 20-5. You can add multiple lights and individually

The Lens Flare filter adds a finishing touch to this glass ball

■ FIGURE 20-3

The light at the end of the tunnel is the Lens Flare filter

FIGURE 20-4

20

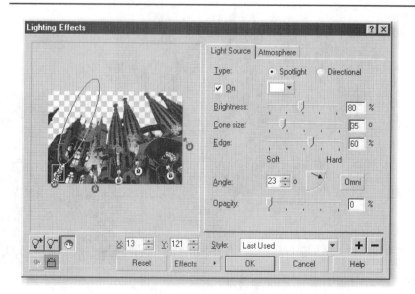

The Lighting Effects filter dialog box

FIGURE 20-5

control the attributes of each light. This is a rather intimidating dialog box. Using it is a little less than intuitive. After opening the filter, the preview window displays what the lighting effect will look like with the default or the last used setting.

Setting Up the Lighting Effects Filter

The first step in using this filter is to choose a Light Type from the list box. The list box contains a drop-down box with several preset light types available—for example, Spotlight and Directional. You can also add and remove your own styles. Each light source has been assigned appropriate settings to achieve a unique effect. For the purposes of discussing the various controls, we will use the Spotlight setting. After selecting Spotlight, our next step is to choose a color for the light; white, which is now the Default setting, provides a good starting point. Remember that colors add a color cast to an image. For example, I recently changed the background of a brightly lit photograph to that of a sunset. The Lighting Effect filter was used with an orange lit to add the color cast that was necessary to make the foreground look like it belonged in the same picture as the background. A more traditional effect is shown in Figure 20-6.

The Lighting Effects filter quickly changes day into night

FIGURE 20-6

The barbell icon representing the light consists of a large node that indicates the focus of the light, and a smaller node that indicates the direction and height of the light. Click the large node and drag the light source to a desired position. As you adjust the position of the light, the X and Y settings on the Position tab indicate the horizontal and vertical position. You can adjust the direction of the light by dragging the smaller node, thereby changing the angle of the line. As you adjust the line, the Directional setting indicates the direction in which light is shining. The length of the line determines how high the light is above the image. As the length of the line (height) increases, the light moves farther from the image and therefore grows dimmer.

This filter allows you to add up to 18 additional lights. Of course, with 19 lights, your rendering time will drastically increase. Clicking the Plus button below the preview window adds another light; clicking the Minus button removes the currently selected light.

Texture Controls

Until now, we haven't discussed textures. This is not to be confused with CorelTEXTURE, which is entirely different. The texture part of the lighting control is located in the Atmosphere tab and creates pseudo-shadows on surfaces that enhance the effect of the filter in some cases.

Lighting Up the Ruins

If you did the exercise in Chapter 8, you have a file that contains ruins of a cathedral with a great gothic looking background. The problem with the image is the original photograph was taken in bright daylight. It isn't any problem to correct with the Lighting Effects filter.

1. Load the file you made in Chapter 8, RUINS.CPT.

2. In the Objects Docker window select the Object (which should be the ruins).

3. From the Effects menu choose Render and select the Lighting Effects filter. When the dialog box opens, select the Style: 5 Up. This puts 5 spotlights in the image pointing up. Click and drag the big end of the icon to move the lights. Click and move the smaller point of the icon to control where it is pointing. The Cone size makes the light coming out of the light wider or more narrow. Add a few more lights by clicking on the lightbulb

button with the plus on it. You can position the lights anywhere you want. Figure 20-5 shows where I placed mine. Click OK to apply the effect. The result is shown below. Don't worry if yours is darker as I lightened mine up with the Tone Curve because it looked like it would be too dark when printed.

This is only a sampling of some of the many things that you can do with the Lighting Effects filter. As you work with the different features you will discover more and more things that can be done with it. Now let's go on to the strange world of the Artistic filters.

21

The Artistic Filters

The Artistic filters group contains five filters—Canvas, Glass Block, Impressionist, Smoked Glass, and Vignette—that are best described as unique. These filters are for the creation of special effects.

The Canvas Filter

In Corel PHOTO-PAINT 5, the Canvas filter is a roll-up. Changing it to a filter was a good move on Corel's part. Canvas does not need to be kept available as other roll-ups do. Actually, Canvas was always a filter that thought it was a roll-up. It lets you apply any tile pattern or bitmap for use as an image background. If you set the transparency level to a higher percentage, Canvas can also be used to overlay an existing image.

Using the Canvas Filter

Canvas is a simple filter that will allow you to add unusual looking effects with little experience or effort. A Corel PHOTO-PAINT canvas can be made from any 24-bit or 32-bit color image (mono or grayscale images have to be converted to color first). The Canvas filter applies the selected bitmap pattern to an image to give it the texture of the applied pattern. The canvas can also be used with a high transparency to overlay an existing picture. The canvas shows through the image and any future application of paint. The Canvas effect is used to load a bitmap pattern over an existing image (creating a screening effect) or to serve as a background image (or canvas).

The Canvas Filter Dialog Box

The Canvas filter dialog box, shown here, is accessed by selecting Artistic in the Effects menu and choosing Canvas.

Descriptions of the settings follow. Canvas map, located below the preview window, displays the selected canvas.

Transparency sets the level of transparency, expressed in percentage. High levels make the canvas more transparent and the underlying image more visible. Lower levels make the canvas opaque, and less of the image is visible. Emboss gives the canvas a raised relief effect. X and Y Offset values allow you to control the size/placement of the bitmap tiles through scaling.

The Rows and Columns settings in the Tile Offset section provide control over the placement of the bitmap tiles in relation to one another. For example, changing the Row Offset value to 50% means that each successive row of bitmap tiles will overlap by 50 percent. Row and Column settings are mutually exclusive, meaning that if a value is entered in one, the other is zeroed out. The Stretch to fit option simply takes the tile and stretches it to fit the image. If the image is large and the tile is small, the results can get either very artistic or very ugly, depending on your viewpoint.

Clicking the Load button displays the Load a Canvas from Disk dialog box. Select a canvas from the PHOTOPNT\CANVAS directory, or choose another image.

Corel PHOTO-PAINT installs ten PCX files for Canvases in the CUSTOM\CANVAS folder. Each PCX file is 128 x 128 pixels at 300 dpi in 256-color mode.

Finding Custom Bitmaps to Use for Canvas

You can use any color bitmap file that can be imported by Corel PHOTO-PAINT to create a new canvas by loading it into the Canvas dialog box through the Load Canvas map files dialog box. The files that can be used for canvases include photo-CDs and the files that you create with Corel PHOTO-PAINT 8. If you have a vector-based file that you want to use, simply load it into Corel PHOTO-PAINT and save it as a color bitmap file.

If the Canvas Bitmap Is the Wrong Size

If the bitmap image that is selected for use as a canvas is too small to fit the image area where it is being applied, the image will be tiled by Corel PHOTO-PAINT to fit the image area. If the image used for a canvas is too large to fit into the image area, it will be cropped (not resized) to fit the image area.

 TIP: *If the image is going to be tiled, you may want to consider cropping the bitmap with the Cropping tool, feathering the edge of the object with a small value, and dragging the image into the Corel PHOTO-PAINT workspace to create a new cropped image. The feathering will reduce the lines and therefore the "kitchen tile" look.*

Applying a Canvas Background

I may be going out on a limb here, but it seemed appropriate to make a background that looks like canvas with the Canvas filter. In this hands-on exercise, we are going to make a photograph look like a painting.

 1. Load the file PHOTO\COASTS\557039.WI. Select Resample from the Image menu, and change the Width to 7 inches. Click the OK button. The original photograph is shown in Figure 21-1.

The original image

FIGURE 21-1

2. From the Effects menu, select Auto F/X and choose Photo/Graphic Edges 3.0.... (If you haven't installed the filters yet, please be aware that this step isn't necessary to apply the Canvas filter. If you want to install the Auto F/X filter, follow the instructions in step 3.) Click the Select Outset Effect button. You will be asked for the CD-ROM that contains the Photo/Graphic Edges (Phot_edg folder) if it is not in your CD-ROM drive. Click on the file named AF109.afx and click the Open button. It will take a few moments for PHOTO-PAINT to generate a preview. Click the Apply button. The resulting image is shown in Figure 21-2. When you have completed this step, skip to step 4.

3. Select Options in the Tools menu. Click the Add... button on the Plug-In Filters page. Locate the folder PLUGINS\AUTOFX and click OK. Then click OK again to close the Options dialog box.

4. Open the file EXERCISE\TILES\PAPER01L.CPT located on the same CD-ROM that contains the photos. This image contains the right pattern, but it lacks the contrast necessary to work with the Canvas filter.

The Photo/Graphic Edges makes the image look more painterly

FIGURE 21-2

5. Select Adjust from the Image menu and choose Auto-Equalize. Use the Save As command in the File menu, and save the file as a PCX in PHOTOPNT\CANVAS as PAPER01L.PCX. Close the file.

6. Open the Canvas filter by selecting Artistic in the Effects menu and choosing Canvas…. When the dialog box opens, click the Load… button and select the PAPER01L.PCX file. Change the Transparency setting to 92% and the Emboss: setting to 20%. Click the OK button.

7. For the finishing touch, select 3D Effects from the Effects menu and choose Emboss…. Click the Reset button, and then change the Emboss color to Original color. Change the Level: to 135. Click the OK button. The result is shown in Figure 21-3.

8. Close the file. It is not necessary to save this image.

The finished image looks as if it were painted

FIGURE 21-3

Considerations When Using the Canvas Filter

If you are going to apply the canvas to an image, be aware that it will make the image more opaque to some extent. The best canvases are those with little color, lots of white area, and contrast. Cement is a good example of a canvas to place on top. It is a high-contrast canvas and therefore the effect of the embossing really stands out.

There is good news and bad news about using the Canvas filter. The bad news? One of the effects can be that the resulting image looks washed out. The good news? There is a cure. After you have applied the canvas, apply the Auto Equalize filter in the Image menu under Adjust. This generally restores most of the tonal depth that is lost when the canvas is applied.

Canvases can be placed on top of and behind images. They can be applied to objects. In fact, the canvas provides a way to add texture only to an object.

Although it has been mentioned before, remember that the preview for this filter does not always faithfully reflect what the final output will look like.

Adding texture to text or other objects is another use for the Canvas filter. Figure 21-4 shows the application of a canvas (default settings of Stucco) to the text with

The
application
of the
Canvas
filter to the
text gives
the image a
photo-realistic
texture

FIGURE 21-4

the background locked. Only the objects that are unlocked have the canvas applied
to them.

The Glass Block Filter

This filter, which is only available with duotone, Paletted (8-bit), 24-bit, 32-bit color,
and grayscale images, creates the effect of viewing the image through thick
transparent blocks of glass. The dialog box is very simple. The two sliders,
Horizontal and Vertical, can be set independently of each other. The setting range is
1 through 100. The lowest setting (1 Width, 1 Height) produces glass blocks that are
1 x 1 pixels in the image area.

Some Things to Do with the Glass Block Filter

Figure 21-5 is a standard studio photograph that has had the Glass Block filter
applied (obviously) as square blocks. I used this photograph to illustrate the fact that
the filter appears to have little effect on the background. That's because of the lack

This is
either an
example of
the Glass
Block filter
or the result
of one drink
too many

FIGURE 21-5

of contrast in the background. Even though there is a difference in shading, there aren't any lines of hard contrast for the filter to act upon. Knowing this about the filter, we can take advantage of it.

Figure 21-6 is a glass ball I made using the Map To Object filter. (I told you back in Chapter 19 that I spend too much time making these things.) The background has hard horizontal lines but no areas of contrast in the vertical. By applying the Glass Block filter to the background (the glass ball is a separate object we learned to make in Chapter 19), we can make the wood on which the ball is lying change shape to appear to be much smaller pieces, as shown in Figure 21-7.

Enough of the Glass block already. Let's move on to the Impressionist filter.

The Impressionist Filter

Like the Glass Block filter, the Impressionist filter is only available with duotone, Paletted (8-bit), 24-bit, 32-bit, and grayscale images. This filter gives an image the appearance of an impressionist brush. Not really, but that's the official description. The amount of Impressionist effect can be applied independently as Horizontal or Vertical values. The range is 1-100 and is measured in the amount of scatter (displacement) in pixels. For example, a setting of 10 in the Vertical will diffuse the

Glass ball
on large
wood poles

FIGURE 21-6

The Glass
Block filters
change the
poles into
sticks

FIGURE 21-7

image over a ten-pixel region in the vertical. Using a setting larger than the default (or 10) will scatter the pixels in the original image to the point that it becomes unrecognizable. In the previous edition of this book, I referred to this filter as "one of those 'what-were-they-thinking-about?'-type filters that ends up in every photo-editing package." I have since changed my mind This filter has taken on a new life.

The real key to using it is to be aware that when it scatters pixels on an object, it replaces the scattered pixels with the current Paper color. This would seem to restrict the filter's usefulness. It doesn't—if you remember another part of PHOTO-PAINT that thinks in such a binary format. I am referring to the mask! Here is a hands-on exercise that I think you will like.

Making Cut Metal Objects

This hands-on exercise may seem complicated but the results are worth it. In it we are going to make a title screen for a multimedia presentation that introduces one of the rock-and-roll categories. Using several filters, we are going to make letters that look like they were cut out of metal flooring.

1. Locate and Open the file 537099.WI in the EXERCISE\PHOTOS folder. Select Resample… in the Image menu and change the Width to 6 inches. Click the OK button.

2. Select the Text tool from the Toolbox and type **HEAVY METAL** on two lines with a line spacing of 80. The font is Kabel Ult BT at a size of 96 and centered. The result is shown in Figure 21-8. The figure has white type so it will stand out in the book. The color of the type is not important.

3. Open the Objects Docker window (CTRL-F7) and check Lock Transparency. The text should be selected.

4. In the Edit menu, select Fill… and click the Bitmap Fill button. Then click the Edit… button. In the Bitmap Fill dialog box, click the Load… button. From the Import dialog box, locate EXERCISE\TILES\METAL01M.CPT on the Corel CD-ROM. Click the OK buttons to close all of the dialog boxes. The text will fill with the metal texture.

Note—Heavy Metal is not a reference to the tuba section

5. Click the Create Mask button (CTRL-M). Click the Paint On Mask option in the Mask menu (CTRL-K) or the Paint On Mask button in the Standard Toolbar. From the Effects menu, select Artistic and choose Impressionist…. Change both of the Scatter settings to 6. Click the OK button. The result is shown in Figure 21-9.

6. The edge of the mask needs to be smoothed out a bit. From the Effects menu, select Blur and choose Gaussian Blur…. Change the Radius setting to 1. Click the OK button.

7. Click the Paint On Mask button again to return to the image. In the Objects window, uncheck Lock Transparency. In the Object menu, select Clip To Mask. There won't seem to be any difference at this point.

8. From the Effects menu, select 3D Effects and choose Emboss…. Change the Emboss color to Original color; Depth: 5; Level: 120; Direction: 128. Click the OK button.

The Impressionist filter scatters the edge of the mask

FIGURE 21-9

9. From the Effects menu, select Sharpen and choose Sharpen.... Change the Edge level (%) to 45 and the Threshold to 100. Remove the mask.

10. Select the Text object and choose Drop Shadow...in the Object menu. For settings, use a Distance setting of 0.1, Color of Black, a Feather of 10, and an Opacity of 100. Offset direction is bottom-right 315. The result is shown in Figure 21-10.

11. Close the file. You do not need to save it.

You can use this technique on just about any object to get a rough cut effect. The Sharpen filter was applied to add specular highlights to the edges of the metal. You can also use this technique (without the sharpening and the embossing) to make text that looks like a stencil.

The Smoked Glass Filter

The Smoked Glass filter applies a transparent mask over the image to give the appearance of smoked glass. You can determine the color of the tint (before opening the filter), the percentage of transparency, and the degree of blurring.

537099.wi

We are now
ready to
rock and roll

FIGURE 21-10

The color of the tint is determined by the Paint (foreground) color, which is controlled in the Tool Settings roll-up before opening the filter dialog box, or from the color controls within the dialog box. The Tint slider controls the opacity of the tint being applied. Larger values mean greater amounts of color tint applied to the image. A value of 100 fills the area with a solid color. The Percent slider controls the amount of blurring applied to the image to give the appearance of the distortion caused by glass. A value of 100 percent produces the greatest amount of blurring, while 0 percent produces no blurring of the image.

The Vignette Filter

The Vignette filter applies a mask over the image through the creation of a transparent shape in the center. The remainder of the mask is opaque. It is designed to appear as an old-style photograph when the image is placed in an oval or other shape.

A vignette can be applied to the entire image or just a masked area. By clicking and dragging the Offset slider, you can control how large the selected shape appears around the center of the image. The larger the percentage, the smaller the transparent oval. The Fade slider controls the fade (feathering) at the edge of the oval. Using the Vignette dialog box, you can determine the color of the mask, either by selecting black or white or by selecting a Paint color from the drop-down swatch.

Figure 21-11 shows the standard application of this filter. The attention is focused on the little girl by fading the rest of the background to black. But do you wonder what would happen if you applied a small amount of the Vignette filter to a mask? I did, and came up with a cutout filter as shown in Figure 21-12. It's not as simple as it may seem. Here is the recipe:

- Make a mask in the shape of the cutout. I recommend squares and circles.

- Apply the Vignette filter by adjusting the filter settings using the onscreen preview.

- Use the local Undo tool to remove shadows from one side.

The only restriction in using the Vignette filter is the inability to select the area that is to be the image center. This is logical when you consider that the vignette is supposed to be equal on all sides, and therefore always uses the very center of the image as its center. The problem occurs when your subject is not in the center. The only way to correct an off-center subject is to crop the image so the subject is centered

21

A typical
vignette
style of
image

FIGURE 21-11

A little
mask and a
little
vignette—
voila! A
cutout

FIGURE 21-12

and then, if the resulting image is too small, use the Paper Size command to restore part or all of the image size after applying the filter.

That wraps up the Artistic filters. While these are not the most powerful filters on the planet, I think we have seen that they can be used to create some unusual effects, even if they are not what the original filter programmer had in mind.

22

Fancy Filters

The filters in the Fancy category of the Effects menu offer unique special effects that cannot be obtained through any other means.

The Fancy Filters

The Fancy Filter neighborhood is getting a little lonely now that the Glass and The Boss filters have moved to the 3D Effects category. As diverse as the remaining are, they all have one thing in common—they are all popular third-party plug-in filters in their own right. Two of the filters, Paint Alchemy and Terrazzo, were previously only available as plug-in filters on the Macintosh, and Julia Set Explorer 2.0 is from Kai's Power Tools. Together they represent an awesome array of special effects capability.

 TIP: *Are you looking for The Boss and Glass filters? They've moved to the 3D Effects category.*

Paint Alchemy

Paint Alchemy and its counterpart Terrazzo are both incredible filters that offer many levels of customization. Since there is very little documentation about these filters and they are, without a doubt, the most complex ones, they are presented in greater detail than the other filters in this chapter. To ensure the most accurate documentation, I have been assisted greatly by Xaos Tool's documentation and tech-support people, who have been a world of help. Acknowledgments and kudos given, let's play with Paint Alchemy.

Paint Alchemy applies brush strokes to selected areas of your image in a precisely controlled manner. As with all filters, you can use masks to apply Paint Alchemy to part of an image or the entire image. You can use one of the many brushes provided with the filter or create your own brushes. It is not hard to create effects with Paint Alchemy; the key to using and enjoying this filter is experimentation.

 TIP: *As you learn how to make changes to the Paint Alchemy filter styles, I recommend limiting your changes to one at a time so that you can keep track of the effects.*

Starting Paint Alchemy

The Paint Alchemy filter is located under Fancy in the Effects menu. Clicking Alchemy in the drop-down list opens the Paint Alchemy dialog box as shown in Figure 22-1.

 NOTE: *Paint Alchemy is only available when 24-bit color images are selected. If a grayscale, back-and-white, 16-color, or 256-color image or 32-bit is open, the Alchemy filter is unavailable (grayed out).*

The Paint Alchemy Dialog Box

The dialog box is divided into three sections: control tabs, style controls, and preview controls.

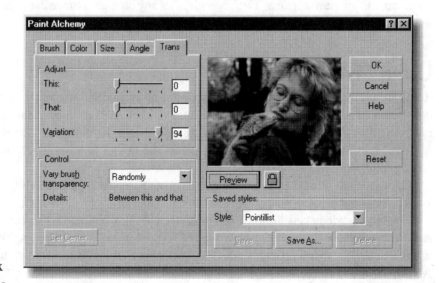

The Paint Alchemy Dialog Box

FIGURE 22-1

The Control Tabs

These are the controls that let you customize Paint Alchemy. They are arranged on five control tabs. Only one tab can be visible at a time, but the controls on all five tabs are always active. To switch between tabs, click on the tab labels tabs at the top.

The Style Controls

The style controls let you select one of the 75 preset styles included with Paint Alchemy, modify an existing style so that it may be saved as new style, or remove an old style. Before you begin modifying the preset styles, I encourage you to work with the preset styles to get a feel for what they do. If you do change a style and like the results, you can save these settings as a style.

The Preview Controls

The preview controls allow you to zoom in or out of the preview image. They also allow you to move the image inside of the preview window. Clicking the left mouse button in the preview area zooms the preview image in; right-clicking zooms it out. Clicking the left mouse button and dragging produces a hand for moving the image around in the preview window. Two seconds after any change is made in the preview window, filter preview is automatically invoked.

Using Styles

You can use Paint Alchemy to create an enormous variety of effects. With 30 parameters to change and the ability to use custom brushes in addition to the brushes provided, the number of possibilities are virtually infinite. To allow you to keep track of your favorite settings, Paint Alchemy offers the ability to save all of the filter settings as styles.

Each style is a complete record of the settings of all the controls. By loading a style, you can reproduce exactly that incredible filter effect that so wowed your client.

Loading a style is very simple. You only need to click on the down arrow to the right of the Style box, and a drop-down list of 75 predefined styles appears. You can use the styles that Corel provides with Paint Alchemy, or you can create your own. Any of the pre-defined styles can be customized.

TIP: *Altering existing styles and saving the new settings under a new name is often the best way to begin creating your own styles.*

Creating a Custom Style

Paint Alchemy, like many paint-oriented filters, can take a long time to apply to an image. When you begin experimentation in search of the custom look that is going to win the Corel Design contest for you, consider selecting a small area of the total image by using a mask. Smaller image areas can be processed much faster. When you find the style you want, you can then apply it to a larger image to make sure all of the settings work before you save it as a style.

The following is a recommended procedure for creating new styles. There is nothing about it that is set in stone; it is only a guideline.

- Find an existing style that is closest to the style you want to create. Use the settings from that style as your starting point.

- Reduce the number of brush strokes (the Density) on the Brush tab until you can see what the individual brushes are doing. Using the Zoom feature of the preview window, zoom in on individual brush strokes and make necessary adjustments to appropriate parameters (size, transparency, etc.).

- Change the attributes on the Color control tab until you can see how the controls change each brush stroke. Once you are comfortable with the color controls, adjust your colors.

- Increase the Density (number of brush strokes) until the angle of application becomes clear. Now you can adjust the brush stroke angle.

- To save a new custom style, click the Save As button. You are asked to enter a name for the new file (it can seemingly be a name of endless length, but you can only see the first 40 characters in the Style box). The current settings are saved with the name you provide, and the new style is added to the Style drop-down list in alphabetical order.

Changing a Custom Style

To change a custom style, do the following:

22

1. Select the style to be changed.

2. Make the changes desired.

3. Click the Save As button. (You cannot change and save a preset style with the same name. With preset styles, only the Save As button is available.)

Saving a custom style will substitute the current style settings for those of the Paint Alchemy style with the same name.

 TIP: *A quick way to return to the default setting for any style is to click on the style name. Then use either the up or down arrow key to move to an adjacent style, and then, using the opposite arrow key, return to the original setting.*

Removing a Custom Style

To delete a custom style, you need only select the style you want to delete and click the Delete button. A warning box (I like to call them "second chance" boxes) asks you if you are sure that you want to delete the style. If you click OK, it's all over.

The Brush Tab

The Brush tab is the tab you see when Paint Alchemy is first opened. This tab is the heart of Paint Alchemy. The description that is in the Xaos Tool's Paint Alchemy manual can't be beat: "The simplest description of what Paint Alchemy does is this: It applies a whole bunch of brush strokes to your image. As a result, the shape of the brush has a profound effect on the look that is produced."

The Brush tab displays seven of the standard brushes. When I first began working with this program, I thought the best brush for the application was displayed along with those were also likely candidates for the effects. Wow, was I ever wrong! The seven standard brushes that are displayed never change, regardless of the current brush that is loaded. The currently selected brush has a highlighted border around it. (On my system, it is red.)

Loading a Custom Brush

There are 30 custom brushes included with Paint Alchemy. They are located in the COREL\DRAW80\PHOTOPNT\PLGBRUSH directory . Click on the Load button and the Load Brush dialog box opens as shown below.

Load Brush

File name:
plusglow.bmp

plusglow.bmp
pntbrush.bmp
pntwide.bmp
pufftext.bmp
pyramid.bmp
ripple.bmp
saturn.bmp
scatch.bmp

Folders:
e:\COREL\CO...\PLGBRUSH

e:\
corel
corel80
photopnt
plgbrush

OK

Cancel

List files of type:
BMP File [*.bmp]

Drives:
e: seagatee2

It allows you to select any .BMP file as a custom brush. Here are the general rules regarding brushes.

You can load any BMP file as a brush as long as it meets the following parameters: 128 x 128 pixels, grayscale (8-bit) and 300 dpi. If any of these parameters are different, the custom brush won't work. The exception is that the resolution can be 100 dpi. The brush icon will appear but the resulting brush may be distorted.

Using the default settings, brushes are completely opaque where white and transparent where black. Gray areas are semi-transparent; the darker they are, the more transparent they are. Black portions of your brush will not change your image, while the white portions define the area in which your selected effect is applied.

TIP: *When making brushes in Corel PHOTO-PAINT, it is not necessary to paint white-on-black. Do all of your work in black-on-white, and then use the Invert filter.*

Styles that are built around custom brushes depend on the brushes remaining in the PLGBRUSH folder. If the brush that a selected style needs is not available when the style is selected, a default brush is loaded in its place.

Density

The Density slider controls the number of brush strokes that will be applied to the selected area. Density is used to calculate how many brush strokes should be used for a given image size. The absolute number of strokes that will be used with the current image size is displayed to the right of the slider. All of the calculations are based on the image size, not the mask size.

 TIP: *The time required to apply the effect depends directly on the number of brush strokes: the more strokes, the longer the effect will take. The other factor that determines the amount of time that it takes to apply an effect is the size of the image or the size of the mask. If the image is large and the mask is small, the processing will still occur more quickly because the effect is only calculated for and applied to the masked area.*

Positioning

The Adjust sliders are far less than self-explanatory. They add randomness to the position of the brush strokes. When the Horizontal and Vertical Variation sliders are both set at 0, the strokes are placed on a regular grid. The Horizontal Variation slider controls side-to-side brush stroke deviation. The Vertical Variation slider controls the up-and-down motion of the brush stroke deviation. With most of the styles applying Multiplying brush strokes one on top of another, there are many styles that seemed to be changed very little by the positioning controls.

Layering Methods

There are three choices for layering methods in the Brush tab: Random, Ordered, and Paint Layering.

RANDOM LAYERING   The brush strokes are applied so that they randomly overlap each other.

ORDERED LAYERING   The brush strokes are applied so that strokes that are above and to the left always overlap those that are below and to the right. With a square brush, this can look like roofing shingles. With a round brush, it can look like fish scales.

PAINT LAYERING   With Paint layering, the brightest portions of each brush stroke take priority in the layering. The effect it produces is highly dependent on the shape and coloring of the brush. You will need to experiment with Paint layering to find out what it can do. Paint layering can also cause brush shape to be lost when brushes overlap too much. The overlapping brush problem is resolved by lowering the Density setting or reducing the brush size (on the Size tab) to reveal more of the brush.

NOTE: *The Paint method of layering can cause aliasing (the dreaded "jaggies") when a brush that has hard black-and-white (or bright) edges is used.*

Randomize

Before you read this, click the Randomize button and see if you can figure out what it does. For those of you who understand techno-babble, it is a *random-seed generator.* For those that do not speak the language, it is the Randomize setting, which lets you set the initial value used in the random-number generation, a value that is called the *seed number.*

Clicking the Randomize button will randomly change the seed. You can also type a number directly into the box that is adjacent to the button. As a rule, forget the button. The fine folks at Xaos Tools, however, give two examples where you might actually want to use this function, as follows.

CHANGING THE SEED TO SUBTLY CHANGE THE EFFECT You may want to change the seed if you like the general effect that Paint Alchemy is producing but not the way some brushes work. Changing the seed puts the brush strokes in slightly different random positions, and this may produce that final correction you were looking for.

MAINTAINING THE SEED TO ENSURE REPEATABILITY Using the same seed number guarantees that the exact same series of random numbers will be used for Paint Alchemy's internal calculations and thus all of the effects will be identical. This application, however, sounds a little fishy to me. How can it be a true random-number generator if identical results occur every time you use it?

BONUS: PICKING THE NUMBERS FOR YOUR STATE LOTTERY This is my idea. The numbers that you get each time you click the Random button are indeed random, so you can use this function to pick lottery numbers in much the same way that they are picked by the state, untainted by the sentimental and unscientific "favorite numbers" technique. The only hitch is that most big-money lotteries are based on two-digit numbers. No problem just use the last two digits of the random number for the lottery. By the way, if you win using this method, it is only fair for you to split the winnings with myself and the editors who let this piece of nonsense get into print.

Creating Your Own Brushes

Creating brushes is one on the slicker things you can do with Paint Alchemy. It is easy to make a brush, but it is a little more difficult to make one that looks great when it is used in Paint Alchemy. Here is a summary of brush-making tips from Xaos Tools and from my own experience working with Corel PHOTO-PAINT and Paint Alchemy.

You can open the existing brush files in Corel PHOTO-PAINT. (The brushes are BMP files located in the PLGBRUSH folder.) You can then use Corel PHOTO-PAINT to alter the appearance of the brushes. If you change one of the original brushes that came with Corel PHOTO-PAINT, make sure you only save it under a new name. All of the styles in Paint Alchemy were designed to use one of these brushes. If you change the brush, you will need to reinstall PAINT to restore the original brushes. If you want to save changes you made, use Save As.

When you create a new brush from scratch, use an image size of 128 x 128 pixels with a resolution of 300 dpi. Also, remember to make the image a grayscale. If the brush you create is too large, it will not load into Paint Alchemy.

 TIP: *To change the brush that is used by a style, select the style before you select the brush. This is because every style has a brush associated with it. If you load the brush and then the style, the style will load its own brush, forcing you to reload your brush.*

The Color Tab

You can use the Color Tab, shown in Figure 22-2, to create effects such as pastel-like colors or even create improved black-and-white styles.

 TIP: *To create pastel-like colors using the Color tab, set the Brush Color to From Image and the Background to Solid Color (white). Then set your brush strokes to be partially transparent.*

Brush Color

Each brush stroke is a single, solid color. To determine the color of your brush strokes, use the Color tab. You can set the colors of your brush strokes by using the colors of the image you are working on or by selecting a specific color using the Brush Color controls.

FROM IMAGE   The color of each brush stroke is based on the color of the image at the center of each brush stroke.

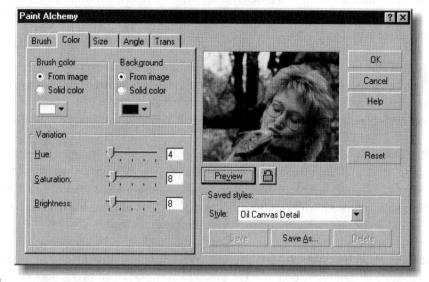

The Color
Tab portion
of the Paint
Alchemy
dialog box

FIGURE 22-2

SOLID COLOR   The color of all brush strokes is based on the color that you select. To select the color, click on the color preview window to the right of the Solid Color button to open up the standard color-selection palette.

Background

You can choose to apply Paint Alchemy brush strokes with a Paper (background) of solid color using the Background controls.

FROM IMAGE   The brush strokes are applied to your image based on the color of each brush stroke.

SOLID COLOR   The brush strokes are applied to a Paper (background) of a solid color. To select the color, click on the color preview window to the right of the Solid Color button to open up the standard color-selection palette.

The Hue, Saturation, and Brightness Variation Controls

These controls operate in a similar manner to the Impressionism or Pointillism brush tools. They allow you to vary from the initial Brush Color settings. The amount of

22

variation can be controlled independently for the hue, saturation, and brightness of the brush color. These controls affect the brush stroke of both the From Image and the Solid Color settings.

HUE VARIATION   Hue Variation controls how much the color varies from the starting color. A small setting causes the colors in the brush to vary just a few shades to either side of the original color. A large setting produces a rainbow of colors, producing a confetti-like effect.

SATURATION VARIATION   Saturation Variation has the least noticeable effect of the three. It controls the amount of gray level in the image. It isn't a simple relationship; for example, 100 percent gives lots of gray. It has a greater effect in images where the color scheme of things contains large quantities of gray. Play with this control, but expect subtle rather than great changes in the image.

BRIGHTNESS VARIATION   Brightness Variation has the effect of controlling contrast. Officially, it controls the amount of variance in brightness between the starting color and the additional colors that are created by Paint Alchemy.

Image Enhancement

As with many of the other filters, you can increase the effectiveness of the Color tab by using the other controls and filters in Corel PHOTO-PAINT to modify the image before working on it with the Paint Alchemy filter. If you have a low-contrast image, you should consider applying the Equalization filter to stretch the dynamic range of the image or increase the contrast of the image to produce more dramatic results.

The Size Tab

The Size tab, shown in Figure 22-3, does just what it says: It enables you to vary the size of the brush strokes that are applied. There are several controls on this tab that are evident when you open it. The Adjust controls vary according to the Vary Brush Size selection. When I first opened the Vary Brush Size drop-down list, I was greeted by a lengthy list of, shall we say, interesting names. However, once you understand the thinking behind the designers at Xaos, these might make a little more sense.

The Size
tab of the
Paint
Alchemy
dialog box

FIGURE 22-3

The Vary Brush Size Control

Clicking on the arrow button to the right of the name box produces a list of eight sets of brush variations. The names of the presets are the same on the Size, Angle, and Transparency tabs. What follows is a description of the action of each of these variation sets.

NO VARIATION   Here's the only set that is self-explanatory. Well, sort of. When this option is selected, all of the brush strokes will be the same size. The size of the brush is set using the Size slider. The size is scaled from the actual size of the brush image selected. In practice, it is a percentage of the size of the original. For example, since the BMP file that makes up the brush is 128 x 128 pixels, a size value of 128 would produce brush strokes of the same size. If the value was set for 50 (50 percent), the brush strokes would be 64 x 64 pixels in size. All of the brushes included in Paint Alchemy are 128 x 128 pixels. Now for the weirdness.

What does a Variation slider in the Adjust section do in a No Variation setting? It overrides the No Variation option in the Control section, of course. Thus, larger numbers cause larger variations in brush size in the No Variation setting. Is that clear? I think I'm getting a headache. By the way, the preceding explanation applies to all of the Variation sliders.

RANDOMLY   When this option is selected, the brush strokes vary in size randomly. I love the two settings for this one: This and That. You use This and That to set the minimum and maximum size allowed. It doesn't matter which is which. The larger setting will be the Maximum and the smaller setting will be the Minimum. Look at the bottom of the tab. Another Variation slider! This one does the same thing as the Variation slider in No Variation: It overrides the This and That slider settings.

BY RADIAL DISTANCE   With this option, the brush strokes will change smoothly in size, in a circular manner. The brush strokes start out one size in the center and gradually change to another size at the edge of the circle.

- **Center slider**   This determines the size of the brush at the center of the circle. Because the size of the brush varies as a function of its distance, this slider and the Edge slider control how the brush stroke will appear.

- **Edge slider**   This sets the size of the brush at the edge of the circle.

Variation Slider: Center and Edge Sliders

To set the location of the center point, click the Set Center button. This brings up a dialog box shown below that contains a thumbnail of the image or of the area selected by the mask. If more than one area is masked, an area of the image that is determined by the boundaries of the various masks makes up the preview image. By clicking on the place that you want to be the center of the circle, a small crosshair is placed on the image at the point where you clicked.

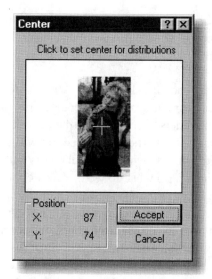

Below the thumbnail is exact X/Y-position information (in pixels) for the point where the circle is centered. Actually, I haven't got a clue why this information is provided. It wasn't in the Mac version, and when I asked some members of the Paint development team, they didn't know either, except that it had been requested from higher up in the command chain.

NOTE: *The Set Center point determines the center of the circle used by the Size, Angle, and Transparency tabs. The Set Center point is available on the Size, Angle, and Transparency tabs when By Radial Distance is selected on each.*

BY VERTICAL POSITION   With this option, the brush strokes change smoothly in size from the top to the bottom of the image. You set the sizes using the Top and Bottom sliders.

BY HORIZONTAL POSITION   With this option, the brush strokes change smoothly in size from the left to the right of the image. The sizes of the brushes are set using the Left and Right sliders.

BY HUE   With this option, each brush stroke is scaled according to the hue of the image at the location of each brush stroke. You set the minimum and maximum sizes using the Warm and Cool sliders. For example, the default By Hue setting for the Spatula style is Warm 5, Cool 30. The warmer colors will be limited to variations of up to 5 percent of the brush size, while the cool colors will be allowed to become up to 30 percent of brush size. So what do we mean by cool and warm? On a color wheel, the dividing line between cool and warm runs through red. Therefore, by using the By Hue option for determining brush size, brush strokes that are applied to areas of the image that contain colors on the yellow side of red are given the Warm size values. Those colors that fall on the magenta side of red are given the Cool size values. (This detailed explanation is so that you know how it works. I have yet to sit down with a color wheel that can calculate this stuff. Experiment on small images or the preview window.)

BY SATURATION   With this selection, each brush stroke is scaled according to the saturation of the image color at the location of the brush stroke. You set the minimum and maximum sizes using the Unsaturated and Saturated sliders. If you are very health conscious, you can use these setting to make images that are high in unsaturates (just kidding). Setting the values for Saturated to be larger than the values for Unsaturated results in brush strokes over richly colored areas that will be larger than the brush strokes over black, white, or gray areas.

 TIP: *While working with this larger/smaller brush stroke thing, remember that smaller brush strokes retain more detail of the original image and may be more desirable than larger brush strokes.*

BY BRIGHTNESS   With this option, each brush stroke is scaled according to the brightness of the image color at the location of the brush stroke. You set the minimum and maximum sizes using the Dark and Bright sliders. Setting the values for Bright to be larger than the value for Dark results in brush strokes over bright areas of the image that will be larger than brush strokes over dark areas.

The Angle Tab

You use the Angle tab, Figure 22-4, to set the angle of your brush stroke and to change brush angle based on its position in your image. Based on the Control option chosen, the Adjust options vary. You can also control brush angle based on the color content of your image, or you can change brush angle randomly. This tab is similar in operation to the Size tab.

Vary Brush Angle

The Vary Brush Angle drop-down list lets you specify what should control the orientation (the amount of rotation) of your brush strokes. You can apply all of the brush strokes at the same angle, or you can have them vary randomly, according to information in the image, or by their position. The following is what each option does.

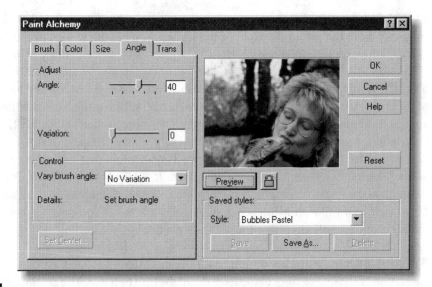

The Angle
Tab portion
of the Paint
Alchemy
dialog box

FIGURE 22-4

NO VARIATION   When this option is selected, all of the brush strokes will be rotated by the same angular amount. The amount of rotation (-180 to +180) is set using the Angle slider. If the Angle is set to 0, the brush strokes will not be rotated at all; they will have the same orientation as the picture of the brush that is displayed on the Brush tab. If the angle is set to 180 degrees, the brushes will be upside-down.

RANDOMLY   With this option, the brush stroke angle varies randomly. You use This and That to set the minimum and maximum angles. It doesn't matter which is which. The larger setting will be the Maximum and the smaller setting will be the Minimum.

BY RADIAL DISTANCE   With this option, the brush strokes will change their orientation smoothly in a circular manner, starting at one angle in the center and gradually changing to another angle at the edge of the circle. The operation of these controls is described in the By Radial Distance section on the Size tab.

BY VERTICAL POSITION   Using this selection, the brush strokes change their angle smoothly from the top to the bottom of the image. You set the angles using the Top and Bottom sliders.

BY HORIZONTAL POSITION   With this option, the brush strokes change their angle smoothly from the left to the right of the image. You set the angles of the brushes using the Left and Right sliders.

BY HUE   With By Hue selected, each brush stroke is rotated according to the hue of the image at the location of each brush stroke. You set the minimum and maximum angles using the Warm and Cool sliders. Therefore, when using By Hue for determining brush stroke angles, areas of the image that contain colors on the yellow side of red are given the Warm size values. Those colors that fall on the magenta side of the red are given the Cool size values. If you set the angle for Cool to be larger than the angle for Warm, brush strokes over the blue areas of the image will be rotated more than brush strokes over yellow areas. (You should feel free to experiment on small images or the preview window.)

BY SATURATION   With this option, each brush stroke is rotated according to the saturation of the image color at the location of the brush stroke. You set the minimum and maximum angles using the Unsaturated and Saturated sliders. Setting the values for Saturated to be larger than the values for Unsaturated results in brush strokes over richly colored areas that will be rotated more than brush strokes over black, white, or gray areas.

BY BRIGHTNESS   With this option, each brush stroke is rotated according to the brightness of the image color at the location of the brush stroke. You set the minimum and maximum angles using the Dark and Bright sliders. Setting the values for Bright to be larger than the values for Dark results in brush strokes over bright areas of the image that will be larger than brush strokes over dark areas.

Angle Variation

The Variation slider in the Adjust section lets you add randomness to the stroke angles. The higher this value, the more your strokes will vary from their set angles.

The variation is calculated as degrees of offset from the brush angle. Thus, if you set Vary Brush Angle to No Variation, the Angle to 90, and the Variation to 10, you will get brush strokes that range in angle from 80 to 100 degrees.

The Transparency Tab

The Transparency tab, Figure 22-5, is used to control brush stroke transparency and to change the transparency based on brush position in your image. Based on the Control option chosen, the Adjust options vary. You can also control transparency

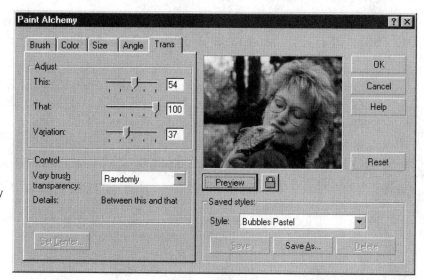

The Transparency Tab portion of the Paint Alchemy dialog box

FIGURE 22-5

based on the color content of your image, or you can control it randomly. This tab is similar in operation to the Size tab.

The Vary Brush Transparency Controls

See the Size Tab for information on using these controls.

The Power of Paint Alchemy

I have given you many pages of reference material about the Paint Alchemy filter. While perhaps not the most exciting reading, this material will be very useful when you begin experimenting with creating your own brushes and styles. What follows is a hands-on exercise to give you a taste of what Paint Alchemy can do.

Making A Travel Poster

The purpose of most travel posters is not to provide information but to convey a thought or feeling. We are going to create one for Europe that has an artistic theme to it.

1. Open the file EXERCISE\PHOTOS\EUROPE\673069.WI. Select Resample from the Image menu and change the Width setting to 7 inches. Click the OK button.

2. From the Effects menu, select Fancy and choose Alchemy. When the dialog box opens ensure the Style is set to Default. Click OK. The result is shown in Figure 22-6.

3. From the Effects menu, select Auto F/X and then Photo/Graphic Edges 3.0. Click the Select Outset Effect button. Select Af073.afx and click the Open button. Click the Apply button.

NOTE: *You will need to have the CD that contains the Edges in the CD-ROM drive to access the edges.*

4. From the Effects menu select 3D Effects and choose Emboss. Click the Reset button and change the Emboss Color to Original color. Click the OK button. The result is shown in Figure 22-7.

The result
of applying
the Default
Paint
Alchemy
filter

FIGURE 22-6

After the
AUTO F/X
and Emboss
filters it
looks more
like a
painting

FIGURE 22-7

5. Click the Text tool button in the Toolbox. Click the cursor in the image and change the Font to Futura XBlk BT at a size of 72. Type the word **EUROPE**.

6. Click the Object Picker tool and open the Objects Docker window and enable Lock Object Transparency.

7. From the Edit menu, select Fill. In the Edit Fill & Transparency Roll-Up, click the Fountain Fill button and click the Edit button. From the Fountain Fill dialog box, choose Red Wash in Presets. Click OK to close the box and OK again to apply the fill. With the Object Picker tool you can place the text wherever you like. I thought it looked good in the upper-left corner.

8. Select Drop Shadow from the Object menu. We are not wanting to make a drop shadow but a back glow to make the letters stand out. Set Distance values to 0 and Direction: Average. Select White shadow color, Opacity of 100 and a Feather of 25. Click OK. Figure 22-8 shows the finished picture.

Ready for printing and hanging on the travel office wall

FIGURE 22-8

TIP: *A problem with many of the Alchemy filter effects is they tend to make an image nearly unrecognizable. A way to reduce the effect is to make a duplicate of the original as an object. Apply the effect to the object in Single mode and then reduce the Opacity of the object, letting more of the original show through.*

Well, there are so many other things we could do with these filters they could fill any entire book. If you want to learn more about using these filters, then check out Chapter 24. In it we learn to use Paint Alchemy and Terrazzo to create seamless images for Web pages.

Julia Set Explorer 2.0

This is the one of the original filters from Metacreation Corporation, (formally Metatools and before that HSC). Just to eliminate a point of confusion, the filter is called Julia Set Explorer in the Fancy menu, but when the dialog box opens, it is called Fractal Explorer 2.0. The explanation is simple. This filter is a hybrid of the Julia I Explorer from Kai Power Tools (KPT) 1.0 and the interface from KPT 2.0. Now you won't lie awake worrying about it.

If this is your first time with the Kai Power Tools (KPT) user interface, welcome to the jungle! Just kidding. I have heard this User Interface (UI), shown later in Figure 22-9, described as everything from the best UI on the planet to a Klingon Control Panel. I personally opt for the latter. A friend of mine who is a big fan of KPT insists that it is really easy to learn to use. On the other hand, he believes that Neil Armstrong's moonwalk was a fake and that wrestling is real, so judge accordingly. Whether you hate it or love it, you have to use it. So, to get the most out of this very powerful fractal generator, you need to spend some time learning your way around.

Fractal Explorer Basics

The Fractal Explorer UI, you may have already noticed, doesn't look like your average Windows dialog box.

TIP: *The Fractal Explorer UI requires the monitor be in 16.7 million (24-bit) color to display properly. If your UI looks horrible (by that I mean the graphics look muddled), make sure you display is in the proper mode.*

To make the UI less confusing, many of the options, like Help, remain dimmed until you place the cursor over them. The dialog box can be moved around the screen by clicking on the title bar and dragging the dialog box anywhere on the screen. When you exit the filter by clicking on either OK or Cancel, the filter will remember its placement on the screen for the next time it is called up within that session. When you leave Corel PHOTO-PAINT and return, all positioning information is lost and the UI restarts in the center of the screen.

Temporary Resizing

Placing the cursor over the button in the upper-left corner with the Kai circular logo on it brings up the program credits for Kai Power Tools. Double-clicking this button reduces (i.e., minimizes) the Fractal Explorer to its preview window. Clicking once repetitively on the preview window magnifies the image increasingly. Double-click on the preview window and the Explorer is returned to its original happy self.

Help

Clicking on the Help button (to the immediate left of the title bar) brings up the Help menu for Fractal Explorer Kai Power Tools 2.0. Be aware that there may be Help references to things that are not in the Corel version of this product. You can also get help by pressing the F1 key, which turns the cursor into a question mark. Clicking on any part of the UI brings up context-insensitive help. No matter what you click, you are going to get the opening help screen.

Options Menu

In the upper-right corner is the Options button. Clicking on this button brings up menu choices that deal with Apply modes, which are discussed in detail later in this chapter.

Fractal Explorer Controls

Here is an explanation of the controls on the Fractal Explorer dialog box. Refer to Figure 22-9.

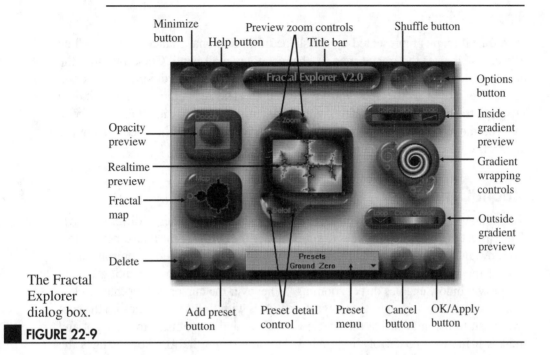

Minimize button
Help button
Preview zoom controls
Title bar
Shuffle button
Options button
Inside gradient preview
Opacity preview
Gradient wrapping controls
Realtime preview
Fractal map
Outside gradient preview
Delete

The Fractal Explorer dialog box.

Add preset button
Preset detail control
Preset menu
Cancel button
OK/Apply button

FIGURE 22-9

Preview Window

The real-time preview window in the center shows the fractal while it interacts with the underlying image. The initial preview window displays a rough idea of the fractal very quickly, followed by three steps of increasingly refined views. Repeat clicks preempt the preview computation, allowing fast exploration of the fractal space. Color choices are instantly mapped onto the set.

Opacity Selector

The Opacity preview selector on the UI controls the underlying image view. It is useful when there is a special Apply mode or transparency in the gradient that is part of the fractal. Click on it to sample one of eight preset test images, or to view the underlying image, the current selection, or the contents of the clipboard.

Fractal Map

The fractal map is represented by the shape of a traditional Mandelbrot set. When the cursor is over the fractal map, it changes to a small hand. Click and drag the small circle around the fractal space inside of the fractal map, or simply click and the circle moves to the spot you've clicked to. The real-time preview window displays the changes immediately, without having to manually input any numbers. As you move around the fractal map, you may stop to zoom in or out, using the controls on the preview window, at any time.

Zoom Controls

Zooming within the Fractal Explorer is accomplished in a number of different ways. The easiest method of zooming is to simply place the cursor in the real-time preview window and click to zoom in and right-click to zoom out. The zoom controls on the top of the preview window frame allow centered zooming, and clicking on the preview window enables direct zooming. Whenever the cursor is over the preview window, the arrow changes to a magnifying glass with a plus sign. Click on the spot you wish to magnify inside the preview window, and it zooms in to that spot and makes it the new center of the preview. Holding down the ALT key changes the magnifying cursor to "magnify-minus." Clicking with the ALT key held down zooms out from that point.

CENTERED ZOOMING For centered zooming, use the two controls on the upper left of the preview window frame. The plus sign (+) zooms in, the minus sign (-) zooms out, and the center of the window stays constant. If you click on the word "Zoom" on the interface, a pop-up slider will appear. Drag the slider in either direction to zoom in large steps. This is a fast way to zoom all the way in or all the way out.

Panning Control

The Panning control allows 360 degrees of continuous panning of the fractal through the preview window.

HOW TO PAN On the outside edge of the preview window are eight small arrows. Click on any of the arrows to move the main preview window in that direction. Clicking anywhere on the frame surrounding the preview (in between the arrows) moves the fractal in that direction.

DRAG PANNING   Holding down the CTRL key turns the cursor into a hand, which allows the fractal to be "dragged" around the preview window for precise positioning. Limitations don't end at the preview window boundaries. Drag as far away as the screen allows.

Detail Settings

Increasing the detail settings on any fractal set adds new elements to the fractal set. Repeated zooms on a fractal set seem to eventually zoom "through" the fractal to nothing. Increasing the detail settings fills the space by increasing the ability to discern small changes, particularly inside the fractal's interior. The higher the detail is set, however, the more computational time is required for rendering. Use the two controls on the lower left of the preview window frame to control the detail in the fractal image. The plus sign (+) increases detail; the minus sign (-) decreases detail. Clicking on the word "Detail" shows a slider for more precise detail settings.

Gradient Preview/Pop-Up Menu

On the right hand side of the Fractal Explorer dialog box are two gradient preview/pop-up menu dialogs. The top gradient dialog governs the interior of the set, and the bottom one governs the exterior of the set (which is most often the dominant area). The pop-up menu for gradients is the same menu that is used by the Gradient Designer, complete with hierarchical categorization of gradient presets. The Triangle/Sawtooth icon shows the looping control and further affects the way that the gradient is mapped to the fractal set.

Gradient Wrapping Control

Also on the right side, between the Gradient Preview controls, is the Gradient Wrapping control. The fractal set may be colored with any gradient you choose. You can obtain more interesting renders with the same gradient by controlling the repetition of the gradient as it applies to the set in two different directions. There are two controls for mapping the gradient frequency to the fractal set.

The Spiral setting, on the upper left, controls how fast the color cycles as it moves from one potential line to the next. The lines are expressing the potential of any point in four-dimensional space to fall toward the attractors, roughly analogous to space around an electric charge with equal attraction to their electrostatic center. Within a

22

ring, the electrostatic pull is the same and there can be many such rings moving toward the center of the charge.

The Spoke setting, on the lower right of the Wrapping control, determines how often the gradient will be repeated over the entire 360-degree circle around the set. This is the Radial control. These two settings interact with each other. Variations in the Spiral setting will result in widely divergent effects.

The Preset Menu

The Preset Menu is where all of the named or saved fractals are stored. When you press the letter "a" or click on Add, a dialog box will allow options for item names, category names, and preset files.

Shuffle Button

The Shuffle button allows selection of different Fractal Explorer parameters to randomize. You may check All, or None, or select from the list. Each time the Shuffle button is clicked, the selected parameters are shuffled. The parameters that can be shuffled are:

- Exterior Colors
- Interior Colors
- Exterior Looping
- Interior Looping
- Apply Mode
- Test Image
- Equipotential Speed
- Radial Speed

Options Button

Clicking on the Options button displays a menu with the Apply Mode list and three other options. Those options are as follows.

WRAP IMAGE INSTEAD OF GRADIENT   This option allows the user to grab color data from an Opacity preview mode, which can be the underlying image, the Windows clipboard, or a Selection. The Fractal Explorer uses the color data contained in the selection, image, or clipboard, and wraps that color around the gradient.

NUMERICAL INPUT   Numerical Input enables the experienced "fractologist" to find previously explored spaces or to explore new fractal spaces by "hard-coding" the algorithm variables.

DRAW GRADIENT ACROSS TOP   This feature creates a bar across the top of the fractal image you create to show you the gradient that was used. It is not active in all modes.

 TIP: *If a bar appears across the top of your image after applying the effect and you are wondering where it came from, it is because the Draw Gradient Across Top option is set.*

A Quick Tour of Fractal Explorer

To do Fractal Explorer justice would take volumes, and it still wouldn't scratch the surface or do you much good. The real secret is to experiment. That said, let's begin exploring.

Making a Title Screen with Fractal Explorer

Maybe its just me but I get tired seeing the same canned multimedia presentations at meetings. Since one of the things that Fractal Explorer does best is make backgrounds, let's create an exciting title screen that doesn't look like everyone else's.

1. Open a new image with a setting of 4 x 4 inches, 96 dpi resolution, and 24-bit color.

2. Open the Fractal Explorer by clicking on Julia Set Explorer 2.0 in the Fancy drop-down menu of the Effects menu. The Fractal Explorer dialog box opens. Now for the tricky part. You need to open one of the presets. The presets on this dialog box are not the same as normal drop-down lists. On the bottom middle is a rectangular area that contains all of the presets. Click and hold the tiny arrow in the lower-right corner until another pop-up menu opens. When this happens, don't let go of the mouse button. You have three choices at this point: Corel Presets, Misc., and Presets. While still holding down the left mouse button, move the cursor over to select Corel Presets.

3. Still holding down the mouse button, move back over to the drop-down list that just appeared and move the cursor down the list to the bottom. As you do this, the list will begin to scroll downward. Keep going down until you get to Totally Tubular. Now let go of the mouse button. After a moment, the center preview window should display the new fill pattern.

4. The Up and Down arrow keys allow you to move through the list of Presets. Click the Down arrow key and watch the preview window. It says "Tropical Island." The DOWN ARROW key selects the next preset. By using the UP and DOWN ARROW keys, you can move quickly though all of the presets and see what they look like. The preview window changes almost instantly to a new shape. Keep watching. The first image you see in the preview window is a really rough approximation of what it will look like. If you give it a moment, the preview window will be refreshed two more times, giving it more detail each time.

5. Now click the UP ARROW key and return to the Totally Tubular preset. Now you are going to make a change. You want to use this effect, but the color is wrong. I picked this preset because the Inside Color setting has no effect on it, so you only need to concern yourself with the Outside Color.

6. Place the cursor over the box that says "Color Outside." When the cursor is over where it is supposed to be, it will change into a tiny representation of a drop-down box. Click on the box and a very long drop-down list will appear.

7. Holding down the left mouse button, move down the list until you reach "Metallic." As you pass some of the names on the list, various-sized drop-down lists will appear. When you get to Metallic, the drop-down list associated with that setting will appear. The default setting for Totally Tubular is Blue Green Metal Cone, which is checked at the top of the list.

8. Still holding the left mouse button, move the cursor down the secondary list to "Gentle Gold" and release the mouse button. The lists disappear and Totally Tubular changes from a blue-green to a gold. Click the OK button on the lower right and you have created an excellent gold background for a presentation, as shown below.

9. Select the Text tool in the Toolbox and type **TURBO GEARS** using Kabel Ult BT at a size of 96. Click the Object Picker tool. Click the Lock Object Transparency in the Objects dialog.

10. Open the Julia Set Explorer and from the presets list choose Presets. Move up the list to Ground Zero. Select it and apply the fill. Only the text should filled.

11. From the Effects menu choose Noise and select Add noise. Apply a Gaussian Noise at a level of 12 and a Density of 50.

12. From the Effects menu choose 3D Effects and Emboss. Click the Reset button and change the color to Original color. Click OK.

13. From the Object menu choose Drop Shadow. Select Flat, Direction of 225, Distance of 0.15, Opacity of 100 and a feather Width of 16. Click OK. The resulting image is shown below. There you have it. A slick new title page for your new product—whatever Turbo Gears are.

The Terrazzo Filter

The next plug-in filter we will discuss from Corel PHOTO-PAINT's Fancy filters group is called Terrazzo. (The name comes from the Italian word for "terrace" and originally referred to a kind of mosaic floor covering.) I again acknowledge my gratitude to the fine folks at Xaos, who assistance was invaluable in creating this part of the chapter.

Terrazzo enables you to create beautiful, regular patterns taken from elements in existing source images. With Terrazzo, the patterns are very easy to create and infinitely repeatable. The best part is that Terrazzo is simple to use. No, actually the best part is it makes great seamless tiles.

An Overview of Terrazzo

The regular patterns you can create with Terrazzo are based on 17 symmetry groups, which are known in the math and design worlds by several names, including "planar," "ornamental," or "wallpaper" symmetry groups. You choose the symmetry you want to use from a Symmetry selection box from the Terrazzo dialog box.

The 17 symmetries in the Terrazzo filter are named after common American patchwork quilt patterns. Each of these symmetries also has a mathematical name. Because these mathematical names (such as p-4m) aren't very exciting or as easy to remember as the quilt names (such as Sunflower), Xaos has only used the quilt names in the interface.

Tiles, Motifs, and Patterns

Each Terrazzo-generated pattern is made from a *motif*, which is the shape that builds a *tile* when a *symmetry* is applied to it. The tile, in turn, repeats to build a regular pattern. These three terms will be used throughout this discussion.

The motif in Terrazzo is very similar to the masks in Corel PHOTO-PAINT. The area that is enclosed by the motif is the foundation of the tile. There are eight different motif shapes. Different symmetries use different motifs.

Although each of the 17 symmetries produces different results, all of the symmetries perform one or more of the following operations:

- *Translations*, which move the motif up, down, right, left, or diagonally without changing the orientation

- *Rotations*, which turn the motif one or more times around a center at a specific angle

- *Mirror Reflections*, which create one or more mirror images of the motif

- *Glide Reflections*, which create one or more mirror images of a motif and move the motif up, down, right, left, or diagonally

The Terrazzo Filter Dialog Box

Terrazzo is located in the Effects menu under Fancy. When you first open Terrazzo, you will see the filter dialog box as shown in Figure 22-10. Terrazzo works on grayscale, duo-tone, 24-bit, and 32-bit color images, but not on black-and-white (1-bit) images. Like Paint Alchemy and all of the other filters, you must have an image open before you can access the filter. Let's take a closer look at it.

The Original preview on the left side of the Terrazzo dialog box displays the masked area of the image, or the entire source image if you haven't selected any areas with a mask.

The large image on the right of the dialog box displays the source image with the current symmetry applied to it which is referred to as the Result image.

NOTE: *The Result image is the one to which you are applying a pattern. Although you can open a new source image from within Terrazzo, you cannot open a new Result image without closing Terrazzo and returning to Corel PHOTO-PAINT's main screen.*

22

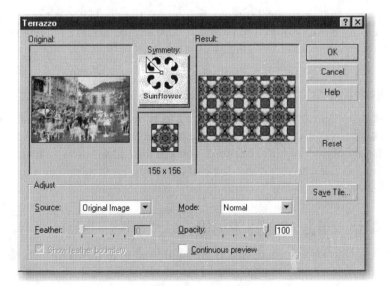

The
Terrazzo
filter dialog
box

FIGURE 22-10

The Continuous Preview Option

When the Continuous Preview check box is checked, the destination image is continuously updated as you change any of the settings in the Terrazzo dialog box. This allows you to see the effects of your adjustments in real time as you are making them.

 TIP: *Leaving the Continuous Preview options selected may slow down some older systems. This is especially true if you are using a large motif, one of the triangular motifs such as Sunflower, or the kite-shaped motif such as Whirlpool. If you experience system slow-down, you may want to consider switching off the Continuous Preview option. That said, I find that having it on really helps in finding some nice patterns quickly.*

By default, Continuous Preview is turned off in the Terrazzo dialog box. When the Continuous Preview check box is not selected, the destination image is updated only when you release the mouse button after making an adjustment to one of the controls in the Terrazzo dialog box.

The Terrazzo Motifs

When you first open the Terrazzo dialog box, the motif is positioned in the center of the source image; if you have already opened the Terrazzo dialog box, the motif is in the position where you last placed it.

Adjusting a Motif

You can change the tile you are creating by moving the motif to a new position on the source image, thus selecting a different part of the image to make into a tile.

In addition to moving the motif, you can also adjust the size and, in the case of the Gold Brick symmetry, the shape of the motif. Each motif has a handle on it that enables you to resize it.

To Adjust the Motif's Position

Place the cursor anywhere inside the motif and hold down the left mouse button. The cursor becomes a hand, and while you hold down the mouse button you can drag the motif anywhere inside the source image.

If the Continuous Preview option is on, the Result image on the right side is constantly updated to show the results of repositioning the motif on the source image.

To Adjust the Motif's Size

Place the cursor over the motif control handle and drag it to increase or decrease the size. The only exception to this is the Gold Brick, which has two handles. The handle in the upper-right corner of the motif resizes the width, and the handle in the lower left lets you resize the height of the motif and skew its shape.

TIP: *To constrain the Gold Brick motif to a rectangular shape, or to return to a rectangular motif after you have skewed the motif, hold down the SHIFT key as you drag the lower-left handle. The motif automatically becomes rectangular as long as you hold down the SHIFT key.*

Selecting a Symmetry

The first time you open Terrazzo, the active symmetry is Pinwheel. This symmetry is displayed between the Original and the Result images in the Terrazzo dialog box. Each symmetry swatch displays a simple representation of the selected symmetry.

To select a different symmetry, click on the currently displayed symmetry swatch and the Symmetry selection box opens as shown below. Clicking the desired symmetry causes it to be highlighted with a blue border. Click the OK button when you are satisfied with your selection, and the selected symmetry appears between the Original and Result image.

22

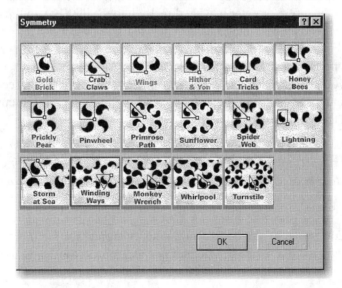

Creating Seamless Patterns

With most of the Terrazzo symmetries, you may notice a visible edge or seam between the tiles. The feather option in the Terrazzo dialog box allows you to feather the edge of a motif so that the seams between tiles fade away. Once you have made a seamless tile you can save it as a seamless tile by clicking the Save tile button. For more information on this see the section on Saving a Tile later in this chapter.

Feathering in Terrazzo is produced in an area outside the motif (called the *feather boundary*), and the pixels inside the feather boundary are dispersed, thus creating a gradual transition between motifs.

 TIP: *Sometimes there is such a thing as too much of a good thing. With certain patterns, using too large a feathering value causes faint black seams to develop on certain patterns.*

Using the Feather Option

You use the Feather option in the Terrazzo dialog box to set the width of the feather edge around the motif. The feather option is dimmed (not available) if you have selected the Sunflower, Prickly Pear, Turnstile, or Winding Ways symmetry. The option is not available because these four symmetries are kaleidoscopic and therefore always seamless.

To adjust a motif's feather edge, drag the slider to increase or decrease the feather edge around the motif, or enter a value directly into the data box to the right of the slider. The value is a percentage based upon the size of the image. For example, setting the Feather value to 25 creates a feather with a width of 25 percent of the distance from the edge of the motif to its center.

When you set the feather value above 0, you will notice that a second border appears around the motif in the source image. This border represents the area included in the feather edge of the motif.

 TIP: *You cannot move the motif by clicking and dragging inside the feather border. You must be inside the motif itself to move a feathered motif. (This little jewel drove me crazy till I figured it out.)*

If you don't want to see the feather boundary around the motif, you can turn it off by clearing the Show Feather Boundary check box in the Terrazzo dialog box.

This only turns off the visible border; if you have feathering selected, the feathering is still applied.

You may notice that setting a Feather value slows down your system a wee bit. The folks at Corel have done a wonderful job of speeding up these filters in comparison to the Mac versions. However, if you noticed that the feathering is slowing your system down, keep it off until you are ready to fine-tune your image.

 TIP: *Some symmetries create mirror lines as they reflect a motif to create a pattern. Feather does not occur on mirror lines, because these are "seamless" lines; feathering only appears on edges with visible seams.*

Feather Boundary Constraints

If the Show Feather boundary is off and you have some value of feathering entered, you will discover that you cannot position the motif any closer to the edge of the source image than the feather boundary.

If the motif is already positioned near the edge of the source image and you attempt to enter a value for Feather, that would create a boundary that goes beyond the image edge. You would then receive a warning and the maximum allowable value would automatically be entered in the Feather value box. The slider or values will not exceed that value unless the motif is moved.

One last feathering note: If you have a very small motif, you may not be able to see the feather boundary, even if you have the Show Feather Boundary option turned on. Although you can't see it, the feather will still appear when you apply the pattern.

The Mode Settings

The Mode drop-down list in the Terrazzo dialog box lets you control the way a pattern is applied to a selection.

The Opacity Slider

The Opacity slider in the Terrazzo dialog box lets you adjust the opacity of the pattern when you apply it to a selection. You may want the effect of an almost invisible pattern (low opacity), or you may want a bold application of a pattern, covering the destination image entirely (high opacity). An opacity value of 100 (100 percent) means that the pattern is completely opaque; an opacity value of 1 means that the pattern is almost invisible (which is not very useful).

Previewing Tiles

A preview of the current tile appears below the symmetry swatch. The pixel dimensions of the current tile are also displayed below the tile. You are provided with a constant preview of the tile you are creating.

Saving a Tile

One of the benefits of having the Terrazzo filter integrated into Corel PHOTO-PAINT is that saving a tile button becomes a real time saver. The Save Tile feature saves the tile created by Terrazzo as a BMP file. This way you can quickly use Terrazzo to make a tile, and by saving it as a tile, you can use it immediately as a bitmap fill.

To save a Terrazzo tile:

1. Choose the symmetry, and position the motif where you want it in the source image.

2. Click the Save Tile button in the Terrazzo dialog box. The Save Tile dialog box opens.

Name the file and confirm where you want the file saved. Click the OK button. When you return to the Terrazzo, click Cancel if you do not want any pattern applied to the image.

TIP: *Make note of where the seamless tile is saved or be prepared to spend some time looking for it.*

Terrazzo is an excellent texture and pattern maker, but its greatest strength is its ability to create seamless tiles. Not only does it make great seamless tiles but you can preview the resulting tile pattern in the preview area.

23

The Color Transform Filters

This is a collection of six filters that run the gamut of usefulness from the essential to the goofy. I used to think they just took up space and were barely worthy of mention, but my opinion of them and what you can do with them has changed dramatically. The first four filters listed below are located in the Color Transform category of the Effects menu. The remaining four are in the Transform category in the Image menu. Except for the Invert filter, none are available with black-and-white files. Other exceptions are noted in the descriptions of the individual filters.

- Bit Planes Halftone
- Psychedelic
- Solarize
- Denterlace
- Invert Posterize
- Threshold

The Bit Planes Filter

This filter, available with all images but black-and-white, applies a posterization-style effect to each channel individually. One of the earlier online help files described the Bit Planes filter as "a powerful tool for analyzing gradients in images." So let's find some images with gradients to analyze. I have a better idea, let's find something creative to do with this little wonder. First of all, what does it actually do? The filter reduces the image to basic RGB color components (even if it is a CMYK image) and emphasizes the tonal changes.

The Color plane sliders control the sensitivity of the effect. Higher settings display fewer tone changes, and gradient steps. At the highest setting, the image contains a large amount of black-and-white areas, since the effect is displaying only extreme tone changes. Lower Color plane settings display more tone changes and gradations. At the lowest setting, a photographic image will appear like color noise, as subtle changes are virtually random. A graphic or computer-generated image will show salient contours of change in tone.

The Color sliders can be used separately to see the tone changes in a specific component color, or together to see all tone changes. The Bit Planes filter is used to provide unusual color effects to an image—as you will soon see.

Creating Special Effects with the Bit Planes Filter

In this hands-on exercise you will learn to use the power of the Bit Planes filter to make a mock cover for a fashion magazine. By now you should know how to use most of the PHOTO-PAINT tools, so the descriptions that follow may seem somewhat brief.

1. Open the file EXERCISE\PHOTOS\712014.WI. From the Image menu, choose Resample and make the image five inches wide. Click the OK button.

2. Use the Magic Wand mask tool to isolate the background. I recommend a Tolerance setting of 7. Mask most of the light brown background and then use the Brush mask tool to finish masking the darkly colored areas at the bottom of the image.

TIP: *You will discover it's easier to touch up a mask by enabling the Mask Overlay button and using it for a guide than to use the Mask Marquee.*

3. When you have completed the mask, invert it (CTRL-I). Select Create Object: Cut Selection (CTRL-SHIFT-UP ARROW) and with the Object Picker tool, select the Background in the Objects Dockers window (CTRL-F7).From the Edit menu, choose Clear. The result is shown here.

4. Select the object and duplicate it (CTRL-D). From the Effects menu, choose Color Transform and select Bit Planes, which opens its dialog box. Move all three sliders to 7 and click the OK button. The result is shown here.

5. From the Objects Docker window, select the original object. Apply the Bit Planes filter again, but uncheck the Apply to all planes option and drag the Blue slider to 5. Click the OK button. Use the Object Picker tool to position the two objects as shown here.

6. Click on the Background in the Objects Docker window to select it. From the Edit menu, choose Fill, select the Texture Fill button, and click the Edit button. From the Samples 7 Texture Library, choose Neon Spandex. (Don't look at me—I don't make up these names.) Lock the two colors that are unlocked and click the Preview button until you find a background you like, or you can enter **8357** for the Texture #: setting. Click OK to return, and click OK again to apply the fill.

7. For the finishing touch, click the Text button in the Toolbox and click inside the image. Change the Paint color to Yellow by clicking on the color swatch in the onscreen preview. Type **FASHION** and then change the font to Futura Xblk BT and the size to 60. With the text selected, choose Drop Shadow from the Object menu to the text, pointing down with a feather of 14. That's it. The result is shown in Figure 23-1(in grayscale) and in the color insert.

23

With the Bit
Planes
filters, a
high fashion
look is a
snap

FIGURE 23-1

A few pointers about using the Bit Planes that I learned while spending way too much time on this chapter. For reasons I cannot explain, the best effects seem to be with the filter at maximum and only one of the channels (usually blue) reduced. The best subjects tend to have lots of solid colors on them and a solid background color—white seems best. Now, on to halftones.

The Halftone Filter

The Color Halftone filter can make a perfectly good image look like it was printed in the Sunday comics. Available with all images except black-and-white, Paletted, and L*a*b files, the Halftone filter simulates the effect of using an enlarged halftone screen on each channel of the image. For each channel, the filter divides the image into rectangles and replaces each rectangle with a circle. The circle size is proportional to the brightness of the rectangle.

The Halftone filter converts color images into color halftone images. Use the Max Radius slider to control the maximum radius of a halftone dot, and the Cyan, Magenta, and Yellow slider bars to control the channel angle in order to determine the color mixture and to produce a wider range of colors.

So what can you do with the Halftone filter? It's great for taking existing nonphotographic clip art and making it look like the Sunday comics. Don't laugh; Roy Lichtenstein made a fortune doing the same thing. Although there is nothing to prevent you from using this filter on photographs, you'll get the best results with solid images. Figure 23-2 shows a clip-art image from the CorelDRAW library with the Halftone filter applied at the default setting.

Using the Color Halftone Filter

You can select Color Transform from the Effects menu, and choose Halftone from the drop-down list. In the Color Halftone dialog box you may enter values in the Dot Control section from 2 to 10, for the maximum radius of a halftone dot. Beware of using this filter on small images. The minimum size of the halftone dot setting (2) will be more than the image can handle. I have had the greatest success with this filter when I use a 300 dpi setting for the rasterization of the image (makes a big image). I then apply the Halftone filter, and resample it back to the desired size. The only note of caution is that the halftone effect can disappear when applied to some halftone screens used by printers.

23

Turning clip art into comics is easy with the Halftone filter

FIGURE 23-2

From the dialog box you can also enter a screen-angle value for each channel. You will see little or no difference regardless of the settings, so I recommend leaving it at the default setting. Click Reset to return all the screen angles to their default values. The values indicate the angle of the dot from true horizontal.

The Psychedelic Filter

If it isn't bad enough that the '60s are showing up in the fashion world, we've got a 60s style filter in Corel PHOTO-PAINT. (It has been said that if you clearly remember the '60s, you weren't really there. Perhaps this filter will bring them back to you.) The Psychedelic filter first appeared in PHOTO-PAINT 3 and I thought it was the dumbest filter ever made. I have since learned that when it is used in combination with another filter, it can be quite a jewel. This filter is available with all images except black-and-white and Paletted images. It changes the colors in selected areas or images to bright electric orange, hot pink, banana yellow, cyan, lime green, and so on. The Level slider in the dialog box spans a range of 256 shades (0-255). Used in large doses, it can induce flashbacks.

Here is a hands-on exercise to show you some of the interesting effects that can be achieved with this filter.

1. Open the image EXERCISE\PHOTOS\678043.WI and resample it down to six inches in Width.

2. Select the Magic Wand mask tool and mask the background. Then choose Clear from the Edit menu. Remove the mask. The result is shown below.

3. Sharpen and then select High Pass. Set Percentage to 100 and Radius to 15. Click OK.

4. From the Effects menu, choose Color Transform and then Psychedelic. Click the On-screen preview mode. There are three different settings I want you to try. First, set the Level to 11, then move it to 33, and finally try 99. The results of the three different settings are shown in Figure 23-3. They also appear in the color insert.

The Solarize Filter

The Solarize filter, available with all images except black-and-white, gives the effect of a photographic negative. This effect will be more pronounced in color images. When applied to its maximum of 255 shades, Solarize results in a negative or inverted image. It simulates an old photographic technique that required the photographic plate to be briefly exposed to sunlight outside of the camera. This resulted in the darkest areas being washed out—just how washed out was determined

The Psychedelic filter produces some interesting and unusual effects

■ FIGURE 23-3

by how long the plate was exposed. (The emulsions they had in the old days were very low speed and very, very slow.)

The Solarize filter operates in a similar fashion, except that instead of entering in the time the image is in the sun, you can control the shades of color that will be affected by the filter (0 through 255). A setting of zero in the dialog box has no effect on the image. A maximum setting of 255 shades makes the image a complete negative.

Like the Invert filter, the Solarize filter transforms colors to appear like those of a negative photographic image. Unlike with the Invert filter (which produces an absolute effect where the image colors are completely inverted), you control the intensity of the effect to achieve different results.

So what can you do with the Solarize filter? Not much. This is one of the filters that begs the question: "Why is it here?" Actually, there are a number of special effects that require the Solarize filter. One is the creation of the chrome effect that everyone seems to want these days. While the procedure to create chrome is too complex to cover in this chapter, at least now you know there really are things you can do with the filter.

The Deinterlace Filter

The next four filters are found in the Transform flyout in the Image menu but can also be accessed from the Effects drop-down menu found on the dialog boxes. The Deinterlace filter, available with all images except black-and-white and Paletted, removes even or odd horizontal lines from scanned or interlaced video images. You can fill the spaces left by the discarded lines using either of two methods available on the dialog box: duplication fills in the spaces with copies of the adjacent lines of pixels, while interpolation fills them in with colors created by averaging the surrounding pixels.

The Invert Filter

This filter, available with all images, is both the simplest and most essential filter. The Invert filter changes the colors in an image so that they appear as a photographic negative. While the ability to make a photographic negative is rarely needed, the Invert filter can be used to reverse a portion of the image to create intense feelings in the viewer and it can also be used to change colors. Figure 23-4 is from my first PHOTO-PAINT book. The procedure used to make it is simple. To make the image

The Invert filter can convey negative emotions to the viewer.

FIGURE 23-4

shown in Figure 23-4, first mask the left half of the drawing using the Rectangle Mask took. Apply the invert filter; then remove the mask and blur the line between the inverted and non-inverted area. The text was made slightly transparent and the water drops were applied to the text using a bitmap fill that no longer exists, unfortunately.

The dialog box doesn't have any settings. Click the Preview button to display the effects of the current filter settings before applying it to the entire image.

Making Day out of Night with the Invert Filter

Many times you will have an image that will not reproduce well in either grayscale or photocopying. While the following procedure won't work with many images, on occasion it might help you out of a bind and everyone will think you're an artistic genius.

1. Locate the image EXERCISE\PHOTOS\555069.wi. Load the image and Resample it to six inches wide. Click the OK button. The original image is shown here.

2. From the Image menu, select Transform and choose Invert. From the Image menu, choose Convert To and choose Grayscale. The result is shown in Figure 23-5.

3. Close the file and don't save the changes.

One of the times that Inverting a photograph works

FIGURE 23-5

Using the Invert Filter to Change Colors

The last exercise for the Invert filter demonstrates its power to change colors. Just because you apply this filter doesn't mean the image will look like a negative. In fact, there are times when it is easier to find the opposite color and invert it than to create it. I know that sounds dumb, but when it comes to creating gold and bronze colors. I do much better finding a rich blue and inverting it.

1. Open the image EXERCISE\PHOTOS\686086.WI. Resample it so it is six inches wide.

2. From the Image menu, choose Transform and then Invert. Quite a change, isn't it? Close the file and don't save any changes.

The Posterize Filter

This is a type of filter used throughout photo-editing. In fact, the term used to describe the breaking down of smooth color transitions in an image is called *posterization*. The Posterize filter, available on all but black-and-white images, removes gradations, creating areas of solid colors or gray shades. This is useful when you need to simplify a complex color image without converting it to 256- or 16-color mode.

Another way to use this filter is to apply the Posterize effect selectively to individual channels through the Channels roll-up. Please note that individual color channels are grayscale images. Posterizing an image with a setting of three and four shades is a standard use of this filter, which removes gradations, creating areas of solid colors or gray shades. This is useful when you need to simplify a complex color or grayscale image for use as a background. The Level slider specifies the number of gray or color channels. The lower the value, the more pronounced the poster effect will be. Figure 23-6 shows a typical outdoor sailing picture, while Figure 23-7 shows the effect of applying the Posterize filter at a setting of 3.

23

The Threshold Filter

One of the many uses of the Threshold filter, available with all images except black-and-white and L*a*b, is to convert grayscale or color images into high-contrast line-art images. When images are scanned at high-resolution black-and-white (not grayscale), it is sometimes advantageous to scan them in as grayscale and then use the Threshold filter to remove the light gray background. See

A great sailing photo with many complex shades and patterns

FIGURE 23-6

A great sailing photograph that has been posterized

FIGURE 23-7

Chapter 5 for more details about how this is done. Another use is to convert specific colors in an image to black or white or both through multiple applications.

Using the Threshold Filter

The ideal candidates for this filter are high-contrast images that do not contain large shadow areas. The photograph of London in Figure 23-8 is such a picture. Figure 23-9 shows the application of the filter using the Bi-level setting. This setting converts the image into black-and-white, almost as if you were using the Convert To command in the Image menu. The difference is that you can control the setting of the threshold of what is converted to white and what is converted to black with the Threshold filter.

Making the Filter Work Better

Adjusting the Threshold slider back and forth helps define the image the way you want, but we can improve the results of the Threshold filter by first applying a High Pass filter (from the Sharpen group). Figure 23-10 shows the result of applying the High Pass at a maximum setting before applying the Bi-level setting of Threshold. Notice how much more detail is visible because the High Pass reduced the parts of

A sunny
(not foggy)
day in
London
town

FIGURE 23-8

Applying the Threshold filter changes the picture

FIGURE 23-9

the image that are not important when applying the Threshold filter. Figure 23-11 used the same (High Pass) image as Figure 23-10 except that the To White option was enabled. Note of confession here—the skies in Figures 23-10 and 23-11 had some spots that I removed with the Eraser tool. I bring up the point because it leads into how to operate the filter.

Operation of the filter is simple, although the filter dialog box at first appearance seems very complicated. This last exercise of the chapter will teach you how to make a woodcut using the Threshold filter.

Making a Woodcut with the Threshold Filter

Woodcuts date back to the 1600s and fall in and out of popularity. The same image rules discussed earlier for the Threshold filter (high contrast, no large shadow areas) still apply. So in this exercise we are going to turn a photograph of a butterfly into a woodcut...of a caterpillar (just kidding).

This is a
photograph
to which the
Threshold
filter was
applied

FIGURE 23-10

Same
photo, same
filter except
the To
White
option was
choosen

FIGURE 23-11

1. Locate and open the image EXERCISE\PHOTOS\720063.WI. Using the Resample command, reduce the width to five inches and click OK. The original photograph is shown here.

2. Just so you can see the difference the High Pass filter makes, from the Image menu choose Transform and then Threshold. By default the filter dialog box has the To Black option set with Threshold set to mid-point. Ensure that you are in onscreen preview and move the Threshold slider either direction to see if you can get a good image. Fat chance. Click the Cancel button.

3. From the Effects menu, choose Sharpen and then High Pass. Set the Percentage to 100% and the Radius to 10. Click OK. Yes, the photograph now looks like it was shot in Los Angeles on a smoggy day.

4. Now open the Threshold filter. Big difference, right? Now click the To White option and you should have the woodcut I promised you, as shown above. Move the Threshold slider to the left and right. Notice that as the detail increases, the background become solid. You should also click the Bi-level and revisit the To Black settings. Click OK to apply the filter.

5. Close the file and don't save any changes.

NOTE: *To learn more: Corel has put a wealth of information about this filter in their online help, and I recommend that you review that for detailed information on the operation of this filter. Open the Help file (F1) in PHOTO-PAINT 8. Click on the Index tab and enter Threshold. Select Threshold filter.*

23

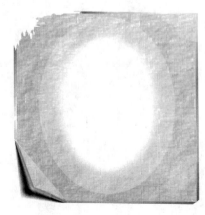

PART

V

Extending the Power of
PHOTO-PAINT

24

Using PAINT as a Web Creation Tool

When Jeff Butterworth of Alien Skin Software originally created The Boss filter, he wanted it to be the best embossing filter available on the market. He put so many controls on it, it can be used to go beyond just plain old embossing. Here are some other things to try with it that even Jeff may not have thought of yet. I really enjoy all of the interesting 3D effects that can be created with CorelDRAW. Here is a technique to produce 3D objects for a Web page using The Boss filter.

Making A 3D Web-Page Button

In this hands-on exercise we will create a basic 3D object that can be used on a Web page or made part of a control panel illustration. Once you have made the basic button, before you add the text, you can duplicate the object and make as many as you want.

1. Create a new image, selecting 24-bit color, Paper Color: White; Size: 4 x 4 inches; and Resolution: 72 dpi.

2. From the Edit menu, choose Fill. From the Edit Fill & Transparency dialog box, click the Fountain Fill button and click the Edit button. From the Fountain Fill dialog box, choose the Gold Plated preset. Click OK to close the dialog box and OK again to apply the fill.

3. From the Tools menu, select Grid & Ruler Setup. On the Grid tab, enable Show grid and Snap to grid. Click the OK button.

4. Select the Ellipse Mask tool from the Toolbox. Click the cursor in the image area and drag a circle mask in the center of the image made up of four squares. Disable Snap to grid (CTRL-Y).

5. Click on the color blue in the onscreen palette with the right mouse button. Select the Fill tool from the Toolbox and click inside the circle mask.

6. From the Effects menu, select Fancy and choose The Boss from the drop-down list. From the Style drop-down select Wet, change the Width to 60 the Smoothness to 100, and the Height to 100. Click the OK button. The result is shown below.

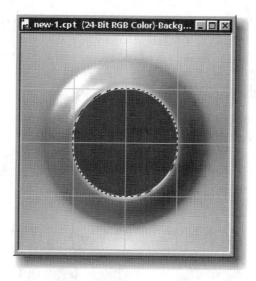

7. Click the Invert Mask button.

8. Open The Boss filter again. Change the Width to 15, the Smoothness to 50, and the Height to 80. Click the OK button. The finished blank button is shown. At this point we have created a blank button and would save it as a blank if we were going to make more of them. In the next part of this session, we are going to add a symbol to make our blank into a button that can be used to move to the next page on a Web site.

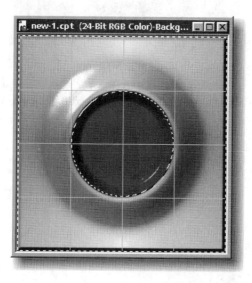

24

9. Change the Paint color to red by clicking on it in the onscreen color palette. Click the Text tool and select the ZapfDingbats BT font at a size of 96. Click in the center of the button and type **ALT+0228**. The ALT key must be held down while entering all four numbers from the numeric keypad.

10. Select the Object Picker tool and use the arrow keys to line up the letter in the center of the image as shown below. After you have it in position, select Create From Object(s) in the Mask menu (CTRL-M). Next, choose Combine from the Objects menu and combine the object with the background.

11. Open the Boss filter again. Change the Style to Wet and the Width to 3. Click OK. The button is finished as shown. All we need to do now is make it into an object so we can place it. Click the Remove mask button.

12. Our next step is to make the button into an object. We now need to make a mask that is roughly the same shape as our button. In the middle of the upper-left grid square, click and hold the left mouse button and then hold down the CTRL key. This action constrains the mask to a circle. Drag a circle that pretty much covers the entire button.

13. With the button masked, click the Create Object: Copy Selection button on the Property Bar. Next, click and drag the blank button object out of the image into the work area. It will look like the one shown below. Once you have made one, you can duplicate it using either Duplicate in the Image menu or just duplicate the object. Next use the Flip, Horizontally command in the Object menu to make one pointing the opposite direction. Use the Resample command to make the button the correct size for your Web page.

24

Making Green French Fries for your Web Page

OK, so maybe French fries wasn't the best way to describe them, but it sounded better than little squiggly-things, right? These "French fries" are actually ornaments

Now your Web page can have really classic 3D buttons

FIGURE 24-1

that are easily made and placed as mappable objects on your Web page. In this session we are going to make a simple green worm. The first step, setting up the grid, is probably the hardest part.

1. Create a new image that is 6 x 2 inches at 72 dpi.

2. From the Tools menu select Grid & Ruler Setup. On the Grid tab, enable Show grid and Snap to grid. Enable Frequency and make it 2.0 per inch in both directions. Click the OK button.

3. Select the Rectangle Shape tool from the tool box (F6). Double-click the Fill swatch on the Status bar. When the Select Fill dialog box opens, click the Fountain Fill button (second from the left) and click the Edit button. In the Fountain Fill dial box, choose the Preset Cylinder: Green 04. Change the Angle to 270 and the Steps to 999. Click OK to accept the settings and OK again to close the dialog box.

4. Ensure the Render to Object button is enabled. If you cannot find the button, double-click on the rectangle Shape tool and check Render to Object in the dialog box.

5. In the image, click and drag a rectangle in the center, leaving unfilled a width of one square all around.

6. Select the Ellipse Shape tool (F7). Ensure the Render to Object button is still enabled. Click and drag a circle two squares in diameter on each end of the rectangle. The results are shown below. Even though there are three objects it appears as one.

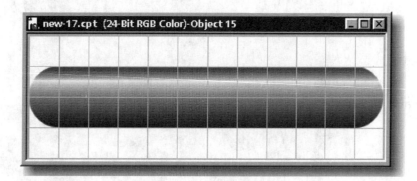

7. Marquee select all three of the objects and using the Combine command in the Object menu select Combine Objects Together.

24

Open the Effects menu, choose 2D Effects, and select Ripple. When the dialog box opens, click the Reset button and change the Amplitude setting to 10. Click OK. The result is an object that looks like a green French fry as shown below.

So, what can you do with this little fellow, other than serve it with green eggs and ham? Figure 24-2 shows an example of using blue to make the ornament and duplicating it to make the entry to the Aquatics sections of the city Web page.

A Quick and Easy Rope Border

Want to get someone's attention? Here is a very easy way to make a rope border either for a Web site or a publication.

1. Create a new image that is 6 x 4 inches at 150 dpi. I know this is an image that is too large for a Web site but it needs to be this large for the Orbits setting on the Brush tool to work. We'll resample it later. Use the F4 key (Zoom to fit) to make the entire image fit on your screen.

These ornaments quickly add a professional touch to your Web site

FIGURE 24-2

2. Drag a rectangle mask in the middle that fills the image with approximately an inch of the borders.

3. Select the Image Sprayer tool in the Toolbox. Double click on the button to open the Tool Settings roll-up. From the Presets select Rope.

4. In order to make the rope border an object ensure the Lock Transparency in the Objects Docker window is not checked and click the New Object button at the bottom of the Objects Docker window.

5. From the Edit menu, choose Stroke, Stroke Mask. When the next dialog box opens, choose Middle of Mask Border. Click OK. This begins the application of a very complex brush structure so it will take a few moments.

6. Remove the Mask. To give it more of a rope and less of a pasta look, I used the Canvas filter under the Artistic category and applied BreadC.pcx (no kidding) at a 40% emboss.

7. The last step is to Resample the image down to the size and resolution (72 dpi) needed for your Web site.

Figure 24-3 shows an example of what you can do with the rope we just learned to make. If you have a stylus you can use the rope preset on the Image sprayer to make rope signs as shown below.

Rope
borders are
easy and
draw
attention of
people
surfing
the Net

FIGURE 24-3

Using the Glass Block Filter to Make a Multimedia Background

This filter is good for distorting an image for use in backgrounds. Here is a quick hands-on exercise to make a background that would be a nice addition for a multimedia presentation.

1. Open a new file that is 6 x 6 inches, 72 dpi and 24-bit color.

2. From the Edit menu, select Fill… Click the Fountain Fill button and then the Edit button. Change Presets to: Cylinder: 11, Angle: 45.0 and Steps: 999. Click the OK button and OK to close the Edit Fill & Transparency dialog box.

3. From the Effects menu, choose Artistic and select Glass Block…. Change both sliders to 30. Click the OK button.

4. From the Effect menu, choose 3D and select Emboss. Click reset and enable Original Color. Click OK.

5. From the 3D category in the Effects menu, select Pinch/Punch. Set the slider to 100 and click OK.

6. Close the file and do not save the changes.

That's all there is to it. The "glass blocks" made by this filter also make good borders for masks by clicking on the blocks with a Magic Wand mask tool. The blocks cause the masks to align with the grid formed by the blocks. Make the mask into an object and then use the Drop Shadow command as shown in Figure 24-4.

Parting Comments

Well, that's all folks. If you have been reading this from front to back, give yourself a gold star. As you work with PHOTO-PAINT remember Dave's golden rule. If you're not having fun with PHOTO-PAINT, you're not doing something right. See you when PHOTO-PAINT 9 ships.

Between now and then I am working with Gary Preister (one of the most talented DRAW people I know) to create a book that should be out at the end of 1997. We wanted to call the book "Grumpy Old Men Do Corel." The title made perfect sense, Gary (the Duke of Draw) is 55, while I (The Prince of Paint) am a youthful 49 (at least until November). Unfortunately, CorelPRESS didn't think the title was appropriate so the official title is (fanfare please) *Corel Studio Techniques*. Yes, we are going to expose all of the secrets of Corel (not really). It will be a full color book in which Gary and I show step-by-step how to do some pretty fantastic stuff with

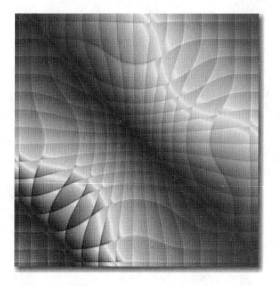

The Glass
Block filter
can produce
excellent
backgrounds

FIGURE 24-4

DRAW and with PAINT. One of my favorite parts of the book is the Gary Does/Dave Does chapters. In it we both attempt to do the same type of effects with DRAW and PAINT. For example, in the Stained Glass section Gary demonstrates how he can quickly produce something that resembles stained glass. In the PAINT side of the chapter I show how to make stained glass that looks so real it will make you think it is a photograph. All kidding aside (not likely) Gary's stuff will knock your socks off. Look for it in your local bait shop or a bookseller near you.

N

R

S

T

U